John Bown was brought up on a small holding on the hills of Derbyshire, where life was tough, but happy. As a teenager he came to a personal faith which informed his future life. His calling was to be a policeman which he undertook for thirty years retiring in the rank of superintendent. He recalls, humorous and frightening incidents during his police career, and identifies critical elements in his development as a police officer. He takes you on a journey through Ethiopia, Jamaica, Nigeria, and South Sudan as he describes his work as an overseas police adviser.

To Edga

Best wishes

John

Dedicated to my late mother-in-law, Barbara Self, who died far too young but had a profound influence on me and my life, as well as giving me her lovely daughter Margaret as my wife.

John Bown

CALLED TO SERVE AND PROTECT

AUSTIN MACAULEY PUBLISHERS™

LONDON * CAMBRIDGE * NEW YORK * SHARJAH

A CIP catalogue record for this title is available from the British Library.

ISBN 9781035808465 (Paperback)
ISBN 9781035808472 (ePub e-book)

www.austinmacauley.com

First Published 2023
Austin Macauley Publishers Ltd®
1 Canada Square
Canary Wharf
London
E14 5AA

This book is the autobiography of the author covering the period from his birth in 1943 to 2022. Family and friends are referred to by their first names only and have given their permission to be mentioned. Work colleagues and contacts are identified by a randomly selected letter so as not to reveal their identity.

Part 1
The Beginnings

Home and Family

My ancestors on my father's (Bown) side have lived around Ashover, for more than three hundred years and before that were in Matlock. A brief examination of their occupations over those years revealed most of the male members of the family were either farmers or worked in quarries. On my mother's side (Dronfield) they similarly resided around Ashover (Stone Edge) during the same period and nearly all of them found employment on the land or in the quarries. On both sides of the family, you can find an occasional example of a family member who was a publican, but there is no history of public service. How was it then that I ended up being in the employment of the Derbyshire Constabulary from January 1960 to November 1992 and then continued working alongside the police at home and abroad until 2014 when I finally retired at the age of seventy.

At the age of fifteen, I made the most critical decision of my life when I made my own personal commitment to follow Christ and that has informed everything I have done since. It was that decision that led me to apply to become a police cadet in 1960.

In the rural area where I lived, there was not much choice for entertainment. Our isolated farm was about two miles away from the nearest bus stop to either Matlock or Chesterfield and the timing of the last bus home meant that if you wanted to go to the evening cinema session you had to leave before the end of the main film to catch the bus. Before I could make up my own mind about what I wanted to do with my time, my mother had insisted that along with my brother we were regular visitors to the local chapel. This involved going to Sunday School in the morning along with the other kids, living down Hungerhill Lane and then returning for the evening service along with mother. Dad had already died when I was just four years old.

My mother was not particularly demonstrative about her Christian faith, but it was very real to her, and I grew up with the belief that there was a God who I could talk to when I found myself in a sticky situation. We only had two bedrooms at the farmhouse where we lived, and I shared one with my mother (being the baby of the family and often poorly as a child). My brother Sam shared the other bedroom with our half-brother Ernest who was twenty-one when I was born. I slept in a single bed and my mother slept in a very old-fashioned bed with an iron frame and a feather filled mattress. If I were awake when she came to bed, I would see her kneel at the bedside to say her prayers and always her three sons were included in those prayers.

We were not a wealthy family as evidenced by the fact that my mother never paid income tax and my brother, and I were on free school meals. My father had been the part owner and farmer of a larger (for those days) farm of approximately one hundred and fifty acres at the time he married my mother. He had been successful in his farming along with his father and had moved from being a tenant at the farm to purchasing it along with his father. My mother already had a son when she married my father. At the tender age of nineteen, a member of a keen chapel going family and living in a rural area, she found herself pregnant.

She occasionally talked about this, and I remember one occasion when she told how she felt deeply depressed about her life and could not see the way forward. One night in her bedroom she had a vision of an angel, who appeared in shining white robes and spoke to her personally telling her that from that night onwards she would be able to cope and to bring up her son. My half brother, Ernest was born in 1921, so when I was born in 1943, he was already an adult, which given what happened later was a great blessing for my mother, my brother Sam and myself.

Like all the other males in his family, my father developed a debilitating heart decease soon after I was born, and it became clear that his health was such that he needed to reduce his workload if he were to survive and see his sons growing up. A decision was made to sell the big farm and move to a smaller one of just thirty acres. In the same year that we moved to the smaller farm, when I was four years old, my father died. I have a vivid recollection of seeing the doctor coming out of the downstairs room where my father was in bed and explaining that my father had died. It is a great sadness to me that I have no personal recollections of my father. As I grew up, I heard lots of stories about my dad most of them focussed on his temper. We had an old-fashioned wireless which ran off a wet accumulator battery, that had to be recharged after a month or so. It was enclosed in a wooden cabinet with a cloth covered loudspeaker at the front.

The cloth covering had a hole in the middle and I remember asking my mum how it had been made. Her answer was quite revealing because she said that I was partly to blame! She then explained that one day when he was looking after me and trying to listen to the wireless at the same time, having failed to shut up my noise, he shut up the noise of the wireless by putting his foot through it! I remember another story about him tripping up over a cast iron wheel from some farm machinery that had been left lying in his way, and him losing his temper and kicking the wheel so hard that he smashed the cast iron rim. I often wondered what it did to his toes.

I have only one or two recollections of living on the big farm, that we left in 1948 and one of those was quite painful. My eldest brother had some hens housed in a shed in the croft in front of the farmhouse and it was my job to let them out in the morning. The problem was that they included a cockerel who was a nasty piece of work. He loved to jump on my head and peck my face, so I had to quickly pull up the trap door that allowed the fowls out and then run as fast as my little legs could carry me back to the house. I remember another time when with my brother Sam we raided the pea row in the field alongside the road, filling our pockets and then leaving a trail of empty peapods along the road and into the farmyard.

As I grew up, I became familiar with the poaching expeditions of my dad, granddad, and great grandad. These mainly took place over the Chatsworth Estate. My great grandfather had been a most notorious poacher and had experienced many a fight to resist arrest by the gamekeepers. The big farm ran alongside the boundary of the Chatsworth Estate. On dad's side the area was cultivated, whereas the area on the Chatsworth side was a grouse moor. The Duke of Devonshire, through his agent sought to persuade my dad to sell him the shooting rights for our farm, but dad was not having that. Whenever the estate had a grouse shoot, my dad would sit himself under the boundary wall, and knock down, quite legally any game that ventured over his field. I started my shooting at the age of eleven with a double barrelled .410 shotgun and I confess to having done a fair bit of poaching myself, it clearly ran in the blood.

There is a saying "Poacher turned gamekeeper" which applied in my case because at one stage in my police career I caught many poachers on the Chatsworth Estate. My son also had shooting in his blood to the extent that he became a gamekeeper as his full-time employment.

My family did have some contacts with the local policeman who lived in the nearby village of Ashover. During the Second World War my mother provided a bit of a café for soldiers who were being taught to drive before joining active service. They were based in Chesterfield and used the roads close to our farm for driving practice and then eventually to qualify to drive the heavy army lorries. By providing this service mother managed to get extra tea coffee and sugar on her ration book. The local policeman was also in the habit of dropping in for a cuppa, but on one occasion he chose a very, bad time to arrive. My father was a licensed slaughter man, and his services were regularly required to kill pigs and either cut them up for use as pork, or cure them to become bacon, ham, or shoulder. The number of pigs a farmer slaughtered was regulated by the Ministry of Agriculture and War, however for a variety of reasons was sometimes exceeded, not least where a pig was in danger of dying but otherwise suitable to be eaten and intervention by killing was the only way to ensure that the farmer got something back for his efforts. It was not just formal farms where pigs were reared for this purpose, many people kept a pig in a garden and reared it for their own consumption, but for which they must have a licence.

At that time the village policeman patrolled in an Austin Devon saloon car. Ashover is one of the largest parishes in the country and was therefore one of the first where a mechanised beat was designated. One day he drove into the farmyard just after my father had killed a pig which had not been licensed for slaughter and the carcase was then being prepared to be butchered. This first action after the killing of the animal required copious amounts of hot water to be pored over it so that animal's hairs could be scraped away. Imagine the scene, my mother is making shuttle runs from the kitchen to the farm building from which a steady flow of steam was emerging, when up pulls the police car.

The bobby quickly surveyed the scene and opening the car window greeted mother saying, "Morning Lillian, have I chosen a bad time to come?"

To which mother responded, "Ey lad it's not the best of times, perhaps tha'd like to come back in a couple of weeks." When he did come back and enjoy my mother's tea, on returning to his car he found a nice piece of pork on the passenger seat. All strictly illegal, and if there was any suspicion of it being done for commercial advantage, my father would not have got away with it.

Living in a remote farmhouse meant that my upbringing differed greatly from anything experienced today. We did not have electricity, so that meant lighting was from paraffin lamps in the living room, and candles elsewhere. We did have paraffin fuelled pressure lanterns to use outside in the winter, carrying them around and then hanging them up in any building we occupied at the time.

We fetched our water from a well across a field and about a hundred yards from the house. Water was heated in the black-lead coated fireplace, with a copper at one side of the fire hole and the oven at the other side. So, no taps, no running water, no bathroom, no central heating, and no flushing toilet. We had an earth toilet situated behind the farmhouse and getting to it required a walk through the garden and into a small croft. It was a double seater so you could have company if you wished. That never did happen for me, and I do not recall any couple ever going there together. The toilet was at the end of a building that housed the pigsty which meant that you could blame the pigs for the bad smell.

In our living room we had a quarry tile floor some of which was covered by homemade "pegged" rugs. My mother made these using used sacks as the backing material into which were pegged scraps of material recycled from worn out clothing. We also had a "front room," which we only opened on high days and holidays. In the early years at Walton Lees Farm, all the cooking was done on the black leaded fireplace. Down some steps from the living room was our kitchen, just a small space with a sink and some cupboards, later we invested in a Calor Gas cooker fuelled by bottled gas which was delivered by a local businessman. Having a wash before going to school involved bringing about two pints of hot water from the boiler part of the kitchen grange, poring it into a washing up bowl, metal before plastic came along where you washed your face and hands and if necessary, your legs. Going back into the living room you would be inspected by mother to ensure there were no "tide marks" on your neck. Baths were undertaken once a week on Saturday evenings in front of the fire in a large tin bath. The entire family of four used the same water so last one in was not sure whether they came out cleaner or dirtier.

In the winter, the only place where there was any real warmth was in front of the open fire. Going upstairs was like walking into a refrigerator. It was not unusual to wake up in the morning and not be able to see anything through the window because of a layer of ice on the inside of the glass. We did not have much in terms of possessions or creature comforts, but it was a loving environment, and we were not conscious of going short of anything.

For some reason unknown to me I was usually the last person to get into the bath, by which time the water was far from clean, and mother had a way of dealing with any of the implications of bathing in dirty water, she added a disinfectant with the brand name "Izal." This used to make the water go a milky colour, but that was not the only impact it had on a small boy, the worst being that it used to make the end of my penis sting like hell, and I would cry out, "My tail hurts!"

One Saturday evening there was a knock at the door just after the bathing had been completed but the full bath was still located in front of the open fireplace. Mother was a bit shocked to find a local character at the door, who was well known for getting drunk and then doing strange things, and although he was in a state of drunkenness, given that he had been a friend of my father, she invited him in. He sat down in a rickety chair which was alongside the tin bath and started to dose off. Sam and I were desperately keen that he should fall asleep and then drop into the bath and were whispering what we would do if that happened. Whilst we were longing for him to fall asleep mother was working hard to keep him awake. Eventually he recovered enough energy and sobriety, to get up and go back to his pony and trap in our yard and make his way home.

Life on a farm involved the farmers kids undertaking farm work and coming home from school I would quickly change into my play/work clothes. There were always tasks to be undertaken which varied according to the season of the year. In the winter months, it was mainly carrying buckets of water from the well to the cattle, or for the house. In the summer, we would help harvest the hay and other crops. This was before the introduction of bailers, so the hay was gathered loose and stored in stacks ready for the winter. We did most of the work by hand, but a contractor or neighbour would cut the grass using a tractor and mower and we would use wooden rakes to turn the grass and prepare it to collect.

Sometimes we borrowed a large black workhorse called 'Jack.' He was a lovely gentle giant of an animal and even as a relatively small child of ten or eleven years I was able to handle him. I remember well, loosening him from the headstall in the stable and letting him out into the farmyard where I would stand on an empty forty-gallon oil drum to saddle him up ready for work. All you had to do was call his name and he would walk over and wait for you to put on his collar and the other harness required for whatever you were doing.

In the spring, I remember using Jack with a cart to carry manure (muck to us) from the farmyard to the fields, where I would get into the cart and throw the contents out in small heaps ready to be spread by hand later. When a small heap of manure was in place I would simply say "Ger on (Go)" to Jack and off he would walk in a straight line until I said "Woe (Stop)" and the entire process could be repeated.

One of his little foibles was that he did not like getting his feet wet and one day an old relative who used to come and help us on the farm was using Jack to pull a roller over a recently sown corn field. Returning to the farm he took a shortcut across the field which involved crossing a very, small stream. Jack jumped the stream and pulled the shafts out of the roller, leaving the rolling mechanism behind!

Some of the time we also had a pony that was borrowed from the same neighbour, but horse riding was never my thing. It is strange to me now that I seem to remember enjoying working with Jack but found no real pleasure in riding the pony. I continue to have that same preference for looking at the heavy working horses when visiting agricultural shows.

We would also grow oats and wheat which we used as food for the livestock. This would be stored in stacks in sheaves ready for the threshing machine later in the year. Threshing days were highlights of the year. The day before the event contractor would arrive with all the machinery. A huge threshing machine (called a drum), and a large stationary bailer pulled by a tractor. My favourite threshing tractor was a Field Marshall which as kids we called a 'Popper Tractor' because it had a single cylinder engine which made a popping sound.

Threshing day involved a lot of workers; the contractor would often supply someone located on the top of the drum, feeding the sheaves of corn into the machine and at least one other located on the ground supervising the machinery. Neighbouring farmers would support each other on threshing days because the demand for labour would exceed that normally available from employers or family. There would be one or two people on the stack throwing the sheaves onto the top of the thrashing drum. As 'kids' we would often help-out on the stack throwing sheaves from the distant parts of the stack to the man who was feeding them onto the machine. Another one or two farmers would be located at the bailer carrying the large and very heavy bails of straw into a stack and others would be located at the rear end of the threshing machine where the grain would come out of chutes into sacks which they carried to wherever the grain was to be stored.

Threshing days were noisy, dusty, and lively and quite different from the quiet days which were the norm and to that extent I enjoyed them. There was a distinctive noise made by the machinery which took the form of a medium pitched humming noise, but this would increase each time a sheaf of corn was placed into the threshing drum. However, being a serious hay fever sufferer right from my early days, the dust played havoc with me, and I would spend most of the day sneezing much to the amusement of the farmers! There were other risks to health on threshing days, rats and mice would have moved into the corn stacks and I have seen occasions when a mouse or rat has dropped inside a farmer's shirt. Jack Russell dogs were an essential element of these days as they quickly disposed of the rats and mice. The machinery also involved some risk and on one occasion one of my uncles lost a finger when he accidentally got it trapped in a drive belt.

My mother would be extremely busy cooking food for all the workers and often the status of the farmer was judged by the quality of the food presented on 'threshing days.' There was always a piece of beef so large that it only just fitted into our coal fired range oven. The roast beef would be accompanied by enormous amounts of potatoes and other vegetables. Hot puddings were an essential ingredient to conclude the threshing day dinner, steamed treacle sponge being my favourite.

Growing Up

I attended the local school in the village of Ashover from the age of five to fifteen. My school days were happy days without being "the happiest days of my life." I was never set any homework; I was never caned or subjected to any other form of corporal punishment and was never aware of feeling under any pressure or stress whilst there.

I was usually within the top half dozen in my class in all subjects undertaken and I represented the school in football, cricket, and athletics, distinguishing myself in the latter by winning the half mile in the South Peak Schools sports event during my final year in school. Whilst I appreciate the importance of academic achievement, I do feel sorry for today's kids when they are subject to such parental pressure to achieve beyond what they are naturally capable of.

Ashover School during the years I attended included infants, juniors, and seniors. Short of passing the 11+ or 13+ examinations, you remained at the same school from five to fifteen years of age, which is what I did. My teachers were surprised when I did not pass the 11+ examination because being one of the top pupils, they expected me to do well. On reflection I had been at home suffering from asthma leading up to the date of the examination and was probably not at my best. Conversely, two years later I was successful in passing the transfer examination, but still missed out on Grammar School because our school had five of us pass the examination that year, but only three places were available, all of them going to children who already had siblings at the school. Reflecting on all of that, what happened turned out to my advantage, my mother would have struggled financially to send me to Grammar school, and lack of academic achievement did not hinder my later police career.

I do remember that I could read before I started school and that I achieved this without any assistance from anyone else. I have distinct recollections of discovering new words even prior to five years when I started school.

Walton Lees Farm where we lived was located on Hungerhill Lane, where there was a small community of us. At Hungerhill Farm lived one family, Charlie (mother's cousin), his wife Lilly and their children, Bessie, Eva, and Ernest. At Glendale Farm lived Bob and Alice and their children Robert and Malcolm plus nephew Leon. This created quite a community of kids and when going to school, we would all make our way to the top of the lane and wait for the school bus to Ashover.

On the opposite side of the Darley Dale Road but at the junction with our lane was an old chapel, which had been turned into domestic accommodation and housed my mother's sister Ethel. She and her late husband had brought up fourteen children. Given that my Aunt Ethel was the oldest of my mother's siblings and my mother the youngest, then by the time I was attending school all their children that still survived were grown up and most had left home.

Two of the boys, Ronnie and Brian had lost their lives in WW2, and they had lost a couple in childhood, but the remainder were still alive. Only the oldest, Abraham remained at home along with the youngest girl Brenda, both of whom had not yet married. It is difficult to imagine how my aunty managed to bring up all those children in a building that had received little adaptation. The heating system comprised a large pop-bellied solid fuel boiler which had been there during the church days. The building was open to the roof and rooms were demarked by wooden partitions up to the height of around seven feet. Uncle Abraham had worked in stone quarries all his working life and had died at quite a young age the effect of the stone dust that was part of his everyday working environment.

Aunt Ethel would frequently come out to talk to us as we waited for the bus often in the warm weather just wearing her long white night gown. My mother referred to Ethel's family as the Old Chapel lot and for her special services at our chapel such as Sunday School Anniversary and Harvest Festival were judged by how many of them turned up. Quite often all those still alive would attend, which for two of the daughters involved travelling from Darlington, quite a journey. I loved it when, after the evening service some of them if not all would come to our home for supper.

Mother would have prepared a feast ready for the events. Home cured ham would have been boiled as would a mature hen or two, my mother selecting ones that were about to stop laying and had plenty of body weight. These hens were boiled not roasted so that the impact of old age was less evident and the meat tender and tasty. Although we did not have much money, we were never short of food, and it came natural for mother to share this with family and friends.

There were three busses running into Ashover School each day, all operated by a local company. We were picked up by the bus that commenced collecting children in the hamlet of Uppertown and by the time we got on the bus most of the other children were all on board. Our bus was always an old Bedford coach which had seen better days. Unlike the Alton and Slack busses, ours had the driver's seat integral with the public part and those who got on early could sit on the front seat which was in line with the driver B. After we had joined the bus, the next pick-up was at the bottom of Belland Lane, where our cousins, Don, Patricia, and Keith joined us, their mother Nellie was one of aunt Ethels fourteen children. I remember one day when Don came and sat close to me and my brother Sam and said, "I reckon you two were in trouble with your mum last night, because I heard her shouting you for about a couple of hours." Where they lived was about two miles from where my mother had been shouting but it is testimony to the volume of her voice that it could carry for that distance.

Certainly, we had no excuse for not hearing her and I cannot remember what it was that was so stimulating us that we ignored mother is beyond my memory. There have been times when I have had cause to be thankful that I inherited her voice and I have used it to good effect in a crowd control environment. The next stop was at "The House under the Rock," which for generations had been one of the family homes of my mother's family. It is so called because it is built under a rock face and has a walk-in larder which has a floor, roof and three walls consisting entirely of rock. My mother's uncle Charlie had brought up his family there and his daughter, Nellie was in occupation, along with her husband Jack. Sometimes they had their grandson staying with them who was none too keen to go to school and had to be coached onto the bus, with us pulling him, whilst Nellie pushed him. The strange thing was that on the return journey we struggled to get him off the bus. Aunt Nellie, as we called her had a habit of blinking and twitching when she was stressed and to be honest getting her grandson on and off the bus was very funny.

My call to serve and protect took place following my decision at the age of fifteen to become a born-again Christian but, looking back over my childhood years there was some evidence of a desire to serve well before that time. August 1952 was extremely wet in Lynton and Lynmouth when those North Devon seaside resorts experienced widespread flooding and associated damage. I was nine years old at the time the youngest of four children living on adjoining farms and we decided that we would respond to an appeal made by the Mayor of Chesterfield for funds to help the people rebuild their homes. We organised our own carnival with sports, fancy dress and the like and I personally picked fresh vegetables from our field and sold them at the carnival and on the side of the main road from our wheelbarrow. I cannot remember how much we collected but we did receive a nice letter of thanks from the town's Mayor.

The following year the flooding theme continued when many towns on the east coast experienced widespread flooding and our town Mayor again appealed for funds. We decided that January was not a good time for carnivals and with carol singing fresh in our minds after Christmas we decided to go singing from house to house and collect funds and once again received our, by now customary letter of appreciation.

Doubtless we were not the only kids to respond to those appeals but the fact that we did reflects an early indicator of a desire to help others less fortunate which has certainly influenced my desire to work in the developing world.

Both these events also indicate something about the ease with which we roamed around the countryside without any fear. I remember these times as an age of innocence when we did not have a care in the world, and I wish that we could re- create such a society for my grandchildren in the twenty first century.

However, the final incident suggests that the countryside was not entirely safe and not everyone's intentions were honest. I am not sure exactly when the incident occurred but was probably around 1956 when I had just entered my teenage years. Along with my mate from one of the neighbouring farms, I went into Chesterfield to the cinema one Saturday evening. This involved a walk of about two miles to the nearest bus stop. The last bus back left Chesterfield at 9.25pm so we had to be sure to be on it and avoid problems at home.

When we got off the bus so did an elderly female neighbour and a man who lived close by our home in a gypsy caravan. We walked along with the former all the way to our homes, and she then continued the short distance to her home. But whilst undertaking her final few hundred yards she was accosted by the man who had also been on the bus and was raped by him. My mate and I ended up being witnesses in the prosecution case and were both interviewed by CID officers from Chesterfield. I remember being impressed by their work and it is possible that the experience helped influence my later decision to join the police.

We are told in the twenty-first century that global warming is causing weather extremes, but as I think back to my childhood, we did have extremes of weather just as much then. I have previously made references to the Lynton and Lynmouth floods and to the East Coast floods both of which occurred in the fifties and extremes were not restricted to flooding. We certainly had weather that was very much colder, and we had far more snow than we have had in the last twenty years or more. The worst winter in living memory was that of 1947 when I was just four years old and therefore have no recollection of it.

However, it was so often talked about in my home that I can tell you much about what it was like. During that winter there were four significant snows each one coming from a different wind direction and with a couple of weeks in between each snowfall. Each downfall completely blocked all the roads and lanes around where we lived. The two farms where I spent my first nineteen years were both located at around one thousand feet above sea level, which partly contributed to the volume of snow, but in 1947 the snow also fell in profusion at lower levels and road transport came to a standstill after each fall of snow.

In those days, normal levels of snow on the roads were cleared by a snowplough, pulled by a farmer's tractor. These snow ploughs were constructed from very heavy and solid timbers in the shape of an arrow and pulled by a chain with the tractor leading. At each end of the open vee shape a council roadman would walk, operating a lever to ensure that the plough covered the intended ground. These ploughs had originally been pulled by horses, but tractors had taken over after the war years. Once the snow started to settle on the roads, these ploughs would be turned out to clear the roads. They only worked effectively if the level of snow did not exceed two feet in depth, and as a result they could not cope with the 1947 levels of snow. Each time the snow fell there were blizzard conditions and the snow drifted across the open fields completely filling the space between the walls on either side of the roads.

The only way the snow could be cleared was by engaging farmers and labourers to hand dig the snow with shovels. At the time my father had a dairy herd of cattle and after each snow it was at least two weeks before he could get the milk to market. My mother used to explain that every single churn and other clean container were filled with milk awaiting the road opening, Given the very cold environment the milk did not deteriorate as rapidly as it would have done at normal temperature. Mother was turning some of the cream and milk into butter and cheese, but there were occasions when they just had to poor the milk into the drains.

Once the roads were open travelling along them there would be a mountain of snow blocks up to sixteen or so feet high. The trouble was that each time they had opened the roads there would be another snow fall blowing the mountain of snow back into the road and requiring the process to be repeated. Apparently, the snow did not completely disappear until late spring, but there followed one of the best summers on record and all the farm crops produced heavy returns.

Winter snow made life difficult for us on the farm and as a child I hated having to go out in blizzard conditions to do tasks essential to keep our farm animals alive and in good condition. With a large bucket full of water hanging from each arm and conveying these more than one hundred yards was difficult enough at any time of the year but doing it in two or three feet of snow was an awful job. Mucking out the cattle was equally challenging because the first task was to clear a path for the wheelbarrow, which was impossible to push through snow. If you have only ever lived in a town you are unlikely to be able to envisage what it can be like at one thousand feet above sea level with heavy snow and gale force winds. The conditions are commonly referred to as a 'white out,' which means that you are unable to see more than a couple of feet in front of you. As children we frequently suffered from what we referred to as "hot-aches," when we came into the warmth from working outside, the sudden exposure to warmth made our hands extremely painful and we would be told to hold our hands in hot water until the pain receded.

Snow, however, did have compensations and given that there were many steep hills around our farm sledging was a regular winter-time activity. All our sledges were handmade often re-using articles that were no longer required and fixing runners, underneath. Once Robert our neighbour used an upturned kitchen table complete with legs, this he pulled behind his pony and we all sat on the table, hanging on to one of the legs and squealing with delight as we were dragged around the fields. The traditional sledging was often undertaken after dark because work had to be done first when arriving home from school.

If there was a good clear moon and snow on the ground visibility was amazing due to the moonlight being reflected off the snow. Whilst it is possible that I am looking at past through rose tinted spectacles, I am sure that winters were much colder and there was much more snow in those days than today. In recent years, my grandchildren who live in the barn in our farmyard often only have a couple of occasions when they can sledge and then only for short periods before the snow disappears. In my childhood we would often sledge every night for a week or more. How we managed to avoid serious injury on those occasions I will never know given that we had no idea about having protective equipment. One year, the snow was so good and the period so long that we managed to create our own version of the 'Cresta' run at our neighbour's farm.

This involved sledging down the field above the farmhouse, negotiating through the farmyard and then down the field below the farm. This required considerable talent in steering with your feet. The run was best achieved on your belly with feet hanging off the back and steering the projectile. On one occasion I misjudged the turning through the farmyard and ended with my head inside the fire hole of wood fired copper used to boil small potatoes for the pigs, fortunately the fire was not lit. I have read of sledging accidents when people have received fatal head injuries in such circumstances and looking back, I conclude that God was looking after us because he had things in store for us as we grew up.

Snow often made it difficult getting to school and when the snow was fresh on the road, we would not bother going up the lane for the bus, because the chances were that it would not appear. On other occasions our lane would be filled completely by snow from wall to wall and we would have to go over the fields to get to the school bus. Play times at school when there was snow covering the school fields would often involve huge snowball fights. This involved getting yourself into a gang and then rolling up massive snowballs with which you created your own base with walls to protect you from the enemy! There would then follow a battle between your gang and another with the aim of destroying your opponent's home base. The brave would lead their mates into the battle and throw themselves at the opponent's snow fort. Great fun!

Looking back on how my mother managed to earn enough income from just thirty acres of land to bring up my brother and I seems to have been something of a miracle. There is no chance that such a small farm would support a family today. Farms in those days were mixed, meaning that we had cattle, pigs, and hens, whereas today the farmers specialise to gain the benefit of scale and the farms are much bigger. We would have a sow from which each year would have a litter of pigs. Sometimes we would sell these to a local butcher for pork and sometimes for bacon, and if it were the latter, we would just keep them a bit longer. The advantage of pigs over cattle is that they mature quicker which means that you do not have to wait quite so long to get your money back.

We always had two or three milking cows and they supplied milk for our own consumption, as well as to feed the calves we had at the time. One of our tasks as children was to 'suckle' the calves, which was done from a bucket. When the calf was newly born it was necessary to teach it how to feed from the bucket, because by instinct the calf would want to feed directly from its mother. Going up to the calf you had to get it to start sucking your finger and then move your hand into the bucket of milk, whilst the calf was still sucking and gradually remove your finger. Eventually the calf would discover that this was the way it fed and thereafter you just held the bucket of milk in front of the calf and away it went.

Generally, the milk from one cow would feed more than one calf, so we would buy in calves mainly the surplus from dairy herds. I cannot recall that we ever kept cattle though to the age in which they would be slaughtered for beef. That would have taken between eighteen months and two years which meant that you had to wait a long time to get your money back. We would sell ours as 'stores,' when they would be between nine months and a year old. The farmers who bought them would fatten them up, feeding them with high protein concentrates, before selling them for beef.

The first milk that the cow supplies is quite different from what it settles down to after a couple of days. It is vitally important that the newly born calf has the first milk because it has a special content that the calf requires at that stage. My mother used to call the second milk produced after a calf had been born as 'beestings.' It had a yellow tint to it and a strong but not unpleasant flavour, and she would use it to make a pudding and a custard. It was always a special treat. Another treat from the new milk would be that we separated the cream and churned that into butter. We had this glass churn container into which we poured the cream and then screw on the top the churning apparatus. As children we loved turning the handle of the churn and observing to cream turning into butter. We could make a meal out of mother's freshly baked bread and newly churned butter.

At least one a year one of our pigs we would kill and butcher for our own consumption. During his lifetime, my father would kill and butcher the pig, but after that his brother, my uncle Jack used to come and do the task. I have childhood memories of these occasions that people these days would be squeamish about. My uncle did not believe in using a stun gun before bleeding the animal because he thought it adversely affected the flavour. One of my tasks as a small boy was to stir the blood as it poured out of the pig into a large pot.

This was in preparation for my mother to use the blood to make black pudding. She had her own recipe with all sorts of grains, herbs, and flour in it along with onion and large lumps of fat from the belly of the pig. These would be placed in large cloth bags and boiled in a copper. The smell of them cooking and the flavour of them when you opened them up and sampled them was quite amazing and far better than anything you can buy today. It is said that the only thing that was wasted on a pig was the squeal. The intestines were washed and cleaned and boiled to make chitterlings. Any meat on the ears, tails, feet, and head was boiled and turned into brawn. The hams, shoulders and sides would be salted and dry cured into the most flavoursome bacon you ever tasted.

These would once dry from the salting process be placed in muslin bags and hung from hooks in the house. They would supply the household with ham, shoulder, and bacon for as much as a whole year. I have happy memories of summer evenings when we would be getting in the hay harvest with help provided by other family members and ending the evening with ham and eggs. I can smell the smell and taste the taste as I write this account of those years on the farm.

My mother also had a large flock of free-range laying hens which provided a substantial proportion of her income. We mainly had hens that were a cross between Rhode Island Red's and Light Sussex which we would buy in as day old chicks and then cull after a couple of years when their egg production would be declining. The day-old chicks would arrive in special cardboard boxes with about twenty in each box. We used to love holding these golden balls of fluff when they arrived. We had a special brooder with heating that we placed them into for the first month or so of their life.

Hens start laying from about twenty weeks old onwards, so creating an income quickly. When they first start laying, they are called 'pullets' and the eggs are much smaller than you would get from a mature hen. They start laying full size eggs after about thirty weeks and generally have completed their commercial life after two years. When we culled them, we did not waste the meat they were called boilers, because rather than roasting they would be boiled so that the meat was tenderised. In the wintertime their egg production would decline in direct proportion to the hours of day light. To overcome this, we used to take in a couple of pressure lanterns and hang them from the foul shed ceiling.

They provided light but also some heat which encouraged the hens to carry on eating and scratching amongst the deep litter, thereby keeping up the egg production when the price of eggs would rise, due to the general decline in output. The lights would go off after about two hours when they had burned away the tank full of paraffin used as fuel. One of my tasks was to fill up these lanterns and light them before taking them to the foul shed. Walking into the shed with the lamps would disturb the rats and it was not a pleasant experience. Wherever you get hens, you inevitably get rats because the hen food provides an easy source of food.

From being a teenager, my mother had supplied egg and chickens direct to people in Matlock walking there a distance of at least five miles with her huge baskets. During my childhood years she had regular customers in Chesterfield, using the same wicker baskets, but travelling on the weekly Saturday Uppertown bus. She would visit with eggs every week and sometimes oven ready chickens, and occasionally ducks and geese. We would buy in day old cockerels to rear for meat, and they would be housed in free range accommodation. The busiest season was Christmas, and this was a time when my mother earned a substantial proportion of her annual income. Free range chickens, taste nothing like what you buy today from the supermarket.

Ours were far more mature and therefore had more flavour, however in those days having a chicken was a treat because they were more expensive than a joint of beef, so you had chicken on high days and holidays. When the chickens were a few weeks old we would inject a pellet into their neck, just under the skin which would slowly release and make the chicken produce more weight. They were called capons, but the practise is banned these days. Whereas chickens without the pellet would typically have an oven-ready weight of perhaps four to eight pounds our capons would weigh between six and twelve pounds, which meant that at the upper end they were about the same size as a small turkey. Our preparation for Christmas involved everybody working our fingers to the bone in the build up to Christmas Day.

Bearing in mind that there were not the cold storage facilities available that we have today for four or five days leading up to Christmas Eve we would be working late into the evenings, plucking, and dressing and then delivering somewhere around sixty birds. We set up something of a production line in one of our sheds, where we had a large boiler powered by a bottled gas. The water had to be at just the right temperature because having killed the bird we would dip it in the water and then pluck off the feathers. The hot water enabled us to remove the feathers a little easier than would otherwise be the case, but if it were too hot it adversely affected the final appearance of the bird.

Once the bird had been plucked, they would be left hanging from the ceiling awaiting the removal of the innards and final oven preparation. Anyone who has plucked a chicken will know that it is a skilled task if you are to avoid ripping the skin and that some of the feathers are quite difficult to remove. By the time we finished our task usually on Christmas Eve, we would be fed up with the sights and smells of chicken feathers and guts and our fingers would be red raw. However, mother would have money in the bank for a while. On top of the chickens one or two of mother's customer would ask for a turkey, goose, or duck and we would buy them in live and then pluck and dress them.

If you think plucking a chicken is challenging, just try a goose where there is a layer of down underneath the feathers, so you end up plucking them twice. Turkeys are a challenge simply because of their size. Compared with today hardly anybody had a turkey for Christmas, then.

Our farm animals were always what you might call "people friendly," because they were hand reared and used to having human beings around them. My brother and I could walk up to our cattle in the fields and jump on their backs, riding them around without any problem. With today's suckler herds you would be unable to get that close to cattle. There were occasions when our relationship to livestock was not so easy, and we had a huge, and nasty gander that used to chase me and my brother and peck us. They can cause quite a bruise and one day I grew tired of having to chase him away and I angrily picked up a lump of wood and threw it at him.

Unusually for me, I hit the target at the side of his head, and he went down on the ground. My brother said, "Tha's killed him youth, tha'll be in trouble with mother now." Fortunately, he came round quite quickly, but never again chased us and was partially blind in one eye. I do not think mother ever discovered what had caused his blindness and I was not going to volunteer the information.

I have a vivid memory of coming downstairs one morning when I would perhaps be eight or nine years old and finding a lovely fluffy German Shepherd puppy in the living room. My brother Ernest had decided to get a dog. He called her Wendy. She was black and tan in colour and grew into a most intelligent and loyal dog and a protector of me and my brother. We loved her dearly and have very many happy memories of her. I have had an affection for German Shepherds ever since that time.

Wendy would always appear to be more aggressive towards others when we were at home on our own or out with her. When in the house she was fastened on a chain secured to a large, heavy, sewing machine and if someone came to the door that she was unsure about she would start to pull the machine towards the door. I remember one occasion when I was alone at home with the dog when an old pick-up truck appeared in the farmyard and a scruffy looking bloke got out and started wondering around the farmyard. I opened the door and asked the man what he was doing, and he said that he was looking for scrap metal.

I told him that we did not have any, but he continued to rummage around. I then put Wendy on her lead and went outside our front door with her, as soon as she saw the man she started to growl and bark and pull towards him. I said, "I think you had better leave because if you do not, I will take my dog off the lead, and she will go for you." There was an immediate reaction as the man ran to his truck and jumped in the cab. Sadly, for him, the engine would not start, so he had to jump out with the starting handle to hand crank the engine. All the time Wendy was pulling hard on her lead and barking and growling at the man. I have never seen anyone hand crank an engine so speedily and fortunately it started, and he was able to drive away in one piece. Well done, Wendy!

On another occasion mother asked us to take something to a neighbouring farm, which involved about a two mile walk across an area of open moorland. We took Wendy with us, keeping her on the lead because the moor was a used for grouse shooting and the gamekeeper might shoot a dog running loose and disturbing the birds. Half-way across the moor the gamekeeper appeared, and Wendy growled and barked, letting him know that he would be in serious trouble if he did anything to us. When the gamekeeper saw my mother and few days later, he told her that she could depend upon the fact that if we were out with our dog, we would be safe because she would protect us.

At one time we also had a lamb as a pet. Joey lost his mum when he was being born and the farmer gave him to us to hand rear. There is nothing so lovely as a newly born lamb and we loved feeding him cow's milk from a bottle with a teat. Initially feeding him was a total pleasure, we would nurse him on our knee. Just occasionally he spoilt his manners and peed on our knee, but the delights of feeding him far outweighed the influence of a drop of urine. Naturally, Joey started to grow bigger and gain strength. It was impossible to feed him on your knee anymore, so now we would bend down with the bottle in front of us and he would feed standing up. He was so enthusiastic for his milk that he would sometime push violently at the bottle and towards the end of the time he needed milk we ended up having to feed him through the bars of a gate, otherwise he knocked us off our feet.

As Joey grew up, he developed some of the characteristics of a dog, following us around, wherever we went and getting engaged in our play. One of his favourite tricks was to knock down the wickets when we played cricket and then run away. Jumping off the school bus and walking down the lane, Joey would hear us and run the half a mile to meet and greet us. Eventually, he became so big and strong that if he ran and butted you, it could be quite painful, and he would stand guard outside the farm and attack anyone who came past. That was when mother decided she would have to sell him, so he could join a flock and start to do what rams are born to do! He produced a record number of lambs that first year, but the farmer had to get rid of him because he taught the ewes how to climb walls and get out of the fields. We never asked what happened to him, but we had certainly enjoyed having him as a pet if only for a limited time.

Each year would be remembered for annual events that formed much of our social life outside of church and school. In the early summer there would be a Sunday School trip to a seaside resort. This is how I first caught sight of the sea, because where we lived you could not have been further away from the coast and as hardly anyone possessed a car this was your only opportunity to see far flung places like, Skegness, Bridlington, Scarborough, Rhyl, Llandudno, and Southport. I remember one year when my nephew Stephen had his first ever glimpse of the sea from the window of the bus and said to his dad, "By gum dad that's a big pond."

Given that the nearest coastal resort would be at least a three-hour, drive in a bus we would have to leave as early as possible. I have recollections of getting up at dawn to do the farm jobs before being picked up at the top of our lane. We youngsters would find the back seats and as I turned into a teenager, I would try to get next to one of the girls so we could have a bit of a cuddle. My mother would have packed a lunch for us, but we would also visit a café for a meal at the resort. I recall one of my older cousins Reg, once got on the bus with a large box containing three dozen packets of crisps and proceeded to eat them all before, we arrived at our final destiny. He was quite fond of crisps and obviously, he was a big bloke.

I would always spend a while in the penny arcade wasting my money in the machines and we would always have a paddle in the sea. Donkey rides were also a frequent treat on these trips. Mother tended to spend the first hour at the resort looking for the best café for us to take our lunch, the packed meal having been consumed at a mid-journey break. Looking back to those trips we would never arrive at the resort until around noon and would be gathering at the bus for the return journey for about 5pm, so rarely had more than five hours at the resort.

Mother would also take Sam and myself on a winter trip to a pantomime. Again, we would travel by coach to the theatre often in Sheffield, but occasionally in Leeds or Birmingham if the star of the performer were more in line with mother's and/or the organiser's requirements. I can still remember the words and tune to some of the songs we were asked to sing on these occasions, just consider the following lyrics for a couple of them.

"Why does a red cow give white milk when it always eats green grass?"

"That's the burning question, gives you indigestion!"

"I don't know, and you don't know!"

"Tell me, if you can?"

"Why does a red cow give white milk hen it always easts green grass?"

Or if you prefer:

"Fish and chips, covered in glorious batter. You can smell them a mile away on a summer's day. Fish and chips covered in glorious batter etc."

Amongst the star performers I remember were, Morecambe and Wise, Ken Platt, Ken Dodd, Albert Modley, George Formby, All Read, Norman Evans, Arthur Askey, and Roy Castle.

Such trips were only complete if we stopped at a fish and chip shop on the way back home.

One year our entire school along with all the pupils from schools in Clay Cross were given a free trip to an afternoon performance of a pantomime in Sheffield, all paid for by Sir G who was a native of Clay Cross and at the time was the Shell fuel distributor for Derbyshire and Nottinghamshire and the main distributor for Austin and Morris cars. His sister was married to the headmaster of our school which is why Clay Cross was extended to Ashover. I recall that the theatre was completely, filled by children and their teachers. At the interval, each received an ice cream and then before the second half commenced, they turned the spotlight on Sir G in the Royal Box. The cheer that went up from us kids exceeded anything we had produced for the performers.

Occasionally mother would take us to Chesterfield on a Saturday travelling on the Uppertown bus. She would take us along as she visited her regularly customers with eggs and over time, we got to know them well, to mother they were not just loyal customers, but her friends. One of them had a town centre, sweets and tabaco shop and the owner would always send Sam and myself a bag of sweets. Another of the customers was a solicitor who had dealt with my father's affaires but was also a good friend to my mother. Her customers were very loyal and had traded with mother for many years. A couple of events were always included in the visit to Chesterfield. We would go to see "Jack the Barber" for a haircut and visit the Burlington Café for our lunch. The café was on the first floor above a cake shop operated by the same organisation as the café. Sam and I always had the same things for dinner, shepherd's pie with chips and peas for the main course and a "blown-up sugar" for desert (a cream filled meringue) from the cake shop.

I remember one Saturday afternoon when Sam and I were seated in "Jack the Barbers," awaiting our turn when a smart gentleman entered the salon and spoke to the barber, who then turned to us and said, "This gentleman needs to be at the football ground soon, do you two lads mind letting him jump the queue?" We instantly agreed as we were in no hurry. When the man left for the football ground which was just up the road, he expressed his thanks to us and gave us half a crown each, which for us was quite a lot of money. We then discovered that he was a Knight of the Realm, a local businessman and the Chairman of Chesterfield Football Club.

Mother used to use the Tripe Shop as her base for her Saturday visits to Chesterfield. She would deposit her baskets in the room at the rear of the shop and then keep returning when she had sold her eggs and/or chickens and brought back shopping. Sam and I would often wait there for her finishing her shopping. Saturday supper at our home usually consisted of a selection of different types of tripe and cowheel with tomatoes, vinegar and salt and pepper. Occasionally mother would make a cooked meal from tripe and onions and mashed potatoes. The room at the rear of the shop served as a little rest area where there was a shelf around the walls with high stools allowing customers to sit to the shelf and eat a takeaway portion of tripe.

One week a mate of the shop owner came in and he was a little worse for drink and not very observant about what was happening. The shop owner's young son was also in the back of the shop talking to us and he had been using a bubble maker, those old-fashioned small containers of soapy water and a bubble stick to dip in a then blow the bubbles. The boy had lost interest in his newly acquired toy and was talking to us when the partially drunk man was supplied with his plate of tripe. We watched with excitement when he poured a liberal supply of soapy water on his tripe thinking that the vessel contained vinegar. Regrettably, I cannot state here what the man said because he used words that we had never heard before and I would not care to repeat. The look on his face and the bubbles issuing forth from his lips amidst the bad language, put us kids into convulsions of laughter so much so that we had to run outside so we could continue to laugh.

On one occasion mother took us on a day trip organised by the Chesterfield branch of the Poultry Association to the Shrewsbury Flower Show. I remember that there was a high wire artist working high above the showground and without a safety net. It was brilliant. More memorable was our lunch in a restaurant at the show. I cannot recall what food we had, but I can remember that Sam and I got uncontrollable giggles. Two smart young men had joined us in the restaurant and ordered a meal. Just after they had been served one of them accidentally tipped up his entire main course onto his knee—a good job it was not soup! We started to laugh straight away and then the verbal exchange between the customer and the waitress just added to the humour.

It took us ages to calm down and eat our food, so much so that the two blokes left before us and as they passed by our table I said, "Did you enjoy your dinner?" and the one who had not spilt his meal replied, "Yes, but he still has half of it in his trouser pockets." That led us into another fit of laughter.

School Days

I have very many happy memories of attending Ashover School between 1948 and 1958 in fact I cannot think of any negative experience. I was never on the receiving end of the corporal punishment that was meted out at our school, although I saw others being caned. I often wonder what that said about me, I certainly was not a goodie, goodie, person and did get into mischief, but either the teachers did not find out or were not interested. One of the tricks we got up to in the summer, was to collect live wasps at lunchtime and then release them in the classroom to disrupt the lesson. We would go to school with an empty matchbox into which we placed an apple core and then during the lunch break we would go to the dustbins where waste food from the canteen was being disposed of and open our matchbox.

This was an invitation to the wasps to go for the apple core and once we had two or three wasp's we would shut the box and take it into the classroom. Over the period of the afternoon in turn we would open our matchbox inside our desks, each of which had a small hole in the worktop cover. The wasps would then escape into the classroom and inevitably some child would be scared and ask the teacher to get rid of the wasp, which provided an interesting interlude. To this day I fail to understand how the teachers did not rumble that we had an unusually large number of wasps invade the classroom in summer afternoons.

My favourite teacher was married to my cousin Harriett. He had been a prisoner of war under the Japanese during WW2 where he had worked on the infamous railway line, where thousands of his fellow prisoners died. I cannot ever remember him talking about his experiences in the classroom, but occasionally a story of what it was like would sneak out. One such example followed a visit to his home by one of his former fellow inmates and Harriett overheard a conversation in which the friend was recalling that Bill had saved his life on one occasion. The friend had stolen a pineapple when they were out on a working party, and the theft had been discovered.

The working party members were lined up by the prison guards and told that if no one admitted the theft, they would all be punished. Bill knew that his friend was feeling week and close to death at the time and would not survive any punishment, so he immediately stepped forward and took the punishment. The incident reminds me of someone who did the same thing for me an act which led me to desire to serve others, that was Jesus. I am reminded of the words of an old hymn, "In my place condemned he stood, sealed my pardon with his blood, Hallelujah—what a Saviour."

I have other memories of Bill in the classroom, he was a brilliant shot with a tennis ball and if you were talking to your next-door neighbour in class when you should have been working, suddenly and without warning a ball would bounce off the desk into your face. There was not much power behind the throw, but the shock was enough to bring the conversation to an end. Looking to the front of the class Bill had a wry smile on his face but, said nothing and we would get back to the work.

I remember one sunny spring morning when at the break he beckoned me over to him and said, "Do you fancy a walk to Whitbank this morning?" At first, I was a bit confused about what he was asking me to do, before realising that for some reason he wanted me to visit his home. He explained that he should pay in the dinner money he had collected earlier in the week but had left it at home. Given that his wife Harriett was one of my favourite cousins, I jumped at the opportunity. The walk to Bill's house was about two miles each way and involved climbing a steep hill out of the village of Ashover. This was an age when very few people had telephones and I therefore turned up at Whitbank unannounced and knocked on the door. Harriett answered the door and exclaimed, "What are you doing here, aren't you supposed to be at school?"

I explained the reason for my visit and having handed over the money we sat down to share a freshly made coffee and a piece of Harriett's delightful cake.

Bill was quite strict as a teacher, but he was genuinely interested in helping us achieve our learning objectives and I recently discovered that he was always the most popular teacher in the school, when I wrote about him in a post on the Ashover History and Genealogy Group on Facebook and many former pupils reported that he was their favourite. Bill was a scout leader in his spare time and helped establish a permanent scout camp near my home and most Sundays after he had attended the local parish church, you would find him doing jobs there. He was a good example of the public service mentality that has informed my desire to "protect and serve" in my life.

Harriet, his wife attended our chapel where she played the organ and where she supported anyone with needs, ranging from just talking to people who needed company, to helping new mums to cope with their household duties when the pressure was on them. A truly lovely lady and a demonstration of the servant mentality that Christians are supposed to demonstrate.

During my time at the school, it was one of the few remaining schools in Derbyshire, where there was an infant, junior, and senior department, catering for education from five to fifteen years of age. I had the good fortune of having Bill Banner teach me twice during my schooling, in the junior department when I failed the eleven plus examination, and again when I took the transfer examination at thirteen years of age. Knowing my teacher that well and he me as my teacher for a total of four years did, I think serve me well and on one occasion kept me out of trouble, when perhaps I should have been punished.

On one isolated incident, I assaulted a fellow student during a break. For some reason he jumped on my back and turning round I punched him in the face. When I spotted a bleeding nose, I became a bit worried and more so when he ran up to Bill. I then overheard the following conversation.

Pupil: "Please sir, John Bown has thumped me."

Teacher: "Well he has never done anything like that before, so you must have asked for it." Thank you, Sir!

Bill was also accomplished in a variety of arts and crafts, and he introduced us to various skills that I would later use to earn a bit of money. He taught us leather work and my brother, and I used to make purses and wallets which we sold. Another skill he taught was jewellery making which we again took up as a money-making hobby. I used that skill to impress my girlfriends on birthdays and at Christmas. The first recipient of a jewellery gift was Jackie, she was quite surprised by the gift because I had never expressed any devotion to her or so much as had a chased kiss. I was I think thirteen at the time. My next girlfriend was Sheila who also benefitted from my jewellery making skills. By this time, I had discovered the wonderful pleasure of kissing, so for a time Sheila and I did a fair bit of that.

Significantly on a school trip to Liverpool she and I along with two other couples occupied the back seat of a bus driven by her father, who could see us through the mirror. Undeterred we wone the competition for the couple who

37

could kiss for the longest period. Our relationship just faded away, but she remained a good friend although we tended only to meet very occasionally at Ashover Show. In 1997, when I experienced my fifteen minutes of fame and appeared on national television, she wrote to me and said how much she had treasured the jewellery I had given her and how upset she had been when the item was stolen in a burglary at her home. More recently I wrote extensively about my school experiences on a Facebook group for Ashover including the trip to Liverpool. She commented on my post saying that she remembered it well, with some pride! Sadly, she died suddenly during the summer of 2020, that is what happens when you get old, your school friends start dying. Rest in peace Sheila, you will always be special to me.

As a teenager I was very fit, and sport occupied a fair amount of my time at school. Living on an isolated farm about two miles away from the nearest bus stop and about three miles from school I had a natural training environment, often running in preference to walking. In the junior department of school, football was my favourite. I played for the school team from an earlier age than most of those who were in the team. I was big and strong and fitted well into my role as a full back. However, I did not really possess outstanding ball control skills and once I got ahead of the half-way line, I completely ran out of ideas. Ashover School always did well in the annual South Peak football competition for the Bunting Cup.

That my elder brother Sam had been in the winning team a few years before, I was keen to match his achievement. Because I had joined the team younger than the other team members, I was going to be able to have two attempts to reach this pinnacle of achievement. At the first attempt things were looking good until we got knocked out in the semi-final. However, the following year we went a stage further by getting into the final only for the competition to be abandoned due to an outbreak of chickenpox. What a let down!

Competing with other schools in the senior department was more problematic for we Ashover kids because we were competing with schools where students could be up to eighteen years old, and we left school at fifteen. I did distinguish myself in the annual area senior school sports day in my final year at school when I was fourteen. Knowing that I was a good runner in distance events, the school entered me in the half mile event, which was the nearest thing to a distance event, given that I frequently ran two miles in my going out clothes to catch the bus to Chesterfield, a half mile felt like a sprint for me.

When we lined up for the start of the race at Causeway Lane, the Matlock Town, football ground, the portents were not good. Many of the other blokes were much older than me and many were equipped with proper running gear. I was turning out in football shorts, an old vest, and the cheapest gym shoes money could buy. The running track was just marked out on the grass of the football pitch and the race involved two full circuits. My aim initially, was to stay close to the leading pack for the first circuit and then to respond to what the others did.

At the conclusion of the first lap, I was in the group of four runners who were likely to be competing seriously at the conclusion. Rounding the penultimate bend, I started to realise that I had quite a lot of fuel still in my tank and started to pick up speed, by the final turn with about a hundred yards left, I moved into second position, when I decided I should go for a sprint finish and left the other runners standing. Crossing the finishing line, I could hear my fellow pupils and teachers from Ashover, shouting me on and I think I could have gone on running for another couple of hours! What a wonderful feeling it was to come first!

Most play times at Ashover School, whatever time of the year there would be an impromptu football game, often this took place in the playground where in the centre was a surface water drain, from which we kicked off each game and resumed after a goal had been scored. One day we were forced to abandon our game when one of the little kids came running across our pitch from the school playing field, heading as fast as he could towards the school toilets, unfortunately as a he crossed over our centre dot a large 'turd' dropped out of his trouser leg— end of play for that break!

At other times if there were not enough volunteers for a proper game we would have 'shooting in,' with the playground side of an external urinal wall as the goals because it happened to be about the same size as a junior football net. The problem was that standing the other side of the wall peeing into the urinal there was a severe temptation to try and propel the urine over the wall, thus spraying the head of the unfortunate goalkeeper on the other side. What a sight it was half a dozen kids, red faced pushing with all their worth to achieve their unpleasant objective!

In the wintertime, we farm kids who wore our work boots with metal segs delighted in creating slides on the ice in the playground. Our boots quickly polished the ice making super ice runs. That continued until the headmaster fell on one of our slides, he was a big bloke and he hit the floor so hard that folk in the village thought there had been an earthquake. You can guess that we lads thought of the situation, bursting into uncontrollable laughter. When he said, "You should not laugh at other people's misfortune," it made it even worse.

My mother did not have a high view of education, in fact she would sometimes say to me, "Just thee see education will be t'ruination of t'world." I still have a copy of my school report for my penultimate year and mother's lack of support for my schooling is evident in the fact that I had forty-five absences in the year. To my recollection I was not absent because of sickness but because my services were required labouring for various members of my extended family. Nevertheless, that report describes me as one of the top students in the class.

There were phases in school when some new craze took on and one of these was the discovery of roller skates. These were not the roller boots that are used these days but adjustable metal strap on wheels that you fitted to the soles of your shoes. Farmers' sons were again at a certain advantage because we tended to wear sturdy leather boots throughout the year, and these stood up to the pressure placed upon them by the roller skates. If you were wearing flimsy shoes, then the weight of the skates could pull the soles off your shoes. Those of us who became accomplished skaters could reach some high speeds, which in the context of a crowded school playground was far from safe.

On one memorable occasion I was reaching maximum speed when the headmaster stepped in front of me. My head sunk deeply into his generously proportioned abdomen, and he let out the noise of expiring air. That was the end of roller skating for while!

One of the better aspects of Ashover School was that there was a huge garden which was set out in allotments and in the final years of schooling each boy was allocated an allotment. We were each allocated an agreed sum of money with which we could purchase vegetable seeds of our own choice and then later in the year we would harvest the crops, taking the produce home. The gardening sessions were always great fun and lasted one entire afternoon. Regrettably, we had not yet discovered that girls can garden just as well as the boys, and that boys can cook just as well as the girls, sexism reigned, with the girls' doing cookery whilst we gardened.

The headmaster conducted the gardening sessions and was very enthusiastic about the subject. Because he was rather large and quite slow moving, we gave him the nickname "Slug." The garden suffered from slugs and there would be frequent statements to the affect that there had been a slug on a particular allotment after the headmaster had walked across it, who would respond by bringing some slug bait which just added to the humour of it all. There were some mature fruit trees in the school garden which we would try to raid when the fruit was ripe. There were some well-developed techniques used to remove the fruit from the trees into our pockets to be consumed later. A Victoria plum tree was located near the potting shed, where at the end of a session we would return our tools. Working in pairs, one would carry a tool over his shoulder so that it raked through the lower branches of the tree, and if you were lucky some fruit would fall off into the waiting hands of your mate, who would pocket the proceeds and then share them in the playground.

There was also a productive cherry tree which one year had a record crop. Before the cherries were properly ripe the tool technique had been used to remove the low hanging fruit and we were now left with ripe and spectacular fruit in the top of the tree which could only be reached by climbing, something which could not be achieved whilst the teacher was present. It was our good fortune that one afternoon the teacher was called away and like a flash one of the most, nimble members of the class climbed into the higher branches of the tree, throwing the fruit down to us. We were just a few minutes into the task when the warning signal came that the teacher was returning, but unfortunately the climber could not get down without being seen so had to remain hidden up the tree for the remainder of the session.

In the autumn season quite a few of us lads would leave the school premises at lunch time, mostly to go gathering fruit from trees in local gardens and orchards. We called it scrumping and the main target was a Siberian crab apple tree located in a hedgerow, just a few hundred yards from the school. Every year it would be festooned in yellow/orange fruits and no one else seemed to pick them. We would fill our pockets and then quickly return to the school where we consumed our ill-gotten gains. Legally speaking it was theft (actually, the offence then was larceny because this was before the introduction of the Theft Act, of which more later), but we lads did not view it that way. When October came along, we would be collecting conkers from beneath the numerous horse chestnut trees and every break at that time of the year we would be playing conkers.

If you started with a new conker, yours did not have a score. If it got broken, then you started again with another new one. Your opponent would add one to the score of his conker, conversely if you broke you opponent's conker then you picked up their score. Some of the boys would come up with all sorts of ways to make their conker more resistance to damage, these included baking, soaking in vinegar, or saving them from the previous year so that they were dry and solid. I gather that today kids are not allowed to play conkers at school for health and safety reasons.

Youth Activities and Life

Growing up into my early teens, along with my brother and our neighbour's children we started to look for ways to occupy our time and thinking. Responded to an invitation to go to the Wednesday evening meeting at the local chapel, we were encouraged to take part and three of us (Sam my brother, Robert, and myself) started to sing together and Eva who lived down the same lane would play the organ to accompany us. I must have been about thirteen at the time, the youngest of the trio and still a boy soprano, Robert was about a year older than me, and Sam had just left school and was working on a local farm. We were not new to singing in public, we would always take part in the school Christmas concert as well as singing in the chapel for the annual Sunday School Anniversary service.

This service took place in the early summer and all the Sunday School pupils would be seated on a raised platform area at the front and facing the congregation. These were special occasions, and the church would always be full, in fact so popular were they, that for a time we had to repeat the event a second week so that everyone who wanted could attend. The three of us were accomplished solo singers and would get a good response to our performances. Given that my brother and I both had very fair hair at the time, people had said that we looked quite angelic sat on the platform singing our hearts out. The fact that Sam and I were fatherless played on the heart strings of some of our elderly relatives and nearly always one or two would shed a tear or two. Once we had spotted this, we had an annual competition to see who could tap the most tear glands.

I have some memories of incidents involving children on the platform that caused considerable laughter in the congregation. We would always try to find a preacher who related well to children and young people, and I remember one guy working hard to involve them when he decided to ask if any of the children had a favourite song, I think he intended to lead them in singing it. My cousin's daughter Ann, about five years old shouted out loudly, "Roll out the barrel."

Well, the preacher nearly fell out of the pulpit and the rest of us on the platform, burst into laughter. If he had known the song, he might have said the next line, "And we'll have a barrel of fun," which would have been about right. On another time, my brother was preaching and on this occasion one of the young lads had volunteered to play his violin. Well, he was obviously a beginner, and some awful noises can come out of a fiddle being played by someone inexperienced, which was what was happening.

Suddenly one of the other little kids shouted out, "What is he playing Sam?"

And not turning a hair my brother responded, "I think it's a fiddle" and he said, "I know that I meant what tune was he playing?" Everyone tried extremely hard not to laugh, but it was difficult not to do so. As we grew up, we tended to do more complicated things, and some would recite poems. Our neighbour Eva one time said a poem which opened with the line, "Wanted a man." At the time Eva was beginning to have boyfriends at school and we lads just laughed out loud when she announced the title. For many years after that event, we would have a good laugh about it. Eva did eventually find her man, thankfully.

Stone Edge Wesleyan Reform church was very much a family affair for me because a large proportion of the congregation were related to me, indeed, members of my family had been responsible for building the place. There is a plaque on the wall to the memory of Charles Ernest Dronfield and Benedicta White. Charles was my mother's uncle, her father's brother, and Benedicta (more commonly referred to as Benny) was her aunty, her mother's sister. Uncle Charlie was frequently referred to by those who remembered him with great affection. My mother said that he was especially keen on encouraging the children and young people in the church and would always end his public praying by saying, "God bless these young people," and I have a feeling that what happened to myself and many of my young friends in 1958, was a direct answer to that prayer, even though he had died many years before.

I have previously referred to my aunt Ethel living in the 'Old Chapel,' which was at the top of our lane and just why that building was abandoned in favour of the new one remains at least in part as something of a mystery. My recollection is that the old chapel had a Primitive Methodist inscription on it. Given that the event that gave rise to the Primitive Methodist movement was quite a late development in Methodism it could not have been in use for a long period of time. It occurs to me that there must have been some sort of a split over church governance. I say this because the Wesleyan Reform Union of Churches, whilst sharing theology with mainline Methodist churches, differs in church governance with each church being entirely self-governing whereas the Methodist Connexion exercises central control over church governance. Certainly, many of the leading members of our chapel were very independent minded and they remain so. I assume that there was a fall out and some of my ancestors decided to leave Methodism and create a new church where they were more in control.

We trio of boys started to sing regularly at our Wednesday evening sessions at chapel and made quite an impression, so much so that one of the elderly gentlemen who worshipped at our chapel decided that we deserved a bigger audience. At the time he sang with the Peak Sankey Choir and asked us if we would come along and do a guest spot. We willingly agreed and he provided the transport. The choir was led and conducted by a guy who had been at one time the leader of a dance band. He had two attractive daughters, then probably in their early twenties who had received lessons in singing and it showed in their performances. Most of the choir members came from the chapels within the Bakewell Circuit of the Wesleyan Reform Union of Churches, although a few attended Methodist churches. We had by this time discovered that we could update traditional hymns to give them a bit of a swing and this proved popular with the audiences.

I do not remember the detail of how long we sang with the Peak Sankey Choir, but it was probably just one winter season. The older folk in church were keen to capitalise on the popularity of our singing and decided to form the Stone Edge Gospel singers of which 'The Boys,' were an integral part. Within a short space of time, we three had persuaded three of our mates to join us and had moved from a trio to a sextet.

Chapel was not the only place where our group of lads met together as we grew up. One of the newcomers was a leading light in the Ashover Young Farmer's Club and he persuaded us to join him there. Whilst I was sure that I was not going to become a farmer when I left school, meeting together in Ashover once a week was something interesting to do and got us out of the house. It was also true that some good-looking girls attended as well. One of them was Sheila with whom I had enjoyed some romantic encounters that I have described earlier.

If I remember correctly Sheila became the press officer, and although we were no longer kissing, we had remained good friends. One of her best friends was Anne the daughter of the owner of the bus company in Ashover, for whom Sheila's dad was a driver. She was a good-looking young woman, and I took a shine to her and for a time we were a couple. If the activity in the room where the club meeting was taking place was not that interesting Anne and I would walk across the road to the church yard where we could have a kiss and cuddle without being disturbed.

Our club was part of the Derbyshire Federation of Young Farmers Clubs, and we would have an annual summertime rally on some local farm, where we would compete against members of other clubs in various agricultural related skills. I competed in the chicken plucking a dressing competition. Each competitor was given a live chicken which you had to kill, pluck, remove the guts and other unwanted parts and tie it up ready for sale and display.

Marks were awarded for both speed and the appearance of the finished article. I also took part in stock judging competitions where you were provided with a group of the selected farm animals which you were required to judge and then place in your selected order. I remember enjoying these events and the competitions, but I do not remember ever being placed in the top three.

Conversely, the main winter event was the public speaking competition in which we lads from Stone Edge performed with distinction. Each year there would be a class for novices called, 'Have a Go,' a junior and a senior class. Each team had a speaker, one who gave a vote of thanks and another who seconded the vote of thanks. I have a recollection that one year we woned all three competitions, with a substantial percentage of the participants being our mates from Stone Edge chapel.

Along with the singing at church we were often invited to take part in other aspects of the midweek session at church including reading the Bible, saying prayers and, giving talks and all these activities were developing our skills and building our confidence. Reflecting on this period of my life I recognise that we grow as people and as Christians mainly through doing things. Yes, it is true that we need to listen to good teaching and have good role models, but there is no substitute for learning by doing.

Another noteworthy event in the Ashover Young Farmers Club year was the New Year's Eve Dinner and Dance at the Country Hotel in the village. For someone raised in a remote farm, we were not used to eating posh meals and sometimes getting things right was a bit of a problem. On one such occasion I started to put salt on my main course when some better-informed person informed me that the large salt pot was in fact a sugar sifter. I remember another occasion when I drank the contents of the finger bowl that was intended to be used for the washing of my fingers after I had consumed my barbeque spare rib starter.

Recently I published on the Ashover Genealogy and History some photographs of events including the New Year's Eve dance, explaining how I had enjoyed my time with the Ashover Young Farmers club and looked back with great affection to those days. I was pleased that one response was from the former girlfriend I used to have a cuddle within the church yard when activities in the club were not as interesting as the alternative, who said she also remembered those times with affection.

The Stone Edge Gospel singers became popular in Derbyshire, South Yorkshire, and Nottinghamshire. And each winter season we would travel by coach to various locations to deliver a programme of choral numbers, solo's, duet's recitations (poems) and the older members of our church would lead and preach the message. By now our group of young people had grown to about a dozen, a mixture of boys and girls, and these people became my best friends. We were finding new songs from a series of books called "Gospel Songs and Solos," which were much more modern in their beat and more understandable in their language.

During the autumn and early winter season of 1958, the Bakewell Wesleyan Reform Circuit decided to invite an evangelist to conduct a series of meetings around the Peak District of Derbyshire and the Stone Edge Gospel Singers were invited to provide the musical items and these meetings were to create the foundations upon which my life ever since has been built.

Formerly a pastor of a Church of the Nazarene H felt called to become the Connectional Evangelist for the Wesleyan Reform Union of Churches and originated from Barnsley. He was a powerful preacher, and it was difficult to avoid the intensity of his gaze when he was delivering his message. Every night he would make an appeal for people to get up out of their seats and come to the front as a sign that the wanted to give their lives to Jesus. Now I had been taught much about Jesus, you could have asked me quite serious questions about his nature and purpose and my answers would have been theologically correct from a conservative evangelical point of view, however it is possible to know a lot about someone but not really know the person.

Travelling back home after these sessions we would be talking about the appeal and those who had responded, and I for one was saying that I did not believe that going out to the front was a necessary part of becoming a Christian.

At the end of one of the sessions, the evangelist approached me and said, "How long have you been a Christian?" This was not the sort of bloke you could stand in front of and tell a lie, and throughout the sessions we had already attended he had made it abundantly clear what had to happen for a person to claim to be a Christian.

I said, "Looking at the question from your approach I have not become a Christian," and I then expected to get the whole Bible from Genesis to Revelation, but in fact he just looked me in the eyes and quietly responded, "Why not?"

Over the next few days that question seemed to have been stored in an echo chamber and out of the blue, when minding my own business, I would hear those words, "Why not—Why not—Why not—Why not?"

However, on the bus on the way to the little chapel in Stanton-in-the-Peak I discussed with my mates that the evangelist was not going to get me going to the front. It turned out that there was no need to go to the front of the chapel because the Stone Edge Gospel singers were allocated the seats directly in front of the pulpit and facing the congregation.

I cannot say that I have a vivid memory of the sermon that night, we did our part very well and had only one item left to sing when the preacher made his usual appeal. After a few moments just a small number of people made their way to the front, and he then invited the choir to sing our final item which was, "Jesus is passing this way, today."

As we sang that hymn, I could see in my mind Jesus walking along the seashore and inviting the fishermen to follow him and I knew he was inviting me to respond to his call and I found it impossible to resist him. As the hymn came to an end I turned to my brother and said, "I'm going lad are tha?"

He joined me at the communion rail and then others followed suite. That night of the young people in our group eleven made their way to that communion rail along with a couple of our more mature members. To put this into context that meant that about ninety percent of the youngsters attending our church made that decision that night and how things changed afterwards, what an adventure that decision has led me into over the succeeding sixty plus years.

At the front of the chapel those of us who had responded to the invitation, were addressed corporately about the decision we were intending to make, and we were told to make a simple prayer to the Lord. I cannot remember the exact words we were invited to use but it would be along the lines of what has been termed the A, B, & C of salvation; A—admit you are a sinner in need of salvation, B—believe that Jesus the Son of God, died and rose again so that your sins may be forgiven, and C—Claim Jesus as your own personal saviour. I cannot say that I instantly felt euphoria or excitement, but I did feel an overwhelming sense of peace and I realised that whereas before I knew a lot about Jesus, now I knew him because I had just met him properly for the first time and he had come to stay in me through the power of the Holy Spirit.

There was a lot of hugging and hand shaking from the older members of our church in celebration of what they had been praying for had been achieved. We then gathered around the organ and sung a few songs together. One of these songs was, 'Blessed assurance, Jesus is mine, Oh what a foretaste of glory divine." As we sang, I did feel that I was in heaven and all the angels were singing with us.

Our mother had not been with us on the trip and as I got off the bus at the top of our lane, I ran as fast as I could and dashing into the house shouted, "We've got saved mother!" She looked up and not showing any emotion said, "Good I hope it lasts." Not a one for many words our mother but living as she did until the age of eighty-five, she saw that it did last.

In the recent past Sam and I were having a conversation about our mother and some of the things she said about us and to us that touched on the nature and outcome of our faith. He recalled an incident, well before December 1958, when the three of us were together in the garden and out of the blue she said, "It's my prayer that one of you two will one day become a preacher." Well, within a few months of that decision we had both started to preach. Another conversation we remembered was when the gospel singers were delivering a programme at a church where a meal was being provided.

Neither of us can remember which way around it was but one of us led the meeting and the other preached. As we sat eating the meal one of the members of the church we were visiting turned to mother and said, "Mrs Bown, I should think that you are very proud of your two sons." Mother simply responded, "Nay lass not proud just very thankful." She had such a way with words!

From that moment on 1st December 1958, I have never doubted that I began a personal living relationship with God in Christ. At the time I would have been hard pressed to explain theologically what had happened, but I was certainly aware of the witness of the Holy Spirit that I had become a child of God. I would hate to give the impression in telling my story that I have lived a completely holy and sanctified life. The reality is that I have failed God on many occasions and continue to do so, but I know the power of the cross to forgive sins and restore a right relationship with God.

Although the decision to follow Jesus happened at a specific time and place, there had already been a process whereby we as a group of young people were learning more and more about the nature of Jesus and the Christian life. Some of the mature people in our church had a strong and positive influence over us, and generally they were very welcoming of us. A good example would be arriving late for the Wednesday meeting and in our smelly farm clothes, but not being critical of us. In turn we were inviting friends to join us. As other youngsters heard about us our group continued to grow and this added to our popularity when we were undertaking our winter programme of evening ministry and entertainment, often travelling miles in a coach to get there.

Around the sixtieth anniversary of the Stanton in the Peak outpouring of the Holy Spirit, many of us got together again for a service, and a celebratory meal. Much of our discussion centred on a recognition of the strong influence over us of particularly people in our church. Foremost amongst them was Jack and Barbara (who later became my in-laws, when I married their lovely daughter, Margaret). Their house was always open to us and many an evening would be spent with them.

Given that Jack was never in a well-paid occupation and Barbara was a full-time housewife and mother we have often wondered how they managed to do everything they did. Jack taught us in Sunday School, and both were local preachers. Quite apart from the teaching we received from them what we learnt most was their example of hospitality and gracious caring for us.

I experienced my first taste of preaching when we young people were invited back to Stanton in the Peak to take a Sunday afternoon and evening service there. One of the elderly gentlemen in the congregation invited us to accompany us in a walk around the village for an open-air service. What took place was very impromptu, with no loudspeaker equipment and no set format. It started with the old chap shouting as loud as he could, "Open your windows and your doors and listen to what these young people have to say about their relationship with Jesus."

We had been forewarned so had prepared something simple, but Bible based to say something about Jesus and our new-found faith in him. I am not sure whether anyone heard what we said but at least we were bearing witness to what had happened to us a few weeks before. I am sure that we had been reminded of the Bible passage where we are told that if we believe in our heart, and confess with our mouth the Lord Jesus, we will be saved.

Early in our Christian lives we young people were learning that we should be active in our faith and developing a serving mentality. Many were the occasions when we were reminded that we had been saved so that we could serve.

Part 2
The Calling and the Career

The Calling

There is no doubt most of my contemporaries at Stone Edge Chapel and I, identify the day in December 1958 as the moment when we began a new life in Christ. Jesus said to Nicodemus, "Ye must be born again." And that is what happened to us, but at least one of our number would say that his conversion experience took place over a year or more and he could not identify a specific time and place where he trusted Jesus for salvation.

For my part as I think back, there was in me a process taking place for at least a couple of years before December 1958, I was thinking more and more about the Christian life. Through our involvement in the chapel and the gospel singers we were being exposed to Christian teaching. The hymn book that we used in chapel was the Methodist Hymn book and by singing the words of John and Charles Wesley we were verbalising theology in what we sang, for that is what they set out to achieve in an age when most common people could neither read nor write, they sought to teach Christian belief through their hymns.

I read somewhere that Charles Wesley alone wrote more than 6000 hymns, some of which remain amongst my very favourites. To illustrate what I mean about his hymns I am setting out the words of one of the best, "And Can it Be?"

> And can it be that I should gain—
> An interest in the Saviour's blood?
> Died He for me, who caused His pain?
> For me, who Him to death pursued?
> Amazing love! How can it be?
> That Thou my God, shouldst die for me?

'Tis mystery all! The immortal dies!
Who can explore His strange design?
In vain the first-born seraph tries
To sound the depths of love divine.
'Tis mercy all! Let earth adore,
Let angel minds inquire no more.
He left His Father's throne above—
Se free, so infinite His grace
Emptied Himself of all but love,
And bled for Adam's helpless race.
'Tis mercy all, immense and free!
For, O my God, it found out me!

Long my imprisoned spirit lay—
Fast bound in sin and nature's night
Thine eye diffused a quickening ray-
I woke, the dungeon flamed with light!
My chains fell off, my heart was free!
I rose, went forth, and followed Thee.

No condemnation now I dread.
Jesus, and all in Him, is mine!
Alive in Him, my living Head,
And clothed in righteousness divine,
Bold, I approach the eternal throne,
And claim the crown, through Christ, my own.

Given that most people would not possess a Bible of their own, the Wesley's set about teaching Christian theology through the words of their hymns. "And can it be," is a supreme example and apart from what it says about me and my relationship with God, it is a great old hymn to sing.

Increasingly after December 1958 many of our group were doing more than we had previously done in the service of our Lord. Within a short time, some of us started preaching on a regular basis and more and more we were sharing our testimony both in public and in private meetings with other young people. Frequently when travelling on the bus to engagements with the Gospel Singers we would discuss possibilities for other adventures we may embark upon as part of our faith journey. We were impressed by the stories of John Wesley and his travels on horseback and wondered how we could become travelling preachers.

Going around on horseback did not appear as a likely way of doing this, then we wondered whether the equivalent would be to use a tractor and trailer, but soon abandoned that idea as well. What eventually materialised from these discussions was that we decided to undertake a week of beach mission at the seaside town of Lowestoft.

At a personal level, I was beginning to think much more about, my own future and asking God to guide me. Within a short time, I made the two most important decisions of my life. I decided that God was calling me to be a policeman, where I could work to create a safer society, something I considered important and because I wanted to serve people in that capacity. I therefore wrote to the Chief Constable enquiring how I could become a police cadet. This must have been very soon after making my commitment to Jesus because I was scheduled to leave school in December 1958 within a few weeks of making my decision. I then discovered that I could not join as the minimum age for the cadets was sixteen, so I went to work as a farm labourer living in at my uncle Jack's farm.

The second decision was that after many romantic encounters I realised that I was designed to end up in a long-term married relationship and started to think and pray about finding a partner for life. One of my best friends at the time was a lovely girl, Margaret and I found myself falling in love with her. We had from time to time had the odd cuddle on the bus travelling to engagements with the gospel singers, but what was developing was much deeper than that. On Christmas Eve 1959, a big gang of us old and young had been carol singing around Stone Edge and Wingerworth, and on the way back home, at the top of Stanedge Hill, me and Sam were going to go up the Darley Dale Road and I presume that Margaret was going to her grandmother's, either way we needed to say goodbye and Happy Christmas.

This kiss that we engaged in was rather more passionate than anything I had experienced before, and my heart strings were set alight. I continued to be very friendly with Margaret into the spring of 1960 when Billy Smarts Circus arrived in Chesterfield, and I invited Margaret to come with me to the event. During the evening I managed to explain to Margaret that I felt I was falling in love with her and that I believed that she was the one for me, my recollection is that she responded in like manner. We are still together as I write this during the lockdown of 2020/21, in our fifty seventh year of married life, before which we had enjoyed five years of courting.

I have many happy memories of our annual beach missions to Lowestoft which commenced in either 1959 or 1960, I am not sure which, but we certainly did them for quite a few years. These events came about out of our increasing desire to share our newfound faith and serve the Lord as the main motive in our lives. Lowestoft happened because there was a Wesleyan Reform Chapel there, and the leader was a local councillor, and he was able to give us permission to preach on the beach. That first year we hired a camper van which most of the team travelled and lived in. Three of us had to work on the Saturday morning so we travelled separately in an old Post Office van we had purchased for the princely sum of £25.

In the build up to our trip to the east coast we had spent time together at church praying for the event. The nearer we got to the appointed time, the more anxious we became and the more aware of our own lack of experience and this drove us to prayer. We really got down to opening-up to God during our final preparation sessions and on the final one, it felt like heaven had opened, and we concluded that so long as we continued to rely on our dependence upon God, then we would see people respond to our invitation for them to received Jesus as their saviour. It should be stated here that with other than the two oldest members of the team the rest were teenagers, and we were all inexperienced in preaching, let alone leading a full week's mission with Sunday services at various places of worship and afternoon and evening sessions on the beach.

So it was that on a Saturday in August the advance party of five set off in a camper van we had hired locally. The van was to be the sleeping accommodation for five of the team and the remaining three would sleep in a rather old and barely waterproof tent. My brother, our friend Terry and I were to set off as soon as possible after working on the Saturday morning. The van had been off the road for some time before we purchased and taxed it and Sam and another member of the group, Harold had given it a full service, but it was a bit of an unknown quantity. The van had just two seats, but three of us were travelling in it along with all the luggage for the other members of the team.

Within the first couple of miles of home, we realised that our journey was not going to be high speed when we had to drop down to about fifteen miles per hour to climb the first hill we encountered. Sam and Terry shared the front seats and I sat in the back along with the luggage, but with no seat. Goodness knows how my body did not seize up completely on the 180 miles journey from Chesterfield to Lowestoft.

Fortunately, once we got into Nottinghamshire and Lincolnshire there were few hills and the little van lolloped along at 40-50 miles per hour without protesting too much. Our route along the A17 took us through the small town of Long Sutton, where there is a swing bridge over the river. Just as we approached the bridge the traffic in front of us stopped because the red lights were flashing to indicate that the bridge was closing to allow shipping to pass by on the river. Given that big boats were in short supply in the hills of Derbyshire, like others we jumped out of the vehicle to have a look at the boat. Well, jumped out was a bit of an exaggeration for me, cramped in the back I had to wait for Sam and Terry to get out before I crawled over the seat backs and out onto the street. Things were going great, we were just over halfway to our destination, enjoying our journey, and taking in unfamiliar sights and sounds.

When we got back to the van things took a turn for the worse, having scrambled back into the vehicle the engine failed to start and we were holding back a long line of cars driven by frustrating dads, who had been telling their kids that they would be at the coast soon and now blasting their horns at us to get moving. We all disembarked and pushed the van to the side of the road where my brother tried to diagnose the problem and get the engine running again. Fuel starvation was the cause, and the fuel system was cleaned as best we could and with engine now running, we pulled back into the traffic and headed off towards Lowestoft. After about ten miles the engine started to splutter again and we pulled into the side of the road, which by this time was increasingly busy with holiday traffic making for the Norfolk and Suffolk coastal resorts and not happy that the vehicle in front stopped.

Everybody out, bonnet up and fuel unblocking procedure repeated. We set off again and after about five miles the engine splutters and stops, this time near a filling station, where we use the airline to try and clear the fuel blockage. Back into the van and after a mile, same procedure repeated. Back into the van and after two hundred yards splutter, splutter, and stop. And this time nothing works on the engine. Here we are miles from nowhere travelling to convert Lowestoft to the Lord in our opinion directed by God and yet we are stuck. We do not have the money to call out a garage, what are we going to do? The truth is we turned to God and cried out to him in prayer, "Lord, you want us to get to Lowestoft and we need this van to start running again" Pull the starter, engine sounds as sweet as a nut and runs beautifully the remaining fifty miles to Lowestoft.

In Lowestoft we made our way to the North Denes camping site and joined the others who had travelled down in the camper van. Sharing our news about the journey, the others were overjoyed to hear about the answered prayer on the way down, which they regarded as further confirmation that God was with us.

I just want to depart from the story of Lowestoft to consider the subject of prayer, and the first thing to say is that in my experience God always answers our prayers, but we do not always get what we asked for. I also want to say that nothing is outside of the capacity of God to intervene, repairing a car engine is not what one would normally think of praying over, but it worked.

The only limitation over the power of prayer is the one we place there. God is able, to do exceedingly abundantly above anything we could expect or desire. The Bible encourages us to pray without ceasing and in everything give thanks to God. Later in my story I will share painful times when I prayed for the healing of someone I loved, but who still died young and only received her healing in the next life. It is important to recognise that prayer is not just us asking God to do things, it is primarily about communicating with God and that involves listening to what he is saying to us.

I have never had a problem in crying out to God to make urgent requests, but I have struggled in the day-to-day aspects of prayer on many occasions. There is a need for a disciplined approach to prayer, setting aside a regular period or quiet time and I have not always been good at that. But I have always had prayer moments when God speaks to me, and I respond to him. In my teenage years, these God moments often occurred when I was out in the countryside around my home. The beauty of the countryside frequently spurs me to be thankful to God and that sends me to prayer. You will discover that over the years there has been occasions when God has answered prayers in amazing ways, but you will also discover that sometimes I have struggled. However inadequate we may think our prayers are the Bible teachers us that God loves our prayers, and he describes them as like perfume.

Lowestoft North Denes campsite was located on flat ground to the north of the town of Lowestoft. On the seaside of the campsite was a high and wide sea wall beyond which was the North Sea. We were surrounded by areas of tents and camper vans, and we pitched our tent alongside the camper van, which became our home for the week. I slept in the tent with Peter and another one (I cannot remember who).

Just to put the whole situation into perspective, most of us had never had a holiday before and I had certainly not slept in a tent before. All our cooking was done in the campervan, and I can tell you that with eight lads the food certainly was not of restaurant standard. The lovely folk at our chapel had been baking cakes for us, and we could probably have survived on them for the whole period away, there was so many. Contributions also included boxes of cereals, tinned foodstuffs including soups, vegetables, and fruit. The only shopping, we needed was fresh bread and milk which could be obtained at the camp shop. The group comprised Don, Peter, Paul, Harold, Terry, Sam, Don, Robert, and me. I was the youngest member of the group at sixteen years old and I think that Harold would have been the oldest member of the group, at that time in his early twenties. Compared with the usual groups that conducted beach missions, we were young and, inexperienced but very enthusiastic.

Let me give you a brief description of each team member along with a summary of their subsequent lives:

Don—One of the oldest of the team. Worked at Gladwin's Mark Farm along with my brother Sam. Had already started preaching and leading services. Was a bit more sophisticated than the rest given that he was a native of London and could jive! Bass member of the singing group. Had a Triumph Tiger Cub motorcycle.

Left farming to become a representative for an agricultural supply company. Trained to be a teacher and had a successful career teaching retiring as Head of RE at a large comprehensive school. An elder of his local evangelical church and regularly preaching into old age.

Sam—My brother, three years older than me. Worked at Gladwin's Mark Farm. Was already preaching and leading services and could be very funny. Tenor member of the singing group originally but then joined the bass section. Had a Triumph Tiger Cub motorcycle. Like the others who started out farming he subsequently left agriculture. At one time combined a mobile shop with market trading. Later had a scrap yard and then a haulage company in partnership with another member of the group Harold. Had to give up the haulage business because of a heart condition but, became an agricultural foodstuff representative retiring at the age of eighty. Continues to be an elder at Stanedge Chapel and a popular local preacher.

Peter—About the same age as me. Came from Chesterfield but joined us because there were no lively young Christian's in Chesterfield. Worked in an administrative role at the Derbyshire County Council Officers. Was a regular preacher and fancied himself as a Billy Graham sound alike! Tended to sing the lead part in the singing group. His first vehicle was an autocycle—a bicycle with an engine built into the rear wheel—not exactly a speed machine. Trained to be a physical education teacher which was a remarkable achievement given that he was quite seriously disabled at birth and had to have a series of operations on his feet as a child. Became pastor of his local church and has a ministry overseas.

Harold—worked as a mechanic/fitter and tended to get covered in grease and grime. Had many stories to tell about his escapes from possible death at home as a child and when abroad with the armed forces in Cyprus during the terrorist campaign there. Always had an old car showing signs that it would not be long before it finished up in a scrap yard. Was already preaching and leading on a regular basis. Joined us from the Methodist Church, became a local preacher. Joined my brother Sam running a scrap yard and then a haulage business. Sadly, no longer with us.

Don—my cousin. Worked as a maintenance engineer in a factory in Chesterfield. Tall, dark, and handsome, he fancied his chances with the girls, and we gave him the nickname, "Cassabow." Did not preach but sang bass in the group and gave his testimony and read lessons. Continued to work for his original employer into retirement. Currently in quite a poor state of health in old age.

Paul—joined us from Curbar where there was another Wesleyan Reform Chapel, but few other young people. Had a beard and ate copious amounts of cornflakes earning him the nickname, "Cornflakes." Sang lead in the group and was already preaching and leading. Married a lady from Bradford and moved there. Became a drystone wall builder. Continued to work and preach in his local church into old age.

Terry Bown—worked locally as a farm worker. Sang lead in the group. Never preached but would read lessons and give testimony. Had a BSA 250cc motorcycle. Not given to over statement, but thoroughly reliable. Terry ended up running his own farm and continued to faithfully attend his local chapel until ill health prevented it. Sadly, no longer with us.

Robert he also started his working life as a farm labourer. Robert had a beautiful voice and was a natural singer. His role was mainly in singing and giving his testimony. He could also play the piano and guitar. Robert became a prison officer for a time but then set up his own building and scaffolding company.

John Bown—much more being said about me in this book. Was a police Cadet and was already preaching, sang tenor or lead in the group, had a successful police career, and then worked as a police adviser in Ethiopia, Jamaican, Nigeria, and Sudan. Continues to be involved in local Anglican Church.

On the ministry side of our mission, we had created a full programme with Sunday services at a variety of places of worship on the Sunday along with an open-air session in the town centre. Most of our planned activities were conducted on the Lowestoft Beach where there was a wooden stage provided by the local authority. We had planned afternoon sessions where the main emphasis was children and then afternoon and evening sessions focussed on the grown-ups. The kid's sessions included, action songs, games and simple Bible stories and messages. We had leaflets and booklets available to hand out during the week and posters advertising our beach sessions had been printed by the leader of the Lowestoft Wesleyan Reform Church, who was also a member of the Town Council and had been instrumental in getting us permission to use the beech platform.

Our formal programme commenced on the Sunday morning on a WW2 bomb site on London Road, where we planned to have an open-air service. Having been enthused by the answered prayer for the old van we gathered, eager to get started, but our opening shot was somewhat inauspicious to say the least. What could not have been foreseen is that the local "Mods" group had chosen the exact same time and place to have a rally with their motor scooters. We could not compete with the noise made by these motor scooters and eventually we had to curtail our activities because there were few people around and, they could not hear what we said or sung because of the noise made by the engines of the motor scooters.

We also took the Sunday services in the Lowestoft Wesleyan Reform Church and the Fishermen's Mission and had our opening session on the Beach. Lowestoft has a long, raised promenade overlooking the beach, the level of which is about ten feet below the level of promenade. Looking inland from the beach, is a high wall and about six feet back from that wall, the local authority had erected a sturdy, wooden stand which provided our base for the beach mission. For each session we had a programme including, leader, speaker, reader, songs we would sing and hymns we would use for people to join in. Our children's sessions included games, choruses, and other children's activities.

During the days and into the evenings we spent most of our time around the beach and if we were not involved on the stage then we would be on the promenade talking to young people about our faith in Jesus. Some of the people we spoke to were holiday makers, but quite a good proportion were local youngsters. All our beach sessions ended with us making an appeal for people to respond if they wished to commit their lives to Jesus. We would ask them (whilst everyone had their eyes shut) to raise their hands and then request that they stay behind to speak to us.

Throughout the week, small numbers responded to the invitation, some local and some visitors. If they stayed behind to talk which most of them did, we would provide them with a St John's Gospel, which has a response page included. A couple of teenage girls from Nottingham were regular supporters of our sessions and before the week ended both made a commitment to Jesus. One of them Claire became a regular visitor to the home of Margaret my girlfriend (subsequently wife) and we stayed in touch with her over the years. Sadly, she died during 2020 and we attended her funeral service on-line, when her eldest son paid tribute to her strong Christian commitment that she had lived out from her teenage years onwards. He identified that he had become a Christian as a direct result of his mother's influence.

These stories of people coming to faith will appear in my memoirs and I confess that there is nothing more thrilling than to see a person come to a living faith in Jesus, particularly when you have had some involvement in the decision making.

After one evening session, a local girl, Mary responded to the invitation and I spent some time counselling her about the Christian faith. The discussion went on for quite some time and it was decided that we should catch the bus back to North Denes, but just as the rest of the team were getting on the bus, I got engaged in a further conversation with Mary. Suddenly, my mates decided that they had better stay with me, so they trooped back of the bus leaving Don on the top deck wondering what had happened. We stayed in touch with Mary and her younger sister Yvonne for many years and her sister visited Margaret's home.

It is difficult trying to remember exactly what happened during the first year we visited Lowestoft for our beach mission because we made the trip for at least five years in a row, each year taking a bigger team with us and subsequently staying in a hotel/guest house. Memories tend to blend into one experience rather than be the specifics. The first year was in many ways the most memorable because it was our first experience and we had to cope with cooking and looking after ourselves.

Whilst we did not go short on food, we certainly did not produce fancy meals and occasionally what we ate left one or two people with stomach problems. I well remember that Harold was suffering belly ache and at the conclusion of our powerful evening prayers together my brother came out with the words, "Please bless Harold's belly." We all collapsed in laughter.

One of our favourite evening entertainments was to visit an ice cream parlour situated on the promenade. Here we would often get engaged in conversations with holiday makers of our own age and with local youngsters because it was the place where teenagers congregated in the evenings. Often these informal discussions provided us with the opportunity to explain how our faith was important to us and give testimony about how our lives had been transformed following our conversion to Christ. Sometimes those we engaged in our conversations would then come along to the beach meetings.

We would also meet up with other teenagers walking along the promenade and engage them in conversation. Clearly the fact that we were a group of very ordinary and unsophisticated youngsters meant that there was no barrier in communicating with them. On one occasion we came across a couple of lads who were shaping up for a fight and Peter decided he would step in between them and said, "If you want to hit somebody hit me."

Peter had a jaw that protruded abnormally, and I thought to myself, "Peter, lad you are going to get cracked on that jaw of yours." I was slightly disappointed when the tension seemed to evaporate, and Peter was able to communicate with them about the love of Jesus. Brave man!

Although I have chosen to dwell on our beach mission as an example of our desire as Christians to serve God and witness for Jesus, there were many other occasions much more local. In Matlock, the Mary Dobson Memorial Chapel were active in the town and sometimes we joined in with them. They had a regular Saturday evening youth event where we got involved. Our main role was to go out onto the streets inviting fellow teenagers to come back with us to the chapel, were there would be music playing in a café environment.

Someone would be a giving brief message suitable for teenagers and there would be free drinks and food. We had many good conversations with the young people of Matlock, sharing our faith and inviting them to respond to Jesus. I recall one occasion where a young motor cyclist we engaged in conversation responded by saying that he realised that he should have a relationship with Jesus, but he thought that he would put off the decision until he was older. The next time in Matlock, when we saw his mates and we enquired as to where their mate was, they explained that he had been killed in a motorcycle accident. We were reminded of the Bible passage that says, "Now is the day of salvation," putting off a decision such as that is not a good idea.

Early in my Christian life I concluded that a follower of Jesus is not passive but active and I realised that having been saved through the sacrifice of the "Servant King," I had a duty to serve Him in the totality of my life. My motivation in deciding to join the Derbyshire Constabulary as a police cadet was that I wanted to serve the community and contribute towards a better and safer society.

Derbyshire Police Cadetship

As I approached the minimum age to be a police cadet (16 years) I commenced the application process and was successful. On Monday 20th January 1960, I caught the bus to Matlock and then walked up Bank Road to the offices of the Derbyshire County Council, housed in the former Smedley's Hydro. I noticed that another teenager also got off the bus and walked up the hill and then just like me, walked into the County Offices. The Derbyshire Constabulary Headquarters were at that time located on the top floor of the County Offices and both myself and my travelling companion jumped in the lift and went up to the top floor.

Walking along the corridor we arrived at the door of the recruiting officer, who sticking his head out of the door said, "Come in Bown, and we both entered the door together."

What a coincidence—sharing the same family name, he was from Pilsley, near Chesterfield and it was also his first day. The first day was occupied in going through the various registration processes required, including a visit to the Stores Department to be measured for a uniform. From that day onwards until I became a police constable in 1962, I was known in the Derbyshire Constabulary as Cadet 44 Bown. The descriptive form completed on that day recorded me as having, "manly physique and boyish appearance."

The recruiting Inspector responsible for making the decision was known by his initials KRU, he retired many years later in the rank of Chief Superintendent. He was himself a farmer's son and there was some evidence that he favoured recruiting young men from farming families because they were not clock watchers and I think I benefitted from his bias in favour of what he sometimes called his "hill-billy's."

The fact that I have previously related how I felt called to be a policeman, indicates that I recognised that God is able to communicate with we human beings. People have often asked me how God speaks to me, and the answer is quite complex. In so far as joining the police was concerned it was a combination of my own assessments of the positive role of police officers, in bringing about a better, fairer, more safe society, which I considered important. The job also promised security and a good pension, with the opportunity for promotion available to those who work hard and do a good job.

At a deeper level I had spent time praying about what I should do for a living and although I did not hear a voice telling me what to do, I did have a confidence that applying to the police was in line with God wanted of me, an opportunity to 'serve and protect,' which was directly in line with my Christian commitment. Looking back over the years God has sometimes given me specific words including facts about someone I was witnessing to and includes visions. The direct speech and vision examples have been regular but not frequent, and most often God has spoken through an inner conviction that what I was doing was right.

It is always good to check that you are hearing God speaking and there are many ways that can be achieved. Check out what you feel God is saying against what the Bible says, God is not going to ask you to do something that does not accord with scripture. It can be a good idea to check with a trusted friend or family member. Sometimes it is a matter of going for something and asking God to open or close the door.

Police Cadets were introduced at a time when it was quite difficult getting sufficient recruits as constables. At that time, the minimum age for a constable recruit was nineteen years of age and the normal maximum age thirty years, although that could be exceeded in the case of people recruited from the armed forces. There has always been a high attrition rate in the police force, I think mainly because the job affects your entire lifestyle and is not just a job. In my opinion another major contributor to the wastage rates at that time was the extremely poor people management skills of police supervisors (sergeants and inspectors) of which you will hear more as I tell my story. Statistics showed that police officers recruited as cadets were much less likely to leave the job when appointed constable.

The first six months of my career as a cadet were occupied moving around the various departments at police headquarters. That was good for me because I could catch the Chesterfield to Matlock bus, that got me into Matlock for about 8.45 giving me time to walk up Smedley Street to arrive at Smedley's Hydro in time for my 9am start. Knocking off at 5pm there was just enough time for me to get to the bus station for the return journey leaving Matlock at 5.10pm. After a couple of weeks, I was issued with my uniform which was similar a Constable's other than the Cadets had a flat peaked cap with a blue band. Putting my uniform on I felt quite proud. Once I started to travel on the bus in my uniform, I found that some of the conductors would give me the money back and let me travel free.

After the first six month of my Cadetship, I was posted to the Alfreton Divisional Headquarters of the Derbyshire Constabulary. Whereas at Police Headquarters I was one of about a dozen police cadets, I think at Alfreton there was just two of us. Getting to Alfreton by public transport was quite a problem. I had to catch a bus into Chesterfield and then connect with another bus to take me to Alfreton, a journey that took at least an hour. On arrival at Alfreton, I found that I had followed KRU (recruiting inspector when I joined) who was now the Administration Chief Inspector at Alfreton.

Over the years I continued to follow KRU, experiencing his bullying attitude, but also benefitting from his recommendations for promotion. For quite a while I worked in the police station, enquiry office. My two main duties were operating the telephone switchboard and dealing with complaints from members of the public attending the police station.

Telephone switchboards were quite complex pieces of equipment in those days and given that we did not have a telephone at home, coming to terms with operating this item became the first requirement of the job. Looking at the switchboard from the operators seat you were faced with a collection of jack plugs protruding from a desk. The jack plugs were attached to electric cable and were used to connect different people within the building or to an outside telephone line.

Above the desk was a wall of circular discs each displaying the number of the telephone extension to which it was linked and, below each disc was a socket into which the jack plug was to be placed. At the side of the switchboard was a hand which you turned to make the call ring out. In addition, there was I think two outside lines used for incoming and outgoing telephone calls. Let us imagine the Superintendent wants to speak to the CID General office—he cannot dial it direct his telephone does not have dial attached to it. He picks up his receiver and his disc on the switchboard opens-up and I stick one of the jack plugs into his socket and say, "Switchboard, Sir." He then says, "CID General Office" and I take the jack plug that is lined up with the one already in use stick it in the socket for the required extension, operate a switch that connects the two and wind the bell handle.

When the extension is answered I then switch them through so that they can hear each other, but I cannot hear them. While ever the call is live the discs are open showing the line is in use but when they replace their receivers, the flaps close and I take out the cables and put them back in their resting positions. At busy times of the day the switchboard looked like a knitting machine and care needed to be taken to ensure that you did not disconnect the wrong person.

Sitting in my seat by the switch board, I was also just a few feet away from the enquiry window, where people would come to report incidents and the like. There was a bell on the other side of the window, but generally you would see the person through the frosted glass and open the window before they pressed the bell. Also in the office at another desk was the office constable and beyond him a teleprinter used for urgent written messages for force headquarters.

I have no recollection of being taught how to deal with enquiries at the desk, but it certainly became clear that I was expected courteously to ascertain the reason for the visit before referring the person to the correct department or person. Most frequently they would be producing their driving documents following a motoring incident. There was a national standard form on which these details were recorded and then sent to the officer who had made the original request. If there was a problem, where an offence had been committed then I would have to ask the office constable to deal with the person because he would have to report them for prosecution.

Working in the enquiry office I was soon exposed to things that were quite alien to me coming from my sheltered rural home, and I came to realise that some people do things that at that time shocked and surprised me. One dowdy looking middle aged lady said she wanted to complain about her husband's insatiable appetite for sex. At this stage, given that I had no personal experience of sex, I felt I should hand her over to someone with more knowledge, but I could not stop her going on. She told me that when she was having her periods, he insisted on having annul sex, something that I was totally unaware of. When I found a constable out of her hearing, I reported what the lady had said including her line, "I am browned off, I don't know which way to turn."

Sometimes I worked shifts in the enquiry office and that was a major problem for transport. When I worked the afternoon shift (2pm—10pm), I missed the last Chesterfield to Matlock bus and therefore had to walk from Walton to my home, about four miles, resulting in me not getting there until about midnight. The village bobby in Ashover worked a rural mechanised beat using a Morris 1000 Traveller. Sometimes he would turn up with a delivery from police headquarters and time it so that he could give me a lift home, which was kind of him. On one memorable occasion he arrived about 9.30pm and seeing me in the office said he would wait until 10pm and then give me a lift home.

Within a few minutes of him making the offer it was snowing heavily and when we set off in the police car there was a thick covering of snow on the road surface. Travelling down Alfreton Hill, we came across a car that had skidded off the road. We stopped and assisted the car driver to get his vehicle back onto the road. It was undamaged and thanking us profusely continued his journey. Jack and I, then started to walk back towards the police car when we saw another car coming down the road towards us, clearly travelling at too fast a speed for the road conditions. Seeing the police car, he applied his brakes and completely lost control of the vehicle. Jack said, "Oh bloody hell, John," when he realised that this car was going to collide with the police car. Our car was undriveable, and we had to arrange for it to be taken to the police garage, and for us to get a lift home.

Jack was an excellent local policeman, knowing everyone in the area and policing in a firm but fare style. He continued to police Ashover until his retirement and stayed in the village until his death many years later. My annual visit to Ashover Show each August would see me bump into Jack and we would have a chat about old times and often we would have a laugh about the night he gave me a lift home. Jack had retired after 25 years rather than the usual 30 years, because he could count his war time military service towards his pensionable service.

He would always tell me how long he had been receiving his pension, and the last time we had the conversation he had been receiving his pension for 10 years more than he had been paying it in. As I write this, I have been receiving my pension for 29 years, but I served for 30 years and am now 77 years old. I will have to live to 90 to match his record!

The theory of the police cadets was that training would be provided through specific activities along with the "one the job," learning from the task in which the cadets was engaged in on a day-to-day basis. Certainly, in the enquiry office at Alfreton, I was developing skills in dealing with members of the public at the enquiry office and over the telephone. Cadets were regularly recalled to the

County Offices for training sessions which were mainly being engaged in collective drill movements. I remember one occasion when we were marching up and down the car park in a gale, when the hat of the cadet in front of me blew off and I put my foot on top of it, crushing the whole thing. We all collapsed in laughter and the trainer had to nip round to the stores department and get the unfortunate cadet a new cap.

The development of life-saving skills was also a regular activity, and we would be taken to the swimming baths in Belper on Sunday mornings. Given that there was no way I could get from the farm to Belper by public transport, I would be picked up by Traffic Patrol Car—a Ford Zephyr Mk11, which was quite an experience for me. On one occasion we got engaged in a chase of a stolen car and I was just amazed at how fast the trained driver was able to proceed along little country lanes. The criminal did not get a chance to get away and eventually the car was stopped, and the driver arrested. That week I did not get to the swimming baths, but I had a story to tell my mates the following week. During those sessions at the swimming pool, I obtained the Bronze Medallion award from the Royal Life Saving Society along with their Advanced Resuscitation Certificate.

During our cadet training we were also programmed to undertake a couple of residential adventure training courses in the Peak District. The first was a daytime exercise over couple of days and the second one a night-time exercise for a similar period. Our base was the Barnsley Mountaineering Club Hut on the Snake Pass about a mile east of the Snake Inn. It was not exactly luxurious we slept on straw beds and washed in cold water. There was a chemical toilet that had to be emptied every day, and I drew the short straw being allocated that task.

Given that I was used to emptying the earth toilet at home, it was not so upsetting for me as it might have been for some of the others. As well as the practical exercises we received lectures in survival skills and care of the countryside. The day-time course concluded with a team exercise where we had to bring a member of our team on a stretcher from the summit of Kinder Scout to the Snake Inn, in the form of a race against the clock. Setting off at intervals and with our team being towards the last to set off you could see how the others were progressing. The main thing that contributed most to the success was to get your lightest member strapped to the stretcher and tell him to keep his eyes shut and pray for safety!

The two biggest members of our team were me and another John, so we decided that we would be the anchor men holding the ropes at the back of the stretcher. Anyone who has climbed Kinder Scout from the Snake Pass will know that other than the final half mile it is all downhill, so holding the stretcher back becomes the most important part of the task. Coming down from the summit we quickly overtook two of the other teams, but the leading team was still ahead of us, and we two Johns made an executive decision to depart from the path. Spotting that we could descend quite steeply into the river valley and come out much closer to the Snake Inn we reckoned that we could get back to the rendezvous point much quicker than via the footpath the lead group were taking. It does have to be said that the descent was going to be at a very steep angle and our stretcher man was none too keen on our suggestion, but he was outvoted and told to keep his eyes shut and pray.

There were times before we reached the river valley that I thought we were going to lose control of the stretcher, or that it was going to flip over, but thankfully neither of those possibilities occurred and we were on our second pint at the Snake Inn before the second team arrived. Naturally, our competitors said that we had cheated, but we responded by saying that we had never been told we must stick to the footpath, and if we had genuinely been carrying a casualty speed would have been important. Our opinion prevailed and we were one happy group on our way back to the hut for the night.

The night exercise took place over Bleaklow which is the area of high moorland to the north of the Snake Pass. Each team were allocated a guide who was accustomed to map reading and following compass readings as well as being familiar with the area. We all had different starting points, but the plan was to rendezvous at a shooting cabin on the summit, where we would eat our packed meal before making our way back to base. On the first day we undertook the route in day light so that we would have half a chance of success. The only problem was that from about late afternoon on the day of the exercise it rained cats and dogs right through the night.

Well before we got anywhere near the summit we were saturated through to the skin and our packed meal was a soggy mess. We had a set window of time for meeting with the other groups, but what with the downpour of rain and the poor visibility we never found the shooting cabin, so we consumed our soggy meal on the hoof and set off back to base. When we met up with the others, we discovered that just one group out of four had found the cabin, but thankfully we all got back safe and well.

Back at Alfreton Divisional Headquarters I was posted into the CID office, where my duties were mainly administrative, and I worked normal office hours of 9am to 5pm. At that time, I purchased a James Cavalier motorcycle which I used to travel to work. It was great not having to catch busses, but within eighteen months of buying the machine it gave up the ghost, so I was back on public transport for the final few months of my time as a police cadet.

One of the interesting tasks I was given in the CID office was to type up the diary sheets of a couple of officers who had been seconded to a murder enquiry operating out of Chesterfield CID office but whose home base was Alfreton. The two linked murders became known as the Carbon Copy Murders. The murder enquiry continued for at least two years after the second of the two murders. The bodies of both victims, W and G found dumped at the side of Clodhall Lane in an isolated quiet location and the victim's cars were then abandoned at Park Road, Chesterfield.

The victims were both homosexuals who frequented a couple of Chesterfield pubs where gays congregated. A former soldier, M became the major suspect, but there was a shortage of evidence to put before the courts. However, on two occasions, but to individual police officers and with no witnesses he had admitted the crimes. M had met up with the victims in Chesterfield and then travelled with them in their cars to the grounds of an isolated manor house near the village of Wingerworth, where the murders took place.

At that time my girlfriend, Margaret lived at Pond Head, Wingerworth and my route walking the three miles back home took me right past the place where the murders took place. It was a bit spooky, because the murders had not yet been detected, so the murderer was still at large. But the good thing was that a plain clothes police car patrolled around the lanes at night and when they first stopped me to check who I was and where I was going, they gave me a lift home. Thereafter, they would just pull up and say, "Jump in and we will give you a lift home." My mother was quite disturbed the first time the police delivered me home. But once I explained she no longer worried about my safety.

M was eventually found guilty of both murders along with the murder of a couple of lovers who he had killed after observing them having sex in some isolated woods whist he was a serving soldier in Germany. I believe that I am correct in saying that it was the first time that a person had been convicted in an

English court for a murder overseas. He was sentenced to life imprisonment and sent to Rampton, a secure establishment for violent and disturbed offenders. So far as I am aware, he is still incarcerated there.

On a couple of occasions as a Police Cadet I performed duty in Derby at the Assize Court. In those days, a Circuit Judge would visit the Assize Court in Derby where he would try the most serious cases. There was always a formal opening ceremony when the High Sherriff and other notables would gather and there would be a contingent of police officers including cadets, who would form the guard of honour for the arrival of the judge. Thereafter we would spend the rest of the day listening to the cases. It was always an interesting day.

Sport played a part in my time as a police cadet when I competed regularly in cross country events held by the Police Athletics Association (PAA). The height of my cross-country running career was in 1961, when finished in third place in the Regional Police Athletics Association Championships and eighth in the National Championships. Police cadets were not eligible to be members of the PAA, but we were invited to appear as guests. At the National Championships I was by far the first cadet to finish the race and at the reception afterwards, I was approached by the secretary of the Metropolitan Police Athletics Association who told me that if I joined the Metropolitan Police in London, I would in effect become a fulltime athlete. At that time some of the best runners were Met policemen and I am sure that I would have been given every assistance to become an accomplished athlete, but I had been called to be a policeman and not an athlete, so I graciously declined the offer.

My cadetship was concluded on 7th November 1992, the day before my nineteenth birthday, after which I became Constable 201 Bown.

Initial Police Training and Probationary Period

At the conclusion of WW2 many former members of the armed forces, were looking for employment and a career in the police service was an attractive option. To cope with the massive influx of police recruits a regional system of police training was established. These regional police training schools were operated by the Home Office and staffed with police officers seconded to them from the constituent forces, usually for a fixed period of two years. Those officers selected for the role were provided with a national training course for Student Instructors.

The Derbyshire Constabulary was in the Number 3 Police District, and the training venue back in 1962, was a former public school located in the village of Pannal Ash, on the outskirts of Harrogate. I was originally scheduled to start my initial training in December, but at short notice my date was brought forward one month resulting in me visiting the local magistrates court on my 19th birthday, where I swore an oath to serve the Queen in the office of constable.

Back in 1962 there were many more police forces than exist today. Our region included the counties of Derbyshire, Lincolnshire, Nottinghamshire, and the West Riding of Yorkshire. Each county had a police force, but there were also the following city and borough forces:

Derby Borough Police, Nottingham City Police, Sheffield City Police, Leeds City Police, Bradford City Police, Lincoln City Police, Halifax Borough Police, Dewsbury Borough Police, Rotherham Borough Police, Grimsby Borough Police, Wakefield Borough Police, and Doncaster Borough Police. Most of the smaller forces were amalgamated into the surrounding county areas in 1967, or in subsequent amalgamations that saw South Yorkshire being created along with other metropolitan areas.

We were housed in dormitories at the police training school, some of them were large with as many as thirty beds. I considered that I was fortunate to be allocated to a smaller dormitory with just a dozen of us, many of whom were mature married men, who were less likely to behave stupidly or disturb your sleep pattern that younger recruits away from home for the first time in their lives would have done.

Each class of recruits had a dedicated police trainer who in our case was Sergeant T a member of the Nottinghamshire Constabulary. Much of the instruction was concerned with police laws and built around legal definitions, which had to be learned by rote. These definitions could be lengthy and were all included in a little book published by the Police Mutual Assurance Society (PMAS), who supplied copies to every police recruit. I still have my life, house and car insured by PMAS!

These legal definitions were often complex and lengthy. For example: Larceny—A person steals who, without consent of the owner, fraudulently and without a claim of right made in good faith, takes, and carries away, anything capable of being stolen, with intent at the time of taking permanently to deprive the owner to owner thereof. Notwithstanding that he, being the part owner or bailee thereof, fraudulently converts the same to his own use, or to the use of another person other than the owner.

It is a measure of the learning that took place back in November 1962, that I can still recite the definition more than fifty years later. Truth is the definition was so complex and the cases around it that had built up over the years, so many that I could not properly understand it. I was thankful that in 1968, the Theft Act provided a new and much simplified definition which was: "The dishonest appropriation of property belonging to another, with the intention permanently to deprive the other of it."

The idea of having an experienced police officer responsible for the teaching of recruits had much to commend it. They were not just teaching theory but imparting the benefit of their practical experience. It was also true that they were able to project the values of effective policing and the importance of police public relationships. During that period of training, I concluded that T had exemplified the best approach to policing, and I determined to emulate what I learned from him.

The initial training course of thirteen weeks duration was part of a two-year probation period, during which you could be dismissed on the basis that you were unlikely to become an efficient police officer, without any right of appeal. At two intervals during the probationary period, you returned to the police training school for a two week-long refresher course. Courses commenced monthly and during the first month we were designated 'Juniors,' the second month 'Intermediates' and the final month 'Seniors.'

Immediately after breakfast everyday Monday to Friday we had a parade and inspection which was led by the Drill Sergeant, a former Guardsman from the Grimsby Borough Police. The parade involved a march past and salute to whoever the inspecting officer happened to be. My helmet size was the largest made and there was a Leeds City policeman in our group who had the smallest helmet size. One day we decided to have a bit of a laugh and we swapped helmets for the parade. It caused a fair bit of hilarity, his helmet clearly did not fit my head and I had to use the chin strap to make sure it did not fall off my head, whereas my helmet dropped over his eyes and ears. When he did the "eyes right," although his head turned to the right the hat just continued facing forward and we fell about laughing. We were all put on the 9pm discipline parade, but we had expected that to happen, so we were not unduly worried, and we were made very welcome in the student's bar that evening!

Each course is programmed to have a competitive sports event towards the end, where classes and individuals competed, and I was happy to discover that our event was the annual cross-country race. I shared with my class members that I had a record of success in PAA Cross-Country Running and persuaded some to train with me so that we had a chance of winning the event. The drill sergeant was also the physical training instructor, and he was also a bit of a betting man, he had said that he was sure that one of the members of another class would win the cross-country race, but what he did not know, and my class did was that I was training every day, and that I had been placed third in the PAA Cross Country Championships, and on the same Harrogate course that we would be running. All my mates bet him half a crown that I would win, there was a lot riding on the race.

We were assessed through written examinations held at the end of each stage of the course plus a final round of practical tests. My record in the examinations always put me in the top half but I was far from outstanding which did not worry me because I was confidence that I would pass the final examination and practical assessment. One of the major practical things to learn was maintaining our pocketbooks, which is where a police officer records evidence of an offence and based upon which would be his report. You will note that I keep saying his with no reference to her. This is not because of sexual bias it was because our training school was for male officers only and the establishment of the Derbyshire Constabulary at the time was for 819 men and 20 women.

We would start out learning the theory and then undertake a demonstration where the offence would be dealt with, and we would all complete a pocketbook entry and later a report. The documents would form part of the course work assessment.

Soon after the commencement of the course we were informed that there would be a Christmas Concert and recruits were invited to join the choir and undertake solo acts. I joined the choir and started attending the rehearsals. At the time, the Black and White Minstrel Show was top of the bill entertainment on BBC television on Saturday evenings, so we performed as the Black and White Minstrels of Harrogate, wearing cricket whites, and having faces and hands blacked. I do not think we would get away with that today! We sang a medley of negro spiritual songs. and it went down very well.

From lunch time on Saturday to 11pm on Sunday evening we were free to go home if we wished. Not many of the recruits had cars so one person would order a taxi and then their mates would jump in with them until the taxi was full. It was always a rush to catch the train in Harrogate Station that would get us to Chesterfield in reasonable time and getting back in time was also a bit of a challenge. One weekend the train from Chesterfield to Leeds was late and I missed the connection to Harrogate. The later train would not have got me in for lights out, which would have meant trouble for me, so I had to take a taxi from Leeds to Harrogate which was quite expensive. Before the Christmas break, I managed to sort a lift with another recruit who was travelling my way and with whom we shared the fuel costs.

The annual cross-country run took place about a week or so before the end of the course. The weather was extremely cold and everywhere was covered in snow, far from ideal for running 6.5 miles through woods and fields. As well as the recruits, well known guest runners were invited to take part although they would not be counted in the results for the recruits. The trouble for me was that some of the guest runners would clearly finish ahead of me but I had no way of knowing which of those in front of me were competitors in the annual training school event.

Being heavier than a typical runner was a disadvantage when the course was on the level, and the weather conditions good, but conversely, I had reserves of strength that kept me up with the leaders where the course was difficult. The course was extremely hilly, and the ground snow covered, it could hardly have been worse, which gave me a degree of confidence that I could win. The final mile or so was on local roads and up a steep hill, before entering the long, level drive into the training school. Coming up the hill I felt strong and overtook a few runners but was not sure whether anyone else was in front of me. On turning into the drive, I saw a couple of runners about fifty yards ahead of me, which caused me to break into a sprint finish. I was able to overtake them and at the finishing tape I was told that I had won the race. Once all the scores were calculated we were pleased to find that our class had also wone the team award.

All my fellow class members duly collected their half a crown bet from the PTI which cost him quite a lot of money. Thereafter all the police holds' he demonstrated he used me as the stooge to get back at me for all the money he had lost.

On the night before we had our passing out parade, we had a special dinner when presentations were made to all those who had been awarded a prize. I did not get any awards for academic achievement, but I was proud to stand up to receive the individual and team award for the annual cross-country run. Many years later I found myself working at Chesterfield College and discovered that my line manager was the son of one of the other team members. I was able to show him a photograph of the team, including his youthful looking dad.

My mother and brother attended the passing out parade and clearly, mother was proud of her son. For my part I was starting to worry a little about commencing my duties at Ilkeston a town on the border of Derbyshire and Nottinghamshire, a place I had never visited in my life. Arriving at the local railway station with all my luggage I was picked up the police beat car driver and taken to my lodgings at 69 Cavendish Road Ilkeston.

I had never resided in lodgings before and did not know my way around the town. I was told to report for night duty commencing at 10pm on the Monday evening. I would then work seven shifts of nights without a break, followed by a rest day. At that time at Ilkeston the foot beat officers were divided into five groups. At any given day one group would be taking their weekly rest day, and the remaining were split between the four shifts; 6am—2pm, 10am-6pm, 6pm—2am and 10pm-6am. New recruits always started work on nights in the basis that it was easier to get to know an area with fewer people about. I shocked a member of the public on my way to work on that first night, when I asked him the way the police station.

My recollections are that I worked with a colleague on the first night and thereafter I was on my own. Thrown in at the deep end would offer the best description. February 1963 was in the middle of what became known as the big freeze up and night temperatures were extremely low. We wore pyjamas under our uniform and thick woollen balaclava helmets under our police helmets. Prior to going out onto the streets the duty sergeant would brief us on what to look out for, like stolen vehicles or wanted persons and we would be inspected. Whilst the constables worked a four-shift system, the sergeants worked a three-shift system, so you did not have the same sergeant all the time. Within a short time of commencing my duties at Ilkeston I discovered that they saw their role as being to make life as difficult as possible for the constables, especially the new recruits.

One of the sergeants was an old-time bachelor who originated from Scotland and in his broad Scottish accent he would say the same thing every night as his final instruction. "Hang around the Market Place until the hostelries disgorge their noxious contents." The probationer constables were always allocated Bath Street Patrol. This street contained nearly all the shops in the town and was on a hill about half a mile in length. At the top of the hill was Ilkeston Market Place, around which were the hostelries that would throw out their noxious contents onto the pavements at around 10.45pm each evening. Some would be worse for wear and in that state liked to make fun of the police or worse still fight other drunken people or occasionally join forces to take on the police. Weekends nearly always included sorting out a fight and arresting the participants.

From about five past ten each evening the entire night shift and those from the evening shift who were not taking their refreshment break would stand in pairs around the market until the noxious contents had disappeared, usually around eleven o'clock. With it being so cold during that first week of nights the public were not tempted to stay around for long. Picking up my Bath Street duties and I would start to check all the lock-up shops making sure they were secure. Going all the way down one side and back up the other checking both front and rear entrances, generally by the time I got back up the marketplace it would be around the scheduled time for a forty-five-minute refreshments break.

The reader should remember that a beat constable had no means of communication other than his voice and a police whistle. At the beginning of each shift, we were allocated a series of conference points at hourly intervals which would either be on the hour, the half hour, or quarter hour. In a town these would be outside public telephone boxes and you were expected to stand by the kiosk for ten minutes when you could be contacted via the telephone. It was not long before your more experienced colleagues demonstrated how you could use a public phone without having to insert any money. This was called "tapping out," you hit the plunger on the telephone cradle for the required number of times which simulated the signal given from using the dial.

This ranged from ten taps for the number zero to one tap for the number one. Chatting one day to a telephone switchboard operator, I was told that it was a criminal offence, and they could see in the telephone exchange when it was happening, but she said so long as we were only calling the police station, they ignored it! It is no good trying it now, it does not work with the modern telephone system.

All police stations had a mess room, equipped with basic cooking facilities where meals were consumed during the break. Often there were games facilities such as a snooker table, dart board, dominoes, and card games.

After break on Bath Street patrol, I would repeat the property security check. This was important because if a burglary were discovered on your patch, you would be called out of bed and brought back to the police station to account for why you had not discovered it. Another way you could be in trouble on Bath Street, was if the Sergeant came looking for you and could not find you. Often, they would drive slowly up the street and if you did not step out to stop them you were in trouble. The good thing about Bath Street patrol was that in the night it would be so quiet that if anything happened you would hear it.

I quickly learned another good thing was that there was a bakery located at the junction of Bath Street with Station Road and they started working from around 3am, so you could have a warm and get cup of tea. At weekends they would produce doughnuts and patrolling nearby you could smell them cooking. I quickly learned that sometimes they would come out of the fat miss shaped and they would throw them into a big bowl of sugar and invite me to help myself— wonderful so fresh and just the job before knocking off at 6am.

When it was quiet especially in the wintertime there were some shop display areas where there was an alcove and if I felt tired, I would go into the alcove and sit down with my back to the wall and have a rest. Even if I dozed, I would immediately wake up at the lightest sound of movement. Sleeping on duty is not something I am proud of, but anyone who has worked nights will know how tired you become around four in the morning.

It did not take me long to discover that the practical aspect of working as a policeman was not difficult for me. I had a relaxed technique when talking to members of the public and was a good listener. I could handle myself physically so not afraid to intervene in a fight if that were required, which on nights was nearly every shift at Ilkeston. What I found more difficult was the paperwork. During our induction week before going away to the recruit training centre we had all purchased a portable typewriter which we paid for on a loan repaid through our salary.

As a point of reference my starting pay as a police constable was £460 per annum. The trouble with reports was that our sergeants gave us no guidance as to how to complete them and when we submitted them, they often came back to us with "Try again," written across them but no indicator as to what was wrong. Of all the sergeants just one of them would take the time to talk you through your report and suggest improvements, consequently all the probationers tried to submit their reports when he was on duty. The effect of which was that he was doing all the work for the others.

During my first week on nights, I came across a very practical problem related to the limits of the law. As I walked down Bath Street, I spotted a couple in a shop doorway. The lady was crouched with her skirt pulled up and her knickers around her knees. I saw that she was urinating which I knew to be an offence contrary to the byelaws of the Borough of Ilkeston. Waiting until she had re-arranged her clothing, I said, "I have just seen you urinating in a public place, and I am going to report you for summons."

I got out my pocket notebook and asked her for her name and address. She flatly refused to tell me who she was despite being encouraged to do so by her husband. That left me with a problem as I had already started to make a pocketbook entry. At that time, a police officer was not allowed to arrest someone to obtain their name and address, so what was I to do. I told her that I would follow them home, so I would then know who she was. I hope you can see the picture, one angry lady storming home along with one embarrassed husband and one inexperienced bobby following at a discreet distance, hoping that they did not live too far off my beat. After about half an hour of this, husband persuaded wife to supply her details and I completed my pocket-book entry and later my report.

On a typical night shift there would be just two or three constables working on foot, supplemented between 10pm and 2am by another two or three constables. As well as Bath Street patrol, other beats were allocated including:

Nottingham Road, Hallam Fields, Cotmanhay, and Station Road/Ilkeston Junction. On some of the outer beats you could be at least three miles away from the police station.

Working nights was often an adventure but sometimes could also be frightening. Adjacent to the market square is St Mary's Church which is surrounded by a large cemetery, and I often found it a bit spooky walking through the cemetery which was a useful short cut to Station Road. One pitch black moonless night I was wandering between the graves in a state of heightened sensitivity when I spotted something white that appeared to be hovering in the air about a foot above the surface and moving up and down. I resisted the temptation to turn and run and started to move closer to this ghostly object. As I got nearer, I could hear heavy breathing and a moaning sound and thought I had better put my torch on a see what we had got.

What I saw was a young couple engaging in sexual intercourse, the heavy breathing was his and the moaning was hers. But when my torch illuminated them, their delight came to a sudden and dramatic end. The man jumped up, pulled up his trousers and started to leg it. The young woman also did the same thing but unfortunately forgot to pull up her knickers, so that she kept tripping up. It was a very funny sight! I wondered what the young ladies mother thought when her daughter arrived home with "In Loving Memory," printed on the back of her coat!

Whist I was completing my initial training course I had purchased my first car, a Ford Zephyr Mk1 1958 model registration number SWJ 536. It was a lovely car but not the most sensible of purchases given that it had a six-cylinder engine and a top speed of 100mph plus. After about eighteen months I took it off the road because I could not afford to maintain it and went back to public transport to get back home on my rest days and see my girlfriend. Over the years I have spent a lot of money on cars and my decisions have not always been the most sensible.

For the first half of my probationary period, I made good progress. True I sometimes I had problems in writing my reports, but overall, I felt I was doing a good job. I was also sorting out what my policing style would be. My driving desire was to make a positive influence and be as helpful as I could whilst recognising that I had a responsibility to enforce the law. One or two of my colleagues led the way in the number of offences they reported and whilst I had nothing against their approach, I tried to be more selective and sometimes would give advice or reach a practical outcome that satisfied the overall aims of policing intervention. This approach is probably best demonstrated via a couple of examples involving the depositing of litter. Just round the corner from the police station was the Ilkeston Cooperative Society store outside of which was a machine from which cartons of milk could be obtained.

We frequently referred to this machine as the Coop Cow, and we often used her resources if we ran out of milk at the police station. Alongside the milk dispenser was a large refuse container into which the empty cartons could be deposited and one day I saw a young man turning the litter bin upside down and spreading the contents onto the pavement. I told him that he was guilty of depositing litter in a public place, and I would report him for prosecution. He said, "Can I do anything that would persuade you not to prosecute me?"

I told him that if he picked up all the litter and put it back in the bin, I would take no further action. He willingly complied and the objective of a litter free environment was achieved. I took almost identical action when a young man came out of the public toilets on the marketplace with a roll of toilet paper and started to tear of pieces and throw them down. The same conversation took place and he then chased bits of paper around for about half an hour until all had been recovered.

Most of we young probationer constables carried a small handbook around with us. Hopkers Summons Headings listed every offence against the law, and I used to look for offences I had not reported previously. One day I saw a car being driven along with one of the front wings missing and another part revealing jagged metal. I recognised that this was an offence and reported the driver, who responded by saying, "I was stopped by a bobby in Skegness yesterday and he didn't know it was an offence." Which I duly recorded as his reply and which was read out at court when he was prosecuted and my case appeared in the Daily Mirror under the headline, "This Bobby Knew."

Although I have alluded to the fact that I had to learn quickly how to look after myself in the face of potential violence. The reality was that I rarely felt at risk of anything other than minor injury. There was one occasion when I was assaulted before I realised what was happening. Walking along a passageway off Nottingham Road, a well-built young man walked up to me and punched in the face knocking me to the ground. As I got up, I could see venom and anger in his face and he said, "That's for shagging my wife whilst I was in prison." I quickly told him I was arresting him for assault on a police officer and placed him in handcuffs.

The following conversation revealed that a colleague, had been visiting his wife whilst he was in prison, and giving her rather more than advice. My prisoner was very apologetic when he discovered that he had got the wrong policeman. The outcome was that the young man pleaded guilty giving the circumstances which resulted in him not having to go to prison and my colleague being disciplined and transferred. His punishment transfer was into a detached police house in the Peak District village of Hathersage. It did not look like a punishment station to me, still his father was a Chief Superintendent!

Ilkeston had an annual fair when the entire Town Centre was taken over by fairground rides, shows and displays. The roads in the area were closed for the duration of the fair and a great time was had by all. The event took place just after the Nottingham Goose Fair, so most of the equipment came directly from there. You could guarantee a fight or two when the pubs turned out. The first year I experienced the fair there was a strip show across the road from the police station. In between the short shows the girls came out onto a stage, scantily clad and demonstrated their dancing skills. They had tassels at the point of their busts and had a rare and amazing ability to make them counter rotate as they danced.

Sitting in the police station looking out of the window I tried to work out just how they managed to achieve such display of physical control, but despite hours of study I failed to come up with a suitable answer. There was also a boxing booth where locals were encouraged to take on the boxers for a cash prize. I never saw anyone win a prize, but I saw lots of bloody noses and black eyes. One of my mates in the police K, had done a substantial amount of boxing and he said that in the past he had successfully challenged the fairground boxers. He was six feet plus and well-built and he certainly demonstrated that he could handle himself.

The fairground owner if I remember was P, a leading member of the Showman's Guild and a wealthy bloke. He obviously knew of K's ability with his fists and as K and I were patrolling together he asked us if we would be in the vicinity of the coconut shy between 10pm and 12 midnight on the Saturday and handed something to K. This was my first year at the fair but not K's. I said to him, "What was that all about?"

He explained that when the local yobs came out of the pubs' they would pay to use the coconut shy and always end up throwing the balls at the assistants, not the coconuts. He also explained that he had been given a five-pound note for each of us. You might say that it was corruption and certainly was contrary to police regulations, but we earned our money on the Saturday, filling the cells with prisoners and saving the fairground staff from injury or from being arrested for fighting with the yobs.

I remember one night when K and I were standing across the road from the Market Inn when they were, "disgorging their noxious contents." One of their customers in a mild state of drunkenness, came across the road and started making fun of K. I waited for him to respond but initially he just laughed with the bloke, that was, until he flicked out K's tie. The next thing I knew was the bloke was lying on the pavement, where Keith my mate picked him up and arrested him for assault on police. K just pulled back when the blokes hand came to his tie and punched him in the face. I was also in court when the man pleaded not guilty to assaulting K. When the defence solicitor asked him how he could justify punching his client in the circumstances, he replied, "It was a reflex, action I did not know what he intended doing to me, but his action was threatening. The bloke was found guilty!

The chairman of the Ilkeston Magistrates Court was a retired GP who was rather deaf, so you could often hear his discussions with his fellow magistrates. I found over time once he had decided you were honest, he accepted your evidence without question. The other thing was that as a local doctor for years he knew the family histories of many of the offenders appearing before him. In those days, summonses had to be signed by a magistrate. If you were deployed on the Nottingham Road beat, you would often find a pile of summonses and court lists to take to the house where the chairman lived. He would get his wife to provide you with a cup of tea and cake and then discuss all the cases that were coming before him.

The second year I was on duty at the fair, K had been posted into the office and I was the one PC approached to provide protection for his employees. Another colleague, who was useful with his fists was brought in with me and provided with his fiver. We earned it that night because a fully-fledged fight developed near the coconut shy. B and I arrested the ringleader who was large and extremely fit, we struggled so much that we had to obtain the assistance of two other colleagues, eventually half carrying and half dragging the prisoner to the police station. K knew the bloke and told him to quieten down. He said, "Let him loose I will put him in the cells." However, once we took our hands off him, he got up and went for K. The next thing was that we were carrying him into the cells, half conscious.

One night we were called out of the police station because a young man was refusing to leave the top deck of a bus. I have no idea why, but he certainly took no notice of our repeated requests. Assistance was called for and the Inspector and Sergeant duly arrived to assist, but rank made no difference he still resisted. He was straddled between the two seats nearest to the top of the steps and for the greater part kept his fingers tightly around the seats, only moving them to punch us and then resume his fixed position. I decided to take a different approach and climbed over the seats to the back of bus.

I then ran full pelt at the bloke putting my head down and sinking it into his back between his shoulder blades. I hit him with such force that he was catapulted down the steps having a soft landing on the Inspector and Sergeant! When he pleaded guilty to assaulting the Inspector the Sergeant and myself, the chairman said, "We take a dim view of anyone who assaults a constable, you will be fined £50 for that, assault on a police sergeant is a rare event so you will be fined £100 for that, and assaults on Inspectors are unheard of so you will be fined £200 for that."

I was in court on one occasion when the retired doctor was administering justice to a local troublemaker with a long list of previous convictions. His solicitor made an impassioned plea for the accused not to be given a custodial sentence, the depth of the appeal was quite exceptional, quoting a list of reasons why prison should be avoided. The chairman in responding referred extensively to the factors that he had been asked to consider and concluded, "Having considered all these good and valid reasons why you should not go to prison, I am sending you to prison for three months."

The young man responded immediately by shouting, "You f.....r."

Without a blink the doctor said, "Six months, take him away."

When writing about my memories of events that took place many, many years ago, you will inevitably think that life on the beat in Ilkeston was full of adventure whereas the truth was that quite often it was boring and quiet for the entre shift. Some of my funny stories are concerned with what happened when I fell asleep on nights. At the bottom of Bath Street was the Felix bus garage, where there was a night shift cleaning the buses. When there was nothing to do, I would nip in and have a cup of tea with the cleaners. One night, I was feeling very tired, and I had about half an hour spare before making my next conference point, which was within sight of the bus depot. I turned down the offer of a cuppa but said I was going to have a quick kip and asked them to wake me up in about twenty minutes. They forgot and I woke to the sound of heavy rain a few minutes after I should have been at the telephone box across the road.

Looking carefully out of the window, I was shocked to see the duty sergeant there, looking like a drowned rat. I was bone dry, so I asked the bus cleaners to turn the hose on me and then snook out of the rear entrance, jumped over the wall so that I could come up behind the sergeant. I apologised for being few minutes late and explained that I had been investigating because of hearing a noise. A narrow escape.

One summers night I was working the Cotmanhay beat which took in a vast council housing estate and involved doing about twenty miles before the end of the shift. My conference point at four in the morning, when it was still dark was on the edge of the Cotmanhay estate and alongside a bus shelter with a seat. Feeling tired, when no one turned up during the allocated ten minutes I sat down in the bus shelter and fell asleep.

I woke up at about a quarter to six, when it was broad daylight, and a group of workers were waiting for their works bus. There was a lot of laughter and banter about now knowing what bobbies got up to on nights and I got on the bus with them jumping off near the police station and getting in for the appointed signing off period. Fortunately, K the office constable on that shift was able to tell me that no one had been looking for me, so I was OK.

On one occasion I fell asleep whilst walking the beat and only woke up when I stumbled into the side of a telephone kiosk. One of our group, Harold got married to Ruth who was the daughter of a couple of local preachers in the Wesleyan Reform Churches. After my nightshift one day I travelled home and attended the wedding returning the following night straight from the wedding and having only had a couple of hours sleep. I was exhausted.

If someone failed to turn up at the end of a shift, particularly on nights it resulted in concerns for the safety of the officer. One night when K was working, the Nottingham Road beat, he failed to turn up at six and I offered to stay on with the Sergeant and go out looking for him. I was a bit concerned that he might have called in to his lodgings and fallen asleep. I did not want to express that opinion to the sergeant, but when we had not found him, I said, "Perhaps he has suffered some illness and gone back to his digs."

K lived in a terraced house, where the back door was approached through a covered passageway. As we travelled through the covered area, I made sure that my conversation was loud in the hope that if he were asleep, he would hear me saying, "I don't think that K will be here Sergeant." We knocked on the door and after a few moments, it was opened by K, he looked quite disturbed and was walking with a limp. He said, "I am glad you came looking for me, I was checking round the back of some lock-up property and fell injuring my shin and I could not make it back to the police station." Pulling up his trouser leg he showed us an area where his leg looked red and inflamed. I learned afterwards that he had woken to hear my words to the sergeant and had been scrubbing his leg with a scrubbing brush to make the mark on his leg. A narrow escape for K.

At the time I was stationed at Ilkeston (from February 1963 to January 1966), the M1 motorway between Northampton and Trowel, was being constructed and there were quite a few houses where Irish labourers working on the site were in lodgings. Many of these fellers were heavy drinkers and could be a handful when they were fighting drunk. One afternoon I was standing at the telephone box on Park Road, making my conference point when I got a call from the police station, telling me to go to a nearby address where an Irish lodger had returned from a long drinking session and was "Breaking the place up."

Approaching the door, I could hear shouting and swearing and banging and crashing. Opening the door and entering without seeking permission because I feared for the safety of the occupants, I was confronted by a raging bull of a man who was small in height but with the muscles of a big man. He came straight at me and before I could defend myself, he had kicked me in the groin, knocking me to the floor and possibly damaging my marriage prospects. There followed about fifteen minutes of total fighting between the two of us with the landlady and her daughter shouting and encouraging me on like I was in the ring with the featherweight champion of the Irish Republic, which I might well have been judging by the way he handled himself.

Eventually I landed a beautiful uppercut right on the point of his chin, hitting him so hard that his feet lifted off the ground before he dropped in a daze. Standing over him I got out my handcuffs and was about to cuff him when he regained consciousness and up came both feet into my groin. Now I was down on my knees again wondering whether my life would ever be the same again.

Another five minutes of sustained fighting followed before I manage a second uppercut to his chin and knocked him out again, this time I turned him over and handcuffed him with his arms behind his back. He was just coming round when the cavalry arrived in the form of the duty sergeant and the beat car driver. I just managed to mumble, "I could have done with you to a bit earlier." My prisoner was helped to his feet when he said in his strong Irish accent, "Sergeant, you've got a hard man here." From that time onwards the man became my strongest advocate on the beat, making a fuss of me whenever he saw me and saying to his mates, "This is a hard man, but he fights fair." That was because I had not drawn my police truncheon, which he regarded as a weapon and would have put him at a disadvantage.

When I had been at Ilkeston for about a year some aspects of my fledgling police career took a turn for the worse with the appointment of a new Inspector. I had got on well with the earlier Inspector, but his replacement had an extremely negative attitude to the constables, probationers or otherwise. He was never satisfied with anything you did and continually found fault. I eventually reached the stage at which I was applying for other jobs because I just could not cope with the pressure, he was putting me under. His ideas about what amounted to effective policing were at complete variance with mine, but he had the power, so his view had to prevail. For example, he insisted that we increased the number of people we reported for summons.

Given that this usually meant reporting motorists for minor motoring offences, which I thought was counter-productive to creating good working relationships between the police and the public. I would overcome this by going to one or other of a couple of places where there was a 'Halt' sign. Hardly anybody observed signs and I would fill my book, just to satisfy the inspector. Eventually our relationship came to a head, when I decided that I would ignore him, not speaking other than if he spoke to me. Coming through the Parade Room, he said, "Bown, come into my office." We had a long conversation in which I made it clear to him that although I was anxious to continue being a policeman the job was not worth putting up with people like him and I was looking for another job.

I knew that he was in trouble with the Superintendent for the number of officers that were resigning and as my standing with the Superintendent was good, I thought I may as well have a go at the Inspector. Thankfully, he changed his attitude towards me, and I stayed in the job for thirty years. There was a lesson learned, do not submit when being bullied by bosses, stand up strong against them and they will back down.

One of the patrol sergeants had a habit of following constables working their beats, keeping out of sight, but checking up on you. One night on Bath Street I realised that he was following me. I decided that I would sort him out. Sometimes to get from the front of a shop to the rear you would have to go through an enclosed alleyway. There was one where it was pitch black not one glimmer of light coming through. I hid myself in there hiding behind a dustbin and then jumping on him, knocking him to the floor, before switching on my torch and saying, "It's you sergeant' I thought some criminal was going to attack me." To the best of my knowledge, he never followed me again.

During our initial training we were taught the basic approaches for delivering a death message a task that none of us looked forward to. When a policeman comes knocking on your door it can often mean bad news and at the heart of the required approach was to be kind, sensitive and supportive. The joke about how not to go about the task was, "Bobby knocks on the door and says to the lady, are you Widow Brown?"

Lady responds by saying, "No" and Bobby says, "You are now."

My first sudden death did not work out quite how it is supposed to do. I was on the early morning shift on a cold winter's day, when called to an old man who had collapsed on the pavement, whilst out getting his morning newspaper. He was clearly dead, but I rendered first aid until an ambulance arrived and confirmed that he was indeed dead. The man had no means of identification on his person, but enquiries revealed who he was and where he had lived. In these circumstances you can never be sure that you have a correct identification, so we were taught not to give the death message until you had been able to confirm with the relative that you were at the correct home. We were told to have the conversation in the house and preferably seated so that if the relative feinted they would not fall to the floor and injure themselves.

With some fear, I knocked on the door which was answered very speedily by a large elderly lady, equipped with curlers in her hair, who I could only describe as a battle axe of a woman, and without showing anything other than mistrust she said, "What do you bloody want?" I tried to persuade her to invite me into the house before completing my identification process, but she was having none of it saying, "Spit it out what's this about."

Eventually having confirmed that her husband had gone out for the morning paper, I said, "I am sorry to tell you that your husband has died." A huge smile spread across her face and her character completely changed and she said, "That's the best bit of news I have had in years, we have been married for forty years of complete misery, would you like to celebrate with me with a cup of tea!" I willingly accepted the invitation, and it was me that needed to sit down to recover from the shock, not her.

Associated with the unpleasant task of dealing with a sudden death in those days was having to attend the post-mortem examination where the cause of death could not be certificated by a medical practitioner. The mortuary was at the outer edge of the largest local authority cemetery so surrounded by graves, which at the best of times would be a bit scary but then build on top of that having to be present when a human body was opened-up, it was for me very off-putting. During training, the instructors would try to frighten us with stories of gory examinations followed by liver for dinner! My first experience was not that frightening but what was worst was the terrible smell when the stomach cavity was opened. Sure enough, when I got back to my lodgings for my meal, it was liver and onions.

I did not have much social life during my time in Ilkeston, my idea of a night out was not a visit to the local pub and as my girlfriend was back home, I only saw her on my days off. I never got established in a local church, although I got to know a few local Christians. Along with a few colleagues including K we did do a bit of game shooting but that was about the limit. I occasionally had a meal at the local Chinese restaurant where I knew the owner and his wife, and they would invite me to parties at the restaurant from time to time.

On 20th March 1965, Margaret and I were married at Stone Edge Wesleyan Reform Chapel, with the evangelist who had led us to the Lord, taking the service. We moved into a new house that we personally rented from a housing association. We would become eligible for a police house but at that time there was a waiting list of up to a year. By that time, my prized Ford Zodiac was parked up waiting to be scrapped and we had no transport to get us to our honeymoon destination of Newquay.

A year earlier, when my car was still roadworthy and running well, my brother had borrowed it for his honeymoon, so he returned the favour and we borrowed his Rover 75 saloon, which was old but a good runner and comfortable. We did have a bit of problem with it when the silencer dropped off when travelling through Devon, but we did manage to get it fixed without too much trouble. On the day of our wedding, it was foggy and wet, turning to snow later in the weekend. Getting married to Margaret was a great decision along with the one to become a committed Christian. Margaret has been the glue that has held me together as a person and after nearly fifty-seven years of married life I cannot imagine how empty my life would be without her. As we waited for a police house, we pondered on where we would like it to be.

Over the years we had visited Stoney Middleton Wesleyan Reform Church taking services on the Sunday and observed that there were two adjoining recently built police houses and longed to live there. We often prayed together about where we would be posted but did not dare pray, "Lord send us to Stoney Middleton," because we thought it much more likely that I would be posted to a much older house, probably in some industrial town.

One day soon after we married, I was off duty in our house when a couple of small boys who knew I was a policeman knocked on my door reporting that another boy had thrown a cat into the nearby canal and that it had floated into overflow pipe from one of the lock gates. I quickly went with them, and they identified the boy responsible who was running away. I chased after him and brought him back to the canal side with me. Stripping off to my underpants I climbed up the overflow pipe, which was about half full of water, until I reached the cat where it had lodged behind a protruding stone.

I was able to grab the cat and bring it out alive and without injury. We were eventually joined by the RSPA Inspector who took possession of the cat and took the boy home to his parents, reporting him for cruelty to the cat.

Not long after our marriage I was working the 6pm to 2am evening shift and sat in the Parade Room, having my refreshments when a call came in that a teenage boy had run away from his home saying that he was going to commit suicide at a disused colliery near his home. We had responded to a call from the boy's parents about a week before, when we had to physically restrain him until he calmed down. I joined the sergeant and two or three other constables to rush out to the colliery. It was very dark at the colliery with no lighting and searching the extensive abandoned buildings would be a time consuming and possible dangerous task.

At some stage I heard a voice above me and shining my torch up to the headstocks I saw that the young man had climbed up to the winding wheel. I made a quick assessment of the situation and realising that as a newly married with no children I had less to lose than the other policemen there each of whom had children. Although I am not good at heights I volunteered to climb up to the boy and see if I could persuade him to come down. Old time coal mines have a tall metal construction (headstock) located over the shaft. At the top of the headstock is a large wheel around which the cable runs, lowering and lifting the cage in which the colliers are conveyed as well as the coal.

A narrow and rickety ladder was attached to the metal framework which I slowly and carefully climbed. Eventually I climbed onto the narrow walkway that surrounded the wheel, the young man was also on the walkway and before joining him I had spoken to him, using his name, remembered from the previous week's encounter, and asking if it was alright for me to join him. It is crucially important in circumstances like this to be very calm and ask for permission before doing anything.

We had a long conversation exploring why he was concerned about his future and about his state of mind. At one stage a fire engine turned up with flashing lights and sirens. When they started to put flood lights on and begin extending their ladder he climbed over the rail as if he were going to jump. I shouted, "Switch your lights off and stop what you are doing." Fortunately, my very loud voice had the required effect, and I was able to assist him back onto the walkway. After about half an hour of conversation he agreed to follow me down the ladder and he was taken home to his anxious parents.

Earlier that day I had been in court where the boy from the canal incident was convicted of cruelly ill-treating the cat. The next day I had a double entry on the front page of the Daily Mirror, featuring both the rescue of the cat and the boy under the heading, "A busy day for an Ilkeston policeman."

Sometimes in the heat of the summer when we knocked of duty at 2am or 6am we would climb over a high wall across the road from the police station and gain access to the open-air swimming pool. This was always skinny-dipping, but it did not matter because there was no one to see us. On a hot summer's night, it was lovely to jump into a cool pool and swim for an hour. One night a couple of us went into the pool just after 2am, when it was still dark and after a couple of hours by which time it was daylight, we got out of the pool to get back into our uniforms, climb the wall, and return to the police station. Shock and horror, all that was there was our helmets. Can you imagine the scene?

Two large men running across the road to the police station, naked and with a policemen's helmet in front of their prized possessions. K, who was working in the office had nipped over the wall and taken all our clothes, other than our helmets. It was not just policemen who gained access to the swimming pool, and it became something of a problem, so much so that the Town Clerk sent a letter to the police pointing out the dangers from these unsupervised swimming sessions, asking for police action to be taken against those who were taking part in these night-time swims. In handwriting the Town Clerk had put, "This does not affect the longstanding practice of the night shift at the police station having a dip at the conclusion of their duties." And we thought that it was a well-kept secret!

Most beats had elements that were scary or unpleasant on nights. Cemeteries were always spooky, Hallam Fields which was in the middle of a steel works, was noisy and smelly. Just off Nottingham Road and close by the county boundary was a cornmill which was alongside the Erewash canal. The office for the mill was at the far end of the building and contained a safe which in the past had been the object of a burglary when fortunately, they failed to open the safe and it was too heavy for them to remove. We were instructed always to check the office when passing on night patrol. A canopy covered the walkway because in the early days, deliveries had come along the canal and rats as big as cats would be running along the rafters above your head, horrible things that always gave me the shivers.

My challenge to the inspector regarding his attitude resulted in an improved relationship and when I came to the end of my probationary period my appointment as a constable was confirmed and I settled down to the idea of a long-term career in the Derbyshire Constabulary. Quite a few of the constables stationed at Ilkeston had married around the same date as Margaret and I and along with us were awaiting the allocation of their first police house.

Some who married after us were allocated a police house before us, and we began to get a bit concerned about it. One day I bumped into the Superintendent who asked me how things were, and I explained how I was concerned that others were passing us by on the housing list. He simply told me not to worry because they were awaiting the right vacancy to occur for me. Clearly, he had a good opinion of my work and I felt confident that everything would work out for us.

One day the Inspector called me into his office and told me that I was being posted to the village of Stoney Middleton in the Peak district and neither I nor my wife, could believe that we were getting our hearts desire. My inspector made it clear that he did not agree with the posting telling me that I would be working without supervision and would not be up to the job! I was glad to get out of his office and when I saw the Superintendent, he wished me all the best and said, "You are just the man for that posting."

That Inspector eventually retired as a Police Superintendent, but I never changed my mind about him. His people management skills were incredibly poor, and he had been responsible for many young constables leaving the job when they would have become effective in the role if they had been given the chance. In the recent past I found myself in conversation with a lady who had lived next door to him, prior to his death. She told me what a horrible man he was and how is wife had been relieved when he died!

During my period at Ilkeston, I gained a good relationship with the members of the local CID office and from time to time they requested my assistance on an enquiry team with them. I remember my first encounter I had with the Detective Inspector. I had received a report of a case of indecent exposure, when a young woman had been approached in a quiet park by a man who had exposed his penis in front of her. She gave a detailed description of an unusual looking man with a swarthy complexion and wearing a denim suit. Bearing in mind that this was 1962 and denim suits in Ilkeston were just about as rare as rocking horse manure, I was not going to forget what the man looked like.

Standing on Ilkeston Market Place and very much emulating the words of the song, "Standing on the corner, watching all the girls go by," I spotted my suspect. I went up to him and arrested him for indecent exposure. Trying to converse with the man I realised that he was not able to communicate properly in English. I took him to the police station where I was invited into the CID office where one of the detectives was fluent in French which we had realised was the prisoner's native tongue. Leaving him with the French speaking detective I went and got myself a cup of tea and calmed down after all the excitement of my brilliant arrest.

I was still engaging in self-congratulations when the Detective Inspector came to see me and thanked me for a good identification. He said, "What did the

97

bloke say when you asked him to accompany you to the police station?" I replied, "When I arrested him, he said, "Me no speak English." The DI again asked the same question, and I repeated my earlier reply. Eventually he told me that there was no power of arrest for indecent exposure, but not to worry because I had done the right thing. Fortunately, the bloke eventually pleaded guilty.

Policing 'Heartbeat' Style at Stoney Middleton

We moved into the Police House, Meadow Close, Stoney Middleton in January 1966 and lived there for nearly four lovely years. I went from an environment where my supervisors thought I was at the bottom of the scale of ability in my role to one where, I was perceived to be at the high point of the effectiveness scale. Certainly, a part of this was that I was working in a semi-rural environment which was more in line with my background.

On the first day at Stoney Middleton the leader of the Wesleyan Reform Chapel called to see us and asked us to start a youth group providing us with confirmation that our prayers had been answered and we were in the right place at the right time.

There were two adjoining police houses, with an office between the two, on a small new council housing estate, adjacent to the main road through the village. A policeman who had transferred from Liverpool lived next door and we both worked a cycle beat. On days when we were both on duty, one of us would be working 9am to 5pm and the other 5pm to 1am. On days when one of us was taking a rest day the other would often work a split shift with two four-hour periods of work during the day with the first one in the morning and the second in the evening. I quickly established a good working relationship with B next door. We agreed that whenever we were in and the telephone rang (shared line) we would answer and if police action were required by us, we would agree which one and then get on with the job. We were in effect providing a twenty for hour a day service, but we did not mind.

Stoney Middleton was part of the Baslow police area, supervised by a sergeant who worked out of an office alongside a police house in the village. G was an old timer, a former guardsman, decent and honest and a lovely bloke to work for. We were then part of Matlock Divisional Police, where Superintendent

Ewas in charge. We also came under the Bakewell police office, where Inspector W was the boss. It was good to meet up with him again, he had been a detective sergeant at Alfreton when I was a cadet there and had arranged a great coach trip to Heathrow airport and Margaret and I had enjoyed that trip very much. I have much to thank the late W for, he died in 2019 by which time he was well into his nineties.

The Baslow sergeant and the Bakewell inspector had a twenty-four-hour responsibility, using their own cars and receiving a car allowance. In Baslow, there were two constables at the time, P, and G, the later having just completed his probationary period. A rural beat car also covered the area working out of Bakewell, and the regular drivers were K who lived in Baslow, B who lived at Ashford-in-the-Water, and J who lived in Rowsley.

I very quickly got to know people around the area where I worked. The first week we opened our youth group about a dozen of them turned up at the chapel and then often visited us at the police house, where we would play board games drink coffee and chat. This brought me to the attention of many families, and I became known as "Bobby John" to everybody.

At the beginning of each tour of duty, I would obtain a list of my conference points and in the office adjacent to my house complete any necessary paperwork before setting out on my police issue pedal cycle made by Raleigh Industries at Nottingham. Typically, my first conference point would be close to the police office, either at the telephone kiosk in the middle of the village, or just half a mile down the road at Calver Service Station. There was always a cup of tea available with T, the proprietor and with M his young mechanic, and these meetings would always have the potential for finding out what was happening in the area and building trusting working relationships. In addition, T's two teenage sons had become regulars at our youth group and to our home. If cover were needed in Baslow, because no one was on duty there, the next conference point would be at the Police Station there.

The Sergeant would always offer a cup of tea and enjoy a chat. He never seemed anxious to get us back out on patrol and sometimes would tell me that he would take me in his car to the next conference point, particularly if it was a long way from the station, for example, Chatsworth House. The first time I made that conference point, I leaned my cycle again the outer wall of the security office and stood looking around. Behind me I heard a knocking on the window and saw that the security officer was beckoning me inside. Given that it was winter I was glad to accept his invitation.

Naturally, I was expected to introduce myself which I willingly did, telling him my name and where I had originated from. The Security Officer also told me his story. A native of the Chatsworth Estate he had left the area when he joined the armed forces in WW2. On demobilisation he joined the police in Norwich where he completed a full police career, I think retiring as a sergeant. Given that the Chatsworth estate had a great loyalty to families, and I found many people working for them were from families who had been in their employment for generations, it was no surprise that they had turned to a local family for someone to head up their security, and he lived in an apartment in the north wing of that famous old house. In more recent years in studying my family history, I discovered that one of my ancestors, G of Beeley supplied the stone used to build that extension to the house including the security lodge where I made my conference point.

It would be about a couple of weeks later when I next made a visit to Chatsworth House and was invited in for the usual cup of strong tea drunk in front of a roaring coal fire. The security officer quickly got onto the subject of my ancestry, explaining that when he had mentioned my name to the estate gamekeepers it had caused not a little consternation, because they realised that I came from a long line of poachers on the Chatsworth Estate.

It was always interesting to look at the visitor's board in the security lodge where often I would see the names of famous people who were staying there at the invitation of the Duke and Duchess of Devonshire. Sometimes members of the Royal family stayed with them on private visits that were not known to the media or the public. There were other occasions when more formal visits were made, and I remember one occasion when the Queen and Prince Philip were staying there and I worked a couple of nights shifts inside the house, working alongside the security staff. This involved walking though underground passageways that contained the sewage system for the house, and I wondered if I had seen "The Royal Wee."

Each Christmas the Duke and Duchess would give some invitations for police stationed at Baslow to attend the staff Christmas party which was always a lovely and memorable event. They would also supply each Baslow based policeman with a turkey, grown on the estate. I worked very closely with D, the

Head Gamekeeper at the time, and provided the evidence for many successful prosecutions of poachers.

Given that I spent a considerable part of every tour of duty in conversation with people I met on my beat, I often found that I would have to make a last-minute dash on my bike to the next conference point which was alright unless it was at the telephone box in the village of Curbar, which was up a very steep hill. Riding up that hill in a panic I had to stand on the pedals and over the period I was using the bike I manage to smash two lots of pedals, something the manufacturers, Raleigh had never heard of before. At that time, my mother's cousin and her husband ran the shop in the village there, so I would often call in on my way to my next port of call, which would often be the village of Froggatt. Their son, Stuart was already a good friend, as he attended the Curbar Wesleyan Reform Church, where I preached from time to time, became a frequent visitor to our house and a regular opponent in a game of tennis at Cliff College, the Methodist training college, located just half a mile down the road from where we lived.

Curbar and Froggat are beautiful Peak District villages where many lovely homes occupied by wealthy people are located. Many of them had businesses in Sheffield and over the years I got to know quite a few of the families. One such family had moved to the area when he had sold his bus company and retired. He was well known through his sponsorship of some of the leading showjumpers in the country.. Another family I got to know had a daughter who was working in London and quite fashion conscious. One time she was at home visiting when I called in to see her family. She took an interest in my police shirt, which were in those days blue in colour similar, to those used by members of the Royal Air Force. Somehow, she realised that the shirts had a detached collar and she said that without the collar one would make her a unique dress.

She was tall and elegant, and I realised that her legs would look a treat under my shirt, so next time I passed by, I dropped one off for her. After some time, her parents showed me a photograph of their daughter at a posh party wearing my shirt, and as expected she looked a cracker! When she told her friends that she was wearing a policeman's uniform shirt, she was asked if she could supply them with one, but fortunately she declined.

One of the wealthy families with a house at the side of the road between Curbar and Froggatt had a Doberman dog that was always wearing a muzzle for what I thought was obvious reasons. On one occasion when visiting the house on official business, the dog seemed to take a disliking to my police cape and decided that he wanted to bite me. I was none too pleased and thought I had better take care. A few weeks later I was riding my police bike down the hill towards the house when the dog came running towards me. I quickly jumped off the bike and when the dog started to try and bite me through the muzzle, I drew my police truncheon and wacked him at the side of the head. He turned tail and ran away yelping. Thereafter whenever he saw me approaching on my bike he ran out of the way.

Right in the centre of the village of Froggatt was a telephone kiosk where I would sometimes make a conference point and nearby was the office of the local coal merchants owned by a family who were leading lights at the little chapel. I would often nip in there for a chat and a cuppa. The family employed one of our regulars at the youth group, who had some form of learning problems that meant he could not hold down a proper job, but they employed him largely out of the kindness of their heart.

You might by now be concluding that a typical day on my cycle beat involved an endless procession of cups of tea, and to a certain extent that was true. However, on each of those visits I was building relationships and finding out information about people which is part of the core skills for effective policing. It did not take long for me to gain a good reputation for knowing who was doing what and with whom.

One of the more frequent crimes in the area was house burglary, often perpetrated by travelling criminals from the nearby city of Sheffield and the best chance of detection lay in the direction of regular late-night checks of cars travelling back to Sheffield. Carrying out such checks was not possible working a cycle beat and it was left to those police cars that patrolled overnight. I would occasionally carry out checks at the traffic lights at Calver Sough, where there was a reasonable level of street lighting and enough space for me to jump out of the way if a vehicle failed to stop. I did have a particularly active local burglar, P, who I determined to send away to prison if I got half a chance. Indeed, often my meeting with P when I always carried out a stop search resulted him in alleging that I was persecuting him and on one occasion he made the following threat, "You need to look out for your back because one of these days I am going to shoot off your f'ing balls." Thankfully, they are still intact!

P was what we call in Derbyshire, "a dee-darr," relating them to an aspect of the accent of folk from Rotherham or Sheffield who are prone to say, "He de what darr doing down dere den duck?" (What are you doing there?). He had first come to the area to climb the rocks and explore the potholes around Stoney Middleton and then stayed in the locality living at first in a tent and then moving in with his girlfriend and her family in a council house in the village of Calver.

As well as having P residing on my beat, I also had two people who had been convicted of manslaughter. One was a local postman who had killed his own mother when she was in great pain and dying from cancer. The other one, H, lived in a gypsy caravan based in a disused quarry about a mile out of the village. H had a brightly coloured bike equipped with a scissor grinder and he travelled from village to village sharpening scissors and knives. H had been convicted of shooting his brother.

Originally charged with murder he managed to get the charge reduced to manslaughter because he convinced the jury that he did not know the gun was loaded. What I did not know at the time was that he was a bare fist fighter who had competed for the tittle "The Gypsy King." I would regularly come across H when he had been drinking and he could be a bit of a handful, but I had never felt that I needed to arrest him and would eventually persuade him to go home peacefully. Part of the reason for this was that he was a good mate of P, my local burglar and I felt that it was probably a good thing for H to owe me a favour. H had a partner Al who originated from Buxton and from time to time I had sorted out disputes between the two of them.

Late one night, A came knocking on my door in quite a state. She told me that she had been to see her family in Buxton but come back much later than she had planned, and H had accused her of having an affair and threatened that he would kill her. I accompanied A to the caravan and having knocked on the door entered, only to be confront by H with a large kitchen knife and, grabbing me he proceeded to hold the knife to my throat. I offered a very quick and silent prayer and then proceeded to engage him in a quiet conversation. Having successfully calmed H's rants in the past I hoped that I could succeed on this occasion.

After a while I persuaded him to let us both sit down and continuing the conversation over half an hour, he handed over the knife and asked me what I was going to do about his threats. I simply told him that I was not going to do anything official about it, because all had ended well, but I would remember that he owed me a favour. I will not dwell on the how and why, but I did subsequently manage to get P sent to prison for a while. When he came out of prison, he had big fight with his girlfriend's brother who stabbed P and put him in hospital where he nearly lost his life. Thereafter he was not half the man he had been previously and caused me no further trouble. It was many years later that I read, "The Gypsy King," by Bartley Gorman and discovered that H had competed for the bare fist fighter tittle that had been held by Gorman and he included some information about H's strange behaviours.

During my time at Stoney Middleton, policing in Derbyshire changed beyond recognition when a new Chief Constable was appointed. Previously P had been the Chief Constable and the Derbyshire Constabulary was underfunded and out of date, but on the positive side had a family feeling. A good example of this was that our Divisional Superintendent at Matlock, who had been off sick following a serious stroke, which left him partially disabled and unable to drive, but was permitted to return to duty. He was a lovely man and his equally lovely wife used to act as his driver. He was still very able intellectually, so BP considered that he need not pension him off.

S was an entirely different proposition and he proceeded to make major changes to the way the force was organised and functioned. As a manager of resources and an organisation he could not have been bettered, but his people management skills were not always to a similar level. The first major change he introduced directly affected me and were concerned with the development of 24/7 supervision, provided by supervisors on duty and not on call. These changes were also influenced by national changes where the number of police forces were greatly reduced. Prior to 1967, Derby had a separate police force, the Derby Borough Police, but the two forces were amalgamated to become, The Derby County and Borough Police, eventually returning to the Derbyshire Constabulary when further changes took place. Just as a brief comment about the earlier history of policing in Derbyshire, until 1947 there had also been a Chesterfield Borough Police force and a Glossop Borough Police Force, the latter with a total police establishment of just twenty-three. Other examples of changes on our borders included the creation of the Sheffield and Rotherham Police (amalgamating Sheffield City and Rotherham Borough), and Nottinghamshire and Nottingham City Police amalgamating.

By the time I was transferred from Stoney Middleton into the CID in Chesterfield at the end of 1969, the Baslow Section had disappeared, and all the sergeants worked a three-shift system based at Bakewell. Matlock Police Division had disappeared, and we had been incorporated into the Buxton Division. Matlock became a Sub-Divisional Headquarters with a Superintendent in charge and the new Divisions had Chief Superintendents appointed as commanders. Previously the force had only had two members with that rank, the Head of the Criminal Investigation Department (CID) and the Head of Administration, both posts based at Force Headquarters. Within the Bakewell Section two rural beat cars were engaged in providing a patrol function 24/7 which meant that apart from Bakewell where constables patrolled on foot, all other areas were policed via a mobile patrol.

Our police headquarters moved from the top floor of the County Offices to the former Head Offices of the Butterley Company near Ripley, where a state-of-the-art purpose-built residential police training school was created. All those developments were due to the abilities and persuasive powers of S. Following his retirement, I served under four more Chief Constables none of whom achieved what he had achieved and one of whom was a total disaster.

A career in the police force offers many opportunities for development both through specialisation and promotion. To pursue promotion the officer must pass appropriate examinations before being considered. There were at that time examinations for constable to sergeant and then from sergeant to inspector. We were not allowed to take the first of those examinations until we had completed five years in the rank of constable. I duly entered the promotion examination at the first opportunity, purchasing my Promotion Examinations Handbooks and embarking on a programme of private study.

The examinations were set nationally, and the results published, and I was delighted to have passed at the first attempt. Whilst my marks were by no means amongst the top five percent, I had easily achieved the pass mark. The Chief Constable had expressed his concerns that not enough members of the force were qualified for promotion, by examination, experience, and suitability and for the first time in the history of the Derbyshire Constabulary he advertised for officers to transfer to Derbyshire on promotion at both the sergeant and the inspector level, a policy he pursued with vigour for many years.

Within a year or so of me passing the promotion examination Police Regulations were changed to allow constables to take the qualifying examination for inspector, where previously you had to be a sergeant before taking that examination. The announcement was made just a couple of months before the examination was due to take place and we were permitted to enter at short notice. I thought I may as well test the temperature and have a go. I took a week's leave before the examination and studied the syllabus as much as possible in the time scale available. I was not overly disappointed when I failed because I was only a few marks short of a pass and the following year passed without difficulty.

Whilst I had a full driving licence, I was not permitted to drive police cars until I had successfully completed a Standard Police Driving Course. When I had been at Stoney Middleton for about eighteen months, I successfully completed the course coming joint top in both the driver assessment and the written examination. When this became known generally colleagues were telling me that I could look forward to being transferred onto the Road Traffic Division. Given that constables who were qualified for promotion could now apply for specialisation, I started to consider whether I should apply to specialise in Traffic Policing or in the Criminal Investigation Department. On balance given my success in the driving course I was inclined to think that it would be the former. However, following one specific event which I shall describe, I decided to look to the CID for my developmental opportunities.

At the beginning of a sequence of events that unwittingly put me in great danger, I received a report that someone had been sleeping in a caravan outside the village of Froggatt. I was aware that an escaped prisoner with a record of violence was believed to be at large in the area and drew the conclusion that there was a good possibility that the caravan was being used by this man. Foolishly, given the violent nature of the prisoner and in the light of subsequent discoveries, I spent a couple of nights sitting in the caravan (in my own time) with a view to arresting him, fortunately for me he had moved on somewhere else. Before I could attempt another night there, I made a routine property check at a manor house in Froggatt where the owners were away on an extended holiday abroad and had reported their absence to the police.

Checking the security of the house I discovered that it had been broken into. I carefully entered the house and carried out a full search. It was obvious that the burglar had spent some time in the house, using the kitchen and a toilet and I now knew why the caravan was no longer in use. What disturbed me most was that I found a firearms store that had been broken into and I certainly suspected that firearms and weapons had been stolen. We now had the potential major problem of the possibility that our violent escaped prisoner not only being at large in the area, but probably carrying with him a collection of weapons and ammunition.

At this stage I called in the CID and attempted to contact the house owner to establish exactly what was missing. A fingerprint examination eventually revealed that the culprit was indeed our violent escaped prisoner, and contact with the owner confirmed that hand weapons, rifles and ammunition were missing. We now had a potential major incident on our hands.

This was before Armed Response Units had been invented and police firearms officers did not exist in any organised way. In Derbyshire we had a few Traffic Department officers who were occasionally authorised to carry arms. They had no real training for the role and selection was therefore restricted to ex-servicemen who had used weapons in their previous occupation. The weapons they used had been received by the police in firearms amnesties or from persons who no longer required the weapons. The fear of some sort of armed battle with the escaped prisoner was so great that the armed forces personal was placed on standby ready to come to our assistance.

Public announcements were made telling people the identity of the escaped prisoner and warning that he was armed and should not be confronted. Responding to the public announcements we started to received intelligence reports from folk who knew the man. We had managed to get sufficient information that he was still in our area and using a stolen Mini Cooper car. Thus, I found myself allocated to a Traffic Patrol car manned by two armed constables from the Derby area and I was with them as the local officer because of my knowledge of the local area.

One night we were keeping stationary observations of traffic using the A623 road at Anchor Crossroads, Tideswell. We were in a Mk3 Ford Zephyr Traffic Car a vehicle well capable of speeds of up to 120mph and with drivers who were trained to Advance Driver skills, I relished the thought of a high-speed chase. Around 1am I heard the exhaust note of a car coming up the road from Tideswell and knowing the distinct sound of a Mini Cooper, "I said, that's a Mini Cooper it will be him, let's get ready for a chase."

There was no response whatsoever, and when the suspect car appeared and turned towards Stone Middleton, they still sat for a further five minutes before calling the sighting in before setting off allegedly in pursuit. I was disgusted by such behaviour and my judgement of Traffic Officers was that they were lazy. Eventually, the escaped prisoner was arrested by personnel from the army in a remote area of North Wales.

Not long after this incident I became one of the drivers of one of the two rural beat cars operating out of Bakewell Police Station, working the full three shift system and in radio contact with the police control room. This was a move I had coveted because I was often frustrated that on a cycle beat, with no communications available I was missing out on the most exciting aspects of the job.

I certainly enjoyed the cut and thrust of the new role but missed the opportunities for chats with the local people, that I had enjoyed when working my cycle beats. When incidents came over the air, I would always be the first to respond and hone my driving skills getting to the incident as quickly as possible. I was usually driving a Ford Cortina which were nowhere near as fast as the Zephyr cars used by the traffic crews and nearly always got to the scene before them. Over time I concluded that I would not enjoy working on the Traffic Department and applied by a CID attachment, to see if I were suitable to become a detective.

Stoney Middleton is one of the many Peak District villages which hold a Well Dressings Festival each year and it always took place at the beginning of July. The opening ceremony in 1966 coincided with the World Cup Final from Wembley that featured England v West Germany. Although I was working my cycle beat on that date, I was not going to miss the final and the sergeant agreed that during the game I could be at home on call. The opening ceremony for the festival was scheduled to take place just a few minutes after the end of the game.

The only problem was that the game went into extra-time, so I had to jump on my bike and ride about half a mile up the road to the opening ceremony. There was not a single vehicle or person in the road and arriving at the well dressings, the vicar and the appointed VIP were there, but no one else. We agreed that the event was open and rushed back to our respective televisions. Hillsborough, the Sheffield Wednesday football ground hosted some of the preliminary games. Switzerland played their games at Hillsborough, and they resided at one of the hotels on my patch. I managed to attend most of the World Cup games there, courtesy of one of the Directors of Sheffield Wednesday, who lived at Curbar. What a great day that was! "They think it's all over. It is now!"

Sleepy villages are not always as quiet as they appear, and the rural policeman had to cope with the fact that back-up was not available, and that encouraged a careful attitude on the part of the policeman and a more considered approach than would be the case in a busy town.

One night I was making a conference point around midnight at the telephone box in the village where I lived, when a man came out of one of the local pubs in a drunken state. The streetlights were off, and he did not spot me, but I followed him wondering if he intended to drive a car in that state. Sure enough, he jumped into a car parked on a roadside car park. For evidential reasons, I waited until he had started up his car and engaged reverse gear before quickly opening the door and dragging him out of the car, explaining that I was arresting him for drunken driving.

My 'prisoner' was a very fit six-footer who did manual work in a stone quarry, and he decided he did not want to be arrested. For the next half-hour I had an almighty struggle to keep hold of him.

It was impossible for me to handcuff him and equally impossible for me to use the telephone box to call for assistance. Eventually a passing motorist rang for assistance and a traffic patrol car duly arrived. Even with the double crew of the car to help it took us a little time to get the man into the car, by which time I was exhausted. Many years later my grown-up son was having a discussion with a man in a pub who was claiming that in his younger days he was a great street fighter and had only been mastered by two people in hundreds of fights. Eventually my son was told that one of the people who mastered him was a policeman arresting him for drunken driving. Both were quite amused when Gareth told the man the policeman was his father, and he sent a challenge for a return match. I declined the invitation!

My spiritual life whilst stationed at Stoney Middleton was busy, attending the local chapel every Sunday, (subject to duties), having the local youth attend the weekly session as well as regularly coming round to our house. From time to time, we would take them to youth events elsewhere including back to my home chapel at Stone Edge and once a year to a concert at the Royal Albert Hall, "Start the New Year with Jesus," where we heard amongst others, Graham Kendrick, Cliff Richard, and Larry Norman. A few of them formed themselves into a band and performed at various church-based functions. Getting the band members and their instrument into my little Vauxhall Viva was quite a challenge.

Just down the road from where we lived was Cliff College. Part of the Methodist Church, they trained people for ministry, at that time mainly in evangelism, and they had regular conferences and celebrations. I would always attend there on duty when such events took place, helping them with traffic control and the like. My wife and I often got to know some of the students when they came to preach for us in the chapel in our village.

Some were overseas students and missed the comforts of their homes. One or two African students used to visit us in the police house and cook themselves a curry, something that they greatly missed in the college menu. Once or twice a year I was invited to preach in the college chapel which was enjoyable but a bit of an ordeal, given that they were continually making notes!

At the college I came across a young man who was helping in the kitchens. Barry had met the students from the college when they had been on mission at Blackpool and had responded to their invitation to commit his life to Christ. He had been sleeping rough and had got into drugs and came to the college to get out of the way of those who were influencing him into a life of drugs and crime. He became a regular visitor to our home, and we got to know him very well.

Hearing his story, we realised how easy it is for young people to get into a negative lifestyle and how difficult it was to get out of it. Eventually, Barry got a regular job with accommodation provided. He found a local girlfriend and started to rebuild his life. Sadly, he had a problem with the job and got the sack, losing his home. Concerned that he would go off the rails, I invited him to live with us for a while until he got himself sorted out. I was aware that I was breaching police regulations but the call of God to care for this young man was stronger than the fear of breaking the rules. Barry stayed with us for a few weeks, whilst he tried to sort out his life. He was still living with us when I received a telephone call from Inspector W at Bakewell. He said, "Do you know a young man by the name of B?"

I began to realise that I was possibly in trouble and told the boss that I did know the young man. He then said, "Is he one of your deserving cases, John?" I confirmed that he was, and he responded, "He is in custody at Bakewell Police Station charged with theft and he gave his address for the charge sheet as the Police House, Meadow Close, Stoney Middleton. We have recorded him as being of no fixed abode and that's what will be now, John." No further action was taken against me, and I was very thankful. I am sure that my misdemeanour was overlooked because my intentions had been honourable and fully in keeping with my call to serve and protect.

Of the young people who were regular attenders at our youth group, one became a Christian missionary in a predominantly Muslim country, another became a local preacher and others later joined the police force. We continued to support B who sorted himself out, and for many years after leaving Stoney Middleton we maintained contact with quite a few of them. Simple acts of kindness often make a difference.

During my time at Stoney Middleton, I worked very closely with the Head Gamekeeper on the Chatsworth Estate and when he retired, he told me that he might get round to writing his memoirs and if he did, he reckoned that a substantial portion would be taken with adventures we had enjoyed together. During the sixties, a pheasant could be sold for £1.50 a brace and there were circulating around the estates in Derbyshire, Yorkshire, Nottinghamshire, and Staffordshire areas professional poachers who made a living out of poaching pheasants.

The gamekeepers all kept in touch with one another and shared intelligence about these top-level poachers. One of the most successful poachers lived near Rotherham and was known to use a Jaguar XK150 car.

One night, the head gamekeeper rang me and said that his staff had found the poachers' car parked in the village of Baslow. This indicated that he would be poaching pheasants somewhere on the estate. He had turned out all his keepers and posted them across the estate to listen for noises that would indicate the presence of the poacher. I turned out voluntarily and joined him on static observations in a field close to a strategic road junction. After some time, we heard someone coming very quietly down the road towards our position. What we did not know is that the poacher had a dog with him, and the dog obviously scented us and started to growl, which caused the poacher to run for it!

I immediately set off to leap over the fence and onto the road to chase the man but in the dark, misjudged the distance away from and height of the fence and my shins rapped the top rail and toppled head over heels over the fence into the road. By the time I was on my feet our suspect had disappeared, but not for long because he set off back into the fields and through a gate where one of the keepers was waiting for him. He put the poacher down on the ground using a pick-axe handle, and I followed up and arrested him.

Subsequent searches revealed a total of sixty-six brace of pheasants that the poacher had shot and stored in sacks ready to collect before returning to his home. During one of my unofficial interviews with the poacher he told me that he visited every estate in the north of England at least twice per year, and he was netting an average income of about £200 per week at a time when my annual salary as a police constable was less than £1000 per year. No wonder he could afford a Jaguar XK 150.

Whilst I was stationed at Stoney Middleton, we had an outbreak of foot and mouth disease. As a police constable I was authorised to act as a Contagious

Animal Diseases Inspector. It was deeply disturbing to see wonderful herds of cattle built up by dedicated farming families over generations, shot and burned on huge fires. To protect the wild deer Chatsworth Park was closed to traffic during this period. The head gamekeeper told me that he suspected poachers were coming into the park poaching and invited me to join him on patrol in the park.

One night we were outside the park on the Pilsley side and walking down the hill towards Edensor and the park. Behind us we heard a vehicle that had driven through the road closure barrier and he said, "Get out of sight John." I did no more than jump over the fence that surrounds the Chatsworth Golf Course. I got a shock when I discovered that the land on the other side of the fence was about twelve feet lower than the roadside. I hit the fortunately soft soil with an almighty thud knocking the wind out of my body. Once the car had passed, he looked over the fence and said, "Are you OK, I should have told you about that drop?" Nothing more than my pride was hurt, and we had a chuckle together and carried on with our patrol.

Stoney Middleton lies at the bottom of a dale with a river running through it which in winter periods of heavy rain would overflow onto the adjoining A623 trunk road, turning the road into a raging torrent. Despite the regularity of the road floods, they only rarely encroached into roadside properties. About two on a winter's morning with an overnight snow forecast my bedside phone rang as did Ks next door. It was the Control Room at Force Headquarters, and we were told that a traffic patrol car was reporting that the road through the village was flooded.

I responded by pointing out that floods were a regular occurrence, and I was not inclined to turn out, but fortunately K said he would go and investigate. I quickly went back to sleep and thought no more about it until I was woken by him knocking on my door. He said, "The dam at Cavendish Mill has burst the banks and the village has been engulfed in thick mud and water. It is currently about half an inch below your back doorstep, I am going back to bed it is up to you now."

I quickly got into my uniform and stepped out of my back door into about three inches of mid-brown mud, crusted by an inch of freshly laid snow. Going out onto the main road, I was greeted by more of the same and where the walls at the side of the road were splashed by the mud. Walking up into the village, I was confronted by a small disaster. All the low-lying houses near the church were flooded, not just by water but by thick and sticky mud. Employees of the Derbyshire County Council and others were working hard to open-up drains that had become blocked.

Householders were trying to rescue possessions, moving them upstairs out of the mess. My entire shift was occupied trying to help people deal with the aftermath of the flood. It was many weeks before some of the houses had been completely cleaned and made fit for habitation.

Cavendish Mill sits in the top of the hills to the west of the dale through Stoney Middleton. Materials extracted from local mines was processed and washed before being carted away for use in various industrial processes. The tailings dam was what was left when the washing had been completed and the heavy rains had caused a breach in one of the walls, allowing the contents to flow down the hillside and into the river and road. The road at the top of the dale was covered with debris, including large boulders, requiring machines to clear it away. The owners of the mill, Laporte Industries, employed many people in the village, and their machines and staff worked alongside the council employees to get life back to normal as quickly as possible. I guess they were also required to pay compensation to house owners.

Working the rural beat car was for me very enjoyable, although I missed the engagement with the local communities, I did not have the sense of frustration that was part of being out of contact with what was taking place and required a speedy response. Being in the Peak District, the roads were always busy at the weekends and there would always be two or three road traffic accidents to deal with. Nowadays, the police do not normally get engaged dealing with these accidents, leaving them to be settled between the insurers, but then I would often submit a prosecution file for driving without due care and attention. I remember that at one time I had a total of seven such accidents awaiting prosecutions in the pipelines.

I recall one such accident that occurred on the A6 road at the bottom of the Taddington Bye-Pass when an old farmer lost control of his old Ford Anglia and ran into a car coming in the opposite direction. The driver pleaded guilty by letter which was read out in court and caused some laughter. This is what he wrote, "My Ford Anglia is a bit like me, she has seen better days, coming up the hill from Buxton she struggled a bit and on the flat at the top she improved, but down the hill she set of like s..t off a shovel and I lost control."

Over time the area covered from Bakewell was extended to include, Eyam (previously worked from Hathersage), Tideswell (previously worked from Buxton, and Hartington, (previously worked from Ashbourne). Other than during the period between 10pm and 6am the area was covered by two rural beat cars. On the night shift one car covered the area but with a two-man crew. Our area included a slice across the county from the Sheffield border in the east to the Staffordshire border in the west. I always enjoyed the night shift because there was always the possibility that a spot check would result in the discovery of a travelling criminal. I remember one good example.

I was working with J who was based in the village of Rowsley. In the early hours of the morning, we were travelling down the A6 near Ashford in the water, when we came across a car stationary at the side of the road, with two young couples out of the car urinating. The car was a virtually new Ford Cortina 1600E, and the youngsters were not those typically expected to be in possession of what I knew to be an expensive vehicle.

Speaking to the driver, I went through the usual checks. Yes, he could remember the registration number and he answered other questions about the vehicle accurately, but I was still convinced that the vehicle had been stolen. I enquired how long he had owned the car and having been told, just a couple of months, I said I was interested in purchasing such a car and asked what he had paid for it. I knew exactly how much the car would have cost and the driver quoted a figure well below what should have been paid.

I was immediately suspicious, but unlike today, when it is possible to do an immediate check with the DVLA and Police Computer records, then you had to rely on your instincts and a bit of common sense. I asked the driver if he were willing to come to the nearby police station, so that I could make a further check. He said he would be happy to follow us, but I told him that I would sit with him and give him directions. He rather reluctantly agreed and when he drove to the police station, he demonstrated that he was unfamiliar with the controls, and I realised that I had backed a winner!

At Bakewell Police Station I got J to take the occupants through to the kitchen where he made them a cup of tea, whilst I started my background enquiries. Given that the vehicle tax disc indicated that the car had been registered in Stockport, I called the main police station there. When I supplied the vehicle details the bloke answering nearly dropped off his chair and told me that he was just circulating the details. It had been stolen by means of a robbery with violence about an hour earlier and he arranged that a vehicle would come and collect the prisoners. J and I duly arrested the assembled company and locked them together in the cell, awaiting the escort from Stockport.

I recall another night winter's night when I was on patrol with P It was snowing very heavily and we were standing by at the police station because of the poor road conditions, when we received a call from the control room. One of the Bakewell doctors had contacted them and asked if the police could help him attend an urgent call to a patient at Great Longstone. Because of the snow he could not get his car out of the drive. Although a Mk1 Cortina was not the best of vehicles in the snow, ours was better than others because the boot was full of equipment and with the duty Sergeant's agreement, we duly set off to pick up the doctor. Whilst we were parked up outside the house at Great Longstone, we got a call from Control Room to say that a bus full of passengers returning from a pantomime trip had gone off the road at Beeley Bar. We explained that it would be at least half an hour before we could get to the scene, but we would get on our way as soon as possible.

Dropping off the doctor we made our way steadily but safely down the A6 towards Rowsley. At what was then a short stretch of dual carriageway we came across a rather shocking sight. A Mk4 Ford Zephyr car, the Chief Constable's staff car was sitting astride the beech hedge on the central reservation and the night sergeant and Bakewell bobby were looking rather dismayed. At that time S was living in a house on Coombs Road, Bakewell and his staff car was always parked at police station overnight. The night shift bobby in Bakewell had worked on the Traffic Department so was authorised to drive the car, and he and the sergeant decided that the urgency of the request required an exceptional response, so they took out the Chief's car only to lose it when it skidded. We briefly exchanged greetings, and neither were too pleased when we could not resist having a bit of a laugh at their expense.

Without further hardship we were able to arrange the recovery of the bus and get it back on the route home with all the passengers none the worse for the experience. It did not seem that the incident caused too much trouble for our two colleagues, given that the sergeant retired many years later as a superintendent and the constable was promoted sergeant at Bakewell where he worked until retirement.

One of the most difficult aspects of being a rural beat car driver was dealing with fatal road accidents and they become especially difficult if there seems to be a case of causing death by dangerous driving. I had one such case when I was requested to deal with an accident on Cutthroat Bridge on the A57 going over towards Sheffield from Ladybower reservoir. This area should have been covered by the car working out of Hope, but for some reason, was not available nor was there a traffic car able to attend.

Arriving at the scene, I found a high-powered sports car on its roof in a riverbed. An ambulance was in attendance and dealing with two persons, the driver, and the front seat passenger. Before they set off with the casualties, I was able to establish that the passenger had life threatening head injuries. A couple of witnesses to the incident were at the scene and I was able to discover that they had both been overtaken by the sports car in what they described as dangerous circumstances, disobeying the white line markings, and travelling at what they described as excess speed.

Long skid marks on the road provided further evidence suggesting that the driver had been guilty of dangerous driving. I therefore called for a police photographer to attend to take pictures prior to the recovery of the vehicle. Extensive measurements were taken at the scene including lengths of skid and other marks indicating the trajectory of the vehicle. Arrangements were made for the vehicle to be examined by a qualified vehicle examiner, so that we could rule out the possibility of the accident being caused by vehicle defect. Today, a specialist accident investigator would have dealt with this accident, but in those days, we were expected to possess all the skills.

My subsequent enquiries revealed that the car driver was a budding racing car driver. The passenger sadly did die, and I therefore had to visit the hospital in Sheffield and take statements from medical staff to prove that the deceased died as a direct result of injuries received during the accident. The driver was eventually convicted of causing death by dangerous driving which he was clearly guilty of, but I felt sorry for him, and there were no winners.

On another occasion when visiting a Sheffield hospital to obtain a statement as to the cause of death of a victim. The doctor told me the medical name of a condition brought on by a depressed fracture of the skull, and I asked him to explain what it meant. He said, "In simple terms he had a permanent erection because there was something pressing on that part of the brain that causes an erection. He laughed when I said, "Can you show me exactly where that pressure point is?"

During my time living in Stoney Middleton and particularly in the final year of my period there, I would from time to time be seconded onto plain clothes duties working alongside a detective constable based at Buxton. Often, they simply, stayed at Buxton but directed me as to what enquiries to undertake. It was these facts and my decision that I did not wish to work in the Traffic Department persuaded me to apply for a CID Aide attachment of three months. It had been made clear to me that there was a longer-term plan to have a detective based at Bakewell and subject to a successful attachment and Detective Training course, I would probably be appointed to fill that position.

The CID Aide programme had been introduced by S, to allow people like me to plan their own career development. The first requirement was that the applicant must have passed the qualifying examination and the second that you were recommended by your own supervisors. I clearly qualified on both counts and when the list of CID attachments for Buxton Division was published, I found my name second on the list and therefore only waited about three months before spending my period on attachment in the CID at Buxton Police Station.

Given that I had worked alongside some of the detectives when making enquiries into crimes on my patch, I settled in very quickly. I was allocated a few not too complex cases to investigate, most of which ended in a detected crime and the completion of the appropriate prosecution file. This was before the days of Scenes of Crimes Officers, so I also learned how to use the Crime Scene Box, with materials used to locate and lift fingerprints, camera for photographic records, and plaster of Paris for lifting footprints and the like.

The end of attachment interview indicated that I had been successful and would be nominated to attend a residential Detective Training Course when one became available with a view to be appointed as the resident detective constable at Bakewell Police Station.

Detective Training courses within travelling distance of Derbyshire were undertaken in Wakefield, Liverpool, and Preston. During the summer of 1969 I found myself attending a three-month long Detective Training Course at the Lancashire Police Headquarters. I thoroughly enjoyed the course, working and studying consistently so that in the final examination I was top of the course. Derbyshire had at that time a unique system, where our nominees for the course were sent to qualify and train them for the role of a detective prior to appointment.

Most of the other folk on the course were already undertaking duties as a detective and had become part of the heavy drinking mentality that persisted in the CID at that time. Although I would occasionally join them in the bar, I would generally drink orange juice, which was frequently commented upon, but did not worry me. I was not on the course to get drunk or spend lots of money, going out every evening, I was there to work hard. I linked up with an officer from the Cheshire Constabulary who had a similar approach and who came just below me in marks in the final examination.

Margaret was working at the time in the National Health and Social Security Office in Bakewell, so we had to buy an old car for her to use to get to work and to visit her mother on a regular basis. Barbara, her mother had previously been diagnosed with breast cancer a few years earlier and gone through a mastectomy and subsequent treatment. We had always been close, but her illness brought us into even closer fellowship, praying with her that she would be completely healed, and supporting her when required. We had been married for about five years and had deliberately avoided having a family, so that we could enjoy life together, just the two of us for a while.

Most of our friends in the Stone Edge gang had got into having babies within a year to eighteen months of marrying. Everyone thought that we had decided not to have children. Being apart for each week for the first time in our married life, combined with an increasing awareness that we should start a family resulted in Margaret becoming pregnant with our first child. Given that we recognised that having children would place restrictions over our subsequent lives we booked a holiday on the Costa Brava in Spain. The holiday cost us £33 each including the flight and half board accommodation in a hotel overlooking the beach in Callela-de-la-Costa. We flew in a Comet 4, the first jet engine airliner and had a lovely time.

It was a long time before we enjoyed any more overseas holidays (other the Isle of Wight!). By this time, I had traded my Vauxhall Viva for a 1965 Volvo Amazon which thinking back through the many cars I have owned was my all-time favourite. If I had the money and a good garage in which to keep it, I would buy one now—they have become popular with Volvo enthusiasts. Margaret was running a 1958 Morris Oxford which had certainly seen better days, not surprising since it cost me just £35, when we no longer needed two cars, Margaret gave it to her sister Ellen, who ran it for quite a while before blowing the engine up on the M1 motorway.

Reflecting on the Detective Training Course and on my subsequent experiences as a detective, although I enjoyed the course it did not address some of the most frequently required skills of the job. Most of the course was taken up in learning in more detail about the laws governing criminal offences. Most of my time as a detective involved the use of interrogation skills and the preparation of complex prosecution files, neither of which were included, other than superficially.

The Head of the Lancashire CID, M, addressed us at length about the investigation into the Moors Murders and the conviction of Brady and Hindley. He told us some shocking facts about the cases and about serial murderers. We also had sessions with Home Office pathologists and Forensic Scientists.

The course included excursions, most of which were more social than educational. The visit to Thwaites Brewery in Blackburn allowed about an hour in the bar when the products could be consumed free of charge. I found it amazing how much beer a typical detective can consume in one hour! The visit to a factory where valves for radios and televisions were manufactured did not add to our collective knowledge and there were no free samples either.

The most valuable visit was an evening session in Manchester, where one of the national daily newspapers was produced. There were copious amounts of food and drink, but we also learned much about the importance of media skills and what journalists look for when interviewing police officers.

My Career as a Detective

Towards the end of 1969, I was appointed to the rank of Detective Constable, but at Chesterfield and not Bakewell. This meant that we had to move home to Chesterfield Road, North Wingfield, another nearly new police house, one of two with an office in between. Being a detective at the old Chesterfield Divisional Police Headquarters differed widely from what it would have been has the Bakewell detective.

During my time working out of Stoney Middleton I thoroughly enjoyed what I was doing, felt that I was on top of my job and was respected by my supervisors and the public alike. Our church life and social environment was enjoyable and productive, and I could hardly recall a bad day. My spell working in the Chesterfield Division was nothing like so straight forward. I found that I was challenged in my work, and Christian life. The latter not least because my mother-in-law was in declining health due to the cancer spreading throughout her whole body, and the former because my call to serve and protect was challenged by aspects of the practices of some members of the CID. However, living through the difficulties and coming out of the other side gave me foundations of resolve and determination that stood me in good stead for the rest of my police career.

It was around the time that I became a detective at Chesterfield that Sir M was appointed Commissioner of the Metropolitan Police. Having made his initial assessment of the force he concluded that his Criminal Investigation Department was institutionally corrupt and set about reforming the Metropolitan Police. The term that was often used as an excuse for this situation was, "Nobel cause corruption." In practise this meant that some detectives were prepared to tell lies and threaten violence against suspects to secure convictions against those they knew to be guilty but lacked legitimate evidence to secure a conviction. I found myself having to confront these behaviours when I saw they conflicted with what my Christian faith told me.

The CID was housed in one of the larger offices in the building with ten desks occupied by eight detective constables and two detective sergeants. I was allocated a desk near the door and at the opposite end to the supervisors. The desks closest to me were also occupied by two similarly newly appointed detectives. The nearer you got to the sergeant's desks the longer the desk occupants had been Chesterfield based detectives. Over the first few weeks in my role, I discovered that we newly appointed detectives were carrying a case load at least four times that of our more mature colleagues. I find it pleasing to tell you that we newly appointed officers eventually retired in the rank of superintendent whereas the old timers never got beyond sergeant rank.

I have always had an open attitude about my work with Margaret my wife and I recall a conversation when she asked me to talk about my colleagues my answer left her in a state of shock. In describing one of my new colleagues, I asked her to identify as many vices as she could think of and explained that whatever list she came up with, R had close to every single one of them. He spent a substantial portion of his duty periods in pubs in the town centre. Admittedly the pubs he frequented were the ones where local criminals and prostitutes would be in attendance. My brother at that time farmed the golf course farm at Stone Edge, and he was able to report to me that R,' would often park his car in an isolated spot near the farm and interview one or other of these ladies of the night in the back seat of his car.

R was noted for his local knowledge, and he claimed to know everything about everybody in Chesterfield Town Centre. Most of the time he kept the information to himself, but occasionally he would come close to my desk and give me a bit of secret information about some criminal he knew I was pursuing. You knew that he was telling you a secret because he got close to you speaking very quietly and out of the corner of his mouth. He certainly got your attention because if you did not listen with the utmost attention, you did not have a clue what he was saying. If in doubt, try talking quietly out of the corner of your mouth to a friend, spouse or partner and see what they make of it.

R frequently alluded to a 'snout' as the source of his information, by this he meant what the rest of us referred to as informants. A good detective will build up a collection of informants who on occasions are willing to shop other criminals. Most of my informants were people I had successfully prosecuted, and when they had been dealt with and they expressed their appreciation of my honest and straight forward way of dealing with them. When I think about R snout is the first word that comes to mind partly because he was generously proportioned when it came to that part of his anatomy, and he frequently used it to ingest copious amounts of snuff. Sometimes you would be awaiting the snippet of secret information he had promised but clearly, he was unable to force it out of the corner of his mouth without the comfort of his regular fix of snuff.

He would take as much of the brown coloured material he could hold between his thumb and forefinger, which he then inhaled through a nostril. At this stage it was as well to lean away from him, and cover your papers, because there was a danger of a minor explosion in the form of a huge sneeze. Out would come his snuff-stained handkerchief with which he would wipe his snuff-stained face and with a bit of luck you would get your snippet of information.

Working as the late-night detective on New Year's Eve, 1969, having been in Chesterfield for just a month, I found myself attending a burglary at Eyre's Department Store in the Town Centre. In the early hours of the morning a man dressed in a dinner jacket had backed a van into the window with a display containing televisions, radios and other musical equipment and emptied the display before driving away. I was getting nowhere in my attempts to locate the van and thus the driver, when a couple of days after the event, R shuffled up to my desk with his mouth twisted in a southerly direction and said, "A little bird told me that J, had called for a taxi from a flat on Cobden Road, and used it to deliver a brand new boxed television to an address off Chesterfield Road, Stonegravels, where the TV had been delivered to the occupant."

I thanked him and organised the raid on the Cobden Road flat, where J was arrested and some of the stolen electrical equipment was recovered. Over the next couple of weeks or so I worked exclusively on the Eyre's Smash and Grab Raid, recovering most of the stolen property and initiating prosecutions of three or four persons for receiving stolen goods.

When the offenders were dealt with at the Derby Court of Quarter Sessions, I was accompanied by one of the older detectives, P who was notable because he was what would today be described as morbidly obese. He was my exhibits officer, producing the exhibits (mainly the stolen electrical items) as I referred to them in my evidence. Some of the items were large and heavy and I could see that P was struggling a bit to cope and perspiring profusely. Bending down and picking up the largest item, not only did he struggle but his trousers also struggled to contain his backside with the outcome that a three-inch long split appeared in his trouser seem. Fortunately, his backside could only be seen by me

123

and the Recorder. We both looked at each other and exchanged a smile and carried on regardless.

I remained on detective duties working out of the Chesterfield office from November 1969 to October 1970. I was extremely busy throughout that entire period often with a case load that I was barely able to keep pace with. Conversely the old timers in the office were carrying just one or two cases at a time. I would often get behind with my paperwork which got me into mild trouble with the supervisors, but generally my work was appreciated because I had a good detection rate and could produce a more than adequate prosecution file.

Living in North Wingfield, we were now within easy travelling distance of Stone Edge Wesleyan Reform Church, and we returned to worship there. Within a short time, we introduced a 'Teens and Twenties' group which grew and prospered. A couple of our contacts from Stoney Middleton became a part of this group. During this time, the physical condition of Margaret's mum was deteriorating, and I was personally challenged to pray for healing for her, and this prompted me to pray much more. It is a fact that prayer has the capacity to bring us into the presence of God and it is also true that the nearer you get to God, the more conscious you become of your own sinfulness.

This period in the church coincided with the growth of the charismatic movement, which was to have a profound effect upon me before long. Our first child, Joanne Margaret was born on the 15th, April 1970 and we became proud parents. Our second child, Gareth John, was born on 30th June 1972, whilst we were still living there. From a family and Christian point of view the years at North Wingfield were deeply significant as you will learn later.

I cannot remember every case I dealt with whilst working out of New Beetwell Street Police Station, but I will recall a few of the more memorable events. Just before Christmas 1970, I was sitting at my desk when one of the sergeants, shouted out, "There's a bloke in the Charge Office giving himself up for theft of some pens from Woolworths, who wants it?" Nobody was keen to volunteer, but a similar incident at Ilkeston came to my mind, so I volunteered to sort it. As I walked downstairs to the Charge Office, I recalled dealing with a homeless man by the name of H who gave himself up at Ilkeston Police Station for an identical theft and I dealt with him. He had a lengthy criminal record which included an annual theft of pens from Woolworths just before Christmas.

This was his way of booking a ticket for a Christmas break with full board at the expense of the Queen! On that occasion everything was going to plan when the Magistrates fined him £100, or two months, imprisonment in default, and Harry was looking happy. Much to his annoyance someone stepped up and paid his fine, so he was back out on the cold streets.

Opening the charge office door, I saw Harry sitting at the Enquiry Desk, I said, "Morning H, nice to see you again." He looked at me and then replied, "Don't let anybody pay the fine this time boss!" We had a laugh together as I processed him and thankfully, he was able to take his annual Christmas holiday. He was a lovely man who had been screwed up by life and decided he could not cope with the pressures of family and working life. His full story was extremely sad, and I fully understood the reasons for the theft of pens.

My heavy workload on one occasion put me in peril at the Court of Quarters Sessions in Derby. In those days, detectives had to complete an antecedent report in the form of a comprehensive record of their previous convictions and current situation when offenders appeared before the Recorder or in the case of Assize Courts, the Judge. Judges and Recorders were potentially frightening people, who would ask detailed questions about such things as outstanding fines and similar and you would be in trouble if the records were not completely up to date. The outcome of this was that we put together the reports in advance and then on the day before the scheduled court appearance, we would get the final information to compete the report. Each day that these courts were sitting they would circulate the list of cases to be heard the following day and that is what we would act upon. On one occasion I noted that I had one of my cases with four offenders listed for the following day and duly prepared the antecedents and the next morning reported to the court.

Arriving early, I noted with horror that another of my cases with six offenders was included on the list. I immediately rang my colleagues at Chesterfield and got them to arrange with the Traffic Department to rush the paperwork to me so that I could hopefully complete everything working in the CID office in the Derby West Police Station which was next door to the Assize Court.

At the appointed time I went into court and successfully presented my reports. Immediately afterwards I went straight into the CID office next door and with the help of the local detectives started finding out the latest information and putting the reports together. We had about another ten minutes work when I was told that I was required back in court for my group of six offenders. I just picked up the unfinished papers and sat in court waiting for the case to be called, worrying what was going to happen to me and trying to identify a solution.

Suddenly, I remembered that I suffer nose bleeds so bending down I punched myself in the nose. I was greatly, appreciative of the fact that my nose started to bleed. When I was called to the witness box, I was holding a blood-stained handkerchief to my nose. The Recorder asked if I had a problem and whether I would like a short adjournment. I said thankyou to him and as I walked back to the CID office to complete the reports, said a quiet thankyou to the Almighty. The adjournment allowed me ample time to complete the paperwork and ultimately give my reports.

One of my other memorable cases involved the report of a house burglary and theft of a shotgun and ammunition. The house was in the village of Holmesfield and was occupied by a farrier. When taking details from him he told me that he strongly suspected a local teenager. I was warned that the suspect had a violent temper and had sometimes visited the location of the burglary, commenting on the gun. His final words to me before I left him was, "Be careful because one day he will kill somebody."

With those thoughts in mind, I drove to the house where the young man lived. Today, I would have had to call out an armed response unit to carry out the enquiry. I decided I would bluff it out. Knocking on the door, it was answered by the young man, and I addressed him by name and said, "I have come for the gun." He turned tail and started to run up the stairs with me in hot pursuit. We took hold of the gun at the same time and without any struggle he let me take possession of it. Opening the gun, I found that it was loaded. I have no idea what the young man intended to do when he ran upstairs, but I duly arrested him, and he was subsequently prosecuted.

His adopted parents were deeply concerned about their son and his uncontrollable bursts of anger. They commented on the fact that I had been able to deal with him in such a delicate situation without upsetting him. I learned that sometimes when he was in one of his tantrums the only way the only way to calm him was to call on the services of their parish priest. Thereafter, until we moved from North Wingfield, I would answer their requests to talk to their son whenever he was in a mood. Many years later, I was reading the Derbyshire Times, when I saw his name on the front page because he had been found guilty of murder and sentenced to life imprisonment. Very recently I learned that he was out of prison having served his sentence and was living the life of a hermit.

Although I was moderately successful as a detective in the town centre at Chesterfield, there were some aspects of the job that I was uncomfortable about.

Many of my colleagues were heavy drinkers and for a proportion of your time it was expected that you would be drinking in the town centre pubs. Whilst I was not teetotal, I had never been in the habit of visiting pubs and although I liked an occasionally glass of beer when I was thirsty, after a pint I had reached my limit. Sometimes feeling peer pressure to drink along with colleagues, I would drink more. I can remember on quite a few occasions having consumed three pints, my stomach rejected what I was doing, and I would go to the toilet and vomit, getting rid of most of the beer I had just consumed.

Sometimes coming out of a pub onto the street, I would feel that some Christian friend might see me and wonder about the strength of my faith. There was also a party mentality and staying out late at a party with my colleagues was not as attractive as being sober and at home in bed with my wife. I was also observing that some colleagues were inclined to stretch the truth when recording evidence. The oft used expression, 'verballing' described this practise, when admissions and confessions were either untrue or a distortion of what had been said.

Too often, detectives depended upon confession evidence at the expense of all else and that was unhealthy. Over the years the courts became increasingly aware of the fact the Judges Rules for the conduct of interviews and recording of confessions, were not being observed which eventually resulted in much tighter control through the Police and Criminal Evidence Act.

Interrogation skills are at the heart of effective crime investigations of that there can be no doubt, but in those days, there were no training programmes for interrogation and interview skills. We developed our ability through practical experience alongside others more experienced. Whilst I would not tell lies, I certainly tried to persuade the suspect that I knew more than I did. A good example of this was in connection with the theft of stainless-steel billets from the Chesterfield Tube Company.

The Tube Works at Chesterfield was one of the towns largest employees. I had been called to the premises to investigate the disappearance of these items which were used in their manufacturing process. They had estimated that they had been disappearing over a few weeks and their initial stock check suggested that about a dozen had been stolen. The stolen items were valuable, each one weighing at least two stone, so not something that could be hidden in a pocket or under a coat. Staff employed on the premises were regularly searched when leaving the premises and were therefore ruled out as suspects.

My conclusions were that the offender must be someone with legitimate and regular vehicular access to the premises. Following this line of enquiry, I discovered that a contractor's lorry visited the site a couple of times a week, removing waste material and that the route taken on the premises, passed by the open area where the billets were stored. Once I had established the suspect vehicle, I discovered that the driver was a local man (B) with previous convictions for crime, so I now had a suspect and had to decide what to do next.

Discussions in the CID office with colleagues who had dealt with him in the past suggested that bringing him for a speculative interview would be a complete waste of time. His record revealed that he had rarely confessed to a crime. In discussion with the security staff at the works, I agreed to set up observations, with a view to catching B in the act of committing the crime.

Whilst I was sorting out a programme of observations, as is often the case circumstances dictated my subsequent activities. As detectives we were aware that a substantial proportion of the material weighed in at scrap metal dealers was stolen property and when passing by any registered scrap metal dealers, we would call in and check the records for names and vehicles of known or suspected criminals. One of my colleagues called in at one of our scrap-metal dealers and discovered a substantial number of stainless-steel billets that could only have come from the Tube Works, so he gave me a call and I attended the scene to record the evidence and recover the items.

Stainless-steel was a valuable material and the total value of the metal recovered exceeded a thousand pounds. However, thieves rarely receive the proper market value for scrap metal and the lower the price paid, the more likely it is that the dealer suspected the material had been stolen. Checking the records, I discovered that the dealer had paid the market price for scrap stainless-steel, and that the details of the seller had been properly recorded. What I found in the records about the seller was not good news, it was not my suspect. Worse still, the seller was a small-time scrap dealer M who I had come across previously, and I knew that he would have nothing in his records and would never disclose from whom he had purchased the material.

The stolen material was duly loaded into a van and conveyed to the police station where it was secured in the stolen property store. Representatives from the Tube Works visited the police station and identified the material and supplied a statement. I then had to consider what to do next.

It was debatable whether there was enough evidence against B to justify an arrest on suspicion. In those circumstances the detective would either push his luck and make a proper arrest or more likely, invite the suspect to accompany him to the police station. The normal form for this was to knock on the suspects door and when he answered, say, "Get thee coat on tha' coming down to the Nick with me." Experienced criminals like B knew what this meant, and that technique would not have worked.

I decided to rely on the effect of the recovered property and use bluff as my key weapon. On my side was that we had never met before. B answered the door at his home, and I said, "B I am Detective Constable John Bown, and I am arresting you for the theft of stainless-steel the property of Tube Investments Ltd, Chesterfield, to the value of £1500, you are not obliged to anything unless you wish to do so, but what you do say may be taken down in writing and given in evidence." I gave him the opportunity to say farewell to his wife, telling him that he would not be seeing her for a while.

All this was a deliberate ploy to be completely different from how he had been dealt with previously, and to have that play on his mind. Getting in the car I said, "Please do not say anything that would incriminate you at this stage." Normally, the detective would have started his interrogation in the car, so I was deliberately adopting an opposite approach. At the police station I showed him all the recovered material and said, "Here is all the stainless steel you have stolen from the Tube Works over the last three months. Now you can say whatever you wish."

He responded "F…ing hell, I have never been nicked so straight in my life." We sat down at my desk, and he made a complete admission, including that he had sold the material to BM and how much he had received. He indicated that he would plead guilty but not make a statement.

But now to dealing with BM the metal dealer who had received the metal from (B). I knew from processing an allegation against his son, that I was not going to get much cooperation from him. On my side was that he had numerous previous convictions for receiving stolen property. In such cases I could use the Special Evidence Rule to give evidence in court of his previous convictions, whereas normally such evidence is not admitted because it is considered to prejudicial to a fair trial. Arriving at the premises of M I was met with the usual verbal abuse. I resisted responding and simply asked to see his records. With some grumbling he handed over his record book and I said, "Are these records completely up to date and do they contain details of all metal you have purchased and disposed of? He replied, "Yes, officer, you can rely on that."

Looking through his records I could see that there was no entry for the stainless steel. I then said, "There is nothing in your records about stainless steel billets to the value of £1500, purchased from B and recovered by me from the dealers on Chesterfield Road," I then told him I was arresting him and cautioned him. He said, "Can I make a telephone call?" I agreed to that request, and he called his solicitor to meet him at the police station.

As expected, M declined to say anything in response to my questions and he even refused to allow me to take his fingerprints, which would have been normal procedure. But as the law allowed me to ask a court convicting him, to issue an order for the fingerprints to be taken, if necessary, using force, I was not bothered because I knew I had prepared a good case and was confident of winning that battle later.

B was convicted of the theft and sent to prison. M was also convicted and ordered to pay a very substantial fine. Immediately on hearing his conviction, he stormed out of court before I could make my application to take his fingerprints. I later had the satisfaction of arresting him so that I could take his fingerprints. The laugh was that he had one hand missing and only three fingers on the other hand, so it did not take long. Just to show there was no hard feelings I did give him a lift home.

At a personal level, I was dealing with the challenge of my mother-in-law suffering the further development of cancer and as a Christian who in theory at least believed in divine healing, I was spending much more time praying. Our first child Joanne had been born and I was coping with what it meant to have the responsibility of another life. I felt that I lacked something in my Christian life and started to read widely about the Holy Spirit. A few of my friends had been baptised in the Holy Spirit and joined the charismatic movement that was sweeping England at the time. Sitting on the stairs of our police house and reading the book, "Nine o'clock in the morning," I put the book down and started to pray when heaven opened, and I felt the sensation of the Holy Spirit spreading though my body like my blood was warming up and sending the warmth to every part of my being.

As I prayed, I naturally drifted into an unknown language. I had been baptised in the Holy Spirit and the experience was going to lead me into some amazing opportunities to demonstrate my faith. I had continued to preach regularly but planning at that time was difficult owing to the demanding nature of my job. If I picked up a big case on the Friday, I would lose my weekend off and get someone to stand in for me, where I should have been preaching.

From a career point of view, I continued to aspire to promotion, but my opportunities were being limited by the policies of S, who was regularly appointing sergeants and inspectors on transfer from other police forces. I was of course at liberty to apply to other police forces, but I wanted to stay in Derbyshire and accessible to my mother-in-law so we could support her. I did apply for selection for what was then called "The Special Course."

This had been newly introduced to select and train outstanding constables for accelerated promotion. Those selected became Sergeants at the commencement of the course and would normally be promoted to Inspector within two years of completion of the course. I did have the satisfaction of being recommended for assessment at the Central Selection Board, held at the Home Office in London, but was turned down at that stage. I put my promotion aspirations on the back burner and got on with my job.

On 12th October 1970, a London based schoolteacher, left London to hitch-hike to the North East, but failed to arrive at her destination. On the Sunday following her disappearance, a couple out walking their dogs in some woods close to junction 29 of the M1 motorway, discovered her body. She had been sexually assaulted and murdered.

I was deployed to the murder investigation, along with a CID Aide (trainee detective) who was working alongside me, the day after the body was discovered, and I remained on the murder squad for the next sixteen months. The investigation became one of the largest undertaken at that time and was headed by a Chief Superintendent from the Metropolitan Police Flying Squad. Scotland Yard were called in by the Derbyshire Police because of the nature of the investigation.

It was clear from the outset that it would be a difficult investigation, the victim had clearly been given a lift by someone who had subsequently murdered her and dumped her body in the woods. Anyone using the M1 motorway on the day she disappeared was a potential suspect. Our initial enquiries in Derbyshire, were concerned with identifying any persons who had been around the woods where the body had been discovered. The site was off the beaten track, and it was initially considered that this might indicate some local knowledge on the part of the perpetrator. The woods were close to three mining villages; Glapwell,

Doe Lea and Bramley Vale and folk living in those villages were all covered through house-to-house enquiries.

A major incident room was set up at the main police station in Chesterfield, occupying the games room in the building that until 1947 had been the Police Headquarters for the Chesterfield Borough Police. Today, the administration for such a murder investigation would be computer based, but in those days, it was paper-based and built around Actions and Statements. Each morning Actions would be allocated to the investigation teams who would carry out the required work and report back in the form of Statements.

The Senior Investigator in the Incident Room had a small team of Statement Readers, who would mark up the statements ready for the producing a card index of facts. These indexes would include vehicle details, personal descriptions, possible sighting etc. Each statement would also be the source of further actions.

Teams of detectives were dispatched to London, to undertake background enquiries regarding the victim. Contrary to what people believe, murders are most frequently committed by persons known to the victim, so background enquiries feature amongst the early actions to be completed. Each motorway service area between London and Chesterfield was allocated a team of detectives with a view to establishing any possible sightings of the victim. In those days, hitchhikers could often be seen thumbing for lifts at the exit roads to the motorway.

Early in the investigation posters were produced showing a policewoman who had a remarkable similarity to the victim wearing her clothes and carrying a very distinctive bag with an elephant embroidered on it, a copy of one which was missing from the victim's clothing. It was felt that the bag would be remembered perhaps more than the physical description of the victim.

Two weeks after Barbara Mayo had disappeared on Monday 26th October, the murder investigation team undertook a check of every person using junction 29 of the M1 motorway, which was a major operation involving many uniformed officers along with the detectives. Masses of information was forthcoming from these checks which then became the subject of further actions to be undertaken by the investigation teams.

Eventually, what was felt to be a positive sighting of the deceased teacher was located at Kimberley close by junction 26 of the motorway, when she was observed getting into a Morris 1000 Traveller. This model of car was popular at the time, but it was determined that we would locate every roadworthy example in the UK and interview the drivers with a view to identifying a suspect. I joined the team of detectives allocated to carrying out those follow-up enquiries and for a time travelled the length and breadth of the British Isles, making extensive enquiries with a view to eliminating the drivers of the respective cars.

Sometimes considerable imagination and skills were required to find someone who could eliminate the individual concerned. Occasionally we thought we had a possible suspect when the driver resembled the photofit image of the suspect and was unable to account for his movements on 12th October. My CID Aide colleague, and I would then start to get excited that we were going to be the ones that detected the crime but would eventually be able to eliminate the person despite the similarity. We always had a fall-back possibility of elimination using a blood sample. This was way before the advent of DNA profiling and blood and secretor grouping was not able to make an individual identification, but it could be used to eliminate someone who did not replicate the sample found on the body of the victim.

During the first few weeks of the murder investigations, we worked without taking rest days and each day would be on duty for at least twelve hours. Detectives in those days were paid something called, "Supplementary Overtime." Every detective was required to complete a Detective Officer's Diary, where the actual hours of duty were recorded. It was expected that detectives would have to work outside the normal hours and that was part of the accounting when calculating the duty hours, so that you only got paid for a proportion of the hours undertaken, the figure being determined by the average number of hours performed by all the detectives.

Here was one reason why detectives spent hours in local pubs whilst on duty. However, where an incident required regular overtime, it could be designated a "Special Occasion," which resulted in us being paid for all the overtime we performed. The enquiry was so designated and apart from it being a good experience, it became a good earner. About four weeks into the enquiry we decided that we were beginning to smell, so we called into our house and took a shower. My daughter never saw me for many weeks and cried at me thinking I was a stranger.

One of the most promising enquiries lived just down the road from me. He owned a Morris 1000 Traveller. He resembled the photofit produced following the sighting and could not account for his movements on 12th October. After lengthy interviews, he indicated that he had been fishing on the River Trent at

High Marnham near Newark on the date of the murder. We took him to the place where he said he had been fishing and talked him through what he had done during the entire day. My Aid and I then spent days interviewing fishermen and customers at the nearby pub, with a view to confirming that what the man said was true.

After some time, we located a witness who had been fishing at roughly the same place and who had taken some photographs of the riverbank where our suspect was supposed to have parked his car. There did not appear to be any vehicle indicated on the photograph, but we had to have the negative enlarged, to be sure that the car was not there on 12th October. Having reported back our findings to the Senior Investigating Officer (SIO) we were then instructed to find and locate as many people as possible who knew our suspect and might be able to vouch for his character or alternatively provide some evidence of criminal behaviour.

It was during this phase of our enquiries that we visited an elderly couple who the suspect and his wife had befriended and who they took out on trips to the shops and places of entertainment. During our interviews with the couple, they gave some indications that they were suspicious of the motivations of our suspect and the old lady told us that she had seen his wife holding a bag similar in description to the one belonging to Barbara Mayo. As this bag was so distinctive, we were unbelievably excited that we had found the key to detecting the murder. I telephoned the incident room and spoke to SIO explaining the enquiries we had carried out and what we had just discovered. He indicated that he and his assistant would come and join us to make their own assessment of the potential witnesses.

Having spent some time interviewing the couple and taking statements from them the SIO drew the same conclusions that we had, and we returned to the Incident Room where arrangements we made for an arrest of the suspect early next morning. In the bar at the police station that evening there was a sense of celebration and relief. Sad to say, when samples were taken from our suspect, we found that his blood and secretor groups did not match those found on the body of the victim. We eventually concluded that our witnesses had invented the story about the bag. What a disappointment!

This murder remains undetected despite the case being reopened via the cold case review process implemented in recent years. I have deep sympathy with the mother of the victim (now deceased), who was clearly devastated, initially that her daughter had been murdered and then later that no one was brought to justice.

Early in 1972, the murder investigation was disbanded although the file remained open, and I was then transferred onto a small team dealing with crimes arising out of the first of two miners strikes under the Ted Heath government. Some examples of the crimes we dealt with was the burning of the fencing at the side of the motorway for fuel for the pickets on duty at a nearby colliery and numerous thefts of coal from coal merchants and other places used for the storage of coal.

It was not a particularly rewarding task, and I was pleased when the miners returned to work, and I was transferred to become one of two detectives attached to a unit beat operating out of the office adjacent to my home at North Wingfield. Along with a colleague we had responsibility for North Wingfield, Grassmoor, Holmewood, Heath, and Tupton. When we had prisoners, we took them to Renishaw Police Station for processing which was then the Sub Divisional Headquarters for the Chesterfield East Sub-Division. The Detective Inspector at Renishaw seemed to take an immediate dislike to me and for the entire period I was based at North Wingfield he was a thorn in my flesh. Virtually every time I took a prisoner into Renishaw, we would end up having an argument.

On occasions, I observed that he was willing to tell lies to secure convictions and I would not be party to such activities. Sometimes he intervened in my investigations, messing things up. On one occasion, I received information that a local well known young criminal had been seen disposing of new radios and televisions in a pub at Grassmoor. My informant told me that the youth had a load of electrical equipment, stolen during a burglary of a radio and television shop some of which was stored in a lock-up garage and the other in the boot of his car. My informant said I should act quickly before he disposed of the property.

Given that there was going to be large amounts of property to recover and the need for urgency, I picked up my fellow North Wingfield detective and off we went in search of our suspect. He was not at home, but his mother told us that he would be at the local recreation ground at a Sunday league football match. We duly arrived at the football ground where I parked my car in the field as near as possible to where the game was ongoing. There was quite a crowd watching, so we walked around the pitch, but could not see our suspect (I). Talking to a spectator I enquired whether he knew and had seen I. He said, "Yes, he is playing at inside right for Holmgate."

I had never previously had to arrest someone playing football, but I knew I had been recognised and I needed to take immediate action. The next time the referee came near me I said to him, "I am a CID officer and I need to arrest one of the players." He responded "You cannot do that I do not know whether his team will be allowed to put a substitute onto the field. Can't you wait till the end?" He then carried on moving around the field undertaking his duties. The next time he came near, I said "I am coming onto the pitch to arrest him." Seeing that he had no alternative when the ball went out of play, he called I over to him. "What's up ref, I was no-where near the ball?"

I said, "It's not him that wants you it's me and I am arresting you, for burglary and theft." I asked him where his car was, and he pointed across the field to a car with someone sitting inside it. Knowing that the car contained some of the stolen property I asked my colleague to take control of the prisoner whilst I sorted the car out. I found that the car was occupied by I's girlfriend and confirmed that the property was still in the boot. The keys were in the car, so I drove it towards my own car when I suddenly saw our prisoner break away from my colleague and run away. I quickly jumped out of the car and gave chase. My background in cross-country running came to my rescue when I chased him over fields streams, walls, and hedges for a couple of miles before catching him and re-arresting him.

Back at Renishaw Police Station with the prisoner I completed my statement saying exactly what had happened, but the Detective Inspector, subsequently left me completely out of the evidence, handing the case over to a colleague. At the best he was trying to hide the escape from my colleague, at worst he was making sure I was not credited with the detection of the crime. He had made clear to me that he considered me unsuitable to be a CID officer and suggested I ask to go back into uniform.

I made it abundantly clear to him that if he wanted to get rid of me, he should put the report in explaining why. I challenged his assumption pointing out that my detection rates were better than most of his staff, and indicating that I would also report, defending myself and explaining that if his report put me back into uniform, I was not scared about that. But my report against him may get him sent to prison.

One of my most persistent offenders whilst I was the area detective for North Wingfield, involved a juvenile offender, who was a very troublesome burglar. His mother was a prostitute and his father long term unemployed but a regular offender for crime. Despite the homelife and values they had been exposed to one member of the family was hardworking at school, bright, intelligent, and honest, and for many months, a source of information on the whereabouts of stolen property, hidden in the house.

I did have a scary moment following an arrest I made on behalf of the Nottingham Police, from whom I had received a request to arrest a man living on a trailer park in Tupton. He had recently vacated a flat in Nottingham, where the pre-payment meters had been smashed and the contents stolen. Having arrested him on suspicion of the theft I conveyed him to the police office and interviewed him about the allegation. He was clearly very scared of going back to Nottingham, explaining that the police would beat him up.

Explaining that with the agreement of the Nottingham Police I could charge him and release him on bail to appear in court at Nottingham. Part of the deal was that he made a voluntary statement admitting the crime. The officer in the case in Nottingham agreed with the proposals and I bailed the prisoner and sent the paperwork through to Nottingham. A few days later the case officer called me and asked me what interrogation method I used because the man had admitted stealing from the gas and electric meters of a flat with no gas supply!

When I received a warning to attend the court in Nottingham I started to panic as to how I would explain that I had got the man to admit something he had clearly not done (stolen from the gas meter). When the prisoner was called into court, I awaited in fear only to discover that he was pleading guilty to stealing the contents of the electric meter and I would not be called to give evidence.

Working as an area detective gave the opportunity to go out on patrol with a uniformed constable in what we used to call a 'panda car.' One night I decided to have an hour or two with the constable and look out for possible crimes. In the early hours of the morning, I suggested that we go and have a look at the Gypsy Camp at Winsick. Whoever had planned the location of the site had failed to consider the impact of putting it right next door to the largest scrap yard in the Chesterfield area and the owner was convinced that the travellers were going over the security fence that separated the two premises and then weighing the metal back into the scrap yard.

All the lights were off in the caravans when we made our way through the encampment to the perimeter fence to see if there was any evidence to support the suspicions, but dogs had started to bark and turning the car to go back between the vans we were confronted by blokes with large iron bars waiting for us. The driver asked what we should do, and I told him to drive as fast as he possibly could without showing any sign of reducing speed and I hoped they would scatter, which is what they did, and we breathed a sigh of relief. Reading a book "The Gypsy King," many years later, I discovered that bashing police cars up with iron bars was quite a regular thing in the gypsy world.

During 1973, my relationship with the Detective Inspector and the recent experience of the Holy Spirit worked together to cause me to be quite specific in my prayers and to have faith that they would be answered. A major concern was that I was regularly unable to fulfil my preaching appointments and had to persuade someone to stand in for me. Given that I felt I had been called both to be a preacher and a policeman, I was experiencing role conflict. My act of faith was to submit more dates for the forthcoming preaching plan and expect God to make it possible.

Soon after taking this step, I was called to Headquarters for a career development interview with the Detective Chief Superintendent. We discussed my lack of promotion. I had been qualified for promotion to sergeant for more than five years and had passed the inspectors examination more than three years before. I shared with him that I had considered applying for an instructor training course because the role of police trainer carried the rank of sergeant but had not done so because I wanted to be promoted on my current ability not on a specific future role. Towards the end of the interview, he told me that it would not be in my career interests to make such an application, but then explained that I was going to be transferred onto the Special Branch (SB), based at Chesterfield.

I was aware that there was just one detective constable who worked out of his own office at the police station at Chesterfield, and that some aspects of his work were so confidential that the office had a combination lock that only he knew the combination for.

Back at Chesterfield, I knocked on the door of the SB office, where I was greeted by the man I was replacing when he retired. Almost the first thing he said was. "One of the good things about this job, is that you have every Sunday off duty." Praise the Lord for answered prayer!

Before I could take up the role, I had to be Positively Vetted by the Security Service who in the future I would be working alongside. I am severely limited in what I am willing or able to write about my time in the SB because much of what I was doing was then and remains covered by the Official Secrets Act. There were four different aspects of the work; 1) Providing intelligence to police operations on possible major disturbances of public order, 2) Providing protection for visiting VIP's (Members of the Royal Family, Diplomats, Senior Members of HM Government, and others considered at risk) 3) Provision of information to the Security Services in connection with persons who may be a threat to the State, and 4) Dealing with naturalisation enquiries (applications for British Citizenship).

My induction to the role included attending courses with the Security Services at what was then their headquarters in Curzon Street, London and with the Metropolitan Police SB. Whilst I was attending the course at New Scotland Yard in January 1974, we were on a three-day working week and motorway speeds were restricted to 50mph. Margaret's mum was in the final weeks of her life. Over the preceding months I had developed a prayer ministry to Barbara, my mother-in-law. By this time Margaret was having to stay with her during the daytime when her dad was at work. I would drop her off on my way to work and pick her up on my way home. Many times, during the night I had been awake for a couple of hours or more, praying for Barbara, because I could not get any peace of mind without praying. On each of those occasions I would find that Barbara was in great pain during the period that I was awake and went back to sleep when I went back to sleep. I still held out the hope that she may be healed but sadly that did not happen.

During the Friday of one of my weeks at Scotland Yard, Margaret rang me to say that her mother was not expected to live much longer and suggested that I drive straight there to see here before going home. Driving up the motorway in a distressed state of mind, I lost contact with my speed and was pulled in by a traffic patrol car. When he asked me what speed I thought I was travelling at, I answered honestly that I had no idea. He told me that I was travelling at 70mph when there was a 50mph limit. I told him that I was sorry and explained that I was rushing home to see my mother-in-law before she died. He said that he would caution me in the circumstances and take no further action. I expressed my thanks and told him that I was a policeman, but I had not told him before because I did not wish that to influence his decision.

When I arrived at my in-law's home, Barbara was still conscious but obviously in considerable pain, we exchanged greetings, and I assured her of my love and appreciation of all she had done for me. I placed my hands on her and prayed "Lord you are the healer, and you can still heal, but at this moment I pray for peace and freedom from pain for Barbara." I then said my farewells and drove the four miles to my own home, where my wife told me that her father had already rung her to say that mom had died.

We cried together, and I am crying now as I write this. I can offer you no explanation as to why such a lovely person should die when only in her fifties. I can only rely on the deep faith that I have that she is now in a better place and that one day we will meet again.

One of my immediate concerns during the miner's strike of 1973/74 was to liaise with the fifteen coal mines located in the Chesterfield Division, with a view to obtaining intelligence about possible disturbances caused by flying pickets. Sometimes the extra numbers created would lead to the strikers blocking roads to prevent work taking place, with the potential for violence. I had a list of all operators of coaches in my area and sought to establish good relationships with them so that I would know in advance when and where coach loads of pickets would arrive and have a police presence there.

On the terrorist front, the IRA were active at this time, and I would regularly liaise with organisations that had legitimate access to explosive substances that might be obtained by them for bomb making. Where the quantity of explosives used exceeded what might be expected, enquiries would be initiated to ensure that a surplus was not being funnelled into unlawful purposes. The "Black September," movement were regularly sending out letter bombs and where a suspect package was received, I would be required to investigate and deal with the package. I had a bomb container available in which a package would be stored until the arrival of the bomb disposal squad if my own enquiries were unable to establish that the package was legitimate.

My period on SB coincided with the debacle of the Clay Cross Council members who had been disqualified from holding office. Huge demonstrations in support of the councillors took place in Chesterfield, on a regular basis. I would be gathering information via SB officers around the country, so that I could provide adequate assessments of the numbers of demonstrators expected and any potential for violence.

To undertake protection duties, I had to qualify as an authorised firearms officer. Protection officers at that time in Derbyshire carried a revolver which was normally secured in a shoulder holster, thus hiding the weapon from public view. There was an initial training course followed by quarterly re-qualification. The weapon issued for diplomatic protection was smaller than the ones in general use by authorised firearm officers and my extra-large hands made the task of qualifying in the top grade that much more difficult, but I always managed to achieve what was required.

My most memorable protection duty for a member of the royals was looking after the Princess Royal who was down-to-earth and charming, and the most memorable government minister I looked after was Sir Keith Joseph, who I found to be intelligent, and wise.

As a SB officer I carried out a significant number of naturalisation enquiries, the majority being in respect of Polish people who had settled in the Chesterfield area at the end of WW2. Most of them had served alongside our servicemen and hoped to be able to return to Poland but did not want to be under communist rule. They were hardworking people and were seeking to have the protection of a British passport before travelling to their former homes, mainly to see their aged parents and other family members. I found no good reason for turning down any of their applications and one of the delights of the role was to be invited to visit them when they returned to the UK after their visit and shared with me the joys of meeting with parents they had not seen for many years.

There were one or two applications from Hungarians who had come to UK following the Hungarian uprising against the Communist Government of Hungary in 1956 and a few Hong Kong Chinese restaurant employees.

A variety of organisations both to the right and left of the political spectrum who espoused undemocratic means existed both nationally and locally and those that were deemed to be a potential risk to the security of the state were the target of my attention during my time as an SB officer. I am not at liberty to identify those organisations, nor do I have any desire to do so. Suffice to say that they existed, and they occupied some of my duty time.

My experience of the baptism in the Holy Spirit was now providing added impetus to my desire to serve Jesus. I was preaching on a regular basis and sometimes, there would be incidents where the Holy Spirit had prompted me to say something that had not been planned. Sometimes, when talking to people afterwards, one of them would tell me that the words that had been a spontaneous response to God speaking to me through the Holy Spirit, was a direct message for them. I was getting invitations to travel further afield for special meetings in which I would be the visiting speaker. On one occasion I was speaking to a man after a meeting who clearly had mental health problems and was into substance abuse. He had an extremely negative view about the police, and it challenged me that I should try to help him and show a positive aspect of what some police officers would do. I invited him to stay with us for a few days, whilst I found a place for him at a drugs rehabilitation and treatment centre.

I was putting myself back in a risky position having him live in the police house but felt from a humane and Christian point of view, I had no choice. Within a few days I took him to a Christian drugs rehabilitation unit in the Midlands. Sadly, within a couple of days he did a runner. More significantly when my wife cleaned the room, he had been sleeping in she found three knives hidden away.

Out of the blue a group of Christians in Matlock invited me to attend a meeting with them. The group was led by Rev S, who was then the vicar of Holy Trinity Church, Matlock Bath and included other key members of his church plus leaders of other churches in the area. They explained that they wanted to put on a Christian Musical called "Come Together," written by an American couple, Jimmy, and Carol Owens. They wanted to ask me if I would consider being the narrator.

They made it clear that I would be required to do far more than just read out the narration part, as times of ministry and prayer would be included, which I would be expected to lead. The musical director was going to be G, who I knew from my time singing with the Peak Sankey Choir. We prayed about it, and I said that I would agree to undertake the task but that I would first have to prepare myself by visiting a performance elsewhere.

Looking through the list of upcoming performances of Come Together, we discovered one not too far away at a large public hall in Leeds and Margaret and I found ourselves included in the large crowd of people attending the event. The narrator was the l, vicar of St. Michael le Belfry in York. We observed a substantial group of musicians and singers and sensed a growing excitement before the event commenced. At that time D was one of the most well-known speakers and teachers involved in the charismatic movement and I certainly realised that I was not going to be in the same league as him.

What we now know but did not know then that was that the young man who would a few years later marry my wife's sister, was a member of the choir that evening. Chris had responded to the invitation to receive Christ at the first guest service held at York Minster. At the time he was studying at York University. He is now a Church of England Bishop, having spent a successful career working for Shell, first as a research scientist and later as a human resource specialist. He trained to be a vicar whilst holding down one of the top jobs in human resources in Shell, becoming an unpaid vicar and then when he took early retirement, a parish priest, before being appointed a bishop.

The Vicar of St Michael-le-Belfry and a small group of like-minded charismatic priests in the Church of England have had a profound positive impact on the church. Their stories involve contacts with people who have themselves been positive role models in the Anglican Church, including Justin Welby and Holy Trinity, Brompton (from where the Alpha Course was created) as just two notable examples.

I am reminded of the ripple effect when a stone is thrown into water. A significant event sends out ripples of influence sustained over many years and that continue today through the influence of the Archbishop of Canterbury and through Alpha course around the world. Students of church history, noted a similar effect following Billy Grahams' first UK based mission at Harringay in 1956, from which many new converts, eventually became Anglican vicars, who in turn influenced many others.

We were able to see for ourselves what an amazing ministry was possible through Come Together. The singing was amazing, the narration challenging and the ministry time when people came together in small groups, uplifting. Both Margaret and I felt we were deeply blessed spiritually, and we left overflowing with the presence of God, a feeling that persisted for many months.

Back in Matlock musicians were appointed and a large group of at least forty singers selected . Rehearsals commenced and these were expected to replicate the planned performances. The leadership team stood by me to assist and to guide me through areas of ministry in which I had only a minimal experience. We eventually had two nights with a sell-out audience at the Pavilion at Matlock Bath, followed by one night in the Kings Hall in Derby, two nights at the Mortimer Wilson School in Alfreton and a final night at Holy Trinity Church, Chesterfield. Numerous lives were touched, people were healed and delivered, and many received Christ into their lives for the first time.

During late autumn of 1974, on a day that turned out to be cold, wet, and miserable, I took Margaret and our two children along with my mother to Bell

Vue Zoo and pleasure park in Manchester. The whole place was showing signs of decay and it was not the most memorable of trips we had ever undertaken. With a view to improving the day, we left early, and I said we would go back home via the A57 Snake Pass and have a look at the Lady Bower Reservoir. The journey took us through Glossop and my mother said, "This is a miserable place. Is it in Derbyshire? If it is, I hope you never get posted here" Two weeks later, I was called for an interview with the Detective Chief Superintendent at Force Headquarters, where he told me that I was being promoted to uniform sergeant and transferred to Glossop!

Living at Glossop

We moved into a new house on a housing development at Simmondley, a suburb of the town They were still building houses around us when we moved in. Finances became a problem at that time because detective constables were paid more than uniform sergeants due to the allowances, detectives received. On top of that the central heating in the house was heated by an oil-fired boiler, with fuel supplied from an underground tank. I quickly discovered that keeping warm and comfortable was going to account for a substantial part of my income. I found out that I was eligible for family income support but did not feel that it was intended for someone in fulltime employment.

I settled into the role of a police sergeant very quickly, having been a constable in uniform for seven years and then a detective constable for five years, there were very few aspects of the job that I was not capable of performing.

Although we were a long way from our family and existing friends we settled quickly in Glossop. People were moving into the new houses and most of them were of similar age and with children of similar ages. Our daughter Joanne started at the local school which was just a five-minute walk from where we lived. School gate conversations resulted in Margaret making many good friends, when she invited them round for coffee and cake. I was working a basic three shift system of early, late, and night shifts. Generally, I walked to work because it only took fifteen minutes. Glossop is some fifty miles from police headquarters at Ripley and about twenty miles from the divisional headquarters at Buxton. If senior officers came to see us, they usually made an appointment, before setting off.

Moving into a new area always involves looking for a new church. Now we were out of the reach of Wesleyan Reform Churches for the first time, we thought that the Methodist Church would make the best fit. Settling in a new church now involved thinking about the needs of our children, aged four and two years, respectively. The first church we tried was Central Methodist in the Glossop, we tried it twice but given that no-one spoke to us, decided against it. We knew of an independent church at New Mills, where a friend (a policeman) was one of the elders and for some months we worshipped there.

It was a charismatic fellowship, and we enjoyed the liberty of being able to demonstrate what God was asking us to do through his Holy Spirit. I regular preached for them, but it was never going to be a long-term solution, being too far away from where we lived.

On the day I was told I was being promoted and posted to Glossop, I had completed an application for what was then called a "Student Instructor Course," with a view to becoming a police recruit trainer. I had decided that given the problems I had encountered in the CID I should take my career in a different direction. Right from attending my initial training course and admiring the work that my instructor was undertaking I had felt that at some time I would like to follow his example. Subsequent events would prove that the decision I made then would lead me into many amazing experiences and opportunities. This was not a case of God speaking and me following, rather it was an inner feeling that it was the correct thing to do.

In the event, I only worked as a Sergeant in Glossop for a few months. I enjoyed my work and took to the duties of a sergeant with consummate ease. One incident stands out from that period as being significant. On one of the small council estates in Glossop we had a problem family. One or other of the sons of this family would get into trouble and according to their ever-loyal mother, they were never to blame, and she always defended them. Visiting the house to make enquiries or arrest was also problematic.

I remember one night walking into the police station at about 9.30pm ready to commence a night shift and being passed on the way by one of the members of our problem family. He was showing signs of facial injuries and was looking as though he had not enjoyed his experience. About an hour into our shift an emergency call was received from the mother to the effect that someone had been almost murdered. Clearly this called for a mass turn out so we all turned up in force, only to find that the call had just been a rouse so that mum could undertake an identity parade to find out who had nearly killed one of her beloved sons.

I was somewhat surprised that the scarred son identified me, but not worried because I could prove that I was at home and not at the police station when these events where alleged to have occurred. I was duly attacked as the culprit for this allegation of attempted murder and all hell was let loose. Over the space of the next half an hour a running battle occurred between the police and every member of the problem family. At one stage we had handcuffed one of the family with his arms around a lamp post. The funny thing was seeing him trying to shin his way up the lamp post. Eventually, all the family except mother ended up being convicted for public order offences and assaulting police officers in the execution of their duties.

The Student Instructor Course was held at the Police Training Centre located at Ryton-on-Dunsmore, Coventry over a period of nine weeks which included two weeks at the Police Training School at Harrogate undertaking teaching practise. The course covered all aspects of learning and teaching theory, in fact by registering for some additional learning it was possible to obtain an adult teaching diploma. At my final interview on successfully completing the course, I was asked whether I was prepared to serve at one of the Regional Police Training Schools. My response was that I would like to be deployed on those duties but would prefer to work at the one located at Warrington and not at Harrogate. In July 1975, I found myself posted to the Regional Police Training School, Bruche, Warrington on a two-year secondment.

I discovered that whilst some aspects of the initial training course had changed little over the twelve years since I had received my initial training, other aspects had moved on reflecting changes in educational and learning theory adopted in schools and colleges. A good example was the introduction of job-related learning objectives and the assessment of achievement through a series of multi-choice tests at regular intervals. A detailed analysis of the tasks undertaken by recruit constables had revealed that far too many subjects were being taught to a level that was not required.

As an example, the detailed and complex law on murder and manslaughter was taught, but in practice a junior constable would never deal with such a case, other than to take initial action at the crime scene. Similarly, the detailed law on forgery was taught to every recruit despite only about one percent of police officers ever dealt with such an offence.

The physical aspects of police work had also been examined in the light of the practical requirements. Physical training and ultimately fitness tests were therefore now designed around the threefold requirements of strength, speed, and stamina. Strength to arrest a reluctant or violent prisoner, speed to chase after and catch an escaping prisoner and stamina to hold onto such a prisoner until assistance was forthcoming.

The changes marked real progress by comparison with the training I had received, when we were required to learn by rote an extensive list of legal definitions and then required to complete a long subjective examination based mainly upon those legal and some procedural requirements. I do wonder whether the law needs to be so complex and have a suspicion that this has more to do with the excessive number of parliamentarians who have a legal background and their vested interests in making it complicated so that the legal profession may continue to make a fortune explaining it to the rest of us.

Each recruit training class was allocated two instructors who had responsibility for teaching all aspects of police law and procedure during the ten-week course. Inevitably a close relationship was built between the instructor and the recruits for whom they had responsibility. For the recruit, the trainer often represented their first exposure to a real live policeman or woman and generally they displayed a keen desire to learn thus creating an ideal learning environment. They were a pleasure to teach, and I enjoyed every moment in the classroom. Another development in police training between 1962 and 1975 was the creation of practical exercises based upon typical scenarios that a young constable might find him or herself dealing with.

I well remember one day when my class was undertaking a road accident practical exercise on one of the streets within the training centre campus which turned into a real arrest for burglary and theft. I was explaining how to take measurements of the position of vehicles following an accident when I saw a young man climbing over a high wall at the side of the road. He was coming from an area where the kitchens and food store was located and was carrying a bag full of food which he had clearly stolen from the training centre food store.

I am not sure who was the most surprised the thief or me and my recruits. Imagine, you are on the run from a young offender detention centre when the car you have stolen breaks down and you find yourself in what appears to be a semi-industrial area with a large works canteen and kitchens. You are hungry, so you climb over a wall into the site, break into a food store and steal some food and then seek to make good your escape by climbing over another wall with the loot and drop literally into the hands of twelve uniformed and very keen police recruits. Keystone Cops had nothing on it! Twelve police recruits, competing to be the one who affected the arrest of 'Bill the Burglar.' I did have a short conversation with the young man explaining that he should give up a life of crime straight away if the best he could do was to break into a police training centre!

One of the practical exercises involved dealing with someone who was drunk, and I became a regular in playing the part of the drunk. I had a set of old clothes that I sprayed with beer, and I would lie down on a bench as if drunk and incapable. We would have explained to the recruits that there had been many occasions when drunks had died choaking on their vomit. I found that if I mixed Rice Crispies with milk, it looked very much like vomit. I would put a little pile on the ground below my mouth, so it appeared to have come out of my mouth. What the recruit did not know was that I also had a mouth full of it. At some stage when the selected officer was trying to wake me, I would open my mouth and out would come the contents, sometimes covering his/her shoes.

Although at the time I genuinely believed that we were delivering good quality training in a combination of the knowledge, skills and attitudes required to be an effective policeman, I was not without criticism of what we were doing. One of my concerns was the extent to which success was judged purely on the weekly knowledge checks. In fact, three failures in the nine tests that took place would place the recruit in jeopardy of losing his/her job. Conversely whilst practical and attitudinal skills were assessed at the end of the course, nowhere near the same scrutiny was given to the outcome of those tests. The inevitable consequence was that trainers would teach their students to pass the examinations, more than teaching the practical skills and at the extreme end this resulted in a minority of trainers collecting from their students' details of all the questions in an examination and then using those questions for future 'revision' sessions.

I found myself frustrated by the fact that my classes were never at the top of the average marks (neither were they at the bottom), but some instructors who I felt displayed poor teaching techniques consistently did better with their students. Eventually I came to realise that they were the ones who were teaching the questions, but I also discovered that it did not go unnoticed by the management. In fact, every test had a validation score which was worked out based on research into the results likely for that test. The aim was for the validation score to be approximately eighty percent. Scores substantially lower might indicate a poor level of instruction, but scores substantially above that were known to indicate the teaching of the actual or similar questions.

Just over half-way through my two-year secondment I was posted into a specialist department where we designed and administered the examinations and additionally taught on a one-to-one basis (usually in the evenings) students who were experiencing difficulties. I discovered that I had been selected for the post because my students nearly always averaged the validation score.

Unfortunately, the current educational requirements for children and schools are now often based upon results of tests and examinations. I do not like league tables for schools and I do not like the emphasis that is placed on tests and examinations. Generally, schools do well because the children attending come from an area where they are better-off, and schools do poor because they have children attending who are disadvantaged across a variety of measures; hence the scramble to live in areas where 'good schools' are located. It seems that we never learn from experience.

Another problem related to the fact that police officers deployed as trainers reflected both the good and bad aspects of policing culture and sometimes, they displayed inappropriate attitudes, particularly in the form of sexism and racism. Each class of recruits had a class leader who was appointed during the first week of the course and who would be accountable for the behaviour of his/her colleagues when the trainers were not with them. For example, the class leader would march the class onto the parade ground in the morning and he/she would also ensure that every member of the class was ready for the commencement of each classroom, specialist, or practical session.

Often the person selected would be someone with a background in a disciplined organisation. On one occasion the person who displayed the early signs of leadership was a young Afro-Caribbean man who had been a police cadet. Regrettably, some of my colleagues told me that I had made the wrong choice and I had to conclude that they were displaying racism. It was a source of pride over the ensuing years that the young man had a successful career reaching quite senior rank and at one time representing the Black Police Officers Association.

Sport played a significant part of our life at the police training school. A staff football team would challenge classes for a lunchtime game on the all-weather surface. The staff team was dominated by the Deputy Commandant, and it tended to be a bit of a clique, so some of us got together to create a second staff team, calling ourselves the "All Stars." Inevitably there came the opportunity to take on the staff team. I cannot remember the outcome of the game, but one incident will be forever in my mind and earned me a bonus point or two with the other staff members, when I had a physical encounter with the Deputy Commandant, and he came off worst.

We went for a fifty-fifty ball, and it was clear to me that I was going to get there first. Having the ball at my feet and about to pass it I realised he was not going to stop, so I dropped my shoulder and catapulted him into the air. Bravely, the referee refused the bosses appeal for a foul, declaring that I had got to the ball first, and just taken evasive action. Given that the Deputy Commandant was rather unpopular amongst my colleagues, I had plenty of opportunities for drinks at their expense in the bar that evening.

When I arrived at Bruche, I discovered that there had been a Christian Fellowship Group run by an Inspector who was no longer on the staff and with the permission of the Commandant, I resumed the weekly fellowship session. We never had any more than half a dozen recruits attend but we did have some lovely times of fellowship, the Matron who was a lovely Christian lady attended quite frequently. One of those who did attend during his course became a good friend and continues to be so after more than forty years.

Phil was a member of the Kent Police expecting to attend his local regional training school at Ashford, just down the road from Maidstone where he lived, when he was instead sent to Bruche, a place he had never heard of. Because it was impossible for Phil to get back to Kent over the weekends, we invited him to stay with us for a couple of them. We also discovered that a friend of ours was intending to go to her parent's home in Kent for a weekend and arranged for her to provide, him with a lift.

At the conclusion of his initial training course, Phil was posted to Sittingbourne, and he and his new wife moved into a house just a few hundred yards from my wife's sister Ellen and her husband Chris. The connections continue to today, but more of that as I continue to tell my story.

One night in the fellowship group, I was praying the concluding prayer when God gave me a vision of a mountain covered in snow. It was so clear that I knew I must share the picture with the group. I was reluctant only because Matron was a member of a Brethren Church and did not believe in the present-day use of the gifts of the Holy Spirit. I started to explain that I had a mental picture of a mountain covered with snow and as soon as I did words came which I spoke out and this is what I said, "God says put your hand in mine and he will rescue you."

One student stayed behind until everyone had left and then asked if I knew anything about his history. As it was the first time that I had seen him I informed him truthfully that I had no prior knowledge of him. He then told me of an incident when he had been the lead climber on a snow-covered mountain when traversing a ravine, what he was holding onto gave way and he started to fall. He instinctively put out his hand and felt a hand grab his and pull him across the gap, but there was no one there. He made it clear that this had saved his live and possibly the lives of his climbing companions. His final words were, "If I did not know then who rescued me, I know now."

Sadly, it was at this Regional Police Training Centre that the BBC was able to expose racism amongst the staff and recruits when a reporter joined the police and covertly filmed a series of incidents reflecting very badly on the Greater Manchester Police and the training establishment (The Secret Policeman). I have no doubt in my mind that the eventual closing down of regional police training centres was at least partly influenced by this incident.

I absolutely loved being a trainer and knew that the decision to apply for a trainer's course would have far reaching influences over my subsequent life, but I could not have envisaged the detail of how that would work out, taking me to Africa and the Caribbean.

As recently as 2008 (when I was well into my sixties) I was still teaching police recruits, by which time recruit (student officer) training had become once again the responsibility of an individual police force. In my case I was working for a college of further education which had won the contract to provide the student officers with instruction in police law. I replaced a law lecturer about whom the student officers had offered much criticism, mainly because that person was unable to relate the theory to practical examples.

The course was linked to a local university and successful participants completed a foundation degree in policing by the end of the two-year probationary period. It was a source of some pride for me that the end of year evaluation undertaken by the university revealed a transformation in the effectiveness of the course and a high level of satisfaction. My teaching has always been grounded in the practical knowledge and skills required for effective work performance along with the display of appropriate behaviours and attitudes, whether in the UK or overseas.

One of the problems of serving outside of your own police force is that when you complete the secondment, you rarely return to your previous job. In July 1977 when I completed my two years, I had been sergeant for three years and qualified by examination for promotion to Inspector for seven years. There was a vacancy at Glossop for an Inspector, and I hoped that we might be able to stay there in the rank of inspector. We had settled very well in the town. We were worshipping at Hollingworth Methodist Church.

Our third child, Barbara (named after my late mother-in-law) was born in March 1976. Joanne was doing well at the local primary and infant's school. Margaret had a ladies' group she met with each week at our home. I had transferred my preaching qualification to the Methodist Church and featured on the preaching plan for the Glossop Circuit, as well as speaking at charismatic groups in the immediate area and further afield.

Transferred to Chesterfield

When my posting came it was back to Chesterfield as patrol sergeant in the town centre but living in an old and poor police house overlooking the carbonisation plant at Wingerworth. I was extremely angry when I saw this because whilst we were living at North Wingfield, which also overlooked the carbonisation plant our son Gareth had recurring problems with asthma which the doctors indicated was caused by the poor air quality in the vicinity and these facts had been recorded on my personal file. I submitted a report to the boss at the police training college indicating my anger at the complete lack of sensitivity of those responsible for the posting.

Calling me into his office, the Chief Superintendent complimented me on the use of language in the report but said that submitting it might amount to professional suicide. He then told me that he had spoken the Divisional Commander for the Chesterfield Division, one KRU, who I have previously commented upon, who had responded by suggesting that I visit Chesterfield, where I would be supplied with the keys to every vacant police house in the Division and I could take my pick. Margaret and I along with our three children then had a trip to Chesterfield and eventually settled on a detached senior officer house at Shirebrook a coal mining community on the Derbyshire and Nottinghamshire borders. The house had been unoccupied for a few months before we moved in, and the extensive garden was overgrown.

Initially I worked out of the same police station at Chesterfield, where I had been a detective and Special Branch officer. By this time, the Superintendent was the man who had been my Inspector at Ilkeston and who had made my life misery. He greeted me like a long-lost son, but I was not impressed given that I still carried the scars from my earlier exposure to his management style. After a few weeks I was transferred to the Chesterfield East Sub-Division working as the Shirebrook Section Sergeant and replacing an old-timer who had retired. The first Sunday living in Shirebrook we attended the local Methodist Church. In all our travels we have never settled so quickly as we did there.

Although most of the congregation were elderly, they made us very welcome. This extended to inviting Margaret around for coffee and coming and working in my garden. We had spent our removal allowance in fitting new carpets and decorating some of the rooms and thoroughly enjoyed being at Shirebrook. One of the elderly couples let it be known to me that one of the busiest public houses was near the bungalow where they lived, and they were often disturbed in the early hours of the morning by customers leaving the premises, I decided that the first time I was on nights, I would sort out the problem.

Every night that week I took one of the constables with me to the public house about half an hour before closing time, and at 11.10pm (closing time plus ten minutes drinking up time), we walked through the premises and instructed the landlord to collect all the glasses empty or full and shut down the premises as required by law. Outside any disturbance of public order was dealt with by way of arrest. The following Sunday, the elderly couple thanked me profusely and said that their neighbours had all said how happy they were that the licensing laws were now being complied with and they could stay asleep at night. Conversely the licensee hated my guts, but I was not too worried about that.

One of the roles of a sergeant was to develop the skills of the constables, especially those in their probationary period. One night I took out a newly appointed constable with me in the supervision car with the intention of showing him how to issue a fixed penalty ticket. In one street we found some cars parked in contravention of the law and I assisted the young constable to write out and fix the notices to the cars. Having done that, we moved over to Bolsover, where we found a car parked directly outside a night club where parking was prohibited.

He issued a fixed penalty and attached the notice to the windscreen. We then resumed patrol and I then remembered that it was always a good idea to check the registration numbers of the vehicles with the Control Room, to make sure none were listed as stolen or of interest. The first number we sent in was for the car at Bolsover and we got an immediate response when the operator informed us that the car belonged to one of the detective sergeants based at Renishaw. The young bobby asked me if we should go and tell him, but I said that knowing the officer involved it would only end in a fight.

Back at the police station at our meal break, the phone rang, and it was the detective sergeant and for twenty minutes he shouted at me using the widest range of bad language I had ever heard. He assured me that he was not going to pay the money and would complain to the Chief Superintendent (KRU). A few days later KRU rang me and said that he was proud of the fact that I had put a notice on the detective sergeant's car, and he had told him to pay it but also explain why he was in a night club, when he should have been on duty.

The Divisional Commander (KRU) who I have previously identified as a bully was continuing to push his staff into submission and I came across this whilst working at Shirebrook. I was there during the Fire Brigade Union strike, and we were serviced at Shirebrook by a Green Goddess (Army Fire Engine) based in Chesterfield. Our local fire station was regarded as being at risk from the striking firemen and KRU had issued an instruction that these retained fire stations should be visited on an hourly basis.

The schools were closed for the summer holidays, and subject to vandalism, so KRU had instructed that they be visited on an hourly basis. At the police station our cleaner had resigned, and I was reporting on a regular basis to get a replacement. The Deputy Divisional Commander called in one day at the police station and commented on the lack of cleanliness, so thereafter, I went into the station in my own time every other day and cleaned the police station myself. We were extremely busy in other directions as well and because we failed to find a burglary at one of our many schools, I received a nasty memorandum from KRU asking for an explanation.

His memo hit my explosion button and I researched all my officer's pocketbooks showing how busy we had been, and I sent in a lengthy report indicating that where he was requesting so many actions that we could not possibly comply with all his requests, we had to prioritise. I finished with a flourish explaining that following negative comments by his deputy about the lack of cleanliness at the police station, I had been cleaning it every other day in my own time and asking how long it would be before a replacement cleaner was appointed.

A week or so later KRU held one of his regular divisional meetings where we would collectively be grumbled at for our lack of commitment. At the completion of the meeting, he glared at me and said, "Bown, don't you ever put in a report like that to me again." Then he smiled and said, "I have strongly recommended you for promotion to Inspector." I have always believed that the only way to react to a bullying boss is to take them on and I had just proved my case. In any case I knew that he had great respect for my work and that his bark was worse than his bite.

Whilst the firemen were on strike, I remember attending a fire in an old people's bungalow in Shirebrook. There was smoke billowing out of the premises, but no sign of flames. I knew it would be a long time before the Green Goddess arrived from Chesterfield, so I decided I would have to enter the building to locate and rescue the occupant. I noted that the bedroom was unoccupied and the bedding smouldering but not blazing. I then found that the occupant had collapsed whilst sitting on the toilet.

He looked to be dead, but I tried to get him outside without any immediate success and by now I was choaking through smoke inhalation, so I had to get outside into the fresh air for my own safety. Once outside I was joined by one of the local fire officers, who was also the safety officer at Shirebrook Colliery. He had with him his breathing equipment which he quickly assembled and went into the bungalow to retrieve the body. A few minutes later I could hear the fire officer shouting my name. For some reason he needed my assistance.

Going back into the building I found that he had got his breathing apparatus stuck to some coat hooks in the hallway and could not release himself. I was able to release him and together we dragged the man out into his garden where I performed external cardiac massage and mouth to mouth resuscitation until the arrival of an ambulance when they declared the man to be dead.

Whilst working from Shirebrook, whenever the Inspector was off duty, I would be appointed Acting Inspector, working out of Renishaw Police Station where W, who had been my Inspector when I was a Stoney Middleton, was now the Superintendent in charge of the Sub-Division. One day I drove into the car park at the rear of the police station and saw him standing by a metal dustbin from which smoke was rising. I greeted the boss and he then said to me, "I have noticed that you get your fair share of nasty memorandums from KRU," he looked at the blackened remains of some paperwork in the dust bin and added, "I get even more than you and this is what I do with mine!" Well done, W!

Shirebrook Police Station was unique in Derbyshire for the number of times the police station windows were smashed. Drunken blokes making their way back home to the "Model Village," built for the employees of nearby Shirebrook Colliery, would decide to make their little statement by throwing a stone through the windows or by slashing the tyres of cars parked in the yard. I remember one night, having called out a member of the Derbyshire County Council Works Department to fix the window, he told me that his research of the records indicated that Shirebrook Police Station had more broken windows than the combined total of all other stations in the County.

Following the recommended promotion, after just three months at Shirebrook, I was invited to attend a promotion board chaired by the Chief Constable . I was confident that I was doing well when he said, "Mr Bown, would you be prepared to move if offered promotion?"

I replied, "Sir, I recall that when I joined the force, I completed a form indicating that I was willing to serve anywhere in the county at the discretion of the Chief Constable, so I do not intend to give you the pleasure of reminding me of that fact, but I would point out that we have been living in our present house for just three months, our children are settled in a local school and the paint has just dried following decorating, so I would prefer not to move."

He responded, "Twice in my service, I moved within six months" and I replied, "Yes Sir, but you are our Chief Constable, and I am not likely to replace you." He laughed but made no promise.

Two months later I was informed that I was being promoted to the rank of inspector at Glossop, to fill a vacancy that had existed when I moved from there just five months earlier. Although we were sad to be leaving Shirebrook, we were not unhappy to be returning to Glossop where we had many friends and where our eldest child could return to the same school she had previously attended. In the event we remained at Shirebrook for another four months awaiting a police house becoming available.

Whilst living at Shirebrook our two eldest children attended a village school at Scarcliffe, which was just a couple of miles out of Shirebrook. We placed them there because the headmistress of the school in Shirebrook told us that as the children of the local police sergeant they could well be bullied, and she recommended that we did not send them to her school.

Back to Glossop

Glossop was the smallest Sub-Division in the Derbyshire Constabulary and whereas all the others had a Superintendent in charge with a Chief Inspector as deputy, Glossop had just a Chief Inspector and no deputy. Although I was not aware of the significance in the future for my career development it did give me a significant boost in my upwards promotion. As an inspector I worked the three-shift system of earlies, afternoons, and nights. Each shift also had a sergeant providing supervision and we covered the nearby small town of New Mills as well.

Taking up my appointment as an Inspector I was never conscious of there being a need to learn new skills. Given that we were cut off from the rest of the force policing in Glossop was rather insular and certainly there was little interference from elsewhere in the force. The Chief Inspector at that time had a long-term pedigree in the CID and we knew and respected each other. My sergeant was competent in his duties, although new to the rank and he had also come to the rank of sergeant through the CID. Given that I had occupied two years of my career, teaching recruits how to do the job, and explaining the complexities of the law, I was well prepared for anything that might confront me.

Despite the competence of my sergeant, he did have to call on me one night to rescue him from a situation that he and one of the constables found themselves involved with. Whilst he was dealing with a drunk driver, I was out in the supervision car patrolling and checking up on the other constables, when he called me on the radio asking me to return to the station as quickly as possible because he had a problem. He explained that after the drunk driver had been bailed, they had discovered that the blood sample taken by the police surgeon had disappeared.

Just to briefly explain the process then undertaken in connection with drivers under the influence of alcohol, at the time of arrest the driver would have been asked to provide a sample of breath by blowing through a tube into a bag. Where the tube indicated alcohol in the breath the driver would be arrested and taken to the police station, where another breath sample would be obtained. Where the result was positive the driver would be asked to provide a sample of blood taken by the police surgeon. The blood would then be divided into two sealed sample containers, with one retained by the police to be sent for analysis and the other provided to the driver so that he or she could send that sample away for independent analysis.

It was obvious to me that the prisoner had managed to steal our blood sample, and I therefore instructed all the officers on duty to go looking for him and arrest him on suspicion of theft of the blood sample. He was picked up less than half a mile away from the station, but when we searched him, we only found the blood sample that was legitimately his. I then put myself in the place of the prisoner and decided that he would have disposed of the blood sample as quickly as possible and initiated a search of all the roadside surface water drains, starting at the police station and following the route the prisoner would have taken. We created a tool for the job in the form of a saucepan lashed to broom handle. I was delighted when at the third surface water drain, we found the blood sample.

Given that it was lying in water, we took a sample of the water, so that any contamination could be measured against the water sample. I took great pleasure in going into the cell where the prisoner was detained and showing him the blood sample and telling him that he could now look forward to an additional charge of theft.

There was another occasion when, I was in the driving seat and my sergeant in support that turned out quite badly for me. One snowy night on the main street in the town a shop window had been broken apparently by a snowball. I was with the sergeant, and we spotted fresh footprints going away from the window which had more than likely been left by the offender, given that the snow was recently fallen and there were no other footprints nearby. I decided that we would do a tracking job. We followed the fresh footprints as quickly as we could because the snow was falling and beginning to obliterate the tracks.

We eventually arrived at the back door of an end of terrace house, which was partly enclosed in a rickety porch. We knocked on the door, but there was no response. We banged on the door and the drainpipe but there was still no response. My sergeant pointed out that my banging on the door was in danger of making the porch collapse on top of us. I decided to do my party piece (a legal requirement before entering premises without consent of the occupiers) and shouted very loudly, "We are police officers and we have reasonable grounds to suspect that a person who has committed an arrestable offence, namely criminal damage, is inside the premises and we intend to force an entry to arrest the offender."

Still no response. I started to bang on the door again which resulted in me breaking a panel in the door and us being able to see inside the kitchen. Where a couple had now appeared. I repeated my allegation and my intention to force an entry to make an arrest. My suspect was not impressed and whilst I put my hand through the hole in the door with a view to forcing it to open, he got his camera and started taking photographs of me trying to bash his door open. Eventually it became clear to me that I was not going to gain entry and we decided to abandon our efforts.

The next day I went back to the house where I had a doorstep conversation with my suspect. I explained that I was a bit embarrassed about the previous nights' activities and explained that if he offered to compensate the shop owner for the damaged window, I would simply give him a verbal caution, which he willingly agreed to do.

Police are often required to make instant decisions based upon what they see and with no chance of checking beforehand. Late one night I had driven over to New Mills, parked up the car and set off on foot patrol. Coming into a main road I looked to my right and saw a car with the driver's door open and coming along the road towards me, running at speed was a young man. Being only a few feet away from me I had no chance to ask him to stop, so I stuck out my leg and tripped him up. He did a not very elegant nose-dive into the tarmac. I helped him to his feet and was about to tell him I was arresting him when I saw someone step out of the shadows at the side of the road and get into the car—he had obviously stopped to attend to an urgent call of nature, and I was left with egg on my face. I duly apologised and explained my reasoning for the action, he laughed and told me I had made a brilliant tackle and not to worry about it.

I would like to think that career progression relates only to the way a person performs their duties and get recognised for that, but there is far more to it than just the way duties are performed. It is certainly true that being in the right place at the right time has a massive influence on career progress. Most people would point to fate or luck, but as a Christian I have always believed that part of my source of success was Divine Providence.

A good example for me was receiving a report of a missing toddler.. Children go missing on a regular basis and most turn up within a relatively short time without much effort on the part of the police. S disappeared from his family home on the edge of a Manchester overspill estate at Gamesley, Glossop. The Derbyshire County Council had agreed with other local authorities in the Greater Manchester area to build the estate to rehouse people from areas where the existing housing was being demolished. The estate had a fair proportion of people with criminal records and could be difficult to police. On the other hand, there was a good community spirit, which certainly came to the fore in searching for the missing child.

I was on duty when the report was received and initiated a speedy search of the area where the toddler had last been seen, but without success. Given that we were just a couple of miles away from Hattersley, where a few years earlier the Moors Murderers had been operating, I felt that we should be prepared for the worst scenario and established a small incident room. Given that widescale searches would need to be undertaken I purchased a series of large-scale maps and attached them to the walls. But for the fact that I had worked on a major murder investigation I would not have known what was required in setting up the Incident Room.

When people go missing it is important to get the information out to the public as quickly as possible and to enlist their assistance. A media appeal was made within a couple of hours of the report, for all the residents of the Gamesley estate to search their own properties, before nightfall. More police officers were brought in from Buxton and they were deployed to carry out a search radiating from the point at which the child had last been observed. Whenever a search was completed our wall map was updated recording the area searched and by whom.

Alongside the area searches detectives were allocated to interview the parents of the missing child, and a thorough search of his home. Experience shows that where people are murdered it is not usually by strangers, but by members of their own family. House to house enquiries were initiated, seeking general information but also finding out information about the parents and other family members.

By the second day of the search members of the public were volunteering to join in the search, so I publicised a time and place for the public to be briefed and then led in the search by a police officer. Our map was used to allocate search areas and other areas were set aside to be allocated at completion of the first area.

Entries on the map were colour coded for the different days of the search. By the third day following the child going missing with no sightings and no leads, it was decided that we had a major incident on our hands and a trained Incident Room Commander—a Detective Inspector (DI) from Chesterfield Division was posted to Glossop and took over from me. I found it comforting that after just a couple of hours in post, the DI told me that everything was up and running and all he now had to do was to keep the system going.

The searches and enquiries continued for more than a week without any success and then we got a call from employees at a nearby sewage treatment plant to say that a small boy's body was floating on the surface of one of the settling tanks. We were able to show that S had managed to get through the security fence and given that the tank had green algae on the surface and could look like grass to a small child, he had either stepped onto it or fallen in and drowned. It was all an extremely sad affair.

Within a year of returning to Glossop, I found myself occupying the rank of Acting Chief Inspector, in charge of the Sub-Division. This happened because the Detective Chief Inspector at Buxton went off duty long-term sick and our Chief Inspector was appointed Acting Detective Inspector to provide cover. I was one of five inspectors at Glossop, three of them were newly promoted and the other one did not get on well with the Divisional Commander, so I got the job.

During my period as Acting Sub Divisional Commander, a few events gave me the opportunity to prove my worth in the rank and make me a candidate for consideration of promotion on a permanent basis. One involved dealing with a personnel problem, that had the potential of embarrassing the force. From time to time a detective would become rather too fond of booze and often this resulted in them being returned to uniform duties where they would not have the same opportunity to drink on duty. We received one such former detective, who I interviewed on his arrival and pointed out that he was being given a second chance, but that I would not tolerate him drinking on duty.

Reports from the officer's sergeant indicated that his work output was extremely low, and he would often fail to answer his radio when called, subsequently stating that he must have been in a radio black spot. He was given further advice and the Divisional Commander was kept aware of our growing concern that we would have to initiate disciplinary proceedings against him. Late one night I received a call from the night duty sergeant, who reported that the former detective had been out of contact for most of his shift and had returned to the police station in a confused state of mind and could not face going home at the end of his tour of duty.

I duly attended the police station and talked at length to the officer in the process of which he said that he wished to resign. These were days when there were no support structures to help a policeman who was an alcoholic to receive treatment and be rehabilitated and when disciplinary action was the first recourse. He wrote out his resignation which I accepted, although I was not sure that I was doing the right thing and thought that higher up the chain of command someone might suggest that I had been precipitate in my decision making. In the event the Divisional Commander contacted me on the next working day, thanking me for my intervention and explaining how relieved he was that we had removed a potential source of embarrassment for the force.

On one occasion during my period as Acting Sub-Divisional Commander, I ended up in command of an incident that could have had an explosive outcome. The initial report came in as a serious accident on the main road between Chapel-en-le-Frith and Glossop just above the village of Hayfield, where a large commercial vehicle had overturned completely blocking the road. Road diversions were set up at Hayfield to the north and at Chapel to the south. Attending the scene, I found that an extremely large road plaining machine had overturned. These machines are used to burn off and remove the top layer of road surfaces before relaying the road. The heat is supplied from a large volume liquid gas tank (LPG) which sat atop the machine and therefore ended up underneath it.

There was the possibility that the tank had been burst and the fire service were called out to make a safety assessment of the upturned machine. They confirmed that the tank was intact but explained that great care would need to be taken when lifting the machine, to avoid puncturing the tank and causing a gas leak. They explained that in such an event the gas being heavier than air would probably go into a roadside surface water drain and end up in the village of Hayfield. The senior officer advised that we should put the wheels in motion to evacuate the village should it be found necessary.

Along with the duty sergeant, I considered how we should prepare ourselves for a possible evacuation of approximately one thousand residents. We would need to provide transport for those who did not have any and find somewhere to house them, possibly overnight, where they could be provided with a meal and somewhere to sit down in comfort. Contacting a local coach proprietor, we put him on standby to supply two coaches that could be used to provide a shuttle service.

We decided that we needed to set up a forward control point and hired a function room at the Royal Hotel in Hayfield, where there was a large car park. Having considered the most appropriate location for the evacuees we decided on New Mills Comprehensive School contacting and informing them of the decision and requesting their agreement. We also created a plan to bring a team of officers from Buxton and Glossop so that if the public were asked to leave their homes, they would be reassured that their homes were being looked after in their absence.

An extremely large mobile crane was called to the scene, arriving mid-afternoon and the operation to get the machine upright was commenced. Unfortunately, in the process of lifting the machine, the LPG tank was punctured. The senior fire officer ordered all personal to come a safe distance away from the machine, whilst we decided what to do. It did not take long to decide that gas was leaking into the surface water drains and as a result there was a significant risk of a build-up of explosive gas in the village of Hayfield.

We decided that we would have to evacuate the village as quickly as possible, and that the vehicle recovery process would not resume until the evacuation had been completed.

The road closure had already attracted substantial media attention and I therefore contacted radio and television services, doing a down the line interview in which I made it clear that the evacuation was being undertaken as a precaution because we could not guarantee that a naked flame would not ignite gas. I set out the arrangements for busses to pick people up and take them to New Mills Comprehensive School. Those who wished to make their own arrangements were supplied with a telephone number to call (our forward control point) where a record was made so that we could inform them when it was safe for their return home.

Extra personnel arrived in Hayfield and were sent out on patrol to reassure the public and to knock on doors explaining what was happening. A few people decided to stay at home, and we kept a record of them. Police patrol cars with loudspeaker equipment toured the village announcing the arrangements. Within about an hour of starting the evacuation process we considered that we could resume the operation to remove the vehicle. Television, radio, and newspaper reporters arrived at the scene, and I gave an interview explaining the precise nature of the situation.

About 2am in the morning the vehicle had been righted and removed from the scene. The surface water drain had been flushed by the fire service and testing in the village revealed there were no longer traces of LPG, so the residents could safely return home. Around about 4am residents had returned to their homes where they found police officers patrolling, a deliberate policy to reassure them. I got home about 6am completely exhausted having been on duty for eighteen hours without a break but satisfied that we had done a good job. We were featured in all the national newspapers that morning and it was interesting to compare what they had written. According to the Mirror a cloud of explosive and poisonous gas had hung over the village!

Clearly, I had to write an extensive report about the incident. The Chief Superintendent rang me after reading my report explaining that we had done marvellous job. He pointed out to me that New Mills Comprehensive School had been not included in the Peacetime Disaster Plan, but he understood my reasons for selecting it, and the plan would be changed to reflect what we had done. I did not tell him that I was not aware that there was such a thing as a Peacetime Disaster Plan, and I had just been making things up as I responded to the situations developing.

At my career development interview after I had been in the rank of inspector for just one year, I was informed that I had been recommended for promotion to the rank of Chief Inspector and would be nominated for a six-month long course at the Police Staff College. The Junior Command Course, for newly appointed Chief Inspectors and Inspectors who were likely to be promoted to that rank had just been initiated and I was on the queue waiting for a place.

Reflecting on this period of my life, particularly my career development in the police, I had the good fortune to be at the right place at the right time, my face seemed to fit, and I capitalised on that. It was true that I was competent and confident in my work and put a lot of effort into my duties. In the space of eight years, I progressed from a detective constable to superintendent, all of which you will read about later. I do acknowledge that God was also overseeing my career development and putting me in places where I could have an influence for him. Later in my career there was a time when my face did not fit, but God also used that to his and my advantage as you will discover later.

Whilst living in Glossop, along with the sergeant who worked with me we had signed up for a two-year course in Police, Penal and Social Studies at Manchester University. I was conscious that my lack of academic achievement may slow my career development and I was also attracted by the idea of learning more about the whole criminal justice system. I found the course very enjoyable and the lecturer, the son of a retired police officer had a deep interest in the theories of policing. He was also a visiting lecturer at the Police Staff College.

Towards the end of the second year of the course, I was required to attend the Junior Command Course at the Police Staff College at Bramshill House in Hampshire. I thoroughly enjoyed the course and was able to combine some aspects of it with completion of my dissertation to conclude my certificate course at Manchester University, when I passed with distinction. My end of course report indicated that I would be supported to attend university on a fulltime degree course, whilst still being paid my salary as an inspector. Whilst I was attracted by the idea of attending university, I concluded that it would not be in my career interests to be away from the force for three years when I was awaiting early promotion to Chief Inspector.

Being conscious that I have not said very much about my police work in Glossop, I do have one or two stories to tell. I have previously alluded to the fact that being cut off from the rest of Derbyshire, policing in Glossop was a bit insular and things were often done differently. One example involved the Remembrance Day Parade where the end of the two minutes silence was designated by the firing of a signal maroon. This involved using some military grade signal maroons which were fired out of a metal tube like a grenade launcher from the flat roof of a garage at the police station, and when they had reached the required height, they would explode with a very loud bang.

One year on Remembrance Sunday it was very foggy, which caused problems for the bobby setting off the maroon. He was supposed to launch it at a slight angle towards the Town Hall, but he got the angle wrong, and the conclusion of the two minutes were first different because before the bang there was a swooshing sound and then the thing exploded about fifteen feet above our heads. We all jumped about ten feet in the air! Despite the solemnity of the occasion, when we had recovered and checked our trousers, we fell about laughing, but concluded that we would never use a signal maroon again!

I remember another incident outside the Town Hall that caused some laughter. There was a room in the Town Hall that could be hired for functions.

On one Saturday evening there had been a large scale twenty first birthday celebration and we had assisted the organising by allowing them to park their cars in a no waiting area whilst they set up the hall and delivered food and drink and other things required for the party.

Just after midnight when the organisers of the party were leaving, they thanked us for assisting them and gave me a large piece of cake to share with all the officers on duty when they took their break. There we are standing outside the Town Hall me and one of the bobbies, watching the late-night drinkers going home with me with one arm behind my back hiding a large piece of birthday cake, when a drunken man decides he wants to wind me up. I am doing my best to ignore the man and hope that he will go away, but he is getting more and more obnoxious.

Eventually, he does go away, and the bobby turns to me and with a smile on his face says, "Boss that bloke doesn't know how near he got to having lump of cake shoved in his muss, does he?" Laughing together we made our way back to the station where we enjoyed our portion of the cake.

Glossop police station in those days had an open counter which was quite obviously a security risk. One evening a young man came into the enquiry office demanding that his brother be released from our custody. When he realised that we had no intention of releasing his brother, he jumped over the counter and adopting a martial arts stance said, "I am a black belt, just release my brother, or else"

Standing near him was an old-time inspector who had transferred to Derbyshire from North Wales and without flinching his right foot suddenly shot up and hit the black belt in his groin, dropping him to the ground in agony. The Inspector then said in his broad Welsh accent, "I may not be a black belt, but I fight bloody dirty," and then arrested the man.

One of the most disturbing incidents I had to deal with at Glossop was a suicide where a local man threw himself in front of a train. A train is a particularly unforgiving piece of machinery and when it hits the human body it makes an almighty mess. Attending the scene with a young constable we saw an horrific sight and the bobby walked to one side and vomited. I told him that I would deal with the incident, although I was the inspector because he did not look up to the task of collecting the body parts ready for removal to a mortuary. It is not appropriate to go into the detail, but it was a very disturbing task.

It became even more disturbing when I found out that the man was a relation of a good friend of mine. When I informed the man's wife and children, I shed a tear with them I was so sad for them. Many of my colleagues would have said that you must avoid emotional involvement, but I could not help myself. When eventually an inquest had been held and all the paperwork finished, the family wrote a lovely letter of thanks to the Divisional Commander, commenting on the sensitivity in which I had dealt with them, so I felt that was a justification for my sharing in their grief.

On another occasion a man decided to commit suicide on the same railway line by jumping off Dinting Viaduct, which crosses the A57 trunk road high above the road. Although he intended to drop to the road surface below, he misjudged it and got caught up in the branches of a tree from which he had to be released by the fire brigade, with nothing more than a broken leg.

A common way of committing suicide was for people to drive into the Peak District to a favourite spot. Park up the car and then walk up into the hills until too exhausted to carry on they would get down and fall asleep hoping that hypothermia would kill them painlessly. Knowing this, when we found cars parked on the Snake Pass for a lengthy period, we would initiate enquiries to locate the registered owner, which would often reveal someone who was known to be depressed and we would have to turn out the Glossop Mountain Rescue team to carry out a search.

On one occasion the missing person was found alive after a substantial period on the hills and a rescue helicopter took him to hospital, where he recovered. Our enquiries revealed that his pacemaker had kept him alive, when hypothermia tried to stop his heart, the pacemaker overcame that signal.

Glossop was the only place in Derbyshire where one of the area cars was a long wheel-based Land Rover Defender. This was because we were responsible for policing both the Snake and Woodhead passes over the Pennines. Despite that road closure signs were displayed on both mountain roads which were sometimes accompanied by physical barriers, motorists would ignore the signs and get stuck. We would then have a minimum of two officers, put on survival suits, fill an urn full of hot soup and send them off to affect the rescue. I remember many winter days where the only way out of Glossop was into Manchester because all the other roads were blocked by snow.

On one occasion we had just dug a car out of a snowdrift, when we spotted that the Land Rover was sliding down the hill towards us. There was no way we could stop it, so we just had to step out of the way and let it collide with the car we had just recovered. Another time I was on patrol during a heavy snow fall when I found a drunken old man stuck up to his armpits in a snow drift, he was fortunate that I found him because he would have died of hypothermia had he not been rescued.

Returning to Glossop on the second occasion we decided to worship at the Methodist Church in Simmondley which was within walking distance of our home. Although it had a declining congregation, we felt that we should be there despite that one of the regulars had described the church as "As cold as a fish-mongers slab."

We did settle there, Margaret playing the organ and helping in the Sunday School and me preaching. Soon after arriving I decided to start a midweek fellowship meeting. The first week about half a dozen came but then over a few weeks it reduced to just me and my friend who had given us the far from inspiring description of the church. For months there continued to be just the two of us, but we both felt that despite this we should continue. We would always end with a time of prayer, but my mate would never join in the prayers, other than to say 'amen.' He would often explain that he was fully in support of what I was praying about but could not cope with praying out loud. One night I felt I should ask the Holy Spirit to release his tongue and I started to speak out Biblical names of Jesus and invited my friend to join me. Suddenly, he began to exclaim names of Jesus, non-stop for about five minutes. Thereafter he always joined me in our prayers and as new people started to come to the church, so our little fellowship meeting grew again and became a significant part of the life of our church.

During both of our periods living in Glossop we moved in charismatic circles, where I found myself for the first time praying and praising God with people from many different church denominations including Roman Catholics. The Holy Spirit convinced me that these good people, were my brothers and sisters in Christ. We did discover that although we and others were greatly blessed by the outpouring of the Holy Spirit, there were dangers of excess to be avoided. Some groups were into what was described then as "Heavy Shepherding," because the leaders would seek to control every aspect of the lives of their members.

When someone rejected this measure of control, they frequently left with the prospect of being totally cut off from church and Christian things. Margaret and I often built supportive relationship with these people and sought to get them back into main-stream church activity. Whilst this was quite a difficult journey for us and the people involved, we and they were blessed by it, and we thank God for using us in that way.

Near the end of our time in Glossop my brother Ernest rang me to say that he had just found out that I was moving to the Police Headquarters at Ripley, but at that time I had not been informed of such a move. My brother sold eggs and potatoes in Chesterfield and one of his customers sons was being transferred to Glossop to replace John Bown. I did however eventually receive my transfer. I was somewhat disappointed, having already attended the Junior Command Course (designed for newly promoted Chief Inspectors) to find that I was being transferred in the rank of Inspector to the role of Force Careers Officer, a job that I did not know existed.

We were obviously going to have to move home from Glossop and I was given a list of vacant police houses and invited to make a choice, listing three possible options. Margaret and I prayed over the options. In our reckoning were the Police House in Ashover, and Senior Officer type houses at Kelstedge and in Matlock. If we moved to Ashover or Kelstedge we would be within a couple of miles of Stone Edge and go back worship there, but if it turned out to be Matlock then we would look for a church in the town. I was informed that Matlock was the only one on offer to us, so we moved to Matlock and became members at Bank Road Methodist Church and that began a whole new episode in our Christian lives.

Posted to Force Headquarters

As Force Careers Officer it was my job to promote police careers at schools, colleges, universities, and armed forces demob courses. Each year there would be events like job fairs, and career conventions, where I would set up a display and man an enquiry desk along with a selected constable. There were massive display boards which I had to move around from event to event in my own car for which I was paid an essential user car allowance and I had to change my car for one with a boot big enough for the display materiel. I chose a Rover SD1 which was a nice car, although a bit thirsty on fuel.

Settling into the new job, I was working for the first time at police headquarters and the other first was that I now had a non-operational role. In the main I worked office hours of 9am to 5pm with weekends off. From time to time, I would travel out of the force area to take part in careers exhibitions at universities, colleges, and military establishments. The job was enjoyable but nothing like as challenging as other jobs I had undertaken previously. One complication was that the Derbyshire Constabulary had a ban on recruiting, which meant that I could not offer anyone the prospect of being appointed to the force in a short time scale.

I very much viewed my new job as being somewhat temporary in nature given that I was awaiting promotion to chief inspector. In an interview with the Assistant Chief Constable, Administration (ACC), I was asked to look at recruitment for the Derbyshire Special Constabulary, where we were considerably below the numbers we should have had.

The Special Constabulary offers volunteers the opportunity to work as police officers without pay and in support of their salaried colleagues. They have the same powers of arrest and are provided with initial and developmental training. It is a grossly underrated form of public service. My quick appraisal of recruitment revealed that a not insubstantial sum of money had been invested in an annual recruiting campaign using an advertising agency, but which had never featured any market research or follow-up studies of effectiveness.

I determined that I would rectify this anomaly and sent out questionnaires to all the existing members of the Special Constabulary, inviting them to tell me what they enjoyed about the work, what they were unhappy about and what prompted them to apply.

I was amazed at the response, almost all the members of the Special Constabulary filled out my questionnaire. No one had previously shown any keen interest in their opinions, and they relished the opportunity to influence a recruiting campaign. I received masses of quality information in answer to my questions. The only problem was analysing it all when I had no computer programme and no administrative support. I ended up doing a lot of it at home in the evenings, after our three children had gone to bed and with help from Margaret.

My extensive report received supportive comments from the ACC, and I could now approach the advertising agency with detailed information about what aspects of the work was most enjoyed by our existing special constables and what type of events would prompt them to put pen to paper. It was apparent that they really enjoyed undertaking duties at events like, agricultural shows, fairs, and carnivals. They indicated that it would be good if they had their own operating base at these events. I discovered that the force had a caravan that was now surplus to requirements, and I made a successful bid for it to become the Derbyshire Special Constabulary Recruiting Caravan.

The Force Photographer was commissioned to take a series of colour photographs showing members of the Special Constabulary at the sort of events they enjoyed the most. Armed with this information our advertising agency were able to produce a totally focussed recruiting campaign. We even produced a recruitment video in which Brian Clough contributed, talking about winning teams and how people could become part of such a team by joining the specials.

Following the publication of the newspaper campaign and the use of the caravan at various events, where it was both a recruiting display and an operating base, we had an amazing response in new applications. In fact, we generated more applications than had been recorded in the previous five years.

I had not been in post more than a few months when I was asked to go and see the Deputy Chief Constable. I was expecting that it was to learn about my impending promotion, but that was not what he wished to talk to me about. He reminded me that I had reported previously on the fact that the Force Standing Orders were in grave need of amending, because they failed to meet the requirement for guidance for members of the force. He told me that along with a Chief Inspector ((M) from Chesterfield, we would be given six months to produce an entirely new set of standing orders for the force, after which I would be promoted Chief Inspector and then M would be promoted to Superintendent.

Force Standing Orders are the detailed policy instructions for the entire force. Ours were just about useless, having turned into a set of rules rather than guidance. There was no proper index so it was impossible to find what you looked for and they tended to be used has a cover all disciplinary proceeding source where no specific disciplinary offence was proven, one could be done for failing to comply with standing orders.

In our opening meeting with the Deputy Chief Constable, we agreed our overall approach, that we should aim to provide a document that guided members of the force in what they were to do in given situations, but that it should not be used as a tool to hit people with if they made an honest mistake based on known information at the time.

We quickly contacted a few police forces where they had recently reviewed their standing orders and obtained copies to assist us in our work. We were allocated a dedicated member of the typing pool who had to give priority to our work, and we set about our task speedily and efficiently.

Each of us would select a subject, obtain all the policy documents relating to that subject, examine our standing orders where they existed, and look at what the other forces had done. We would then write the first draft of the appropriate order and supply it to the other person to read and check before submitting the material to the typing pool. The Deputy Chief Constable had selected wisely, given that we were both anxious to gain our respective promotions we were keen to complete the task within the allocated time scale. We worked extremely hard producing prodigious amounts of material in a short time scale. We were extremely proud of the new Force Standing Orders.

We had many people contact us and thank us for providing them with a useful guide for carrying out their duties, including the force policy on every given subject and which due to the extensive indexing was easy to use. During the time I was working on the Standing Orders, I learned that I would join the newly formed Operational Support Unit has Chief Inspector in charge of Operations.

When we started attending Bank Road, Methodist Church at Matlock, we found an active church with Boys and Girls Brigades, Sunday Schools, and a wide range of other meetings. I continued preaching but there were no immediate demands upon our time, unlike the life we had left behind in Glossop. We renewed relationships with folk in other churches and waited for God's leading on what we should be doing. Within a few weeks of moving to Matlock I received a letter from the Christian Police Association (CPA).

I had been an isolated member over a few years without having any contact with them other than on one occasion attending a meeting somewhere in Lancashire when we lived at Glossop. They pointed out that it would soon be the centenary year for CPA, and they would like to establish a branch in every force and asked if I would consider helping to establish a branch in Derbyshire. Margaret and I agreed that we would pray about what to do. I was inclined to feel that I should get involved, but we felt that we should look for some confirmation.

We now had an old touring caravan and that summer we took a couple of holidays when everywhere we went, we bumped into members of the Christian Police Association. I was reading a book by the late Fred Lemmon, where he told his story of conversion in Dartmoor Prison and of his early contact with a member of the Christian Police Association, who had in a moment of spontaneous greeting and the grace of God, removed all the bitterness and hatred Fred had for the police.

Sunday morning, we were in Ilfracombe looking for a church to attend, when a Boys Brigade Band came marching up the street and Margaret suggested that we tuck in behind the band and go wherever they were going. They led us to an independent evangelic church, where we were greeted by a tall and impressive looking man who was wearing a tie displaying the emblem of the CPA. It turned out that he was a retired police inspector from the Metropolitan Police and the very man, I had been reading about in the testimony of Fred Lemmon.

Fred had been invited to speak at a CPA meeting and he went with hatred in his heart towards the police and an intention to say that he could not understand how they could be in the police and claim to be Christians. In the event our retired inspector and newly found friend had been the very man who had greeted Fred with a handshake and hug, referring to him as "Brother Fred," and at that moment all the bitterness that Fred felt about the police had disappeared. We joined the retired policeman whose name I have sadly forgotten and his wife and daughter for a meal later in the week and I learned many encouraging things about the work of the Christian Police Association.

Later in the summer we enjoyed a holiday in Hampshire and on the Sunday attended a church in the small town of New Alresford, an area noted for the growing of watercress. Yet again we found a man sporting a CPA tie who turned out to be the Branch Secretary (leader) of CPA in Hampshire, and we joined him and his family for a meal and fellowship. By this time, it became abundantly clear that God wanted me to establish a branch of the Christian Police Association in Derbyshire, and on returning home, obtained the approval of the Chief Constable to form a branch in the county.

We grew quickly into a group of a dozen or more, mainly young constables and started to meet once a month, nearly always at our home in Matlock. My long association with CPA was the source of a great many blessings of which you will read more later in my story. At that time, the ACC (Admin and Training) was a committed Christian and he certainly recruited a few recruits who were keen Christians, and I was able to get them involved in the CPA right from their first days in training.

During my time as Inspector at Force Headquarters the then Chief Constable, , died in post and a formal funeral was arranged to take place at Derby Cathedral, where the great and the good of Derbyshire and Derby would gather to pay their tributes. I was instructed to attend and undertake duties as an usher during the service. At that time, the Derbyshire County was controlled by the Conservative Party and the leader of the opposition had a reputation for not being a friend to the police.

At the Cathedral I was asked to look after the balcony, where I was required to greet people, give them an order of service, and direct them to a seat. Looking from the balcony into the main auditorium, when there was no one on the balcony and just a few in the main body I saw the leader of the opposition on the County Council enter and walk to the front of the Cathedral where there are approximately half a dozen seats that are owned by the Derbyshire County Council. He looked at the labels that had been placed on those seats indicating who should sit there and then turned back walking to the rear of the Cathedral after which he came up to balcony, where I greeted him by name and office, gave him an order of service and directed him to a seat.

The next day I was in the senior officer's coffee lounge at the morning break when the discussion was all about the opposition leader, complaining he had not been given the respect he deserved as the Leader of the Opposition on the County Council. I was able to relate exactly what happened and could rebut the allegations. Returning to my office, I received a call from the Chief Constable's Secretary asking me to go and see the boss, who had been appointed Acting Chief Constable, following the sudden death of the previous one I was asked to describe to him what exactly had happened in the encounter with the councillor at the Cathedral, which I did. It was abundantly clear that he was annoyed about the entirely false allegation against the force.

I learned later that opposition leader had been called for a meeting with the Chief Constable when it was made clear that there were no grounds for the complaint against any member of the Force. Clearly, he had expected to be allocated one of the County Council seats and blamed the police for not doing so, whereas the reality was that those places had been allocated by the Chief Executive of the Derbyshire County Council. So began a difficult relationship between the two of them which would eventually have far reaching consequences for the force, for the Chief and for my career.

The Operational Support Division was created as a response to a collection of national problems, not least the riots in Brixton, London, and Toxteth in Liverpool. It was generally agreed that the police forces in England and Wales had not been fully equipped and trained to deal effectively with major disturbances of public order. The Metropolitan Police had formed the Special Patrol Group (SPG) to provide a rapid response capability for major incidents and provincial police forces were being encouraged to follow their example. As the Chief Inspector Operations, I had responsibility for the Uniform Task Force, the Underwater Search Unit, the Dog Section, and the operational aspects of the Firearms Unit.

The Metropolitan Police had produced a variety of techniques to deal with riots where police came under attack from petrol bombs and other projectiles, these included the use of shields, riot helmets and fireproof clothing. They had created a public order training venue equipped with residential and business buildings so that building entry under attack from above could be developed and rehearsed. Techniques were developed for using protective shields to deal with violent individuals, and to adopt specific formations and movements to clear streets of demonstrators and protesters.

I attended a course run by the Metropolitan Police at their newly created Public Order Training Centre at Hounslow. We were supplied with a manual of techniques which we studied, saw demonstrated and then undertook. I discovered what it feels like to have petrol bombs thrown at you—not nice, where we developed confidence that our equipment would protect us. Our Force Training Department also attended these courses, ready to work alongside my department to train our own personnel in the newly developed techniques.

Back in Derbyshire a dedicated member of the Training Department created our own training venue at a former airfield near Ashbourne and we started to cascade the training throughout the force. After the initial round of training, we would run regular refresher courses. Senior officers were also being trained as Ground Commanders, with the skills required to lead the operations.

As the specialists in dealing with potential riots, my Uniform Task Force, travelled around our region working alongside personnel from other Forces and as national exercises were undertaken, we also participated in those events. Operationally we would be deployed wherever assistance was required by Divisional Commanders, regularly performing duty at Derby County and Chesterfield football matches, carrying out searches for missing persons, and undertaking house to house enquiries following serious crimes.

About six months into my period in the Operational Support Unit, I was sitting in my office when a colleague dropped in for a chat about my job because he had just been told that he was replacing me. I had a quick word with my immediate boss, and he was just as surprised as I was. I learned that I was being transferred into the Training Department to take charge of the Regional Inspector Training Courses. The Deputy Chief Constable told my boss that he would see me later in the week to explain the reason for the move. I therefore decided to go and see the man I was replacing thinking that he might be able to enlighten me about the reason for the move and tell me about the job.

He was aware that I was replacing him, but he said that he could not understand why as the Home Office specified that the person in charge of Regional Inspector Training should have a degree and he was aware that I did not have a one and he felt that I would be unable to cope with the job! I decided that was the end of our conversation. I did undertake a bit of research into his background and found that he had been one of the few officers to fail the Special Course at Bramshill, and his BA had been awarded by the Open University.

Some years later when I was awarded a Masters' Degree in Socio-Legal Studies from Birmingham University, I felt like visiting him and telling him that I was unable to see how he was competent to undertake his duties given that he only had an Open University BA degree when I had a role specific Masters' Degree from one of the top universities in the country, but I never got round to it!

Before I took up the new position, I had an interview with the Deputy Chief Constable, who informed me that I was being appointed to the role because the Regional Inspectors Courses had become far too academic and lacked practical relevance. He informed me that my record as an operation inspector revealed that I was one of the most effective in the force and that was the reason for my selection. The Assistant Chief Constable (Operations) also saw me and explained there had been a major argument about my proposed move to the Training Department, which he had lost, and he was sad to be losing my services.

Derbyshire had been appointed by the police forces within the eastern region to be responsible for delivering a national training programme for police inspectors, comprising a four week-long initial course, followed by a six-week development course after nine months to a year in the rank. Eastern region comprised, Derbyshire, Nottinghamshire, Leicestershire, Northamptonshire, Lincolnshire, Suffolk, and Norfolk. The course content was dictated by the Home Office, but some variation was allowed.

I thoroughly enjoyed both the managing of the programme and delivering substantial elements of the training. Working alongside me was an inspector who had good operational experience. At that time, the force had an outstanding reputation for training provision with a purpose-built residential training centre. Although I had not received either of the training courses whilst in the rank of inspector, my participation in the Junior Command Course, meant that I had covered all the subject material and at a higher level. Being involved in delivering training that helps the participants achieve their own objectives has always been an extremely rewarding experience for me.

At home at Matlock our children were growing up. Joanne our eldest had arrived at her new school, which was just next door to our home, when her new classmates were about to take the 11+ examination, because Ernest Bailey Grammar School, at Matlock still existed. Had she remained in Glossop she would have gone to Glossop Comprehensive School and had not therefore been prepared for the examination. We need not have worried as she passed the examination without any difficulty. In the longer term it would not make any difference because Highfields School, was going to take over and provide comprehensive schooling from two sites, the former Charles White Secondary

Modern School, for 11—13's, and then to a new site at for the remainder of her secondary education.

We quickly engaged in church activity at Matlock and increasingly we involved our children as much as we could. We had always prayed with them and tried to employ the advice contained in a book, "Leading little ones to God." Where they or we were experiencing problems, we would pray together and ask God to help us. Joanne kept having recurring tonsilitis and we discussed that she might have to have them removed. She was not keen in going to hospital and asked if it would help to pray about it.

We did pray and she stopped having that illness. She had been born with a huge and hairy birthmark on her arm stretching from her shoulder to her elbow. We had discussed with doctors about what should be done about it. They indicated that such birthmarks could become cancerous in later years, and they recommended it be removed when she reached the age of five. Having prayed successfully about tonsilitis, she then said she wanted to ask God to remove the birthmark, which to me was a bit more challenging. Although we did pray about her birthmark, she eventually had to have surgery to remove it when she was around seven years of age.

Recently she found a diary she completed when she was at Fullwood Hospital, Sheffield. Reading it reminded us of what a firm faith she had, but also it brought back the pain of leaving her on the evening before the operation, knowing that she would be in great pain the following day. The surgeons, having removed the extensive birthmark, removed skin from her legs to perform skin grafts on the affected arm. Not only did she have pain in her arm, but in both legs as well.

We became quite popular as a family with me preaching and the rest of the family assisting me through songs and readings. On one memorable occasion we were invited to do a session at an old people's home at Darley Dale when every time I started to say something one of the residents repeatedly shouted out, "Get on with it," The children laughed so much that we had to give up and leave!

Quite soon after we arrived in Matlock, the same group of church leaders that had sponsored, "Come Together," decided to have a tent mission in the town and invited me to join them in the planning group. Because they were aware that I had a ministry across the denominational boundaries, they invited me to become the link person with other churches. The evangelist, L who worked with Northern Counties Outreach was familiar to me, but I was not sure why. When eventually we met at a preparation meeting, I remembered that he had been a young pastor at a church in Lowestoft, the first year we had our beach mission. He had led a meeting we attended and preached a message using the text, "Be filled with all the fulness of God," which had made so much of an impression upon me that I still remembered it more than twenty years later.

Along with my family we attended every session during the tent mission. Typical of evangelistic meetings D would end every session with an appeal for people to respond. Our eldest daughter Joanne had by this time found a strong faith in Jesus and would sit on the front row, praying that her friends would respond to the alter call. One night early in the mission D said to me, "I wish I could take your Joanne to sit on the front row for every mission I undertake, she is so expressive in her commitment to what is happening." A scattering of young people from our and other churches did respond to the alter call, and many of them later became part of a large youth group of which Margaret and I were part of the leadership team.

For many years leading up to the tent mission, we had been friends with a family of which the father was a chief inspector in the police. M had previously experienced an encounter with God but was no longer active in Christian things. We would often talk about the faith but not make much progress. It seemed to me that he had abandoned an active faith in favour of pursuing his career ambitions. He had joined the Freemasons, later admitting to me that realising that virtually all the senior officers were involved, and it would enhance his career prospects. However, he was now one of the longest serving Chief Inspectors in the force, so it had not quite worked out how he expected.

M lived in Matlock, and I decided to target him as a potential responder to D's nightly alter calls. On the final night of the mission M came along with his family and during the appeal, our family and his were praying fervently that he would respond to the invitation to receive Christ. Praise God, at the very last opportunity, M responded, and the two respective families wept with joy and relief.

Within a week or so of making his decision M came to see me, looking for advice about his membership of the Freemasons. He had got hold of a tape recorded by a well-known Christian leader, who had identified the anti-Christian nature of some of the activities of the organisation. We prayed together about what M should do and he decided to resign his membership. Not long after that we again prayed together and he shared that his hearts-desire was to be promoted

Superintendent and be posted back to Matlock, so they could see the difference becoming a Christian had made. Within a couple of months, he was promoted Superintendent and posted to Matlock!

Having been the link person for the tent mission and seen the number of young people who had responded I was aware that there were a few small youth groups, for whom it was important to provide something to encourage them in the faith and I came up with the idea of a monthly celebration under the title "YouthReach." Having prayed about it I felt that God had given me eight names of people who might join me in organising and supporting the venture including Mick.

It was wonderful that all of them were strongly supportive and agreed to help from a practical point of view, planning and organising the events and putting their hands in their pockets where there was a shortfall in funding. YouthReach existed for more than a decade and we had some wonderful times through it. Most of the well-known Christian artists and bands performed for us over those years. Although we made a charge for admission, the money only raised about a third of the cost, another third came from local churches, and the remainder from individual Christians, including the founding organisers. The budget for a Saturday night in those days ranged from minimum of £250 to a maximum of close to £1000 and we were always able to pay our bills.

YouthReach was just one of a number Christian activities available in Matlock at that time. Our own group put on Christian Musicals including "Daybreak" and "The Witness." We organised annual trips to the Christian Arts Festival "Greenbelt," and various events put on by Youth with a Mission (YWAM). Once a month they could take a short trip to Derby for the Youth for Christ event. We also supported concerts put on by Musical Gospel Outreach. I despair today at the lack of suitable events for Christian young people in our area.

Over the years I have heard testimonies from people who were regulars at our YouthReach events and often they have identified our events as playing a significant role in either bringing them to faith or helping to retain their faith. Our youth group also set many young people along the way to become preachers, youth workers and leaders. They regularly organised and delivered outstanding services at local churches. I have always been a great believer in people growing through doing.

Soon after we moved to Matlock, another family moved to the area when he was appointed the local representative for "Christian Aid." They had two boys who were similar in ages to our son Gareth and youngest daughter Barbara. We became best friends and together formed a house group, which grew rapidly and became an important element of our growing as Christians. I hold the view that it is in the context of small groups that we are closest to the Biblical model of church, sharing meals together, undertaking activities together, praying and studying God's word all contributed to our growth at that time. We all believed in the importance of being filled with the Holy Spirit and exercising the gifts of the Holy Spirit.

We saw many answers to prayers and examples of following the leading of the Holy Spirit. One Friday night at our house group we were looking at our willingness to share Jesus in our everyday working lives and I felt that I had let things slip in that respect. I asked the Lord to forgive me and help me to do better when I returned to work in the Training Department the following week and I felt that I had simply to be more open about my faith.

Sat in the coffee lounge at the first break on the Monday, I saw that the man sitting next to me had an identity tag indicating that he was a member of the Kent Police Force. I clearly heard God say that he was the man I should witness to that morning. Derbyshire Police at that time ran the National Course in Police and Community Relations and the man from Kent was a visiting lecturer. I tried to resist what God was clearly telling me to do, but in the end knew I must take a step of faith. By that time, my policeman friend from Kent who had come to my Christian fellowship group at the Regional Police Training School, was the Branch Secretary of the Christian Police Association in Kent.

I felt that I should use him as a starting point in our conversation and I said, "I see you are from Kent, I have a good friend there, P who is based in Sittingbourne." I was astounded by his immediate response when he said, "Isn't that strange I have his contact details on my desk at work. He is the Branch Secretary for CPA, and I was going to contact him because God had told me I should be more open about my faith at work."

We shared a few stories about our respective careers and about CPA and went back to our responsibilities. Later, he came into my office and asked if he could talk to me. Very clearly God said to me that he was a Freemason and he wanted to talk to me in confidence. I suggested that we met at lunch time and talk as we had a walk, so that no one else could hear the conversation.

Once we were on our walk the inspector turned to me and said, "You know what I am going to say, don't you?" I said, "I think you are going to tell me that you are a Freemason, and you want my advice about it." He agreed that my reading of the situation was correct. We talked briefly about Freemasonry, and I shared with him my previous involvement with M. I also pointed out that the Methodist Conference had recently concluded that membership of the Freemasons was incompatible with Christian faith and practice. He decided to resign from the organisation.

Inevitably, if these memoirs ever get published someone reading it will be deeply offended. I am sorry, that was not my intent, I am just telling you an honest account of things that happened to me. My mate in Kent, afterwards said I should put a notice up in my office, "Beware of falling Masonry!"

Inspector training was delivered using a nationally agree curriculum, produced by a Home Office organisation based at Harrogate (Central Planning and Instructor Training Unit). There were two elements to the course an initial four-week programme followed about a year later by a six-week development element. The initial element covered a wide range of management and leadership material along with a series of practical exercises and performance assessments. Having undertaken the course at Manchester University and the six month long Junior Command Course at Police Staff College and being a very competent trainer with lots of practical experience I found no difficulty in adjusting to my new role.

Quickly receiving complimentary reports from the sending police forces and from those engaged on the courses. At any given time, I would have a trainer from one of the participating police forces assisting me in delivery of the training along with one of our own inspectors.

The course featured a series of practical exercises., concluding with a paper feed major incident exercise, based upon Harrogate. We had large scale maps and comprehensive information about the resources that might be called upon to assist. Boy soldiers received their training and education at a residential camp on the outskirts of the town and we would expect the course participants to spot this on the map and draw on those resources for help in searches. The major incident involved a train crash with dangerous chemicals leaking and the risk of fire. I was one of just a few people who had carried out an evacuation and I knew exactly what was required.

As the course director one of my major tasks was to write a report on each participant to send back to the force from which the person had been sent. So far as the initial element of the course was concerned there was a set format and little opportunity to elaborate. Nevertheless, I interviewed every participant three times during the four weeks, at the beginning, after two weeks and that at the conclusion of the course. I prided myself on how I could assess the participants and would always make some comment about future potential, which I was told the Chief Officers of the sending forces appreciated.

There was much more freedom allowed in the delivery of the development course, although specific elements of the duties of an inspector had to be covered, how exactly they were addressed involved considerably flexibility. One of the major elements of the development course we delivered was a comparative management study.

We engaged with large local organisations who exposed their management and leadership to a small group of our course members. Included were Rolls Royce, the National Coal Board, Trebor/Sharps, the National Health Service, Tube Investments, and Boots. Participants would attend one or other of the partner organisations where they would study the management and leadership structures and practices and compile a comprehensive report which they were then required to present to the senior managers of the organisation.

We regularly took the course to a coal mine where we went underground right through to the coal face. The idea was to expose the participants to the working life of mine workers and hopefully gain a better understanding of them and their needs and expectations. There were always humorous stories on these visits. The chosen coal mine was not visited down the shaft in a cage, but on a conveyor belt because the mine was built into a hillside, and the coal face could be reached through a steady descent. Leaving the conveyor belt for a while we would walk along a large tunnel, but the final approach to the face required us to get on our hands and knees and crawl along, not good if you do not like being in confined spaces.

It was always, dirty dusty, and noisy and we could feel the air being pumped into the space. Right at the face machines are used to cut the coal and the miners then manually load the coal onto a conveyor. The management of the coal mine would always arrange for the coal face to be moved forward whilst we were there. You had to find yourself a space where you had a degree of protection, until the coal cutting machine had been moved forward. I remember the following conversation. Coal miner to police inspector, "Where are you from?" Police Inspector, "Norfolk." Coal miner, "Bloody hell, I knew we went a long way underground, but I didn't think it was that far."

During my time running the inspectors courses we were approached by the Metropolitan Police and asked to allow them to send some of their inspectors on our course because they had a backlog of inspectors waiting for their development course. We had some interesting and able candidates coming from London. One memorable participant who performed exceptional well during the course and ended up in the rank of Assistant Commissioner was B who very bravely came out as gay and who now has a seat in the House of Lords. I like to think that when I identified him as having outstanding potential during his inspector's course, I helped him in his career progression.

I have previously described the poor relationship between our Chief Constable and opposition leader on the County Council and identified how that came into being. Sadly, the situation got progressively worse when the control of the Derbyshire County Council passed from Conservative to Labour. It became obvious that policing was on a low priority with the controlling group and many of the requests for funding for important projects submitted by the Chief Constable were turned down. P had the potential to have been an effective modernising Chief Constable, but he became extremely frustrated in having many of his budget applications turned down.

One of the responses to this problem was to move expenditure from one budget heading to another. The most significant example was that the police housing budget had an underspend and the Chief Constable decided to transfer some of that money into the financing of improvements in his office. This sort of thing occurred routinely in every other force on the country, without any challenge, but things were different in Derbyshire and our Chief Constable was suspended from duty for spending money without authority.

In the summer of 1983, I was contacted by the Christian Police Association and asked if I would be willing to join a team of members undertaking duties at the International Conference for Itinerant Evangelists being promoted by the Billy Graham organisation at the Rai Conference Centre in Amsterdam. CPA had provided stage security at every Billy Graham mission in the UK and were trusted by the organisation. When their original plans to use Dutch Police officers failed, they sent an urgent request for a team from the CPA to undertake these duties.

I duly found myself sharing a room with my friend Phil in a hotel near the conference centre. The role of the small CPA team was to secure the stage and look after Billy Graham and any special guests. Working alongside the Billy Graham team was a revelation. I have never seen a group of people so dedicated and hardworking in my life as those people. They were all so humble and gracious and very dedicated. The conference was funded by the Billy Graham organisation and the purpose was to provide teaching, encouragement, and support for evangelists from around the world. It was such a blessing to be involved in the event and will remain in my memory as a wonderful experience.

Many of the participants were from the developing world and their faith in praying for support and getting to Amsterdam was amazing. I remember the first time they were all invited to pray out loud in their own language it was unbelievable, about five thousand people praying non-stop, each using their own language to cry out to the Lord.

During our time in Amsterdam, I became friendly with a member of the Billy Graham team who was due to travel to the UK immediately after the event to start the preparation for Mission England which would take place in the summer of 1984. N was a lovely Afro-American man and we agreed that we would make contact when he was in Britain. Our contacts resulted in me booking him to speak at the annual dinner of the Derbyshire Branch of the Christian Police Association, around Christmas 1983. Naturally, I invited the Chief Constable and his wife to attend. I placed them on the top table alongside N.

During the dinner there was a discussion about a former associate evangelist with the Billy Graham organisation who was a relative of the Chief Constables wife who had died a few years earlier.

During my ongoing discussions with N, we decided that when the final arrangements were made for Mission England the Chief Constable and his wife would receive a VIP invitation to attend the event at Villa Park. Every night at Billy Graham missions, senior influential people would be invited and attend a buffet before the meeting commenced when they would have the opportunity to speak to Billy Graham and the other key players. However, before the invitations were sent out, our Chief was suspended from his duties and members of the force were instructed to have no contact with him. N and I decided that our Christian responsibility had a higher priority than any administrative instructions from the police hierarchy and we went ahead with the contact and invitation.

The Deputy Chief Constable then became the acting Chief Constable following the suspension of A and if the decline of the standing of the force had commenced during his term in office, due largely to the lack of support from the police by the Labour led Derbyshire County Council, it accelerated considerably under the leadership of S. He had a favourite saying, "This is not a ditch worth dying in" which he used every time he should have taken on the County Council and completely failed to stand up and be counted. This decline affected the management of the Training Department when an existing Superintendent was appointed as Head of Training who had no previous experience of training and development.

One of the aspects of my role that had been commented upon favourably was the reports I prepared in respect of those attending the inspector's courses. This was particularly true of the development course where I would make some comment about future potential Those conclusions were based upon their performance throughout the total of ten weeks of training, they received. The first time I submitted my final reports through the new superintendent, he suggested alterations, then further alterations, so that in the end we were saying nothing of any substance about the inspectors. Whilst I was deeply disturbed about this, I did not feel that I should complain to the Assistant Chief Constable (ACC), Administration and Training.

Within a few weeks of the first set of reports being sent out the ACC asked to see me. He informed me that he had received complaints from the Chief Constables in the region that the reports had declined in worth and were now telling them nothing about the abilities and potential of their personnel. I produced for him all the paperwork showing my original report, and all the subsequent amendments required by new Head of Training, who was transferred into another role and replaced within a few days, and I was able to carry on as had been the case previously, with my reports being accepted without alteration.

It was a cause of grave concern to me that the Derbyshire Constabulary Training Department which had gained an outstanding reputation under the leadership of S, was now experiencing a terminal decline due in part to the incompetence of the then serving Chief Constable. That decline in standards was not restricted to training and within a few years, the force was unique in England and Wales in not being given a Certificate of Efficiency by Her Majesties Inspectors of Constabulary (HMIC) all this taking place under the stewardship of S.

Being a subscriber to the Police Review Magazine, I was always aware of vacancies for posts outside of my own force and having previously served on what was known as Central Services, when an instructor at a regional police training school, I would look out for senior vacancies on Central Services appointments. I was surprised to find that the Chief Constable's Committee for the Regional Police Training Centre at Ryton-on-Dunsmore, near Coventry had re-advertised for applications for the role of Deputy Commandant (Superintendent).

My knowledge of how things work regarding these vacancies suggested that they had no natural choice amongst the applicants in that region and I thought that I might have a chance of getting the job and a promotion to Superintendent in the process. Being aware that I would not get the job without support from my own force I went to talk to the ACC. He assured me that I would be strongly recommended, by the Deputy Chief Constable, the same one that I had worked for on the Standing Orders task. At that time there was also a vacancy for Commandant (Chief Superintendent) at our own regional police training centre at Dishforth and I was told that my standing with the DCC was so strong that he would have supported me for that post as well. I also learned that the DCC was going to be leaving the force and I should get my application in before he retired to take up the post of Chief Officer of the Police in the States of Jersey.

I was not all surprised when my application resulted in a call to attend an interview with the Chief Constable's Committee. I was aware that there had been a routes and branches review of probationer training and a draft report, outlining major changes had been published and was going through a consultation process. It was clear that the report would form the basis of probationer training for the next decade, and I obtained a copy, studying it at length in preparation for the interview.

Along with three or four other candidates I found myself sitting in the Commandant's Office awaiting to be called for interview. I was encouraged by the fact that I was the only one from a police force outside that region. Being one of the last to be called for interview I was able to gauge their reactions. None of them appeared to be confident and they all displayed that they had found the interview stressful.

Walking into the committee room I found myself being invited by the chairperson, P, then the Chief Constable of the West Midlands Police to take a seat and relax. I was at one side of a huge table and across from me were six

Chief Constables, a senior civil servant from the Home Office and the Commandant and the interview began. A range of questions allowed me to talk freely about myself, my career, and my aspirations. I was reasonably happy that I was saying what I had planned to say and getting an encouraging reaction.

P then asked if I was aware of the draft report into probationer training and when I responded positively, he asked me to tell them what the report was about and my opinion about it. I talked confidently and easily about the report for about ten minutes when he interrupted me and said, "Mr Bown, it is very obvious that you know far more about that report than any one of us on my side of the table."

I knew then that I would get the job, and sure enough, I was appointed Deputy Commandant of the Regional Police Training Centre at Rhyton-upon-Dunsmore for a two-year secondment from July 1983, I was promoted Temporary Superintendent which meant that in eight years I had gone from Detective Constable to Superintendent, quite a meteoric rise in rank! Although I was temporary Superintendent, I was confident based upon previous policy I would be given the substantive rank before returning to the force which is what had always happened before.

In the event, although about a month before I was due to return the Deputy Chief Constable rang me indicating that it was proposed that I would become the Sud-Divisional Commander back at Glossop in the rank of Superintendent. I returned to the Force has Chief Inspector. By way of explanation, I was told that it had become force policy not to give the substantive rank to those seconded to posts outside the force when they returned. It was unfortunate that a colleague who had been seconded to a post at the Home Office in London also lost his temporary superintendent rank and returned as chief inspector. That policy only ever applied to the two of us, because thereafter the status quo applied.

Many years later, after S had retired, I was informed by the Deputy Chief Constable that it was the former Chief Constable who had put an instruction on my personnel file to the effect that I would not be promoted whilst he was Chief Constable.

I still bear the scars of the discrimination I experienced from S, and I have no idea why he acted in the way that he did. Perhaps it was my intervention over the incident at the funeral of the former Chief Constable . What it did do was to force my career into a direction that led me into some quite amazing experiences, which otherwise I might not have had. The Bible tells us that all things work together for good to those that love God and that is how it worked out for me, but I will remain aggrieved by being badly treated and no one having the courage to stand up for me.

Deputy Commandant at Regional Police Training Centre, Ryton-upon-Dunsmore

I found my period at Ryton immensely enjoyable, the role offering the opportunity to bring about a period of change required by the adoption of the new approach to training police recruits which would be far more practical than had hitherto been the case. There had always been a gap between policing as projected through the training institutions and what happened in practise. Often a recruit would be greeted at his or her operational posting with the instruction, "You can forget what you learned at training school and start to see what it is really like."

As the Deputy Commandant one of my specific roles was to be accountable to the Commandant for discipline. The first day of my duty I was informed that I would be expected to deal with a group of recruits who had been deemed to have broken some code of conduct. This ranged from being late for class to not having polished shoes enough or have trouser seems that were not properly pressed. I looked at the paperwork presented to me and decided that I was taking no action in any of the cases because the alleged offences were too minor for me to deal with, all that was required was advice from their instructors.

I just introduced myself and told them I was taking no action. The next day, having discussed my ideas with the Commandant and Chief Instructor I had a meeting with all the staff and explained that in future all minor breaches of discipline would be dealt with by the instructional staff and only serious breaches would be referred to me. This way the recruits contact with a senior officer would reflect that which pertained operationally.

The great thing was that as a management team we all agreed that we should make some fundamental changes to reflect the requirements of the new approach to training. One of the first was to allow recruits to wear jeans and casual clothing in their bar. This met with some opposition from a minority of the instructional staff who felt that we were guilty of lowering standards and turned up in the bar in dinner suits. We just had a laugh with them and got on with other more significant changes.

Right from my time as a recruit all courses ended with a passing out parade to which families and friends were invited in which hardly anything had changed over the years. There would be a display of marching, after which the recruits would be lined up for inspection by a visiting Chief Constable. The inspection would take quite a long time with the inspecting officer spending a brief period speaking to each recruit. It was not the most interesting event and did not in any way reflect what happened during the training course.

At any one time we would have two cohorts of recruits undergoing their initial training. When the senior course was in their final week, the junior course was approaching the halfway stage of theirs. Prior to our changes the junior course members were not involved in the passing out parade. We decided to incorporate the juniors into the programme. We created a written operational order specifying roles to be undertaken by the junior trainees. Some would be performing traffic duty directing cars to the parking areas, others hosted groups of parents and showed them around the premises, yet others undertook a few practical exercises/role-plays typical of what they were being required to undertake as part of their training.

During the inspection we arranged a commentary about the class being inspected including stories about what had happened during the course, amusing incidents, and the like, along with a pen picture of each trainee and all these changes made the day more interesting and relevant to what had been happening during the training course.

The new training programme required that far more practical exercises be undertaken and over time we equipped the establishment for that purpose. In a block of buildings that had been redundant we created a police station with an enquiry desk, and a custody suite including a proper cell. We purchased a small fleet of cars and motorcycles so that they could be used in the exercises involving traffic violations and accidents. All the practical exercises were assessed, and the results included in the final report. Consistently poor performances might result in the trainee failing to graduate.

Physical fitness also played a more significant part in the training and assessment processes and to encourage commitment to improved fitness I would get involved in the physical tests including cross-country runs. We organised a competition between classes where each team had to enter four runners and swimmers. Two of the competitors had to complete both the cross country run and twenty lengths of the swimming pool. We had a staff team in which I participated in the run, but not the swim. The first swimmer could not start until the first runner had entered the pool area, but thereafter it worked like a relay.

The first team to have all competitors finish both the swim and the run was the winner. Trainees were regularly assessed for their physical fitness with a standard that had to be achieved, with failure possibly leading to failure to graduate.

Every course had a dinning in night on the eve of the passing out parade. Dress was formal and along with Margaret and the other senior staff and their wives, we would be on the top table. It cost me a fortune in evening dresses, not for me I hasten to add. There would always be a guest chief officer from one of the forces in the area and a special guest would be invited to make a speech. Often, it would be a well-known person from the Coventry area, one example being D who at the time was an Olympic athlete. I remember that he had contacts with a group of paraplegic athletes from Coventry who needed funding to the get them to the Olympic Games in Atlanta. We, the senior management team decided to enter the Wolverhampton marathon in 1984, to raise funds to send them to Atlanta.

For months beforehand and through the winter we could be found pounding the streets around Ryton, getting ourselves in shape for the event. I had trained up to about twenty miles and did not have any doubt that I would complete the run, but I was not sure how long it would take. The Commandant, who was substantially the oldest member of the team had put on his entry form that he hoped to complete the run that day! I predicted that I would complete it in under five hours. It was an amazing experience, one that I will never forget, and which encouraged me to run three more marathons including the London one in 1991.

Wolverhampton will always be a special one because it was the first. Up to about eighteen miles I was running strong and well ahead of my expected time, but then I ran into the dreaded "wall," when your body says to your brain, "stop because you are hurting yourself," but you must ignore the message. It was a real struggle and I have a vivid memory of turning into a road, that led up a gradient towards the finishing line and reading the road sign, "Legs Lane." I thought I am losing my legs, but I managed to get to the finishing line with a time of four and a half hours. Crossing the finishing line, I felt euphoric and burst into incontrollable tears for a few minutes. What was more significant was that we raised more than £7000 which is all Coventry based paraplegic Olympians required to go to Atlanta.

One of the instructors at Ryton lived in Wolverhampton and he invited us as a family to visit them after the event and then attend his church in the evening. K and I would take the lead when the local Gideons came to give out their special blue version of the Bible (just for the police) to the recruits on each course. I would always say a few words about how the Bible was important for me but made it clear that they were not to feel pressured to take one. Hardly anyone ever refused. I was aware that K attended a charismatic church, and I made it clear that after running a marathon, if they were dancing in the Spirit that evening, they would have to count me out.

Each course was encouraged to nominate a charity they wished to support during their training programme and then events were held, sponsorship undertaken, and other methods used to raise a substantial sum, which would be presented to a representative of the charity at the course dining-in night. These activities were helping to create a sense of community amongst the recruits and a recognition that there were many groups of people who needed help.

Coventry was just an hour and a half drive from our home in Matlock and I would commute weekly, travelling in either on Sunday evening or early Monday morning. Unfortunately, one time on my trip to Ryton in our Rover SD1, the engine seized up and I had to get towed into the training school. It was clearly going to be an expensive job sorting out the engine repair and we bought a Citroen 2CV as a temporary replacement.

We travelled around the country in that little motor for quite a while, two large adults, three children, and a Jack Russell dog. My sister-in-law laughed when she saw our car and told me that you could not have such a car without displaying a "No Nuclear Power," sticker struck on the back. I told her that if she bought one, I would display it. There were very few police superintendents driving a bright red Citroen 2CV displaying a "No Nuclear Power" sticker.

I have always believed that it is good to laugh at oneself and occasionally I would give the recruits a laugh at the morning parade. Soon after I got my little French motor, instead of inspecting the morning parade on foot, I rolled down the soft top of the 2CV, and got someone to drive me up and down the ranks whilst I was standing up and taking the salute. On another occasion I rode up and down on one of the motorcycles used for practical exercises.

There were two lovely houses on the estate at Ryton, where formerly the Commandant and Deputy lived whilst on secondment. Sometimes during the school holidays, I would book one of the houses for my family to stay in. A small charge was made, but our children loved it because they had a swimming pool and gymnasium available to them which they could use. It also gave my wife a rest from housework.

During one of our visits the other house was occupied by G who had been appointed Chief Constable of the West Midlands Police replacing P when he retired. He was a keen country sports enthusiast and had a prize-winning black Labrador working dog. We had a small Jack Russell with attitude called Jack, who decided to take on his lovely gun dog. I had to pull them apart and apologise profusely.

Back at home our Christian lives were becoming increasingly busy our youth group was growing as was our house group. YouthReach was being strongly supported, we were attending events like Greenbelt and Youth with a Mission, discipleship sessions. Our two older children, Joanne and Gareth had each made a response to alter calls, that I made when I was preaching. I organised, "March for Jesus" in Matlock.

We were meeting regularly with the Christian Police Association in our own branch, and I was regularly travelling to other branches to speak at their annual meetings, these included over a couple of years, Northumberland, Grampian (Scotland), Avon and Somerset, South Wales, and Hertfordshire. I became a circuit steward in the Matlock Methodist Churches and was preaching regularly in Methodist and other churches.

I did have a frightening period whilst working at Ryton when I developed a very severe headache that got progressively worse until I could bear neither light or movement and had to be rushed into hospital with suspected meningitis. My wife had contacted people asking them to pray for me and whilst the hospital was carrying out the tests required, I started to show signs of improvement and eventually was discharged with the conclusion that I had suffered a rare and sever virus but was miraculously improving without specific treatment.

Soon after arriving at Ryton, I spotted an advertisement in the Police Review for a Masters' degree course in Socio-Legal Studies at Birmingham University. With the support of the director for the Manchester University Certificate course in Police, Penal and Social Studies, I successfully applied to undertake the degree programme. My lack of a first degree meant that I had to work extremely hard to eventually be awarded the degree of Master of Social Science (M. Soc. Sc).

One of my projects involved an analysis of the development of the police in Nigeria under the heading of Law and Development. That work proved useful when I later worked with the Nigerian Police Force. Travelling from Coventry to Birmingham was not a problem, during the first two years of the course, but was much more of a problem in the third year when I had to travel from Matlock and undertake my studies whilst carrying out operational duties.

During the summer of 1984, I renewed my contact with the Billy Graham organisation when I joined the stage security team for Mission England at Villa Park. In collaboration with N who was managing the event, we invited the now suspended Chief Constable, to attend as a VIP guest. He attended and it was a joy to discover that he responded to the appeal to receive Jesus. The suspension and long-term enquiry had a very damaging effect upon his health.

Eventually, after an enquiry costing a thousand times the amount he spent on his office, it was concluded that the expenditure was irregular, but it was not unlawful, and he retired on a full pension. Within a year or so, sadly he died. I have no doubt that the stress to which he was exposed was entirely responsible for his early demise and I have no doubts who was to blame for exposing him to that stress.

The following summer Billy Graham conducted a mission at the Bramhall Lane football ground in Sheffield and I volunteered to join the team of Christian Police Association members performing duty at the event. I was allocated a role looking after VIP visitors to the event. The VIP guests were accommodated in the Director's Lounge during the pre-mission reception and then moved onto the adjacent Director' enclosure for the meeting. During the reception those who would be appearing and performing on the stage would also join the VIP guests.

The Director's enclosure was not accessible from the stands on either side or below. The area to the right of the enclosure when looking out to the pitch contained the Mission England Choir. I renewed my acquaintance with Billy Graham, and his team, and had opportunity to say hello to Cliff Richard, who was singing and giving his testimony. As usual it was a joy to talk to people and to observe thousand responding when Billy asked them to "leave their seats."

Nine years after this event I was contacted by solicitors acting on behalf of Sir Cliff Richard, who were putting together the case for his defence against an allegation of abuse of a child who had attended the Mission England event at

Bramhall Lane. I met with them at the football ground where I showed them where I had been working and described what had been my areas of responsibility.

Having outlined the nature of the allegation, they obtained a very lengthy statement in which I was able to say that it would have been virtually impossible for the incident to have occurred as had been described by the complainant. It is common knowledge that the South Yorkshire Police and the BBC combined to undertake a grave injustice against Sir Cliff Richard in the reporting of the raid on his home. I was pleased that along with my fellow Christian Police Association volunteers we were able to assist in his defence and the subsequent announcement that there was no basis for the complaint.

Operational Chief Inspector—
Alfreton and Derby

As explained previously I returned to the Derbyshire Constabulary as a Chief Inspector. The gap in pay between the two ranks was the largest one in the police service at that time. Up to Chief Inspector, you are on a set number of hours and generally get paid if you perform overtime. As a Superintendent you have twenty-four-hour responsibility and other than rest days you can be called out at any time and that accounted for the wide pay disparity, so not only was I losing status I was losing a substantial amount of money. I did have a very brief interview with the Chief Constable when he explained his new policy and said that I should look for a promotion to Superintendent in another force.

My wife and I discussed whether I should apply for a post as Superintendent in another force and taking account of the educational needs of our three children, we decided that there was a window of opportunity of six months, to move and that I would apply for every Superintendent post advertised during that period. Unbelievably there was not a single vacancy advertised during that period and we took this as a sign from God that we should remain in Derbyshire.

My post back in Derbyshire was as Deputy Sub-Divisional Commander at Alfreton, one of the quietest areas in the force and not much of a career development move for me. I took up post just as police consultative groups were being introduced and I threw myself enthusiastically into the role, establishing good working relationships with local community leaders and politicians, seeking to ensure that we followed as closely as possible the priorities specified by the public.

Regular meetings were held where public opinion was sought and I attended all those meetings, but I also instructed that the local constable for the area should attend the meetings, so that they could hear first-hand the concerns of the local populace. Over time however, we would just see the same people turning up to every meeting, where they would say the same things and stimulating a wider debate with a larger group of people always proved problematic.

Not long into my spell at Alfreton one of the inspectors based there reported to me that he suspected one of the sergeants had a major problem with alcohol and was believed to be bringing vodka to work in a sparkling water bottle and drinking on duty. Having previously experienced the potential for trouble with police officers drinking on duty I decided I would have to confront the officer.

The female sergeant was working night duty, so I decided that I would turn out for the parade of the night shift at 10pm and observe her behaviour for a few hours before confronting her. By this time, I was much more aware of the support mechanisms available to police officers suffering from addictions and I had in mind to confirm our suspicions before instructing her to seek professional help. In the event there was an incident immediately after the parade and the sergeant was kept busy until the early hours of the morning. I had established that the sergeant did have a sparkling water bottle in her locker that contained vodka. When she eventually returned to the police station, I confronted her with my suspicions.

She denied having a problem, and persisted in the denial even when I pointed out the bottle of vodka. At the conclusion of my interview, I explained that initially I would deal with the matter as a health and welfare problem and told her that she must seek professional assistance within the next seven days and provide for me the evidence that she had followed my advice.

I submitted a report outlining my suspicions and explaining the action I had taken. Sadly, a couple of days later the sergeant was involved in a road traffic collision off duty when she provided a positive breath test and was charged with drunken driving. I found it interesting that the ACC Administration and Training who had been the Divisional Commander at Alfreton, told me that he was aware of the problem of this sergeant when he was serving there. I wanted to say, "Why the hell did you not do something about it?" But I refrained.

The Sergeant retired on an ill health pension, and I wished her every success in her retirement. About six months later I bumped into her, and she had been transformed from her previous self, was working for the Citizens Advice Bureau and free from alcohol. She had never become an alcoholic she had just taken to drink to cope with the pressures of her job.

After a year in post, I received an outstanding annual staff appraisal with a strong recommendation for promotion to superintendent but soon after I was transferred to Derby Central Sub-Division, in the rank of Chief Inspector as Deputy Sub Divisional Commander. Other than policing football matches at the Baseball Ground, I had no previous experience of policing Derby.

I was based in the former headquarters of the Derby Borough Police on Full Street in the city centre. I recall my first time attending a staff briefing when one of the constables used a racist expression. I immediately responded by saying, "If I hear that word or similar racist language used in my presence in future, I will discipline the officer responsible." I was making my statement having been made aware that racism was something of an issue in a city with a large ethnic minority population.

Derby at that time had one of the highest concentrations of late-night pubs and night clubs of any city in the East Midlands. Although I had never worked in the city before, I was aware that a substantial proportion of the work would involve dealing with licensed premises and their customers. When I started to talk to staff at all levels, they would readily identify the licensed premises for the cause of many of their problems but were unable to be specific in terms of blame or cause. I was also aware that there had been a decision in a court, I think in Brighton, where a licensee was held to have responsibility for the conduct of customers, not just inside the premises, but those outside and in the vicinity of the premises where they had got drunk.

I had read about another city where a "Pub Watch Scheme" was being introduced and decided to try and develop one in Derby City Centre. In the first instance I called a meeting of representatives of the licensed trade and explained that I wanted to create a Pub Watch Scheme, part of which would be a system of sharing live information about persons who had been refused entry because of their bad behaviour or been thrown out so there was a consistency in dealing with troublesome drinkers. I made them aware that I would be gathering data about where people arrested for alcohol related offences, had been drinking prior to their arrest and making them familiar with the Brighton court decision. We discussed what might be included in a Pub Watch Scheme and identified people who would be willing to become part of the management of such a group, who would meet on a regular basis, for cooperation and problem solving.

I created a form that officers were required to complete following the arrest of anyone for an alcohol related offence requiring them to indicate where the prisoner had been drinking prior to their arrest. After three months I had my first set of statistics identifying the most troublesome licensed premises. I then called a meeting with each of the licensees for those premises in the top ten and showed them our statistics, making it clear that I expected them to propose how they would improve the situation, and if such improvement were not made, I would oppose their licenses when they came up for renewal.

Generally, the threat of action was sufficient for the licensees to come up with ideas about how they would improve the supervision of their premises. Quite often this touched on the use of doormen and security staff where we had identified a significant problem of people with criminal records for violence being used as doormen and where there was a suspicion that some of them were also supplying dangerous drugs.

It did not take long for the licensed trade to wake up to the fact that they could easily lose their living if things did not improve, and there was considerable enthusiasm for joint problem solving as part of the Derby City Centre Pub Watch Scheme. One example is illustrative of what could be achieved when all the agencies worked together to resolve identified problems. The Pink Coconut was one of the largest night clubs in the city centre and was generally well run, but our data collection showed that they were having a recuring problem of serious assaults on the premises, where customers had used drinking glasses as weapons causing horrific facial injuries from the broken glass ('glassing').

Typically, an argument between customers would result in one of the participants, smashing a glass and pushing it into the face of the other person. Our discussions focussed on how we could remove the weapon. Plastic glasses were not an option in a state-of-the-art nightclub, but we did find that a French company manufactured glasses that when broken shattered into small pieces that could not be used as a weapon. One problem was that they cost about twice as much as the normal ones, but my research indicated that they lasted about three times as long as the ones already in use thereby saving money. These glasses became the norm for the licensed trade in Derby and "glassing" became history.

These were the days before the widespread use of CCTV supervision in the streets although many of the clubs and pubs were introducing them inside their premises. Over time we persuaded many to install CCTV to cover the street immediately outside their premises. This gave us the opportunity to view the actions of the door stewards. This eventually led to the creation of regulations for the recruiting, licensing, and training of door staff, and only those who had qualified in this way were able to be employed in the city. We were the first city to create such a comprehensive scheme and quite often I appeared on East Midlands TV talking about it.

Living at Matlock and commuting to Derby I found that it was advisable to leave home by around half past seven in the morning to avoid huge traffic jams and I would not leave earlier than six in the evening. Every other weekend I would be the duty senior officer for the weekend, and I would always work on Saturday evenings and staying through until the city had quietened down, usually after 4am. Whilst I was in theory the Deputy Sub Divisional Commander with a Superintendent in charge, for a substantial period, there was no Superintendent in post, because my boss had retired, but was not immediately replaced. When he was replaced, it was by a Superintendent who had been a Deputy Divisional Commander who had expected to become a Chief Superintendent and regarded his posting to Derby as a demotion and was not best pleased about it.

On the first day he walked into my office and said, "John, you have been running the show here for some time and you will continue to do so. You will not see me much operationally, but I will help you with the staff appraisals and admin." That was how it worked from then on. For me, it was better than having someone who was constantly interfering in my decision making, I could try out all my new ideas and I did so.

The Divisional Commander at Derby was D, who had previously worshipped at the same church as me in Matlock. I had a lot of respect for him, and he clearly rated my work highly. When my annual appraisal was completed, he was very complimentary, outlining the various successful initiatives I had introduced and making a strong recommendation for promotion. A year later in our discussion, he told me he could not understand why his recommendation had not been acted upon. He repeated his recommendation for an early promotion to Superintendent, but it still had no impact. As I have already stated I subsequently discovered that S, the Chief Constable had instructed his fellow chief officers that John Bown would not be promoted again whilst he was Chief Constable.

My relationship with the Chief Constable suffered still further during my time at Derby. Football matches against Nottingham Forest were always extremely difficult to police, with fighting between opposing football supporters, starting from mid-morning on a Saturday match day through until the early hours of Sunday morning, much of that fighting taking place in the city centre. On one such Saturday we had been struggling all day, when the city was full of shoppers as well as football supporters. During the afternoon there had been an altercation between a hackney cab (taxi) driver and a private hire (taxi), which ended up with the latter being detained in hospital and the former being arrested and detained so that further enquiries could be made before a decision about what action should follow.

In most areas of the country there are ongoing disputes between these two types of taxi operators. A hackney carriage license costs more than a private hire licence because the former can pick-up passengers on the street who have not booked a taxi, whereas private hire taxis must be prebooked. This was the heart of the matter in the case of the arrested hackney carriage driver and the hospitalised private hire driver. The Derby situation is worse because most of the hackney carriage operators are of Asian origin, whereas the majority of the private hire drivers are white British, and there is therefore the possibility of race entering the issue. On top of all that we were in the period of Ramadan when Muslims do not eat during the hours of daylight and have certain obligations to undertake.

Around about 5pm, there was a lull in activity, and I decided to drive back home to Matlock, with the intention of returning for the night shift at 10pm. I had not been home long when the duty inspector called me appraising me of a developing situation. He explained that the police station was surrounded by hackney carriages, blocking the roads and the drivers were threatening to burn down the police station if their colleague was not released. He also said that fixed penalty notices for illegal parking were being issued to the drivers, and I told him to stop that as it would not help, and I set off to drive quickly back to Derby. Just before arriving back in the city, I received a call to contact the Chief Constable urgently, but at the police station I was greeted by a potential riot and the Chief Constable was the least priority in my mind.

I quickly established a spokesperson from the group and learned that they wanted their colleague released in time for him to undertake his religious obligations. I contacted the hospital to establish that the injured person was not in any danger and put the wheels in motion for the prisoner to be released on police bail awaiting the completion of our enquiries, which could be completed within their required time scale. I was about to implement the action when the Chief Constable called me in the charge office and asked why I had not responded urgently to his call. I explained that I had been confronted with a potential riot at the police station and that had taken priority.

I was deeply shocked and disgusted when he said, "You have an Asian taxi driver in custody on a tin pot assault charge, kick his arse out of the police station and forget about it." My response was, "Sir, you have just given me an unlawful order and you should know better. I am a constable in my own right, and you have no authority over me in this matter. I have already decided what I am going to do and if it succeeds you should commend me, if it fails then by all means discipline me." I put the phone down and got on with the job.

On the Monday morning on my return to work I spoke to the Divisional Commander and told him exactly what had happened. He agreed that I had acted correctly in the matter, and he supported my action. I know that he then contacted the Chief Constable and told him that his instruction to me had been completely out of order. In the fullness of time the assault case was taken to court and the offender was sentenced to a term of imprisonment, thus fully justifying my action.

Clearly the Chief Constable had been contacted by someone with some power over him! Many years later when working with police forces overseas, where politicians would give unlawful orders to the police, sometimes involving the arrest of opposition spokespeople or worse still, extra-judicial execution, I would demonstrate from my own experience that attempts at political interference in police operational decision is not restricted to the developing world.

On the 15th April 1989, we were driving up the M1 motorway returning from a visit to relatives in the South of England, when news started coming in on the radio of the Hillsborough disaster. Having listened for a while, I said to my wife, "I know exactly what has happened, it happened to us at the Baseball Ground earlier this season when Liverpool were playing Derby."

Liverpool was playing at the Baseball Ground for an evening game, and I was responsible for away supporters. Evening matches always presented more of a problem than Saturday afternoon games because the arrival of spectators was condensed into a much shorter timescale. Part of my responsibility was to funnel away supporters to the appropriate turnstiles as quickly as possible, to ensure that spectators were in their places before the kick-off. With only five minutes to go we still had a large queue waiting to get in and they were showing signs of impatience, pushing forward with resulting potential for crushing of the people at the head of the queue. I made a quick decision to open the exit gate and allow the spectators to go in without checking their tickets.

We managed to empty the queue just before the kick-off and I then took up my position on the pitch side facing the away supporters. What I saw shocked me because I saw spectators in the ground floor level were jammed in tight with no spare room and some were climbing up into the level above to avoid the pressure of bodies. Fortunately for me no one got injured, but it was obvious that many of the people we let in did not have tickets and they had put the gates under pressure knowing that we would open the gates. At the post match debrief I described what had happened and my conclusion that spectators had come in without tickets. The Divisional Commander agreed that it had been the correct decision saying, "We got away with it, John." Over time I did find out that this had happened in other places with Liverpool supporters.

I have little doubt that the decision to open the gates at Hillsborough, resulting in the death of 96 Liverpool supporters, was wrong in the circumstances because of the impact it had for completely innocent people at the front of the crowd who were crushed to death by those behind them. At least part of the blame must lie with those responsible for the design of the ground and a little blame must also be attached to those supporters who arrived late and without tickets.

Given that my staff at Derby were at their most pressured late at night at weekends, I would occupy most of my time when on duty late at night, out on patrol on foot. Often, I would walk round with a constable, a good way to get to know them and assess their abilities. Unlike some of my fellow senior officers I had not forgotten that I was still an operational police officer and if necessary, I would step in and make an arrest. I recall one night when I was patrolling with the duty inspector, when across the road I saw two youths looking to be drunk and one of them was kicking at shop windows. I realised that eventually he would break one, so I ran across the road, only just avoiding the traffic, keeping my eyes on the youths.

As I suspected when I was getting close one of them did smash a window. I ran up and told him that I was arresting him for criminal damage, pushing him a doorway whilst I asked a couple of witnesses to supply their details. He sensed that he was in trouble and tried to escape, striking me in the face with his fists. I eventually restrained and handcuffed him. When he had sobered up later that night, I had a good conversation with the young man who had been celebrating his eighteenth birthday. Alcohol influences a large volume of crime and in this case, it gave a young man a criminal conviction that would stain his character for years to come. I felt sorry for him.

I woke the next morning to find that I had two lovely black eyes. I was preaching at one of the Methodist churches near Matlock and when I got up to start the service, I pointed to my eyes and said, "This is what happens when you have too much to drink on a Saturday night," I paused for effect and then explained that I had been assaulted in the line of duty. On the Monday morning D rang me and said, "I have your injury on duty report in front of me, I don't think I have ever had an occasion before when a Chief Inspector was assaulted in the process of making an arrest, well done John, you have not forgotten you are a bobby."

Race was an issue in the policing of Derby, and we did have one or two officers who displayed racist attitudes and if we were unable to take disciplinary action against them, we would put them in a non-operational post where they were unable to cause damage to the relationships between the police and the public. We did have a small number of officers from minority groups, and I did my best to ensure that they were not discriminated against in their career development. Whenever I carried out staff appraisal interviews, I would spend a lot of time listening to them, sometimes I did this walking around with them.

On one occasion when I was carrying out the interview of a young black constable, he asked why he had not been considered for acting up in the absence of a sergeant and why he had not been given a CID attachment as part of his career development. From my own knowledge of him I had not seen him display leadership potential, and I explained why at that time I could not support him, even though he had passed the qualifying examination. On the issue of a CID attachment, I said that I would have to talk to those responsible for that department but thought that he should be given a period of development in the CID.

It was to my knowledge that he had been commended for good work in a crime case and I thought that he should be given that opportunity. I spoke to the Detective Inspector, and we agreed that we should prioritise his CID attachment. I did feel that there was the potential for the young man to claim that he had been subjected to racial prejudice and I made sure that everything I had done was fully documented.

Some thirteen years after I had retired from the police, I was contacted by the Derbyshire Branch of the Police Federation. They explained that the officer was being supported in an action against the Derbyshire Constabulary alleging racial discrimination and was asking if I would testify on his behalf, because I was the only senior officer who had helped him and who he trusted. I indicated that I would be willing to make statement explaining what had happened. Before the Police Federation got round to interviewing me, I had supplied a statement explaining about all my contacts with the officer and outlining what I had done to assist him in his career development. I found it amusing that the man who had been the Detective Inspector at the time, was now the Deputy Chief Constable of the force.

Eventually, I was called to give evidence before an Industrial Tribunal in Nottingham, where the officer's claims of racial discrimination were being heard. I spent a day and a half in the witness box being challenged on just about everything I said. Fortunately, I had documented most of my dealings with the officer and the original documents were still available. The tribunal found that the officer had not been subjected to racial discrimination.

I certainly attempted to encourage career development amongst the officers under my command and my main tool for achieving this would be the annual staff appraisal interview. Often, I would spend time in an operational situation with the person who was going to be appraised, observing them performing their duties and engaging them in conversation. On one occasion during the interview with a probationer constable who had completed about eighteen months of his two-year probationary period, I discovered that he was the forces first ever officer recruited under the accelerated promotion scheme.

I was amazed that no special arrangements had been made to maximise his experience, given that after three years he would be promoted sergeant before commencing the Special Course at the Police College, and would become Inspector after a further two years. I agreed with him a series of developmental attachments including a period in the CID. This got me in trouble with the Superintendent in charge of the Personnel Department because he said that I was interfering in his job. He, eventually reached the rank of Assistant Chief Constable in the Derbyshire Constabulary and I was proud to have made a contribution to his career development. I was also proud of the fact that I was able to help a couple of BAME officers to make some career progression.

I remained in the rank of Chief Inspector for more than three years and at every annual appraisal I received outstanding assessments with the highest recommendation for promotion, but it was clear that I was not going to get promoted back to superintendent in the force. When I saw an advertisement for Syndicate Directors of Studies (Superintendent) for the Junior Command Course at the Police Staff College, I applied to undertake their staff assessment programme, but indicated that I would only take up appointment if I were appointed to the substantive rank of superintendent. I was not going to make the same mistake twice and I knew that if the College selected me, the force would find it difficult not to support them.

Having attended on the first ever Junior Command Courses and received a top grading along with the willingness to sponsor me for a fulltime university degree course I was confident that I could perform well enough through the selection process. I was by that time a Chartered Member of the Charted Institute of Personnel and Development and I knew that would also help me, both in the selection and carrying out the duties when selected. I performed very well and was selected to join the staff at the Police College in the rank of superintendent and there was nothing that the Chief could do about it.

Syndicate Director, Junior Command Course, Police Staff College, Bramshill House

The Police Staff College is located at a Jacobean Mansion in Hampshire. The beautiful old house is surrounded by splendid parkland with forests and a large lake. It also has one of the oldest continual use cricket pitches in the world! The institution exists to train selected police officers for middle to senior roles in the police service, and I have always found it a great place to be. I worked there for two years from the summer of 1989 to the summer of 1991 and enjoyed every minute. There can be no greater joy than have a part in helping other people to grow and develop and to achieve their objectives in life and that is what I found myself doing.

Each syndicate of participants in the Junior Command Course (JCC) were allocated an academic director of studies and a professional (police) director of studies. Virtually all the participants were already in the rank of chief inspector, the criteria being that participants should be either newly promoted to the rank or be inspectors about to be promoted.

Building up to my period working at the Police College, I had been studying management and leadership, reading widely on police management styles. My course at Manchester University had started the process and it had continued through my Junior Command Course and studies at Birmingham university. Running the Regional Inspectors Course had further exposed me to ideas about the strengths and weaknesses of police management and leadership. I had also studied Organisational Behaviour particularly in relation to police organisations.

Policing often calls for instant decision making, and a trend could be identified where those who were good at making instant decisions were rewarded through career development and promotion. However, the higher your rank the more likely it was that most of the decisions were not those requiring an instant response and such decisions were best when they were carefully considered, taking account of the views of all the stakeholders.

Management in disciplined organisations was traditionally top down with the bosses thinking that they were in the best position, through experience, to make the decisions and they need not consult with subordinates or other stakeholders. Police managers had tended to be very autocratic and therefore cut themselves off from honest feedback about what life was like at the point of delivery. Organisational theory suggested that the more levels there was in the hierarchy the more difficult it was for those on the front line to influence the strategic decision makers and the most police forces had at least eight levels in their hierarchy. Over my years in management and leadership I concluded that those who were closest to the problem best knew the nature of the problem.

Developing the skills required to be an effective Chief Inspector we needed to help our students understand their own strengths and weaknesses and how the culture of the police organisation could be counter-productive to effective performance. Police organisational culture was identified as insular, authoritarian, and pessimistic. Some police officers saw themselves as the thin blue line, where they stood between an ordered society and anarchy and civil disobedience.

Each member of the staff on the JCC was allocated a subject to research and make suggestions for updating the course material and I was delighted to be given, "Leadership and Teams."

John Adair had written widely on the subject of "Action Centred Leadership." His model involved three overlapping circles each representing actions that a leader must undertake; 1) Complete the **Task,** 2) Build the **Team**, and 3) Develop **Individuals.** I was able to meet him and discuss his work. Good leaders were able to provide a balance between the three elements of leadership. Too much emphasis on one would adversely affect another. Typically, a leader who was only interested in completing the task would cause burnout in his/her subordinates. Alternatively, too much emphasis on the team would have people feeling good but failing in the task. If the leader spent too much time developing individuals there would probably be a lack of team spirit.

Meredith Belbin has studied what makes a team effective and had identified eight team roles that people consistently displayed when working in teams. 1) Resource Investigator, 2) Team worker, 3) Co-ordinator, 4) Plant, 5) Monitor Evaluator, 6) Specialist, 7) Shaper and 8) Implementer.

Belbin carried out extensive research into what made for effective teams and concluded that all eight roles needed to be demonstrated in such a team. He also identified that people consistently occupy the same roles when working in a team. The maximum that one individual demonstrated would be three but might just be one. He also discovered that where a leader was given the right to choose their own team, they would often select mirror images of themselves, which meant that the team would be ineffective, strong in some areas but equally very week in others.

The JCC exposed the participants to a variety of personality profiles all designed to improve their self-awareness and willingness to give and receive feedback about their and others performance. The course included practical exercises, where assessments were made about the extent to which individual participants contributed to the task objectives. The course followed a model of behavioural development used by the University of Surrey, with lots of opportunities to improve self-awareness. I was very much attracted by these ideas because they were something of an antidote to the autocratic management and leadership that we had been exposed to in our police career.

The Police College at that time had four major courses that were being run for the police forces in England, Wales, and Northern Ireland. The Special Course was designed to provide an opportunity for accelerated promotion for constables who demonstrated outstanding ability, some of whom had been appointed to the scheme at the time of recruitment and others, who had been selected in the first few years of their service. The JCC you have already learned about. The Intermediate Command Course was designed for Superintendents to equip them for the next rank. The top-level course for police in England, Wales, and Northern Ireland was the Senior Command Course (SCC), deigned to equip the most outstanding members of the service to progress to Chief Officer levels.

In fact, you could not be appointed to any Chief Officer role without having successfully completed the SCC. Officers from overseas attended the Overseas Command Course. Most of the participants were from countries within the Commonwealth, but there were also participants from Egypt and other Arab nations.

I was aware at this time of the influence of British policing methods overseas and had shown an interest in secondments to the Nigerian Police College and as a training officer in one of our island protectorates but had never pursued them because of family considerations. During my degree studies at Birmingham

University, I had examined the development of the Nigerian Police Force. My studies made it clear that when developing police forces in our colonies, they had modelled the approach to policing on those undertaken in Ireland and not those in those adopted in the remainder of the UK.

The substantial difference being that the police in Ireland, were paramilitary, whereas elsewhere they were an unarmed civilian body. The theory behind a civilian model of policing was that the police were there primarily to protect the public, whereas there was a tendency for a paramilitary police force to prioritise the protection of the state.

The first police force we developed in Nigeria, had clearly been created to protect our commercial interests. Cleanliness being next to godliness according to Victorian standards meant that the UK was importing increasing amounts of palm oil, to be used in the manufacture of soap. The palm oil had been purchased through middlemen who were maximising their profits due to the increasing demand. UK then decided that they would purchase direct from the growers and built warehouses on the coast where they stored the palm oil awaiting shipping to the UK.

The middlemen therefore attacked these warehouses, and our government created a para-military police force called the "Oil River Protectorate," which eventually became the Nigerian Police Force. I had read widely on issues related to our treatment of the colonies and was aware that there was not a universally positive view of our influence around the world. It was with these thoughts in my mind that I felt challenged by some aspects of social events at the Police College.

Every few weeks there would be a dining in night with a special meal, a guest speaker and often a police band. Towards the end of the evening the band would play specific songs associated with some of the areas of the UK. Always when there were members of the Royal Ulster Constabulary they would play "Oh Danny Boy," and there would be great enthusiasm for that song because this was at a time when police officers in Northern Ireland were regularly being killed on duty. They would play stuff like the "Lincolnshire Poacher" and "Maybe it's because I'm a Londoner."

What disturbed me was when we got into the nationalistic stuff such as "Land of Hope and Glory," and I could see of the overseas officers squirming in their seats. Knowing that our colonial past, particularly in Africa was not universally viewed as positive, I felt it highly inappropriate to sing such songs, so I often went out for a meal on my own and did not attend.

A few months into my time at the College, we had a new course director, who I had met previously. Blair had attended the Regional Inspector's Development Course when I was running it and I had reported very favourably on his ability and potential. He had been appointed Acting Chief Superintendent and we struck up an immediate bond. He worked alongside me helping me to deliver the course as part of his induction. It also became obvious that we both had the same egalitarian approach to people, and he also was deeply offended by the nationalistic flag waving that occurred at the conclusion at the dining in night.

We decided to approach the Commandant and express our opinions. He was supportive of what we said and after a period of consultation, the flag waving songs were omitted from the programme. You will read later that I worked with Blair extensively in Ethiopia and Nigeria, where our attitudes towards the excesses of the colonial experience and our desire to make a difference was a strong motivating factor.

There were excellent sports facilities available at the College and I got back into playing squash, participating in competitions with commercial and public sector organisations. I played at the bottom rung of the team and rarely won but I enjoyed myself and it made me fit. I also played in the staff six a side football team and I even turned out for the Police College football team when playing the Officer Cadets at Sandhurst. I would not normally have been good enough to get into the team, but the Special Course students were away on practical exercises when a match was scheduled.

The Army Officer who was refereeing the match told us that he would make allowances for our mature years against his young and fit officers by allowing a few fouls, so he could see how they responded. It was not a good idea, but fortunately no one sustained serious injuries.

Each course would agree a social outing and because I rarely drank alcohol, I would volunteer to drive the college bus. One of the favourite visits was to HMS Victory at Portsmouth, where we would be entertained in one of the bars on board the ship. On other occasions we would travel to London and visit the Tower of London, where the Beefeaters would entertain us, and we would witness the "Ceremony of the Keys" something the public were not allowed to see.

Sometimes a London trip would involve a river cruise in the Police Commissioner's Launch. Visits to London would usually conclude with a visit to a West-End show. During my two years at the college, I saw the Buddy Holly story on three occasions. Having lived through the early Rock and Roll period as a teenager I never tired of Buddy Holly!

During my period at the Police College, I learned a lot about myself and about human behaviour. My knowledge of theories of management and leadership increased, and I became even more convinced of the value of community approaches to policing.

Having not seen or spoken to my Chief Constable since his advice for me to apply for promotion outside of the force, he came to the Police College in the final week of his police career. He made no direct attempt to see me, and I certainly had no desire to have an interview with him. However, I did literally bump into him, and I wished him all the best in his retirement. His concluding remarks to me were, "I think I got things wrong about you, I had you down as a typical county policeman, but I misjudged you."

To be honest at that time I did not have a clue as to what he meant, and it was only when I returned to the force and discovered that he had blocked any future promotion for me, that I discovered what was hidden behind his statement. I certainly did not mourn his loss to the force because combined with the Police Authority/County Council, he had presided over a sad decline in the standing of the Derbyshire Constabulary, for which I have never forgiven them.

Superintendent, Head of Training, Derbyshire Constabulary

Towards the end of my secondment to the Police Staff College, I had a couple of telephone conversations with the Deputy Chief Constable. At first our discussions were about me being posted to a busy operational station, but then I was told that I was going to become the Head of Training for the Force, because the Training Department was in a mess, and I was the only member with the necessary skills and experience to bring about the required change.

My return to the force coincided with the visit of Her Majesties Inspector of Constabulary (HMI). Before being interviewed as part of the inspection of the force, I did have and discussion with the newly appointed Chief Constable. I was impressed by him, he was clearly a modernising chief officer and he shared with me some of his ideas about taking the force forward, they included me working alongside outside consultants to initiate a process of organisational change, and the production of a completely new staff appraisal and promotion assessment system. I realised that I was going to be extremely busy but was excited by the prospect of helping to bring the force back to an efficient and effective organisation.

At the time, the Derbyshire Constabulary was the only police force in the UK that did not have a Certificate of Effectiveness. The situation had been created when on a previous inspection of the force, it was marked below the required standard in some of the key performance areas. On my second day back in the force I was interviewed by the HMI and in his opening question he said, "Ten years ago the training department of your force had a reputation second to none, but now it is near the bottom rung of effective performance. Why is that?"

I was tempted to tell him that I had only just returned to the force, and it was not my fault, but that would not have been an acceptable response. I did refer to the underfunding of the force by an unsympathetic police authority and how that had lowered the morale of the force. I could also have said that the previous Chief Constable had been an unmitigated disaster for the force, but I preferred to keep my opinion to myself on that one. I did share with him some of the plans that I had been discussing with the Chief Constable and assured him that I would do all in my power to bring them to fruition.

My new office was housed in the old hall (Butterley Hall) at the police headquarters and in the stairway leading to my office were the photographs of all the former Chief Constables of the force. One morning passing by the photograph of S I looked at him and said to myself, "You twisted me when you were Chief Constable and I am going to get revenge," Thereafter, if his photograph were straight, I would move it so that it was twisted.

A stupid thing to do but it made me feel better about being wronged by him. I was amused when one day the cleaner said how strange it was that S's photograph was always at a crazy angle and gave me a wink—I had been caught out, so I explained the reason for my strange behaviour.

Back in the training department I was able to observe some of the reasons for the decline in performance and one example comes to mind. The female Chief Inspector in the position that I had previously occupied was continually being complained about by course participants. Her immediate subordinate, an inspector, was holding the course together, but getting increasingly frustrated. It became clear that she had been posted into training because she was failing to perform as an operational officer. I ended up travelling around the region taking statements from course participants who had commented to the inspector on her poor performance. Faced with the damning statements she decided to retire.

Major changes in the way police forces managed their human resources was being proposed by the Home Office in the form of a Home Office Circular. The force had created an implementation group and I was nominated to join the group. I quickly discovered that there had been much talking but little action. Given my previous experience in writing the force standing orders, my recent involvement with the latest policing ideas whilst working at the Police Staff College, and my work on continuing professional development with the Institute of Personnel and Development, I started to produce the recommendations for approval by the other members of the implementation group. The outcome of all that was that I produced a comprehensive staff appraisal and promotion assessment process and therefore left a positive legacy for the force when I retired.

Our previous staff appraisal process, whilst purporting to be an open system was very much a top-down approach. Conversely our new system commenced with a self-assessment, which formed the basis of the initial interview with the line manager/supervisor. Making the individual consider their own opinions about their ability and to include this with accompanying evidence was a wise starting point. Where there was a wide discrepancy between the self-assessment and that of the line manager, the appraisee could ask for an assessment from another supervisor.

Throughout the production of the entire staff appraisal and promotion assessment systems I took account of my own negative experiences and endeavoured to reduce the capacity of one person to block the career development and aspirations of another without providing evidence for their judgements.

The promotion assessment process provided a much more structured and open approach than had hitherto been the case. A decision to promote was based on recommendations from three elements; 1) Recommendation from the Divisional Commander, 2) Successful performance through a series of operational simulations (incidents typical of the tasks required for the rank being sought) and 3) Successful assessment from an executive interview panel. Elements were introduced at each of these parts of the assessment process designed to achieve fair and evidence-based assessments.

Appeals could be made against the decision of the Divisional Commander. The assessors for the operational simulations were trained for the task and were required to produce individual and independent assessments using a numerical scoring system and any wide discrepancies required them to justify their assessment.

It was in the executive interview that most changes were introduced. Chief Officers traditionally demonstrated a belief that they were able to make reliable judgements based upon their interviews. I was familiar with research undertaken by the Chartered Institute of Personnel and Development indicating that unstructured interviews of the type undertaken by Chief Officers, were regarded as the most unreliable of all forms of assessment. Conversely the effectiveness of interviews could be improved by providing a structure for the interview and by posing only behaviourally based open questions.

Fortunately for me our new boss was a very progressive Chief Constable and fully supported me in my recommendations which included me providing training to the entire executive group (Chief Constable, Deputy Chief Constable, and Assistant Chief Constables (2), in the technique of asking behaviourally based questions. Traditionally, Chief Officers would give sets of circumstances and ask how the interviewee would deal with such a situation and would continue to use the same incident racking up the problem to be encountered, putting the interviewee under more and more pressure. I met with considerable opposition from them but given that the boss was on my side they had to go along with me a Superintendent, telling them that their interview technique in promotion boards had been extremely poor.

Behaviourally based interviewing assumes that the best way of assessing future performance is what they have done in the past. For each of the skill areas being assessed I produced a set of open-ended questions. For example, if attempting to assess how the interviewee would deal with a poorly performing subordinate the question would be, "Describe to me a time when a subordinate was not performing to your satisfaction." You are now getting them to provide you with evidence of what they did and not opinion about what they might do.

The first set of promotion boards using the new system took place after I had retired but I was thrilled when the Deputy Chief Constable called me and said, "John, I wish I had known about your questioning technique years ago. I have never seen interviewees having to think so much and where we could use follow up questions to check how honest they had been." That was sufficient reward for me.

Th Chief Constable had shared with me his desire for a change in the management and leadership culture of the organisation, his ideas were very much in line with those I had been familiar with and supported in my work at the Police Staff College. We were both desirous of seeing some devolution of decision making to appropriate levels. Too frequently the organisation was pushing up decision-making and this was partly because of the behaviour of his fellow executive officers. He told me about a consultant who was working with the Metropolitan Police and achieving the sort of change we desired for Derbyshire.

Following an initial meeting with the Consultant it was agreed that I would co-facilitate a course with a Metropolitan Police Divisional Command Team, with a view to the two of us designing and delivering a culture change programme for the force. I was impressed by the style of facilitated learning employed by the consultant and we quickly realised that we formed a formidable partnership.

During my time working with the consultant in London we discussed the specific needs for the work we would do together in Derbyshire. We decided that we would have a series of training workshops for multi-rank groups from Inspector through to Chief Officer. This would be the first time that a Chief Officer was directly involved in training alongside other ranks. Rather than teach the theory of management and leadership, we planned to ask live questions to be discussed in small groups designed to allow the participants to confront their seniors with behaviours that were dysfunctional.

At the time D was the Assistant Chief Constable (Operations). A career detective from Merseyside, he belonged to the old school of management, being autocratic and a bully. Some measure of his habits could be gained from the nicknames he had within the force. One was "Doberman," obviously combining the attributes of a savage bread of dogs with his name. His other nickname was, "Exocet," after the missile used by the armed forces. The latter was accompanied by the expression, "You never know when he is coming, but you always know when he has been."

He would always try to identify something that you were doing wrong and attack you for it Every working morning he would walk into the Control Room at Force Headquarters and study the messages regarding incidents occurring within the preceding twenty-four hours, taking a copy of the various activity logs into his office. He would then call each Sub-Divisional Commander or Deputy and question them about incidents in their area. If you did not know about an incident for which he had the log, then you were in trouble. During my time at Alfreton and Derby, I had refused to play ball with him to the extent that my colleagues did.

I briefed my Inspectors that when I arrived for duty in a morning, they should report to me any incidents that were significant and likely to have repercussions. If he asked me about something I had not been briefed about, I would simply explain my approach and that I would find out about the incident. In the rare occasions that this occurred I usually discovered that there was absolutely nothing to be gained in me knowing about such a minor event and I would then call back to the ACC and tell him that my Inspector had correctly decided that I need not know about it and if I did not need to know then certainly there was no reason why he should be looking into it. In truth he never challenged what I said.

Sadly, most of my colleagues would have the Inspector reporting everything to them, so as not to be caught out which meant that every operational Inspector occupied the entire period between six and eight each morning gathering information. Just this one habit wasted hours of police time for no good reason.

I also became aware that the ACC (Operations) initiated calls from the Operations Room to Sub Divisional Commanders and their Deputies at times throughout the twenty-four-hour period including weekends. Generally, this was just a call to the radio allocated to the officer requesting a location and using this method he would have a quick check on those who were on duty. I was told that during my time at Derby I had one of the best response rates in the force, indicating that I was not a nine to five officer, but regularly still on duty late at night and at weekends.

The Chief and I agreed that the outside consultant would be housed in the VIP accommodation at the Training School and that the Chief Officers would just travel in from their homes and the only Chief Officer who challenged this was D, who called me as soon as he received his joining instructions telling me that he would be staying in the VIP accommodation. I explained that travelling from home had been good enough for the Chief Constable and would have to be good enough for him.

The Chief Constable attended the first workshop, and it was well received by all, who attended with the questions we had prepared proving effective in generating discussions about those things that got in the way of being effective and all participants finding the degree of honesty and openness empowering. Given that I was approaching thirty years in the police service and was planning to retire and start a new career when I reached that milestone, I was keen to leave a positive legacy in the force, but I was not going to be intimidated by the likes of D, because I was not going to be around much longer.

D set out his initial attitude when he arrived at the beginning of his workshop and wanted to park immediately outside the entrance to the Training School but could not because the space was taken up by the canteen assistant's car. She was going to be looking after us over the weekend and using her car to transport food and provisions from the main canteen, so she had a need to park there. I explained this to him and stood my ground and he reluctantly removed his car to the car park. In fairness to him, during the workshop he accepted what was said about how some of his practices were dysfunctional to effective performance and subsequently changed his behaviour.

Although I did not like his management style, I did respect him for his expertise in major crime investigations.

Part 3
Life After the Police

Retirement from the Police—
Group 4 Court Services Ltd

One of the advantages of police service is the opportunity to retire with a substantial pension and start a new career. After thirty years in the job, I could retire with a pension of two thirds of my pensionable pay. I had always planned to retire at that stage for two substantial reasons, 1) I was attracted by the idea of starting again when I was still young enough to learn new things, and 2) staying on in the police was economic lunacy, because although I could have worked through to the age of sixty (eleven more years), I would have continued to pay thirteen percent pension contributions without gaining any increased benefit.

This was the era of the contracting out of public services to private companies and one of the first elements of this in the criminal justice sector was that relating to prisoner escorting. Hitherto this task had been undertaken by the police and prison services and in both cases, it distracted from the core function of those organisations. As an operational commander it was not uncommon for a substantial proportion of your afternoon shift to be engaged in taking prisoners from courts to prisons. I am sure that prison governors suffered a similar depletion of their manpower in conveying prisoners to courts. In both cases the existing system left much to be desired.

The police would often convey one prisoner in a police car with two officers involved. The prison service often used taxis to convey prisoners, leaving much to be desired in terms of security, one notable example of the failures of the system being the escape of Billy Hughes from a taxi in Derbyshire who went on to kill all but one of the residents of the house he took over, before himself being killed by a Derbyshire police officer, all of that taking place within a couple of miles of my birthplace.

I was aware that the area including Derbyshire was scheduled to be the first to be contracted out and therefore was not surprised when I spotted an advertisement for a Training Manager for Group 4 Court Services Ltd based at Worksop in travel distance from Matlock where I lived at the time. Looking at my own cv I reckoned that I was just about the most qualified person in the country for such a role, so I duly applied for the job. It was no surprise that I was called to the company headquarters at Broadway to attend an assessment centre. At that time Group 4 was a privately owned limited company being owned and managed by the son of the founder.

Group 4 was then head and shoulders in the lead in terms of private security companies and operated throughout the world. I was obviously fully familiar with competence-based assessment centres given that I had designed them for the Derbyshire Constabulary and clearly performed very well because at the conclusion I was offered the job with a request that I commence work as soon as possible. It transpired that although Group 4 were the preferred supplier they had yet to receive a contract and they were beginning to panic because the start date was fixed, and they were running out of time to design a training course and operations manual which would have to be examined and approved by the Home Office and the training delivered prior to the operation going live.

I retired from the employment of the Derbyshire Constabulary on my forty ninth birthday (8th November 1992), having joined on my nineteenth birthday. I joined the employment of Group 4 at least two weeks before I retired because I had outstanding leave to take. I was the first employee for Group 4 Court Services Ltd.

The head office of the parent company was in an old mansion house in a small country estate in the Cotswolds overlooking Broadway. The complex incorporated a purpose-built residential training complex with excellent and up to date facilities. The head office of Court Services was Carlton House, Carlton Road, Worksop, Nottinghamshire. I was recruited before any contract had been signed but with the promise that if the contract were not awarded, I would be employed by Group 4 elsewhere in the group.

Having spent my working life in the public sector, I was now being exposed for the first time to a commercial environment. Considering this was happening in 1992 in the early days of the contracting out of elements of the public services, strong opinions were being expressed both for and against these new developments, I was neither a strong advocate for privatisation nor strongly opposed. I was thankful for a new role that would provide a challenge, but also draw upon my previous experience in the criminal justice system as a public servant. Then, and now, I am of the opinion some services are best delivered by the public services and others by the private sector.

I am certainly not ideologically wedded to the idea that only the organisations run for profit are efficient and effective. I have come across private companies that were grossly inefficient and ineffective in roughly the same proportion I had found in the public sector.

I was immediately thrown into a pressure pot where we were doing things that had not been undertaken before and where there would be little time to complete everything within the required timescales. I had sole responsibility for producing a training programme for Prisoner Custody Officers that had to be approved by the Home Office appointed contract Monitor, who was a former prison governor.

The training course had to be informed by a set of operating instructions which were being produced by the second employee of the company, a retired police chief inspector, who had been working for Group 4 at the first privately run prison. At least he had the advantage that he was familiar with the company and had been linked directly with the prison escorts operating from Group 4's privately run prison.

Much of my early days were occupied at Broadway working alongside the Personnel and Training Departments, assisting in the design of staff assessment centres, I think this was due partly to the fact that we had not moved into Carlton House. I was impressed by the professionalism of the training and personnel department. Although I would eventually be accountable to the Director of Group 4 Court Services, I initially reported to the Personnel Director for the parent company, who impressed me as did the Head of Personnel. They were using the latest ideas in staff selection processes, like those we had just introduced in the police.

I spent some time working alongside a highly qualified occupational psychologist, who had previously worked as a Prison Psychologist for the Prison Service. We were analysing the functions of a Prisoner Custody Officer working on prison escorting to identify the skills and behaviours required to be successful in the role and then creating assessment processes for those aspiring to the role. This work then informed my design of the training course in conjunction with the operational procedures being produced by my colleague in Group 4 Court Services.

My official start date was my 49th birthday and the company delivered a new top of the range Peugeot 405 saloon car, and thereafter whilst I worked for them, I had a new car delivered on my birthday. Moving into Carlton House which would be the operating base and training centre for Group 4 Court Services there was much to do before we could deliver the first initial training course. We created a prison set up with cells and a locking system like they would encounter at courts and police stations. We equipped classrooms with state-of-the-art learning aids, and I grabbed myself an office.

For the greater part of the first few months working out of Carlton House, I was the keyholder and would arrive around 7.30am and depart about 6.30pm. The Home Office did eventually sign the contract and we could then start recruiting staff, but they did not extend the commencement date, so we were certainly working under severe time constraints, and I personally felt the pressure. At some stage, the Personnel Director decided that I was being pulled into too many other tasks and would need to set aside specific time to produce the training course. I moved into the Broadway Training Complex, where I worked from a residential room, from early morning through till late evening for more than two weeks. My meals were brought to me, and other than a walk out in the grounds I just worked. At the conclusion of that period, I had produced an extensive training programme for the training of Prisoner Custody Officers, which was approved by the Home Office without any amendment. To be honest I was justifiably proud of that achievement.

Our contract was for a substantial part of the North Midlands, Lincolnshire, and Humberside regions and we established operating depots at Gilberdyke (Humberside), Lincoln and Worksop. We were concerned that there should be a phased introduction, to allow us to settle at one operating depot before moving to another, but the Home Office insisted that the going live date applied to the entire contract area. Due to that fact the first couple of weeks of the delivery of the service was a bit of a nightmare and subsequent contracts were all phased in.

Much of my time in the build up to the start of the operation was occupied in working alongside staff from the Group 4 Personnel Department running recruit assessment centres. Quite a substantial proportion of our recruits were recently retired police or prison officers, with a scattering of bus drivers and a broad selection of others including people from the armed forces. One of my tasks was to scrutinise successful candidates to find ones with some experience of training delivery, who would be recruited early, and I would teach them the course before they delivered it. We had a shortfall, and I appointed some former trainers on short term contracts, those who wanted to be trainers, but did not want to be Prisoner Custody Officers.

The training course included a variety of written and practical assessments all of which had to be concluded satisfactorily for the participants to be certificated by the Home Office as qualified Prisoner Custody Officers. Weekly progress through the course was also documented by the trainer/training manager.

From the trainers who were also Prisoner Custody Officers, I appointed one to be my deputy. He had been a trainer in the Royal Air Force and had performed very well during the assessment centres. I was also taking on board the personnel management functions and in truth I was having to work long hours to keep pace and although I was coping, I was reaching my limits. We did appoint an administrative assistant to work in the Personnel Office, alongside me and she was supported in pursuing qualifications in personnel management.

Our operation was built around the use of custom-built cellular vehicles, where each prisoner was secured in an individual cell within the vehicle. Our fleet ranged from coach sized vehicles with twenty cells, down to vans with just a dozen cells. Each vehicle operated with two Prisoner Escorts, one driving and the other supervising the prisoners. This was quite different from and much more secure than had been the case with the police and prison officer escorting system in either police patrol cars or taxis.

By some sort of a miracle by the allotted commencement date, our staff had all been trained and posted, our three operating depots had been commissioned, our Worksop based operations room was equipped and manned and in theory we were ready to go. The first day was chaotic, influenced partly through a policy of non-co-operation by some prison officers, who delayed the handing over of prisoners, but also that this was an entirely new organisation, undertaking an entirely new task, with previously unused equipment. It took at least a couple of weeks to settle down to anything like a normal operation.

Given that there was a lot of criticism of the contracting out process, the media were watching our every move and yes, we did have an occasional escape of a prisoner. We were able to show that our escape statistics were considerably better than the combined ones for the police and prison service, but the media never reported that fact. One joke that was circulating at the time, (when Nottingham Forest was struggling at the foot of the old First Division) was,

"What's the difference between Group 4 and Nottingham Forest?" Answer, "Not even Forest lost three in a week!"

Our worst disaster took place within the first month of the operation, when a prisoner was found dead in the cellular vehicle on arrival at the prison. He had choked on his own vomit having consumed a bottle of vodka that was labelled as "Sparkling Water." It appeared to be a sealed and unopened bottle, but a syringe had been used to extract the water and refill the bottle with vodka. Relatives of the prisoner had visited the court where the prisoner was appearing and handed over the bottle and contrary to our written procedures and the training received, he had been given the bottle and allowed to consume the contents.

Just a day after the event a senior detective from the Humberside Police along with a detective sergeant came to interview me. It was a bit of a shock when before the interview, he cautioned me explaining that given the initial training course was so recent and the conduct of our Prison Custody Officer so lacking, he had concluded that the training course must have been defective and therefore they were considering prosecuting the company for criminal negligence amounting to manslaughter.

The first thing to say is that the Prisoner Custody Officer in charge at the court where the incident occurred had retired from the police where he had been working as a Police Custody Officer to join Group 4, and arguably should have known not to hand anything over, due to his previous experience, even without having the training course. The interview took two full days, when I ran through the entire training course, producing the training record of the staff member involved.

I was able to show that a written examination had included a question about items from members of the family of prisoners, indicating that they should not be accepted. He had answered the question correctly, but clearly his behaviour did not follow. He had also received training about what to do when there was a suspicion that a prisoner was unfit to travel, and I could show that he was aware that a doctor should be called to decide whether the prisoner was fit to travel. At some stage it must have been realised that the prisoner was drunk but admitting that would have meant admitting to a failure to comply with procedures, so they decided to carry on as if nothing had happened, a decision that had dire consequences. All our Prisoner Custody Officers had qualified as First Aiders, their course including how to deal with drunk people, so that they did not choke on their vomit.

After a stressful two days of interview under caution, it was made clear to me that neither I nor the company would be prosecuted for a criminal offence, but they did not need to tell me that I would be heading for a hard time when the inquest was held. My interrogation in the witness box at the inquest lasted three full days and each day as I arrived and left the inquest, television reporters followed me from the building to my car, stuffing a microphone in my face and asking me questions to which I replied, "No comment."

A legal representative from Group 4 Head Office was listening each day, but I was not allowed to speak to him until I had concluded my evidence. At the conclusion of my evidence, we did have a debrief and he thanked me for doing the best I could to represent the company. However, we realised that a civil action for damages and compensation would follow. I discovered later that the family were given a settlement out of court. The Prisoner Custody Officers involved directly in the incident were dismissed for gross misconduct.

Over the next four years Group 4 Court Services grew rapidly and by 1996 we had been awarded two further prison escort contracts and now had about sixty percent of England and Wales under our control. Following our successful launch, I had suggested to Group 4 that we copywrite the Home Office approved Prisoner Custody Officer course and sell it to our competitors, before they poached my trainers and stole the course. The idea that we should do anything to assist a competitor was alien to them, but my predictions came true when the first time a contract was awarded to another company they head-hunted my deputy who took with him my course, saving them an awful lot of work.

Sitting in my office one day I received a call from one of the bosses at Group 4 Training asking me to recommend any retired police officers who would be suitable to work for them on a project in Ethiopia. The company had been invited to bid for a contract funded by the Overseas Development Agency (ODA) working at the Ethiopian Police College, Addis Ababa. By this time, I had a small number of experienced and talented former police trainers who had worked for me in delivering Prisoner Custody Officer training courses in East Anglia and the North-West Region, and I submitted the names of a few of the best of them along with my own name. I had always been attracted by the idea of working abroad and was in any case getting ready for another new challenge.

After a month or two had passed, I was invited by the ODA along with Rogera retired Metropolitan Police Chief Inspector, who had managed for me the delivery of the initial phase of training in East Anglia, to attend an assessment centre at the Headquarters of ODA at East Kilbride in Scotland. Rather than select an organisation to deliver the contract they had decided that they would select people from a selection of bids and assess their ability in what was an assessment centre for staff to be directly employed by them overseas.

The outcome of the assessment centre was that ODA indicated that they would like to invite a joint bid by the Royal Institute of Public Administration (RIPA) to be led by Blaire, who I had worked alongside at the Police Staff College, and from Group 4 Training with myself and Roger as the selected trainers. I was about to start another new phase in my life.

Part 4
Working Overseas

This next section of my story is largely made up of accounts of my life working overseas sent back to Margaret, my family, and a few close friends, to keep them in touch with what was happening to me. Initially, in Ethiopia communication was difficult as there were no mobile phones and landline telephone charges were excessive. I did have an email facility once we had established computers with an internet connection.

Prior to that we sent fax messages. The style of writing reflects that I was using them as a diary of the most memorable events and tends to differ somewhat from that used elsewhere in this account of my life. It includes accounts of my life working in Ethiopia, Jamaica, Nigeria, and Sudan. I count it a privilege to have been able to undertake this work and am deeply thankful to my wife for allowing me to spend so much time away from her and the family. It was often quite difficult for her and sometimes, challenging for me.

Blown Up in Addis Ababa!

"Oh God it's a bomb." I will never forget hearing those words and then almost immediately catching the sign of some movement on the floor near my feet. Looking down I saw a bright shiny blue metalled hand grenade roll to a standstill just a few inches away from my right foot. People have reported that when faced with the potential of a quick death in a road accident or similar, they have seen their lives flash before them, but it was not like that for me. All I remember is a dull aching feeling of impending disaster before noticing the poof of smoke that comes immediately before a hand grenade explodes. Then the lights went out—I do not mean the electric lights—I mean my lights—everything went inky black.

What happened at that precise moment I can only guess from a reconstruction of the evidence that became available afterwards, but it should be clear to the reader that by some undeserved yet greatly appreciated miracle I survived the explosion. At the time of the incident (April 1997) I was in an Italian restaurant called 'Blue Tops,' in Addis Ababa, the capital of Ethiopia, I was accompanied by my wife, a colleague (Blair) and his wife (Pam) and we were seated at a typical restaurant table. Blaire was to my right, Margaret to my left and Pamopposite me. Blaire and I along with another colleague had been working in Ethiopia since June 1996 helping to develop training capacity in the Ethiopian Police Force, funded by the then Overseas Development Agency (now Department for International Development).

Our wives had arrived in Addis Ababa a few days earlier for a visit and I had arranged the restaurant trip out on the Friday evening both as a welcome for them and a celebration of a successful series of workshops for key stakeholders from the regions of Ethiopia when the participants had committed themselves to create police training establishments within their territory in line with a blueprint that we had been producing since our arrival in the country.

My first recollection following the explosion is finding myself on my feet and some distance away from the table where we had been seated. The restaurant was hazy with blue smoke and, broken tables, chairs and crockery littered the marble tiled floor.

I became aware that my trousers from the waistband to my feet on my right side were soaked with blood. Of more concern initially, was the fact that my trouser crutch was also soaked in blood, and I clearly had some significant wounds between my legs. Having read about soldiers in battle having limbs blown off and being unaware of the fact I carried out a quick check that nothing was missing, thankfully all my equipment was still in situ, but on the other hand I was not sure to what extent everything was intact.

The strange thing as I think back to that time is that I was not aware of substantial physical pain, just an overpowering sense of debilitation and shock. I noticed Blaire was also on his feet and was bleeding profusely but in his case down the left-hand side of his body including what appeared to me to be a chest wound. His skin was very pale and in fact, my mother would have said he looked, 'Like death warmed up.' I felt deeply concerned for him as he limped out of the restaurant.

I followed him outside into the grounds of the restaurant but could see no sign of either Pam or Margaret. Thinking that she may have gone out to the exit to the road, I wondered around still in a daze from the explosion but managing to note that immediately outside the part of the restaurant where we had been sitting an injured man was lying on the grass. I found out later that he had been sitting with his wife at the adjoining table and he had been blown straight through the window—he was about half my size so there is apparently some benefit from being of substantial size. Sadly, the man's wife lost the sight in one eye. I still had not found Margaret and given that Pam had already joined us outside the restaurant, I started to worry that she might be lying dead in the restaurant.

I repeatedly shouted her name and got into a panic, remembering that I had made the booking for the celebratory meal and starting to blame myself for the entire event and the incident, which is a bit silly really but not untypical in such circumstances. In the event, she had crawled under a table and played dead, thinking that the terrorists may still be there. When she heard me shouting her name, she realised that it was safe and got up and made my terrible night a little better by joining me outside.

It is difficult for people living in the so called 'developed world' to imagine the lack of facilities and services in the developing world. If a similar incident occurred in London, the emergency services would quickly arrive at the scene and an ambulance would convey the injured to a hospital where you could make use of adequate emergency services. However, in Addis Ababa at the time such services were not available. and we were left to sort ourselves out.

One of the waitresses at the restaurant arranged a mini-bus taxi to come and pick up the injured persons. Over the next hour or so we visited many clinics and hospitals attempting to obtain emergency treatment without much success. It is difficult to relate what we felt like at that time. The reality appeared to me to be that we had just miraculously survived being blown up by a hand grenade only to die in a taxi whilst trying to get treatment.

Eventually we found the Menelek Hospital where a doctor was on duty and who started to examine Blaire and myself on the basis that we were clearly the most seriously injured. Our wives although deeply shocked only received minor injuries, in part because he and I had moved quickly to get away from the explosion and in effect put our bodies unintentionally between the hand grenade and our wives. My wife reported later that she had seen the hand grenade explode with a large flash and but for my sudden movement the shrapnel would have hit her in the face whereas instead my rather generously proportioned rump took most of the shrapnel and shock wave.

Whilst at the hospital my condition started to deteriorate, and I found breathing extremely difficult. I was making a gurgling noise in my chest just like I had heard road traffic accident victims making immediately before they died. I was convinced that I was about to die and said goodbye to my wife and offered a prayer to the Almighty. I just lay and waited to die thinking to myself "How did I get here?"

Welcome to Ethiopia!

Ethiopia is in east Africa, south of the Sahara Desert and was previously known as Abyssinia. The UK would fit inside the borders of Ethiopia about ten times, and it has a population just a little more than that of the UK. Less than twenty percent of the population live in the cities which mean that, even in the twenty first century it remains an agrarian economy with the majority being subsistence farmers. The expression 'subsistence farmers' trips of our tongues without necessarily knowing what is meant by it; in Ethiopian, it means that the family will live in a traditional tukul (circular house with mud walls and thatched roof) often it will be shared with some of the family livestock. They will have some hens and a few sheep or goats and occasionally a cow. They will grow crops which for the greater part they will consume as a family. Rarely will they have enough produce to sell to others for cash after they have fed themselves. Every member of the family will work from dawn to dusk to sustain the lives of the family and most will be unable to afford to send the children to school.

Ethiopia, unlike much of the remainder of the African continent is not a creation of a colonial power. It existed as an independent nation long before the 'race for Africa' began. Mussolini's Italy did occupy Ethiopia for five years during the Second World War, but it was liberated in 1941 by a joint British and Ethiopian force. Italy also briefly occupied Ethiopia before the First World War, but the Ethiopians defeated the Italian forces at the battle of Adowa the anniversary of which is celebrated to this day as a public holiday.

Ethiopians believe that the Queen of Sheba ruled much of what is now Ethiopia, when her territory included land on both sides of the Red Sea. Axum in northern Ethiopia is reputed to have been the site of her palace. They also believe that when she visited King Solomon their relationship was much closer than the Bible records and that their union produced a male child who became the first of the dynasty of Ethiopian emperors that trace their line back to King Solomon; the last being Emperor Hellie Selassie who was deposed during the

239

communist revolution that took place in 1974. They also claim that the Church of St Mary at Axum contains the remains of the Ark of the Covenant.

The history of Ethiopia is so different from the rest of Africa that Ethiopians are prone to tell you that they are Ethiopians and not Africans. The nation was declared to be Christian from the fourth century and the Ethiopian Orthodox Church is still powerful and influential. Christian festivals are celebrated with colourful and sometimes noisy exuberance, featuring huge parades through the streets led by priests wearing elaborate garments and musicians playing instruments that have featured in these events for many centuries.

Christian and Muslims do coexist in Ethiopia generally without problems and the walled city of Harar in the north of the country is said by Ethiopians to be the third most important city in Islam and has 99 mosques, so the culture is not exclusively Christian. Both the early Christian and Islamic influence, along with the geographical position of the country have resulted in a people and a culture that reflect close historical relationships with the Middle East. For example, the national language, Amharic includes words with both Arabic and Hebrew origins,

The Marxist government led by Mengistu Haile Mariam was a very brutal regime, and hundreds of thousands lost their lives and their property during the period that was called 'Red Terror.' The country was strongly influenced by the former Soviet Union, until the communist government was overthrown after a long civil war. The victors were led by Meles Zenawi a Tigrynian from northern Ethiopia who became Prime Minister of a government that indicated a desire to become democratic and which requested aid from the British Government, hence the police project.

Ethiopia is one of the poorest countries in the world with life expectancy currently averaging 55.2 years. According to CIA statistics Ethiopia has the lowest per capita income in the world currently standing at $90. Sadly, when folk in the developed world think about Ethiopia they tend to dwell on poverty and famine, although these elements are never far away, the nation has a rich cultural heritage and Ethiopians are justifiably proud people.

In one way, my first engagement in Africa came out of the blue, when I received a call from the organisation that I worked for at the time asking me to recommend police trainers for a project in Ethiopia and I put my own and a colleague's names forward. Truth is however, that I had frequently considered applying for a secondment for overseas work in Africa when I had seen them advertised during my police career but had not pursued them due to family circumstances at the time.

Some recent research suggests that the entire human race have common African origins, if that is so then going to spend time in Ethiopia may be a little like going home after an extremely long period away. Such a trip would normally invoke nostalgia and trigger memories of past experiences. That could not be the case because I had never previously set foot in Africa, but nevertheless Ethiopia was a special experience right from stepping of the plane at Bole Airport, Addis Ababa. The first part of my 'Ethiopian Adventure' lasted for the best part of four years and improved my self-awareness no end. To that extent it was a little like coming home.

From time to time, I had crossed paths with people who had lived and worked in Africa. They nearly always had a faraway look in their eyes when they talked about their experiences. For all my poor listening skills, I could recognise that Africa had an ability to attach itself to the souls of those who had tasted its riches. In truth, I was an African adventurer waiting for a time and place to happen.

Bole International Airport is not exactly a pearl amongst airports, being functional more than decorative. My first arrival was at night and all that I could see before landing was the usual patchwork quilt of bright lights, but with an occasional dark area. I later discovered that the dark area was not as I had thought some unpopulated public park or impossible building area, but that segment of the city scheduled for no electricity that night, a signal that I was entering a developing country where services were not completely reliable.

On alighting from the plane onto the tarmac there were not only the usual aroma of kerosene, but also the distinctive smells of Africa. At night throughout Ethiopia there is always the intoxicating effluvium of burning eucalyptus wood and leaves. This water-sucking, fast growing tree, a native of the Antipodes and not Africa was introduced to Ethiopia by Emperor Menelek in response to the rapid deforestation around Addis Ababa and has proved to be something of a saviour for the people. Eucalyptus trees can be seen in profusion in many parts of the country.

The timber is harvested on a regular basis, cutting the tree back to the stump which then obliges by quickly producing the new growth for future wood cutters. All parts of the branches that are anything more than an inch in diameter are used for building material and the remaining twigs and leaves are dried after which they become fuel for cooking and heating. Some indication of the practical nature of Ethiopians can be gained from the Amharic name for the eucalyptus tree 'barsaf' which means literally 'from across the sea.'

I can honestly say that my first exposure to Addis Ababa left me breathless! It should be pointed out this was a physical reaction to the altitude of this the third highest capital city in the world, rather than the spectacular beauty of the place, but there is spectacular beauty in profusion in Addis and throughout the country. The beauty is not restricted to the landscape; the people of Ethiopia are amongst the most attractive in the world.

As I waited to have my passport examined and stamped, I saw the usual airport boredom and bureaucratic machinations, but I also noted that Ethiopians are quick to see the funny side of any incident. They quickly laugh and smile and when they do their natural friendliness and attractiveness becomes very evident. The men are often most handsome being mainly small of stature but with fine facial bone structure. The women are extremely attractive their almond eyes shining out of milk chocolate skin like bright stars in the twilight sky.

The road from the airport into the commercial heart of the city takes one along a modern dual carriageway. I remember travelling along it that first night on my way to the Hilton Hotel. This was my first visit to Africa and although I was tired from the journey I was also buzzing with excitement at the beginning of my adventure. In such heightened state of awareness, one takes in a myriad of pictures without properly understanding the significance of what is being observed.

There were occasions when a beautiful Ethiopian girl would peer into the vehicle, smile, and wave. In my ignorance, I took this to be simply a sign of Ethiopian friendliness, which it was but born out of a desire to engage in a 'business relationship.' Sadly, the absence of work means that too many Ethiopian girls find themselves supporting their families through work that would only be undertaken in the most extreme of circumstances, selling their beauty and their youth to foreign visitors.

The road into the city provides evidence of the changes that have been taking place since the government of Meles Zenawi came to power. There is a considerable amount of building development, and the new buildings look to be sturdy and safe, in fact far better than I have observed in more developed places.

During the daytime, the entrepreneurial character of Ethiopians is revealed in the numerous street traders that are evident selling anything from cigarettes to local crafts. At night, however most of the local street traders are in bed and the women of the night take over from them. It needs to be said that neither these girls nor the daytime beggars are intrusive or objectionable. They are basically good people forced into a way of life they would prefer to avoid but having little or no alternative. They are, like all Ethiopians, good mannered and friendly.

I remember on one occasion returning to Addis Ababa following Christmas leave and being told by my driver that some of my beggar friends wanted to see me. I assumed that my contributions to their welfare had been missed and that they were ready for their funds to be topped up. The reality was quite different—they gave me a Christmas present and card as an expression of their thanks. Could this happen anywhere other than in Ethiopia? I was moved to tears by this expression of gratitude. In the context of European values, I had given them so little, but for them it amounted to the difference between life and death.

The Hilton Hotel was at that time the only truly international hotel in the whole of Ethiopia but since then it has been eclipsed by the Sheraton which is said to be the most luxurious hotel in East Africa. The Hilton is a typical 60's multi-story hotel that might be found in any capital city in the world. It is still attractive and has beautiful gardens surrounding an open-air swimming pool with thermal heated water provided from the nearby Filowa spring, the reason for the decision of a former Emperor to build his new palace nearby.

Sleep on that first night was welcome but relatively short-lived due to a combination of jet lag, minor altitude sickness and excitement at being in Africa for the first time. I will never forget stepping out onto the balcony at about five-thirty in the morning as the dawn arrived. My room was at the side of the hotel with a view not of the beautiful gardens but of some of the surroundings of the city.

That first glimpse of Ethiopia was amazing for a whole range of various and sometimes conflicting reasons. My senses were unable to grasp the complexity of mixed signals. I saw reflections of poverty in a large shantytown of tin roofed mud walled buildings set against a background of surrounding majestic mountains. Modern buildings blend with mud huts and hills and valleys extend as far as the eye can see all interspersed with tall eucalyptus trees.

Addis Ababa offers economic extremes varying from the opulence of the Sheraton to the plastic sheets stretched over thin poles that represent the only shelter that the extremely poor can afford. The difference here against some capital cities is that everything is thrown together in a complete mix without it causing any apparent jealousy. Rich and poor live alongside one another, as do

Christian and Muslim with relatively little evidence of ill will. Ethiopians are wonderfully friendly and generous of nature.

Driving around Addis Ababa is an exhilarating experience and occasionally frightening. There are many extremely ancient vehicles and a few modern ones. Private car ownership is low, and the most cars are either taxies or government owned vehicles. Driving standards are not good and have obviously been influenced by the Italian personality. They drive into difficult situations without any real understanding of what lies ahead, so consequently what would have been a minor interruption becomes a major traffic jam.

However, there is no evidence of road rage, the drivers simply get out of their vehicles and laugh at one another, discuss all manner of problems, and wait for someone to get a bright idea about what to do next. This usually happens eventually and, the day's difficulties having been sorted in the discussions, the drivers return to their vehicles and recommence their journeys.

The most challenging driving experience is negotiating through Meskel Square. During the communist regime, this area was used for the frequent parades of military hardware and the saluting dais is still in existence but unused. The square is massive in size with six lanes of traffic in each direction and having three feeder roads at each end of the square, each road being traffic light controlled. When the lights change, it feels like you are involved in a Grand Prix grid start. There is little or no lane discipline so you may find drivers crossing six lanes from left to right. At the same time, other drivers will be crossing six lanes from right to left with little thought for the fact that at the end of the square they are all going to have to stop again because the lights are on red.

Often your way is likely to be obstructed by a flock of sheep being driven across the carriageway so that they may safely graze on the central reservation between the two carriageways! From time to time the animals blocking the road will be cattle on their way to the slaughterhouse or donkeys delivering local produce. Addis Ababa does not feel like a city. Locals born and brought-up here will frequently talk about their 'village' meaning that part of the city where they have spent their life. It is really lots of villages joined together.

Given that my reason for being in Ethiopia was to work with the police my welcome to the country involved being greeted by Ethiopian Police officers at the Police College located about forty kilometres out of the capital city at the small town of Sendafa. We discovered that so far as our Ethiopian colleagues were concerned, we were long overdue as they had expected our project to commence two years earlier and they put pressure on us to run a course for trainers immediately. We were amazed to discover that although having a full complement of staff not a single course had been undertaken over the previous two years. How did they occupy their time?

We quickly discovered that many of the senior police and other government officials were former 'freedom fighters' who had been appointed not based on their skills or experience, but just because their loyalty could be guaranteed. For example, the Police Commissioner had no police experience whatsoever, was extremely quiet even shy, and walked with a very distinct limp. Not at all what you would imagine as being the requirement to be an effective Police Commissioner conversely, he clearly had a good relationship with Meles Zenawi the Prime Minister and in the event, that worked to our advantage and obviously his.

Over the years that we were working in Ethiopia I had a few personal discussions with the Commissioner, none of which lasted for more than a few minutes because he was a man of few words, but each of which were significant. The first one occurred soon after our arrival and a few weeks into the first course we delivered for police trainers. He spent most of the morning in the class with me observing what was happening but taking no part. At lunchtime he met with the trainees who had been in class, and they did not complete their meeting until mid-afternoon, so my session was delayed.

About half an hour after we had resumed the afternoon session, the Commandant of the Police College came into the classroom and told me that the Police Commissioner wished to see me immediately. I was nervous about this and imagined that he was perhaps unhappy with something that he had observed and wanted a lengthy conversation to impose his will on what we were doing. I walked outside the classroom into the corridor with some trepidation thinking that I would be meeting the Commissioner in one of the offices. He was just standing in the corridor and stuck out his hand a said "Mr John I want to say thank you" and then turned around and walked away leaving me 'gob smacked.'

You will read about similarly brief and revealing conversations with the Police Commissioner in later chapters.

A Miraculous Recovery

As a police recruit, I remember being taught police law and procedure and recall that the law of evidence included details about 'dying declarations.' This is a rule that allows what a person said when they were 'in hopeless expectation of death' to be given in evidence at court by the person to whom the statement was made. Otherwise, such a statement would be regarded as 'hearsay evidence' and would be inadmissible in a court of law. The reasoning behind this rule is that a person who believes him/herself to be dying will speak the truth. I tell you the truth that as I lay in the Menelek Hospital in Addis Ababa on that Friday night in April 1997, I genuinely thought that I was about to die.

I told my wife that I was sorry, but I could not stay alive any longer and was fading, I shed a tear or two as I said goodbye to her and thought about the children I would never see again. For her part, she just reached out and held my hand—words were inadequate and unnecessary. It may seem strange that I did not sense any fear of dying just regret for the things left undone that I would like to have done and a quick and simple prayer to God to forgive my sins and receive my soul.

The lack of breath and the accompanying overwhelming feeling of weakness eventually passed, and I regained some strength. I learned afterwards that an explosion at such close quarters compresses the lungs and the symptoms that I displayed quite frequently occur and can sometimes prove fatal.

Sometime after our arrival at the hospital a familiar face appeared when the then head of security at the American Embassy arrived. He had heard of the terrorist incident and his visit was in a professional capacity to make sure that American citizens were not involved. We had met previously and in fact at our most recent meeting I had collapsed into his arms! I had just completed a 25k walk in aid of the local Leonard Cheshire home in hot sunshine and feinted from heat exhaustion.

We had a laugh about my habit of meeting him under difficult circumstances. He contacted senior members of the staff at the British Embassy and before too long we experienced the welcome support of representatives of the British Government. All four of us were overwhelmed by the assistance we received from the staff at the Embassy. They were so kind and helpful arranging for Blair and me, to be transferred to the Black Lion Hospital the location of the only intensive care unit in the whole of Ethiopia and our wives to the Embassy clinic.

Given that Blairs's injuries were slightly more serious than mine and the British Embassy ambulance was only suitable for one seriously ill patient at a time he was dispatched to the Black Lion Hospital first. Whilst I was waiting, members of the police arrived and started to interview me. In fact, they delayed my journey to the hospital for a considerable period whilst they questioned me about the incident.

When I asked them to let me go for treatment, they told me that they could not allow this as they understood that I may die before they had obtained information from me. At other times, I would probably have responded angrily but I had no energy to be angry and simply let them get on with their interview.

It was in fact after 10pm when I eventually arrived at the Black Lion Hospital at least two and a half hours after the bombing incident. I was taken straight to the operating theatre and passed Blair in a corridor as he was wheeled out and I was wheeled in. We did not speak as he was still asleep from the effects of the anaesthetics, they had administered to him.

My injuries were cleaned and dressed, and I was told that I had some thirty-seven significant wounds. We both learned later when we had recovered at home and returned to Ethiopia that the consultant in charge of the intensive care unit was convinced that we would die overnight due to a combination of blood loss and shock.

Most of my injuries were down the right-hand side of my body starting on the sole of my right foot and continuing through to my upper arms. I had some major injuries between my legs with one piece of shrapnel lodged quite close to the femoral artery. One block of large pieces of shrapnel must have struck the outer side of my right thigh and chopped up the muscles resulting in so much damage to the nerve endings that I lost the sense of feeling in that part of my leg. My backside was liberally splattered with shrapnel injuries.

Assistance from the British Embassy was not limited to getting us to the Black Lion Hospital, they provided clean bedding for our beds which otherwise would not have been available. They brought us food and visited us frequently and cared for our wives in their clinic. They arranged for staff members and others from the British community in Addis Ababa to give blood ready for blood transfusions which the consultant had thought would be necessary. We have nothing but praise for their contributions to our wellbeing, treatment, and recovery.

At the clinic, my wife was operated on to remove a piece of marble from the floor which had become lodged in her leg and both she and Pam were comforted, treated, and cared for. Their main problem was that they were unsure that we would have survived the incident and the reassurance from those treating them was not automatically regarded as being truthful, for that matter during that first night the medical staff at the clinic was just as aware as those treating us that we may well not survive.

Shock does strange things following incidents such as those we were involved in. Both Blair and I were extremely weak and not fully aware of what was going on around us. Margaret was conscious enough to realise that she needed to contact our family but could not remember our own telephone number where her father and our younger daughter was located but could remember her sisters telephone number. She called Ellen her sister and told her what had happened and explained as best she could the current state of health of the four of us.

Ellen in turn contacted our close family, but then started to alert a very wide network of people who knew us, to ensure that they found out directly about the situation rather than hear through the press and to encourage them to pray for our recovery.

During the day after the incident, we were visited by the then Commandant of the Ethiopian Police College, Colonel T, a gentle giant of a man who had managed to serve through three different government regimes as a senior policeman. This lovely man was so disturbed at what had happened to us that he wept unashamedly as he looked at us lying in adjoining beds all wired up to life saving instruments measuring every aspect of our systems and designed to ensure that the staff could respond immediately to any change in our condition. He was full of apologies for what his compatriots had done to us. For our part, we felt no sense anger towards Ethiopians, just relief that we were alive.

During the same day, we also had a visit from a news reporter who had managed to gain access to us by purporting to be a colleague. We had a brief discussion about the incident, and he discovered that whilst we had been seriously injured our wives had received relatively minor injuries. We explained that although we had no direct memory of precisely what happened, we must have moved quickly to get out of the way and in effect put ourselves between the hand grenade and our wives. Clearly, he saw a good story and subtly changed our account to turn us into heroes who had jumped on the hand grenade to save our wives. This was to have serious implications for our families because as well as having to deal with the worry of whether we would survive, they were chased by reporters from national television channels, radio, and newspapers for interviews about the sort of people we were.

In my case I can tell you that I am not the sort of person who is ever likely to jump on a hand grenade. What I did say when I returned to the UK was that it was much more likely that my wife offered the best opportunity of a soft landing!

The day after our incident corresponded with another event of major significance to me, when my local team Chesterfield played Middlesbrough in the semi-final of the FA Cup. All the Chesterfield supporters and many of the non-partisan supporters believe that Chesterfield should have won the tie and been the first team from the old third division of the league to reach the FA Cup Final. Watching the video of the game indicates that Chesterfield should have been awarded a goal late in the game which would probably have resulted in a win instead of a draw, and the referee has subsequently admitted that he got the decision wrong.

However, the hand grenade incident did result in me attending the replay of the semi-final at Hillsborough as a guest of Littlewoods Pools. One or two of my mates suggested that I had arranged the hand grenade incident just so that I could get to the match!

The consultant in charge of the intensive care unit told us on the Sunday that she was concerned that if we stayed in Ethiopia, we were likely to become infected with viruses that our bodies would not have been exposed to and therefore would be serious in our run-down state and she explained that she was negotiating with the British Embassy for us to be flown home for ongoing treatment as soon as possible. We left Addis Ababa with our wives on the Lufthansa night flight on the Monday. At the airport, we had an emotional reunion with our wives who had spent a part of the weekend convinced that we had died, and the truth was being withheld from them.

It was only when they received handwritten letters from us that they accepted that we had survived. We took over the first-class cabin of the flight and were cared for throughout by a doctor who had been flown out from the UK by my employers Group 4 Securitas.

We were loaded into the aeroplane via the lift that is used for loading freight and just before being hoisted into the cabin the Police Commissioner and other senior police officers came to see us off. The Commissioner again made one of his by now customary short speeches. He touched his gammy leg and my bandaged leg and said, "You are like me now."

My employers' activities had not been restricted to making the medical care arrangements; they had also contacted and visited my family, liaised with the media agencies, and the local hospital. My immediate manager was on hand at the hospital to greet us on our arrival and arrange access to my family. The hospital was also being inundated with media representatives wanting to interview us.

Margaret and I have three grown up children and they were all at the hospital when we arrived there. Given the media interest, we were housed in the private wing of the hospital which is where our family were waiting for us. There were lots of tears from all of us and we became more aware than previously of how difficult it had been for our children receiving the news about the incident and having to handle press enquiries about every aspect of our lives. I remembered the moment when I had said goodbye to Margaret and sadly accepted that I would never see my children again, I gave a quiet thanksgiving for my safe return to Chesterfield and the reunion with my family.

Whilst clearly, I was still in some pain from my injuries on my arrival back in England, my priority was to have a bath. I had become aware that I was giving off an unpleasant odour as washing had not been a priority at the Black Lion Hospital, Addis Ababa. Following an initial examination by doctors who indicated that my many wounds were showing the early signs of healing, I was given permission to take a bath. So far as I am concerned that bath did more for me than any treatment I had already received or would receive later. My recovery was quite remarkable; I was discharged from the hospital on the Thursday (my wife being discharged on the previous day). I made two visits to the outpatient clinic and one month later, I resumed work back in Addis Ababa!

True, my body is still full of shrapnel, in fact when I had an X-ray examination some years later the radiographer said that the film of my body looked like the sky at night with the lumps of shrapnel representing the stars. I also still get a few twinges in my right leg from time to time and am inclined to jump out of my skin if there are unexpected bangs, but otherwise my healing is complete. I have no flashbacks, and no nightmares.

Margaret and I attended a press conference at the hospital before she was discharged when all the media representatives were present. I tried to correct the wrong impression that had been given previously indicating that although in practice my movement had prevented my wife from having more serious injuries, it had happened simply as an instinctive action not by deliberate intent. My son-in-law had made some comments to me about arranging everything so that I could be back home for the FA Cup replay, and I repeated this as a joke during the interview. The Yorkshire Post picked up on this comment and arranged for the two of us to be the guest of the sponsors Littlewoods Pools at the replay. Although I was still quite weak I did manage to get to the game and enjoyed being there but not the result as Chesterfield did not repeat the form of the previous game and never challenged the opponents. My biggest problem was that lots of balloons were released in the stand and every time one burst, I jumped out of my skin and felt like running for cover.

The national publicity continued when Margaret and I were invited to appear as guests on The Big Breakfast, when on the famous settee we were interviewed by Sharon Davis about our Ethiopian experiences, Following on from that an organisation that reward acts of bravery decided to give Blair and me their Gold Award.

We had a lovely time we had with our wives at the award ceremony at the Café Royal in London. Sitting at our table was the actress Lois Maxwell, the original Miss Moneypenny and the lady on whom the character was based and had worked alongside Ian Fleming at MI5. An elderly lady, she was also being recognised for her bravery when she had resisted an attempt to steal her Rolex watch by two thugs on a motor cycle. She was far more deserving than we and was a great conversationalist as was Lois Maxwell. The Ethiopian Ambassador to London was also seated at our table.

Back in Ethiopia

Within one month of the hand grenade incident, I was back in Addis Ababa, picking up where I had left off and re-joining my other colleague, Roger. Blair was still in the UK recuperating from his injuries. When I called to see the Police Commissioner, he indicated his delight that I was back in the country, but again the conversation was quite short. He slapped his own gammy leg then did the same to my injured leg and said, "Mr John, we are brothers thank you for the sacrifice you are making for my country." But that was about the sum of his contribution to our conversation. As I have said before, he was a man of few words, but over the years he has been given increasing responsibility and when I last heard (2013) he was Head of State Security, but we are still brothers.

The Police Commissioners reaction to my return was not untypical of the general response amongst my Ethiopian friends and colleagues, although there was some surprise that I had decided to return to a country where I had been on the receiving end of such an atrocity. The fact was that Blair, and I felt no animosity to Ethiopians, and we had already grown to love the country and understood that what happened to us was outside the norm. I have no anger towards the people responsible for the incident who were thought to be members of the Oromia Liberation Front a movement seeking regional independence.

Shortly after our original arrival in Ethiopia we witnessed first-hand the debilitating effect of years of oppressive government. We had ordered a large amount of equipment for our own use and that of the people we were to train at the Ethiopian Police College. Getting agreement for the equipment to come through the customs officials proved extremely difficult, partly because we were not prepared to offer bribes and partly because no one was prepared to decide about important matters.

When people have been denied the right to use their initiative for more than a decade, they are not prepared to risk the possible negative outcomes of making the wrong decision. In these circumstances people look for ways of avoiding making any decision by finding some minor irregularity. For example, when we submitted our applications for resident's permits, they were turned down on the basis that they were not 'neat.' Eventually we found that the reason they were not acceptable is that the forms had been folded to fit in an envelope!

When our equipment arrived at the Police College on a large open top truck, we could find nowhere to store it, so it stood on the lorry at risk of being drenched and valuable equipment ruined, just because neither the Commandant nor the Head of Administration were present. Eventually Lieutenant T a young officer intervened and used his common sense to find the keys to an unused classroom and helped us unload the equipment.

Over time, as the people we worked with developed a trust in us the stories of what they had been exposed to during the years of the Dergue regime came into the open. The roads around the police college still bore the marks caused by the armoured tank tracks when the communists had moved in and taken over, but the human stories were the more revealing. For instance, one of the members of the staff had been sent for political re-education on three separate occasions.

When during the third session he realised that he would probably be redeployed from the police to the army and posted to the front line where he would be called upon to kill his fellow Tigrinyans who were leading the civil war against the communists, he decided it was time that he took a change of directions. Picking his time carefully he escaped and hid in caves as he made his way to the front line of the war and joined his kinsmen as a freedom fighter.

One of our drivers had also been subjected to political re-education after a fellow pupil at his school had reported to the authorities that he had spoken critically about the government. He was held prisoner for quite a long time until being released as a reward for writing a song in support of the communist government. Many families reported how sons had disappeared without any warning and when they enquired from the authorities all they received was a demand from the authorities for the cost of burying the bodies of the relatives that had gone missing.

After a while we discovered that the spy system favoured by the previous jurisdiction continued when we noticed that on each course, we had at least one participant who came from some agency other than the police and eventually we were told that they were government spies who had obviously reported back favourably to those who had instructed them to attend. We capitalised on this later when we encouraged the authorities to send trainers from other government organisations, including the military, civil service, customs, prisons, and immigration departments with a view to developing skills outside of the police.

Countries that are emerging from long periods of conflict or developing democracy for the first time in their history have problems arising from the effect of years of oppression. Citizens in the UK or other developed democracies who feel aggrieved can express their dissatisfaction to the decision makers, but how does a citizen of Ethiopia or Sudan complain to the government and what notice will they take? We have developed networks of organisations and pressure groups that are able to mobilise members in opposition to declared government policy they feel inappropriate or to influence the direction of future policies, but such civil society organisations are not so developed in the new democracies.

The greatest need in developing world organisations including the police and civil society is empowerment. I often liken the situation to a bird in a cage that has had the door opened to let it go free but remains in the cage because the world outside is unfamiliar and possibly dangerous.

Within a few weeks of our original arrival in Ethiopia, we had located and moved into houses in Addis Ababa. The three of us lived within a short distance of each other in a suburb of the city close to the airport road. My residence was a sixties style bungalow with two double and one single bedroom. Like most of our neighbours our houses were enclosed in a compound and mine came complete with a guard/gardener and a maid, neither of whom spoke a word of English. I confess that moving out of a hotel where the three of us were in adjoining rooms to my own house where conversation was impossible, and the only in-house entertainment was Ethiopian Television made me feel quite lonely.

Trying to explain to my maid what I wanted for meals proved quite a challenge. I was keen to have eggs for breakfast so the previous evening I had described and drawn eggs on a piece of paper. I was quite pleased that I seemed to have got the message across, so the next morning it was a bit of a shock to be presented with boiled potatoes for breakfast. I eventually achieved my objective by strutting around the house imitating a hen laying an egg and making the appropriate clucking noises, quite a sight!

Fortunately for me but not for her I soon found a replacement who spoke good English and had previously worked for an Italian family and had been taught her cooking skills by the Mama of that family. She remained in my employment until I left Ethiopia permanently in May 2000. Selam and her sister

Sarah became a part of my family and we also got to know her family as we visited them, and they visited us on a regular basis.

They were both relatively well paid but never had any money because they would hand over a substantial part of their income to family members who had none. This is a common feature of Africa where those who are in employment are the exception and where families support each other, which often results in one worker supporting half a dozen or more unemployed relatives. In the absence of the type of safety net that our government provide, there is no alternative but to support one another.

Ethiopians as a people are generally very friendly, kind, and hospitable people. Addis Ababa was a low crime area and our terrorist incident apart was a safe place to move around and enjoy life. We grew to love Ethiopia and thoroughly enjoyed our time there. There was no shortage of restaurants of a reasonable standard ranging from very expensive ones like the French restaurant at the Sheraton Hotel, or the Jakaranda at the Hilton Hotel with prices comparable to those in London or other capital cities to local inexpensive cafes housed in the lounge of a house.

Many restaurants featured local entertainment an essential element of which is always cultural dancing. Dancing in Ethiopia is a national institution with at least half a dozen regional versions. Each variant has unique movements and involves costumes that reflect those of the region. A night at a good local restaurant offers an amazing cultural experience and an interesting meal at prices that just about anyone could afford.

I will never forget the first time we saw Ethiopian dancing in a local restaurant. We had already started to discover something that many visitors to Ethiopian have written about; the women are general beautiful and the men handsome.

Naturally the most beautiful and handsome are inevitably included amongst those who dance for a living. There we were enjoying our meal whilst observing the early stages of the dancing performance. Both the men and women dressed in spectacular white outfits favoured in the Amhara region of Ethiopia. These have complex and colourful embroidered patterns featuring the various crosses used in the Ethiopian Orthodox Church and often include items of silver attached to the upper body part of the dresses of the women. The silver items shake and rattle when the women dance.

After a while the dancers move out from the stage area and go from table-to-table dancing in front of the customers who are expected to stand up and dance with them. Many of the regional dances feature upper body movement only, but the upper body moves at an incredible pace. Head, shoulders, and chest (bust in the case of the women) move in an extraordinary fashion. The overall effect when the women dance; their breasts bouncing around in time to the music and the silver attachments rattling away, is quite sensual, but believing that our reaction may not be the one intended we tried to focus just on the faces of the dancers for fear of being regarded as immoral westerners.

Over time we plucked up courage to talk to our male Ethiopian colleagues about our observations and they indicated that many of the dances were intended to be sensual and we should just enjoy it! I was never quite sure that we would have had the same response had we talked to the women though.

One of my favourite local restaurants where some of the best dancers, musicians and singers performed was a small intimate place that frequently got filled to overflowing. Customers sat on traditional Ethiopian stools around circular tables. When completely full it probably housed about forty people. The food, though local was good and inexpensive. If you do not enjoy spiced food, then it is advisable to go for fish. Typically, your circular table will be covered by a large circular metal tray onto which is placed all manner of Ethiopian food.

Your meal will be notable by the absence of cutlery and you will be expected to eat with your fingers but remember that culture dictates that you use your right hand, because your left hand is regarded as being 'unclean.'

You can wash down your meal with a local beer or wine. The best beers include 'Bedele' and 'St George' and the best wines include 'Gudar' (red) and 'Crystal' (white). If you prefer not to take alcohol there is a local, naturally carbonated water 'Ambo' which comes from the town of the same name. I remember turning on a tap on a visit to a hotel in the town and finding fizzy water coming out, nice to drink but not so good for washing your hair!

Following your meal, the dancers and singers will entertain you taking a tour of the entire nation of Ethiopia as they work through the various regional dances and songs. You will observe which regional grouping is most represented in the audience by their reactions. Getting on your feet and trying to emulate and copy the Ethiopian dancers will make you popular with the locals and give you a greater sense of engagement.

I recall attending a wedding in Addis Ababa when I spent quite a lot of my time dancing. As we were all leaving at the end of the event one of the principal guests approached me and said, "I don't know who you are, but I appreciate you."

When I enquired as to the reason for his observation he said, "You have the face of a foreigner, but as you danced, I saw that you had the heart of an Ethiopian."

Soon after I returned to Ethiopia following the hand grenade incident and whilst Blair was still recovering in the UK, our colleague Roger had to return home at short notice to attend a family funeral. I found myself contemplating a weekend on my own when I received a fax message from our masters at the Overseas Development Agency (ODA). They told me that they were cutting links with the Government of Ethiopia and ordering me to leave the country not later than the weekend (it was Thursday when I received the message), if necessary, by driving over the borders into Kenya. Having just narrowly escaping death, I was certainly not going to risk my life travelling through the bandit country I knew existed on the borders with Kenya.

I quickly established that there had been an incident in Addis Ababa where police enquiring into the terrorist attack at Blue Tops had shot a suspect who turned out to be one of Ethiopia's leading human rights activists. This had been done from a vehicle supplied by the British Government as part of our aid programme and pulling the plug on relationships with Ethiopia was the reaction back in London. These are the sort of actions that annoy me intensely and amount in my opinion to neo-colonialism. I determined that I was going to respond by gently reminding them of commitments that we had in Ethiopia.

Referring to their guidelines about what needed to be done before closing a contract, I pointed out that we had three houses we were renting along with domestic staff who would need notice of the termination of their contracts. Using their own documents as a source I explained that it would take at least a month to do everything we were required to do.

I had a discussion with the Commandant of the Police College and explained what was happening and submitted my written response via fax to my masters in the ODA. I then visited the British Embassy and had a discussion with our Ambassador, showing him the message received from ODA. He was extremely critical of the decision and indicated that there was likely to be a diplomatic incident in which we would be at the centre. He was delighted when I then supplied him with a copy of my response.

This gave me some reassurance because the status of the Foreign and Commonwealth Office is higher than that of the ODA and I knew I could count on support from the former. Back home I contacted Roger and Blair explaining what was happening and they responded by indicating that they would return to Addis on the first available flight.

Over the weekend I was informed by ODA that we would be given one month in which to shut down our work and commitments but was instructed not to continue work at or with the police college. Once my colleagues were back in Ethiopia, we agreed that we would carry on our work almost as if nothing had happened but put in extra effort to ensure that what we had started would continue in our absence. Deep in our hearts we believed that we would return at some time, although everyone else thought it would be the end of our project.

I had kept the Commandant of the Police College in the picture about the instructions from ODA and our responses to them. For his part he informed the Police Commissioner and he obviously had discussions with Government of Ethiopia. After a few days we were informed that their government were going to expel us from the country as spies and make us persona non grata, but this would only take effect from the day we had already planned to leave. This is what passed for diplomacy, tit for tat actions! Far from diplomatic, but all taking place because someone in ODA had not got any bottle! We were not exactly front-page news, but we were the subject of press reports and the same newspapers that had reported we were heroes after the hand grenade incident were now describing us as spies.

The three of us were informed that Government of Ethiopia were impressed by our work and had told our government that the only ODA initiative in Ethiopia they would really miss was ours and they would do all in their power to reinstate it.

We had lots of parties before leaving Ethiopia with our Ethiopian contacts giving us many presents of Ethiopian artifacts and there was a great amount of crying at the airport, particularly from our drivers and house staff, who would now be without work.

Back in the UK I started to look for work given that we were still paying off a substantial mortgage taken out when we restored the farmhouse were we now lived. I quickly got involved with a man who had produced a computer-based management and leadership programme, doing development work on the material, and delivering courses. The programme was interactive, and I thought it had great potential. I was working from home for most of the time and we agreed a daily rate for my work. It by no means amounted to full time work, but at the time it did bring me in enough to help me pay the mortgage and later my youngest daughter's wedding.

Within a few months of being pulled out of Ethiopia, our government realised that they had made a mistake in cutting themselves off from Ethiopia and they sought to open-up relations between the two countries. We found out later that the Ethiopians had agreed but on one condition, that the work at the Ethiopian Police College resumed, with the same personnel involved.

Within six months of being pulled out of the country as spies, we were back there undertaking our work and picking up where we had left off. Whilst Blair and Roger went back to Ethiopia full time, I worked about half of the time in Ethiopia and continued finding work on a contract basis back in the UK, mainly working with the computer-based training programme.

Joyful Chaos; An Account of an Ethiopian Wedding

Invitations to Ethiopian events of whatever kind, tend to arrive not long before the scheduled day, indeed I have in the past received written invitations after the event, having already attended and enjoyed the particular celebration but we had plenty of notice for the wedding of one of the police officers we worked alongside.

My first recollection of the wedding day was the thunderous noise of rain falling on the corrugated roof of my house at 4.00 a.m. or if you are Ethiopian, at the hour of ten in the night. This was rainy season rain arriving ahead of the rainy season, but in quantities usually preserved for that time of the year. The heavy rain continued almost without break throughout the day and the following night, eventually disappearing at 11.00 a.m. on Monday. My colleague Blai and I decided to take two vehicles in case either of us wanted to return home earlier. Pam his wife was accompanying him in the Toyota Landcruiser, and I was driving an old and rather tired Toyota Corrola.

If you are interested in language construction in Amharic my car would be called a "tinnish, nech machina" (small white car). A thirty-ton lorry is a "tillick machina" (large car). I can quite imagine the confusion that would occur when a traffic-policemen tries to describe a multi-vehicle pileup.

Driving in Addis Ababa is always a challenge. Trying to miss donkeys, sheep, cattle, pedestrians, potholes, and other vehicles tests one driving skills and nerves. In torrential rain, the skill required is increased considerably add to that two vehicles driving in convoy and you can imagine that we had an interesting journey.

Houses in Addis are contained within a compound the perimeter of which is often marked by a tall corrugated-iron fence. The size of the compound will determine either the size of the family, or the wealth of the occupants. The construction of the houses will add further to an estimate of the status and wealth of the people living there.

Walls constructed of stone or concrete blocks indicating more wealth than those with mud walls do. T, is a moderately wealthy person. His compound is large enough to house three separate buildings, none of which are constructed of mud. Speaking of mud there was a lot of it about and Pam began to have some doubts about the wisdom of wearing black suede shoes with medium sized heels. They are not exactly designed for coping with mud.

On arrival at the house, we saw many of our colleagues from the Ethiopian Police College, each of them greeting us with the statutory five kisses, (irrespective of the sex of the person you are meeting). Four of the men were dressed in identical black suites and bow ties. S explained that they were all "best men," but he was the lead best man, so to speak. All four of them were very handsome and smart, and full of the natural joy which is a characteristic of Ethiopian people.

T then arrived and greeted us. He was attired in a dress suit, mid green in colour with black bow tie and looked very smart in a sort of 60's Elvis Presley style, but minus the blue suede shoes. Following the statutory kisses and exchanges of compliments he accompanied us into the house and introduced us to his mother. She was dressed in traditional Amharan clothing and had a grace and charm that I have noted so often amongst Ethiopian women.

Once inside the house we could distinguish other signs of wealth like large rooms and good quality polished wooden floors. I complimented T on his house and he explained that it had been built about 60 years ago. To me that indicated he belonged to a family with some wealth and status, particularly at the time the house was built.

Whilst we waited to set off for the bride's house, we saw many members of T's extended family. There was a feeling of excitement, joy, and anticipation. I love to listen to Ethiopians talking to one another. Their conversation is always so animated, punctuated with laughter, smiles and obvious signs of love and friendship. The tonal variation in normal conversation is much greater than one would experience in England. This is especially true when women are talking. Their voices display natural characteristics of irrepressibly good humour, and affection. They laugh and we laugh with them.

S is showing some signs of organising things and before long we are told that it is time to go. As I get to my car, he informs me that T will travel with me along with three of the best men. My small white car is going to have a struggle negotiating the major potholes between the house and the main road, but why worry today is a happy day. This is Ethiopia the land of joyful chaos, worrying about trivial things is out of place here.

Because I have the groom as a passenger, I lead the way. Somewhere behind me will be Blair and Pam, who I have no doubt will also have collected a car full of passengers. On our way to the family home of the bride we meet up with her car. It is festooned in balloons, colourful ribbons, and other decorations. The car belongs to the Commandant of the Police College. I have no doubt that he would have been enjoying the celebrations himself but for the fact that he is in America. His car makes a nice wedding car, so does mine for that matter.

Blair has the senior bridesmaids with him, so he also has an official role as well. There does not appear to have been a plan involving the use of vehicles, it just happened, but with a little help from Samson and his fellow best men.

Parking is a problem at the bride's family home but eventually we all find somewhere in the middle of the mud at the roadside. To get to the house we walk down a steep track that has been surfaced with lumps of rock, now mud covered. Pam found it quite difficult keeping her feet. She explains that she recently purchased some good walking boots that would have been more suitable for the terrain. They would not have been appropriate with the dress, I think to myself.

As we approach the house some of the guests commence a rhythmic clapping. There are joined by drumming and singing. Amidst the laughter, the excitement, the joy, the mud, and the rain we now have African improvised music played and sung mainly by the younger members of the families.

The compound of the bride's family is rather smaller than that of her husband to be. The wall on either side of the compound has been used to create the sides of an extremely large tent. Poles have been placed from wall to wall and canvas spread over them. The floor of the compound is wet with sticky mud thanks to the overnight rain. A substantial amount of shredded wastepaper has been spread over the floor and is quite effective in soaking up the mud. We all slip and slide to our places accompanied by clapping, singing, and drumming. No one complains about the weather. We are happy we are celebrating who cares about the weather. Let the partying begin.

We have been given places of honour alongside the bride and groom, the best men and the bridesmaids. This happens very frequently in Ethiopia and I find it somewhat embarrassing, but I know that it is simply an expression of Ethiopian hospitality. I have often been told how honoured my Ethiopian hosts feel that I have visited their home or shared in their celebrations. I know in truth that the privilege and honour is all mine. Thank-you Ethiopia! Thanks for the love, friendship, hospitality, joy, and affection you have shared with me. I value it deeply and it will be remembered to my dying day.

This part of the celebration was recorded in the itinerary as a picnic, but it is much more than that. The bride and groom and their party lead the way to collect their food and we follow. The food is laid out on a large table. It is all traditional Ethiopian the core of it being injera and wat. Injera is the Ethiopian equivalent of bread and wat is a stew, often with meat and usually highly spiced. There are many other foods, all very Ethiopian. My first selection is a roll of injera with which I line the plate the other food I select is then placed on top of the injera.

We return to our places and enjoy our food and take in the atmosphere. Food is eaten with your right hand. There is no cutlery. Consuming a stew with your fingers is a skill that takes a while to develop. I am fairly accomplished at it. I tear off a piece of injera and grasp some wat in the injera and pop the lot in my mouth. Handsome S from time to time goes through the first part of the process but instead of popping the package in his own mouth; he pops it in the mouth of one or other of the senior bridesmaids.

I have read somewhere that this is an expression of love. It appears that S loves all three and they love him. All three are dressed in dark green, long velvet dresses with side splits and decorated in white sashes. They each have identical diamond earrings. To say that they were beautiful would be something of an understatement. Their skin is like velvet soft chocolate. Their eyes have a magnetic influence and mine must be on positive not negative poles because they are attracted rather than repulsed.

The younger bridesmaids are dressed in plum red dresses and there are three or four of them. They are also beautiful, but the mature ones take my eye more, given my own age. The bride is resplendent in her elaborate white dress. She is beautiful, but does not smile very much, whereas the girls in green seem to be smiling all the time. Maybe it is the trick of those eyes!

I am conscious that I need to try and paint for you a word picture of this event, because it is so completely different from anything you will experience in

England. This wedding is not silver service. The plates are plastic and as you have heard, there is no cutlery. There are no tables and therefore no damask tablecloths or candelabra. We hold the plate in our left hand and eat with our right hand. This mud floored, canvas covered space, between two high walls is packed with people and they are all Ethiopians, other than us.

We have about one hundred Ethiopians for each "forenji" (the word used to describe foreigners). Many of the Ethiopian women are wearing their traditional dresses; White cotton with colourful embroidery representing their original region. The whole meal may be summarised in the title "Joyful chaos." That description comes to my mind during the meal, and I tell Pam, and she also seems to share my impression.

For drink we are provided with "tella." This is a homemade beer. Various leaves are soaked in water and then mashed and drained. The fluid that is left is fermented and the result is tella. I have been offered it on many occasions. I always accept, but drink relatively little. For one thing, I am not sure of the alcohol content and for another my colleague Blair was once so ill from drinking the fluid that at first, he thought he was going to die, and afterwards felt so ill that he wished he could die. One of the problems with the drink is that one has no guarantee about the water from which it is made, or on the fermenting process. This tella was to my liking and I had one full glass, but no more.

Towards the end of the meal a group of young men and women join us and sing traditional Ethiopian wedding songs to the accompaniment of drums. Some of the best men and bridesmaids get up and dance. I would like to join them but feel a little self-conscious so instead I imitate the upper body movement, shaking the shoulders. I notice that many guests are amused by my actions. I laugh with them and they mimic back to me my actions. We laugh even the more!

We eventually leave the house to visit another location for what is described as the signing of the register. The journey is undertaken in convoy, I am the second vehicle behind the lead car that carries the bride and groom. Pam is with me along with one of the best men. The rain is torrential. Our venue for the next ceremony is like a small park designed for weddings. Today is the last day for weddings for quite some time.

There are periods when tradition says that you do not get married and one of them starts tomorrow. There seems to be a last-minute rush to get married, or perhaps it would be better described as a stampede. The little wedding park is bursting at the seams with couples wanting to "pledge their troth." We are in a queue to get married and not at the front. The bride and grooms' cars are allowed into the wedding arena, for want of a better name. So yet again I have a privileged position. It is clear two types of weddings are taking place simultaneously, civil, and religious. A lot of the activity is taking place in the open air and therefore under a rain torrent of equatorial proportions. The only acknowledgement of the rain is a forest of umbrellas and extensive use by the ladies of plastic bags to cover up their expensively prepared coiffures.

Another wedding car pulls in alongside mine and is immediately surrounded by a small flock of Ethiopian Orthodox Priests. The word flock is not selected out of disrespect for the Orthodox Church. I do not know that there is a collective word for priests. A flock does at least have a Biblical influence, although perhaps the priests would consider themselves shepherds rather than sheep. Anyway, these sheep/shepherds are not exactly dumb. They are singing and dancing to the accompaniment of large drums. The effect is intoxicating.

I enjoy listening to and watching the priests, drummers, and singers. The rain does not dampen their spirits or mine. Eventually we enter the building for civil marriages, pushing our way through the crowd to get there. The ceremony is brief. At key moments men and women guests burst into spontaneous applause and the women participate in African intoning. I think that is what it is called (voice modulating from the back of the throat—done throughout Africa).

We now have an interesting interlude whilst we get all the thirty or so cars in the correct order. Leading is a pick-up truck with video camera man in the back. He is there to video the procession. The bride and groom are next, followed by me and then Blair with the beautiful bridesmaids and so on. There follows a lengthy journey out into the country. Every one of the cars has their lights and indicators flashing and horns sounding. When we pass people on the roadside they applaud and sing traditional wedding songs.

We drive into the centre of Addis and go around some of the big traffic islands three or four times just for the sheer fun of it. Because this is the last day of the wedding season, we meet up with many more other wedding processions all doing the same thing, but on different routes. It must be some sort of a miracle that Addis does not come to a standstill.

Our next part of the wedding is marked in our itinerary as 'Recreation.' We will probably need it after this journey. When we arrive at the Recreation Park, we are too early for them. Never mind folks we will just drive out into the country and kill a bit of time. So off we go halfway to Ambo, thirty plus cars all in convoy, before turning around and coming back. This time they are ready for us. We are directed to a circular area covered by a thatched roof but with open sides. The perimeter is a circular seat covered in dried grass. We sit on this facing inward with the bride and groom seated side by side on chairs opposite the entry point to the circle.

Blair asks M one of our colleagues at the Ethiopian Police College what we will be doing here, and he replies, "Killing time until dinner" and laughs. We find it hilarious, but we are not sure whether he is joking or not. After a while we discover that the Recreation Park is also a 'Tech Bete.' Bete is the word for house and tech is a moderately strong alcoholic beverage made from honey. It is yellow in colour and tastes sweet and pleasant to my pallet, but it is advisable not to consume too much, particularly when you are driving, and the day is still young. We are also served with more food, pieces of warm stewed mutton eaten off the bone. I laugh when I see one person return a well chewed piece of bone to the dish and take another untouched one. I wonder if another person may try to extract a little more meat from the same piece of bone. Each time they come with more meat I make sure I select a piece with no teeth marks!

A group of youngsters including the beautiful bridesmaids start to sing. The audience laughs at the singing and M tells me that the singers are insulting us. They are saying that we are like fat pigs coming to a wedding celebration and eating all the food but not dancing. When they start to dance, I join in, I try to avoid any further insults. Later, I teach another colleague from Sendafa an English song "Show me the way to go home."

I think it might be appropriate for him since he has consumed four bottles of tech. There are more songs, and everyone gets insulted other than the bride and groom. We laugh a lot and discover that this part of the programme is a little more than filling the time.

It is beginning to go dark when we leave the Recreation Park and head for the home of T and his bride. The journey is undertaken at a slow pace with even more blasting of horns and flashing of lights. The rain resumes having treated us kindly at the Recreation Park. Dinner in the evening is like our lunch during the day. We have the same sort of food and the same process. The difference is we now have a disco featuring Ethiopian cultural dancing.

During the meal, I have exchanged glances with the bridesmaids and received back some lovely smiles that I think no more about. During my first attempt to dance I find one of the bridesmaids pushes herself alongside me and stays there, quite close. I look at her and she smiles, and her eyebrows lift-up as she smiles. I think this could be intended as a signal, but I am not sure what, although I think I have a good idea. It could of course be the delusions of an old man. I think it would be a good idea to sit down and try not to look in her direction anymore and I take a well-earned rest.

I get back on the dance floor and concentrate on dancing with the men. This happens in Ethiopia and is a sign of brotherly love. We have a good laugh at my feeble attempts to imitate a form of dancing they have perfected from being small children. More people are now dancing, and I move into another space and find a tall attractive Ethiopian girl in a red trouser suite offering to show me how to dance with a woman. After a while I say "Baka" (enough) and sit down. My minor problems apart and they were probably more imagined than real, I have enjoyed myself immensely.

The final part of the wedding is the cutting of a large circular bread cake and the supplying of a 'bread name' to the bride. Each side of the family supplies three suggestions for names for the bride and the assembled company vote on the name to be selected. The chosen name was that of the groom's mother. To be supplied with a piece of the wedding bread you are asked to state the new name. I succeeded with a little help from the traffic policemen sitting next to me.

I said my farewell to the bride and groom, complimenting them on the day's events and wishing them a happy future together. When I got to my car, I saw the woman in red and panicked. I said "Chow" and jumped in my car, but I had promised to wait for Blair. Some boys knocked on my door and I opened my window to hear one of them say "You want business?" I was not sure what business he had in mind but seeing the women in red standing nearby I decided to drive to the top of the road and wait for Blair at a safe distance.

At the top of the road, I waited for him. When he arrived, he told me that he had some passengers to drop off on the way. He was not as familiar with the road as I was, so I led the way, and we agreed that he would flash his lights when he wanted to stop to drop off his passengers. About half the way home he duly flashed his lights and we stopped. Two female passengers got out of his car and waved to me. One was the 'lady in red.' All she wanted was a lift home! My mother would have said, "There's no fool like an old fool," and as was often the case, she would have been right.

It was still raining when I went to bed at about 10.30pm. What a day! It was still raining at 4.00 a.m. when I woke up and started a few hours of processing between my bed and the toilet. It was not food poisoning or too much drink. I knew from past experience that too much highly spiced food would disagree with my system and I was not disappointed, but it was all very worthwhile.

Joyful chaos, that expression just about sums up an Ethiopian wedding, perhaps it sums up Ethiopia!

A Difficult Week in Addis Ababa

Living away from home can be difficult and my account of one week illustrates the nature of the problem. I spent most of it in hospital in almost continuous excruciating pain. Just to record what happened, I was fine on Monday and went to bed about 10.30 p.m. with no sign of a problem. I woke up at about midnight with this terrible pain in my stomach. Given my propensity for upset stomachs I just assumed that I was suffering from food poisoning or severe indigestion. I spent the next five hours trying to be sick or to empty my bowels neither, of which I succeeded in doing. Some of this time I was leaning over the toilet bowl and putting my fingers down my throat to try and make myself sick. At other times, I was walking around the house to try and take my mind of the pain. At no time did I manage any sleep. It felt as though my stomach was on fire and when your stomach is as big as mine is, that is a big fire!

By the time five o'clock arrived I was getting quite desperate, clearly whatever I was suffering from was rather more than an upset stomach. What was I going to do about it? How was I going to get help? I decided that my best option was to ring Blair and get him to take me to a hospital. The problem was that I could not disturb him from his slumbers. After numerous attempts, I decided I would have to try the British Embassy. That proved a waste of time, there was a recorded message giving an emergency number, but there was no reply from that number either. Eventually, just before 6.00 a.m. I managed to contact Blair and he then took me to the St. Gabriel Private Hospital, where there was a doctor on duty.

She thought I might have some sort of abdominal obstruction and arranged x-rays, but no treatment and therefore no relief for the pain. They eventually decided that the doctor's diagnosis was probably correct and gave me some treatment, including a pain-killing jab at about 9.00 a.m. I had suffered nine hours of sheer agony.

Ultra-sound examination later in the day revealed one and possibly two kidney stones with a possibility that they could be obstructed. The pain killers worked but only for two or three hours, after which I was again in agony and not wanting to demand injections too often, I spent about half of the next two days with no real relief.

An IVP examination was scheduled for Thursday morning and on Wednesday I was instructed to eat only a small amount of food, and drink only a small amount of fluid. I did not feel much like eating—it was I thought, pointless putting much into the bonfire that represented my stomach, but I felt like drinking a fountain dry.

About midnight on Wednesday, I was requested to drink a bottle of castor oil. Thick, horrible tasting oil did not exactly quench my thirst, and it set in motion a sequence of events that I find difficult to describe. My stomach started to sound like a volcano about to erupt and produced a separate set of pains in my abdomen—sleep was impossible.

At four o'clock I had my first enema. What a shocking experience! I am told that some people volunteer for them at health farms to clear out their system. They must have something wrong with their heads as well as their stomachs. The next problem was holding out long enough to get to the toilet. Whilst the nurse was still putting fluid into me, I felt I was getting desperately close to flushing her out of the bedroom altogether. Taking short breaths and holding on like grim death seemed to do the trick.

When I eventually got to the toilet, well what can I say? The speed at which my bowels emptied and the force of the expulsion of it all, left me thinking that I was at risk of turning into a supercharged rocket and disappearing through the toilet ceiling!

When I was a child and sick—my mother would hold my hand and it did not seem so bad. At home, my wife would have comforted me. In Addis Ababa I am on my own and I cried out "O God let me die," but he did not, and the emptying eventually stopped. Believe it or not immediately afterwards I slept for an hour which was the only sleep I got that night.

At six o'clock I had my second enema. Well, when you have had one the second is not quite so bad, but rest assured I am never going to volunteer for that treatment, however beneficial it might be.

At eight o'clock I had a normal abdominal x-ray—to check if my stomach had been properly emptied. Whilst waiting I said a quick prayer something like this "Lord you remember that termination request few hours ago? Keep it on hold because if this chap says I have to have another lot of preparation—I still might want to join you" Happily I was told that everything was OK.

An IVP examination is a form of x-ray where you have a dye injected into your blood and a series of pictures are taken over a specified time scale with the aim of identifying, (in my case) whether the kidney stones were being obstructed. It was slightly nauseating but by comparison with everything that had gone before was quite tame.

Back in my room I was still in pain throughout Thursday, but not quite, I thought with the same intensity as before. Despite this Thursday night required pain-killing treatment and offered little sleep.

When Friday morning dawned, the new day brought welcome relief from the pain and the news from the IVP revealed I had probably already passed the kidney stones out of my system. They had certainly been there on Tuesday. I have no doubt that they exited my system at about 4.05 a.m. on Thursday morning! I certainly knew I had parted with a hell of a lot of something.

If you are considering going to a health farm and they suggest that an enema might be good for you—I have some advice—treat it like marriage—do not enter into it lightly.

Ethiopia for the Tourist

Ethiopia is an extraordinarily beautiful country and quite apart from the natural beauty of the scenery there are many places of historical interest. The 'historical route' normally involves a day's drive from Addis Ababa to Lake Tana for the first couple of nights in the tour, before taking in the ancient capital of Gondar and the rock hewn churches of Lallibela.

I recall making some of that journey along with my wife when attention to detail on our part prevented serious problems later in the journey. Our vehicle was an old and high mileage Toyota Landcruiser that started its' life on a relief programme during one of the frequent periods of famine. To say that it was a well-worn vehicle would have been an understatement.

Addis Ababa is situated in the central highland area of the country and surrounded by mountains. The first part of our journey took us along steep and winding roads out of the city and over the Entoto Mountain. Whilst we were negotiating these precipitous roads, I was sure that I had felt some unusual vibration under the front of the vehicle. Our driver was reluctant to stop because of the long journey ahead of us, but when I insisted, he discovered that a part of the steering assembly had broken away from the bodywork of the car, so it was back to the garage for a quick welding job, before restarting our journey.

The Entoto Mountains feature large areas of eucalyptus forests, used to provide firewood for the citizens of Addis Ababa. As you travel out of the city you will observe donkeys heavily laden with firewood and probably have some sympathy for the donkeys which often seemed to be overworked. You will also observe women and children carrying huge piles of sticks on their backs, the only means they have of obtaining money sufficient to put a meal on the table for their families. Sadly, they suffer greatly from the debilitating effect of carrying heavy weights on their backs from childhood and end up being crippled by arthritic conditions.

Beyond the mountains that fringe Addis Ababa, your journey takes you across an extensive high plateau, dissected by the occasional river. The plateau areas are used extensively by the local farmers to grow crops of barley and teff, the latter being a grain crop peculiar to Ethiopia and the source of the flour used to make injera, one of the staple foods for locals. They also graze sheep and cattle on these highland plateaus. There are no field boundaries, so the grazing cattle could in theory eat up the grain crop, and to avoid this, the livestock is often tended by the children of the family.

Throughout any journey in Ethiopia, you will observe people at the side of the roads and close by, there are small settlements of mud walled circular houses. The natural friendliness of Ethiopians will be evident when they wave to your vehicle and shout some greeting. One of the most frequently used greeting is "You, you," which may well be the only English word in their vocabulary. Alternatively, they often shout 'Ferenji' which means foreigner. One of my responses to the later was to shout back 'Abasha' a derivation of the original name of the country, Abyssinia.

Most journeys across Ethiopia are on dirt roads and therefore in the rainy season they become quite difficult to traverse and in the dry season extremely dusty resulting in your vehicle leaving a dust storm behind. Overtaking through a dust storm is quite a difficult manoeuvre to undertake, but at least you have plenty of notice with the evidence of a moving vehicle being visible from at least half a mile away.

With no air conditioning in our elderly Toyota our dry season journey to Lake Tana, was undertaken with the windows open to keep us cool, but this also allowed the dust to penetrate our vehicle and on our arrival at our destination, our skin colour was not appreciably different from the locals.

Two to three hours out of Addis Ababa the journey to Lake Tana brought us to the Blue Nile Gorge, a dramatic geographical feature where the Blue Nile River has cut about three and a half thousand feet into the surrounding highlands. Looking across from one side of the gorge it looks and is quite close, but it takes around two hours or more to get down one side and back up the other. It is a spectacularly beautiful route featuring wonderful views, frightening stretches of roadway clinging to the edge of sheer drops, and total climatic change, with grazing grass and grain on the plateau and pineapple, bananas, and other tropical crops around the riverbanks at the bottom of the gorge.

At the far side of the Blue Nile Gorge is the town of Dejen, where we decided to take a break. The town looks like the set of a 'Spaghetti Western' movie with drab wooden buildings on either side of the road, outside of which are covered verandas, where locals sit and watch the world go by. We selected one such veranda which turned out to have a floor covered in cut grass, ready for a 'coffee ceremony.'

Coffee was used as a drink first in Ethiopia and the Kaffa area of the country gave its name to the beverage. Ethiopia grows some of the best coffee in the world and it is the nation's leading export earner. The 'coffee ceremony' is a regular feature of Ethiopian life and my wife often spent a substantial proportion of her day when visiting me, attending the houses of my Ethiopian friends experiencing coffee ceremony hospitality. Each ceremony takes at least an hour, involving roasting the green coffee beans on a charcoal fired burner and hand grinding the freshly roasted coffee.

Special coffee pots, with many regional variations in design are then filled with water and an appropriate amount of ground coffee added, whereupon the pots are placed on the charcoal burner until the water boils and the coffee is ready to drink. The coffee is served with sugar but without milk in small cups without handles. Three cups of coffee are normally drunk using the same coffee grains to which more water is added before being warmed up again, so the first cup is strong, but the subsequent ones get weaker as more water is added to the original ground coffee.

Typically, the lady host will have spread cut grass on the ground and added flower petals in front of the burner where she prepares the ceremony. She will also wear traditional dress. As the coffee roasts and gives off a beautiful aroma, she will waft the smoke from the beans in front of you so that your anticipation is built up. The coffee ceremony is a very relaxing and pleasant way to experience Ethiopian hospitality. Many hotels feature the ceremony, but the context is better understood and experienced as a guest of a local resident in a typical Ethiopian home. Given the hospitable nature and generosity of Ethiopians we were never short of such invitations, in fact fitting work into the available spaces was sometimes quite a problem!

Having experienced seeing a large rat jump out of grass gathered for a coffee ceremony in the past and my wife's well-known fear of the rodents, I quickly shuffled my feet around before she arrived and sat down. The residents of Dejen obviously had not seen many 'forenjis' previously so quite a lot of them stopped by for a chat, even though they spoke no English. Our driver gave one of them a sandwich I had given him, obviously, the ham was not to his liking, but the stranger quickly disposed of it. Ignorance is bliss and little did he know that he had just eaten pig meat, 'unclean' both for a Muslim and an Ethiopian Orthodox Christian.

Passing through one of the small towns on our way to Lake Tana, we came across a funeral procession. The deceased person was being carried on his bed at the head a long line of people. The emphasis of the procession seemed to be celebration of the deceased person's life rather than mourning his death, because there was a lot of singing and dancing.

Our delayed start to the journey resulted in a later that intended arrival at our destination, one of the many hotels on the shore of Lake Tana at the town of Bahir Dar. Although it was dark before we arrived, we did notice that as we got nearer to the lake, so the vegetation changed, and the soil was obviously more fertile.

Crops of maize and sorghum were being grown and we noted that structures of bamboo poles with a platform above the level of the crops were dotted around and from time to time we spotted one or two boys sitting on the platforms. Eventually we realised that they were armed with slings and stones which they used to scare away monkeys or birds which would otherwise eat some of the harvest. Some people holiday in Ethiopia just to see the birdlife where there are calculated to be more than eight hundred and fifty species.

As the light started to fade and we drew near to the lakeside town of Bahir Dar we observed farmers driving their cattle back to the enclosures that surround their homesteads or carrying a wooden plough on their shoulders as they returned from a day turning the soil using oxen and ploughs, like those that would have been used many centuries before. We could also see the womenfolk cooking the evening meal over open fires and smell the very African mixture of burning wood and cooking food.

Most of the hotels in Bahir Dar are situated on the shores of the lake with gardens that front the lakeside. During daylight hours, it was a wonderful experience to sit by the water and watch the world go by. Local papyrus reed boats ply between the shore and the closest of the thirty-seven islands located in Lake Tana, the largest in Ethiopia, carrying firewood, charcoal, fruit, and vegetables and sometimes even animals. They look very unstable but as the locals have been using them for centuries accidents are few and far between.

Water based birds including fish eagles and kingfishers dive into the water and bring out wriggling fish trying to avoid being the next meal for the bird. In some of the trees we spotted the nests of weaver birds hanging in profusion. At night, however it is a good idea to avoid the waterside due to the abundant supply of mosquitoes and other insects that clearly enjoy feeding on white flesh!

Lake Tana is one thousand eight hundred metres above sea level, some seventy-five kilometres long and sixty kilometres wide. There are numerous monasteries along the shore of the lake and on some of the islands and a visit to at least one is an essential part of a period at Bahir Dar. We chose to visit the church of Ura Kidhane Gebriel which is situated on the Zege Peninsular. We joined up with another couple to hire a motorboat complete with crew and capable of accommodating twenty or more people for an afternoon visit. The round trip of outward and return journey and a reasonable amount of time for the visit takes about three hours.

The boat journey is quite impressive offering a view back over the coastline and out into the lake that is more expansive than the one available from the shoreline. Our arrival at our intended arrival point was greeted by lots of locals lining the shore all hoping to benefit from the arrival of the wealthy tourists by offering some local products for sale including religious pictures painted in very bright colours on goat skins (miniatures of the ones we would see later in the church) or handmade baskets and knitted scarves. Others offered to be our guides for the visit.

Getting off the boat and onto the shore involved an interesting arrangement. Metal chairs were used as stepping-stones, but as these were deposited onto surfaces that were loose and often uneven, the whole experience involved some strange balancing acts and not a little faith in the powers of the Almighty!

The walk from the shoreline to the church takes about half an hour and follows a well walked path through tropical rain forest. As we walked, we saw monkeys following our progress from the safety of the canopy of trees above us and on one occasion in a small clearing we saw an amazing variety of large and colourful butterflies. Children walked alongside us but were friendly and not demanding.

There is a relatively small entrance charge for the church, but this comes with the supply of a guide, usually a junior priest to take you around and explain what you see. The church is noted for some wonderfully colourful five-hundred years old murals.

On our return journey to the church one of the boys who had walked with us asked for our address so that he could practise his English by writing to us. These requests are quite frequent and generally we had batted them off but on this occasion my wife did supply him with our details and over a few years afterwards she corresponded with him.

Lake Tana is the source of the Blue Nile and on one of our journeys we observed where the river leaves the lake on its long journey to the Mediterranean via Khartoum where it joins the White Nile and Egypt. At this point the locals told us that you may often spot the hippopotamus, but they were either very shy or had moved elsewhere because we never spotted any. Finding the source of the Nile had excited many of the great explorers who were not aware of the fact that there are two distinct sources, but we found it very easily—the nature of modern travel and a shrinking world!

Just thirty kilometres from the source of the river is located the Blue Nile Falls or Tis Isat (water that smokes). We drove out to the nearby village where we found lots of local craft produce available for purchase. There were lots of scarves in typical Ethiopian colours. Many youngsters offered to be our guide and we duly selected a couple of these volunteers to accompany us. Our visit was timed shortly after the rainy season which is a good time to visit because of the heavy volume of water, makes the falls even more spectacular than at other times of the year.

The walk from the village takes about half an hour and passes over an attractive 17th century castellated bridge known as the Portuguese bridge. As we walked along towards the waterfalls, we could hear the roar of the water in the distance and we also passed by 'tuckuls' where the locals were weaving the scarves we had observed for sale when we parked our vehicle.

The roar from the falls became much louder as we approached them and for the last half mile of the journey, we were aware of a fine mist falling on us. We rounded a corner and there in front of us was this amazing expanse of cascading water and a rainbow created as the sun shone through the water vapour. The falls are about four hundred metres wide and involve a drop of about forty-five metres down a sheer cliff.

Looking down into the abyss below us we saw the water foaming and gushing into the gorge that leads away from the falls. On our side of the water at lower levels were some small areas covered in lush grass and vegetation obviously benefiting from the continuous supply of water created by the spray from the nearby torrents. It is a truly spectacular sight!

At the falls and along the entire journey to and from Lake Tana we saw evidence of the influence of the river with maize, banana and other crops growing at the sides of the road and many birds displaying bright colours including red, blue, green, and yellow.

From Lake Tana we continued our journey to Gondar one of the former capital cities of Ethiopia. We were travelling for the greater part of the daylight hours and during much of the journey the lake remained visible alongside our route which gives some indication of its size.

Along the road from Bahir Dar, we saw evidence of the civil war with abandoned military machinery at the sides of the road. It is a disturbing fact that the people of Ethiopia are probably still paying the Russians for the hardware supplied to a previous regime. The so-called great powers of the world have a lot to answer for in the way that they have helped to perpetuate wars across Africa through finance and hardware. Whilst these issues are immensely complex it may well have been better for most Africans if we had not engaged ourselves in these arguments.

The Goha Hotel in Gondar is located on the top of a hill overlooking the town and for that reason alone it is probably the best place to stay. The Goha group is a national chain of government owned hotels and may be found in many towns across the nation, but particularly in the north. Our visit coincided with a wedding reception over the weekend and as most of the activities were outside in the grounds, we observed the celebrations, which added to the delight of our stay.

Gondar was founded by Emperor Fasilades around 1635 and it is famous for the number of medieval castles there are and for the decorations in the Church of Debra Berhan Selassie (light of the Trinity). There is a pleasant little coffee bar/café in the town square where we negotiated the services of a local guide. The cost was insubstantial, but the benefits were considerable as he guided us professionally through the visits we made during the greater part of a day.

Although the castles are no longer in use, they are maintained sufficiently for the shell to remain intact and for the public to climb up the towers from where excellent views are available and we could envisage the former grandeur of the area. After our tour of the castles, we continued to the baths of Fasilades, which feature a small castellated building which is in the centre of a large pool surrounded by a wall designed to retain the water.

The whole object of the construction was so that baths could be taken in privacy. The baths are now used for the religious purposes of baptism into the Ethiopian Orthodox Church. Most of the year the pool is empty of water, however in January each year the festival of 'Timkat' is celebrated at the baths of Fasilades amongst great splendour and excitement. The people gather on the eve of the celebration and sleep by the edge of the water so that they are the first to be baptised when the festivities begin. Our guide told us how he attends the event every year and it was clearly a highlight in his annual calendar.

Although our visit to Gondar did not coincide with the Timkat ceremony which comes early in the New Year, we have attended the celebrations in Addis Ababa which are held on a former racecourse. Thousands of people attend the event parading from their various churches in bright costumes lead by priests wearing expensively decorated and colourful robes. Just because we were very obviously visitors the locals directed us to the front of the crowd, where a rope barrier prevents the priests from being crushed by the onlookers. A huge portable pool had been erected and at the appropriate time the priests splashed those who were nearby in the annual baptism ritual. The people are driven into a state of frenzy by the excitement of the day. It is certainly worthwhile planning any visit to Ethiopia to coincide with this festival.

The walls surrounding the water of the baths are notable for the way in which huge tree roots cover them—it's quite a strange but impressive sight and a clear indicator of how long the structure has been in existence.

Our next visit was to the Ethiopian Orthodox Church of Debra Berhan Selassie. Churches in Ethiopia often have quite elaborate and very colourful paintings and this one is no exception. The entire roof of the church is covered by hundreds of angel-like faces each one distinct and giving the impression that each angel is looking in a different direction. The mural brings to life the passage in the Bible where the writer describes how the angels keep watch over us.

A service was taking place during the period of our visit, but as is usual the activity was in the grounds and not inside the building. Ethiopian Orthodox practices have a clear link with Judaism, so men and women worship separately, and there are parts of the building that are reserved for the priests alone. Often at the very core of the building is the 'holy of holies' which may only be entered by the senior priest on special days in the year.

Generally, tourists continue their journey from Gondar through the majestic grandeur of the Simien Mountains to Lallibella for a visit to the famous rock hewn churches and from there to Axum where the Queen of Sheba is said to have lived and where the sacred Ark of the Covenant is claimed to be hidden in the Church of St Mary, but sadly my leave time was limited and we returned to Addis Ababa, retracing our outward journey.

Working at the Ethiopian Police College

The focus of our work in Ethiopia was building the capacity of the Ethiopian Police College to develop a community approach to policing. The college is located in the small town of Sendafa about forty kilometres north of Addis Ababa. The daily journey from Monday through to Saturday (no five-day weeks in Ethiopia) was a delight, offering a visual exposure to the difficulties and delights of the country and the obvious contrasts with life in Britain.

Farming in Ethiopia is conducted just as it would have been thousands of years ago. We would often observe huge areas of land being ploughed by teams of oxen pulling wooden ploughs. Sheep and cattle grazed the open grassland under the supervision of the farmer or more likely his small sons.

Our journey took us through a village where there was a large abattoir and as a result a long line of butcher's shops. However, some description is needed to overcome any impression that these resemble what may be observed in Britain. Firstly, there was no electricity, so consequently no refrigerators, and secondly there were no fancy marble or wooden slabs. A whole side of beef is fastened to a rough framework of wooden poles all out in the blazing sunshine. Passing one day we would observe that the meat was bright red which meant that it had just arrived from the abattoir but as the days passed so the meat got darker in colour and we guessed less healthy to eat.

At various points along our journey, we passed through river valleys and here we would see the women and children carrying water either in locally produced clay water pots or plastic containers from the river. Often the women folk would be observed washing their clothes in the same river and the cattle drinking from the same river. Hence, water born infections are a regular feature of life in Ethiopia.

The road often left much to be desired. Although it had once been surfaced with tarmac in places this had been washed away by the floods that come during every rainy season. I can recall journeys where the water running down the mountains through which the road passed had cut a new river course straight across the road, making the journey impossible other than with four wheeled drive vehicles. The amount of surface water created at these times has to be seen to be believed and the huge roadside drainage culverts become blocked by debris and silt, every year and have to be dug out afterwards. In the dry season, the temperature is sometimes so hot that the sun melts the tar and breaks up the surface.

Africans generally are entrepreneurial by nature and Ethiopia is no exception. Roadside markets and traders sell just about every commodity that one would wish to purchase.

Returning to Ethiopia for some follow up work during the early part of 2009, I observed a transformation taking place on the road to Sendafa. New dual carriageways have been or are in the process of being completed. New housing estates have been built and there are obvious signs of a developing economy.

The college is housed in substantially built and reasonably maintained sixties style blocks of classrooms and accommodation. I understand that the complex was built by the Swedish government as part of an aid programme. By comparison with the buildings housing the Nigerian Police College in Jos, it is palatial. I really cannot understand how the Government of Nigeria have allowed their police college to deteriorate to such an extent when they have so much more wealth than Ethiopia.

On our original arrival at the police college in Ethiopia there was very little equipment available and the quality of training had suffered as a result. Consider what it was like to be taught how to preserve a crime scene and collect evidence when there was no equipment available. Everything was undertaken from an entirely theoretical point of view and practical exercises were a sham with photographs taken using an imaginary camera, or with a very old camera but no film in it.

Many of the staff members had a collection of different degrees, but it was difficult to see any of them putting into practice what they had learned. In Ethiopia, as in most other parts of the developing world the possession of a degree was seen as the only certain way of ensuring gainful employment and there is no recognition of the fact that work ability is not necessarily related to academic achievement. Truth was that many of the degrees were awarded by universities in Soviet countries and lacked credibility elsewhere.

When teaching how to carry out a training needs analysis I recall one such a graduate of several Soviet universities explaining to me that he did not require the training because the subject had been included in one of his courses in Bulgaria. He could certainly explain the theories associated with training needs analysis, but when tasked with undertaking one as part of the course he had no idea where to start let alone how to complete the task.

Throughout my experiences in Africa, I have found the same problem. Learning is assumed to have taken place when a person is able to describe the theory associated with the given topic, but the model of learning we espoused was that true learning has only taken place when behaviour has changed. In every area we were teaching we would try to ensure that the participants could demonstrate what they had learned through practical exercises.

Whilst most people we worked with at the Ethiopian Police College were supportive of what we were doing, a minority remained unconvinced and probably wished that they were still being sent on courses in the Soviet Union.

Quite early in our time in Ethiopia we were able to identify a small group of very able junior police officers who we felt would be able to carry forward the work in the long term and we did our best to encourage and support these officers. The four most impressive of these were D, A, T and S and what has happened to them over the years since we completed our project in 2000 is in some way indicative of the problems they encounter. They worked with me on a consulting project during the final few months of our stay at the college. I was commissioned by the then Organisation for African Unity (OAU) now the Africa Union, to undertake a security analysis for their newly extended premises in Addis Ababa, produce an operational manual for all security staff and design a training course for all security personnel.

Ethiopian Police officers were (and still are) very poorly paid and it was virtually impossible to raise a family on the pay of a junior officer, so they undertake other work supplementing their income. D was already working as a part time lecturer in the University of Addis Ababa and had been engaged as a consultant by a Swedish based organisation working with street children and A and S were looking to find similar opportunities. I saw the OAU project has an opportunity to further develop their skills. What happened to each of them subsequently is illustrative of the changes they experienced prompted by our work, but also of the difficulties they have faced.

S is a very handsome young man as I commented upon in a previous chapter when describing a wedding I attended where he was the chief best man. During our spell in Ethiopia he was extremely popular with a collection of very beautiful Ethiopian ladies. S and I were very close and we would often refer to each other as brothers. I remember on many occasions walking along streets in Addis Ababa with he and I holding hands, not something I would have been likely to do with a man in England. My brotherly love for S was eventually put to the test when Ethiopia fell out with Eritrea over a border dispute.

There were many Eritreans, living in Addis Ababa and as the relationship with their country continued to decline life became difficult for them. The Ethiopian government was concerned that within the Eritreans living in Ethiopia would be some who would spy for their country of origin, and they started to forcefully repatriate them. Shad been born and lived his entire life in Addis Ababa, but his parents were both natives of Eritrea and before long he was dismissed from the police force and ordered to return to Eritrea.

He was in a perilous situation, if he went to Eritrea, he had no doubt that as a former Ethiopian Police officer he could expect to be put in prison, but if he stayed around in Addis Ababa, he would suffer a similar fate. He decided to go into hiding in Addis Ababa and I agreed to meet his financial needs during this time. About once a month he would appear at my home late at night and we would talk together before I handed over enough money for him to survive for another month. This continued for many months before the situation improved and after representations were made on his behalf, he was allowed to return to work at the police college.

During the period when he assisted me with the OAU project it became clear to him that although he had his job back, his career progression would not follow as expected and he started to look for another job. After some time following our return to the UK, the OAU advertised for security personnel to police their new buildings. Given his background and previous experience of working with the OAU he applied for and was appointed to the security staff.

When I returned to Ethiopia in 2009, I met up with S who is now married with lovely son of around six years of age. When we met, we greeted each other with a huge hug and wept unashamedly. He told me how happy he was and how well paid his job was with a salary of more than ten times what he had been earning in the police. He said, "Thanks to God and you I am alive and well." I was very pleased for S but also very sad that the police had lost a man with such ability and potential.

A christened me his big English brother quite early in our spell in Ethiopia and I decided to call him my little Ethiopian brother. Quite apart from having a very close relationship with him our names reflected his diminutive size and my fairly large physical stature. He impressed us with his quick thinking and general ability during his trainer's course.

Our relationship with the police officers were wider than a professional working relationship and we would often meet up with them in our off-duty hours, and attend their weddings and other family events. A was always good fun to be with at these parties and a very good dancer. We often danced together at celebrations, particularly the end of course graduation parties at the Ethiopian Police College. Generally, men dance with men and women dance with women in Ethiopia.

The Ethiopian Police Force has a very good brass band, dance orchestra and dance troupe and they would perform at the police celebrations. Some of the dancers were amongst the best in the country and regularly appeared on Ethiopian television. From time to time the best dancers would turn professional and leave the police force. I remember that one such dancer travelled the world dancing for Ethiopian communities in America, Europe and the Middle East and earned a much better living than in the police.

The legendary distance runner Haillie Gebrial Sellasie was also a senior police officer as were most of the well-known and successful Ethiopian athletes. He was one of Addis Ababa's most wealthy residents during our time in Ethiopia. He is hugely popular and has established many businesses each of which employ Ethiopian people, but he has never performed any police duty and was recruited into the police force just because of his ability as an athlete.

A and I would often have discussions into the night reflecting on what the future might hold for him, the Ethiopian Police Force, and the Ethiopian Police College. More than once I would explain that he had the ability to undertake the consulting type of work that I was performing and I also indicated that there was every possibility that the police college could become a model for East African police forces. Following the completion of my work in Ethiopia I remained in touch with A and over the years I followed his career progression.

He became one of the youngest officers in the rank of Assistant Commissioner in the history of the force but still found it a struggle to support his family on his income. In Ethiopia those family members with an income are expected to support those without an income and both A, and S were paying for younger family members to be educated at university.

A had joined D working as a part time lecturer at Addis Ababa University whilst undertaking a higher degree and his supervisor drew his attention to a job with an organisation working under the umbrella of the Africa Union training police officers from across East Africa. Out of the blue, he wrote to me inviting me to contribute to one of these courses. Although I felt sad that he had left the police force I was very pleased for him. He now has a job that is satisfying both financially and professionally, and he is able to influence the behaviour of police officers not just in Ethiopia but in many other African countries.

When I visited Ethiopia again in 2009, we spent some time together and I was thrilled to meet his handsome young son. We also managed to do a little more dancing together!

D always impressed us in the early days of our project. His enthusiasm for what we were doing and his commitment to his own development were outstanding. Our project sponsored him to undertake a Masters' Degree in Disaster Management at Cranfield University, and during his time in England he was a regular visitor to my home. He had also been sent on a police course in Germany where he had equally impressed those who were training him. They were astounded at his grasp of the most current training methodologies and learning theories, which had been at the core of our training programme in Ethiopia.

D was a lovely, intelligent, and friendly man and it was a delight to have him visit us and observe our way of life. He reported his surprise at the closeness of our family which was not what he had expected. Our regular Sunday lunches with our grown-up children, their partners and children and other family and friends reminded him more of life in Ethiopia than he had expected. He acquitted himself so well at Cranfield that he was offered the opportunity to continue his studies there with his fees and living costs financed by some part time lecturing. An offer which he declined on the basis that he should resume his career back at the Ethiopian Police College and his decision proved sound when along with A he was promoted to the rank of Assistant Commissioner and subsequently became for practical purposes the Director of the Police College. It was due to his work that the institution was granted degree awarding status and became the Ethiopian Police University College.

The subsequent developments at the College have been quite remarkable particularly considering that when we commenced our project there in June 1996, no officer training had taken place for two years and the institution had been completely discredited. It was as a result of D's representations to the Ethiopian Government's Minister for Capacity Development and the World Bank representatives in Ethiopia that the three of us returned to the College in 2009 and undertook a short project to upgrade the skills of the existing trainers and provide assistance in moving the institution forward. Sadly, for the Ethiopian Police Force, D was recruited by another African organisation and he had a senior role based in Kenya where he trained police officers from across East Africa. However, he continued to use the skills we helped him develop for the betterment of policing in Africa and he was able to care for his wife and children to a level beyond anything he would have achieved locally. Even more sadly D died in 2013 the result of liver cancer.

T joined us on the staff team for the courses at the Police College because of his expertise in computers and computer software, and apart from his specialist skills we noted his intellectual capacity and general ability. I got to know T particularly well because he would travel with us from Addis Ababa to Sendafa and return when he was contributing to our courses and when he attended our executive leadership programme and our conversations about Ethiopia were very informative.

My wife and I learned much more about T when he lived with us for some months when undertaking a Masters' Degree in Change Management at Sheffield University. He was a delight to have around and our young grand children were extremely fond of him. Our eldest daughter had children similar in age to his own and they were like substitute children for him. He had great fun on our farm when we had extensive snow falls and he joined us all on our sledges.

T now has his own consulting company in Ethiopia and undertakes extensive work mainly in the public sector, teaching managers how to improve organisation performance. Whilst I have some regret that he is no longer employed by the police, it is good that he has remained in Ethiopia and is using his skills to benefit his compatriots. Back in Addis Ababa in 2009 my wife and I met up again with T and spent some time with his wife and children. We shared many memories of his stay with us and learned more about his current work.

The Ethiopian Police Force has an ongoing problem retaining their best people after they have obtained degree qualifications and increased their employability elsewhere. They continue to allow staff members to undertake appropriate additional work for payment to supplement their pay, but the long-term solution must be more realistic salaries for police.

Jamaica

What do you think about when you hear the name Jamaica? Perhaps you have visions of a beautiful, picture postcard holiday island; may be your mind suggests a place where safety cannot be guaranteed because of continued violence or alternatively you may ponder on the history of slavery and as an English man or woman feel some sense of guilt about what your forefathers were responsible for. All these images are in some ways correct and as a regular visitor I have come to love the island and its people, but not without some pangs of conscience about the past.

Jamaica is one of the largest of the Caribbean Islands and was one of the first to be regarded as a holiday destination for the rich and famous. Indeed, during the fifties, it was a popular place for some of the stars of the stage and screen to reside with Noel Coward and Ian Fleming included amongst them. Today, it does attract many holiday makers, but they are more likely to work in a factory than in the theatre. Whilst a subsequent chapter will describe for you a holiday I arranged for my colleagues in Jamaica, my purpose in visiting in the first place was not recreational.

Over a two-year period, I made numerous visits to Jamaica undertaking work with the Jamaica Constabulary Force (JCF) on a DFID funded police reform programme. Each visit occupied between two and five weeks when undertaking a specific piece of work and I would calculate that over the two-year period I would have been working on the island for a total of around twenty weeks.

Jamaica is substantially the most obviously violent place I have visited. During a five-week visit to the island a police officer was shot and killed each week. In none of the cases of police murder was a police officer killed in action. They were all assassinated whilst driving their cars off duty. A motorcycle with pillion passenger carrying a high-powered weapon drove up alongside the car and shot the driver.

On my initial journey from the airport to the hotel I was told in advance to avoid one area which would have been on my normal route. At the time, there was a turf war going on between two rival gangs and the road was the dividing point between the two areas. Cars travelling along the road regularly got caught in the crossfire.

Whilst it is true that Jamaica is a violent place it is also true that I never felt threatened there and I travelled extensively across the island without ever feeling at risk other than from careless drivers of which there are many. Add to that the fact that the island of Jamaica is fabulously beautiful, and the people are friendly and good fun to be with then it gets my vote as an ideal holiday destination and a really nice place to work.

My operating base on the island was Kingston the capital where I lived at the Courtleigh Hotel in New Kingston and I worked in an office block in Downtown Kingston overlooking the harbour. Kingston is a large, modern city built around one of the world's largest natural harbours. It was probably for this reason that the British built their original fortifications on the spit of land that creates the enclosed area of water. The original settlement at Port Royal was said at one time to be the most sinful city in the world and it is reckoned that this was the reason for a massive earthquake in the eighteenth and earlier centuries that destroyed substantial parts of it.

Jamaica's capital provides a very strange mixture of impressions ranging from the 'downtown' slums to luxurious hillside houses that would be better described as palaces, according to rumours often financed out of major drug dealing. Despite the inner-city degradation that may be spotted in many areas, Kingston is also attractive combining the expansive harbour with a backcloth of the Blue Mountains, home of the best coffee in the world.

An island nation has the potential for lots of fish and Jamaica has an abundance of excellent fish restaurants. I frequently visited the 'Fish Place' on Constant Spring Road one of my favourite dining experiences. The restaurant is in the back yard of a large bungalow. It does not look particularly impressive from the front and around the back the visible appearance is not greatly improved. It is comprised of a collection of slatted wood tables and plastic chairs on a raised but open concrete base and covered by a pseudo thatched roof supported by wooden struts. They have a very extensive menu and I have just about sampled every fish dish on it. My standard starter was very Jamaican; 'fish tea' a moderately spiced fish soup. My favourite main course was 'seafood combo' a collection of lobster tails, giant prawns, crab backs and fillets of fish mostly fried in breadcrumbs or in the case of the lobster barbequed.

English visitors unaware of what is behind a name may not be attracted by something like 'fillet fish in brown sauce' thinking that the sauce may be synonymous with gravy, however it is more like a mild form of sweet and sour sauce and the fish is wonderful, coated in a crispy covering. The crispy Thai fish is also excellent. The Fish Place is noted for the sizes of the portions so, if you are planning a trip there, prepare by eating nothing all day—you have been warned! If you are into deserts and have any space left, I recommend the rum and raison cheesecake it is just heavenly and if you cannot eat it all they will supply a container so that you can take the remainder away.

The Fish Place is extremely popular with local families particularly on a Friday night and there is a nice friendly atmosphere. Just occasionally you may find yourself in the middle of some celebration, on one occasion my visit corresponded with a farewell dinner for some visiting US citizens who had been working at a local church. I sat in my quiet corner and observed their entertainment, speeches, and presentations.

Initially my major piece of work was to provide a training course for supervisors (non-commissioned officers) and equip divisional trainers to deliver the course. The JCF is equipped with a Police Staff College where commissioned officers are trained but there had hitherto been no training provided for supervisory ranks (corporals, sergeants, and inspectors).

My first task was to carry out an extensive training needs analysis of the duties of supervisory officers and then to specify the skills and abilities required for those duties.

I then designed a course and delivered a pilot to a group of supervisors. Once the content of the final course had been agreed, I then designed and delivered a course to equip field trainers to deliver the programme at their local stations. The final stage of the project was to provide support for the field trainers as they delivered the course.

During the training needs analysis stage and the supporting of field trainers I travelled extensively across the island visiting all the main police stations. Whilst people in Jamaica are apt to refer to their nation as third or developing world, travelling around I realised that by comparison with say Ethiopia or Sudan, Jamaica is close to first world. The roads are generally in a good state of repair, police stations are clean and reasonably well equipped and there is a regular and reliable supply of electricity. By contrast in Nigeria the electric supply company was NEPA (Nigerian Electric Power Authority) which was referred to by the locals as; 'Never Expect Power Always.'

Police training sessions in Jamaica always commence with the singing of some Christian songs and a time of prayer, which is undertaken with unbridled enthusiasm. Clearly, they were not accustomed to the experience of the English trainer joining in these sessions. Such a way of starting the day's events in a UK police training establishment would be frowned upon, but I was happy to be a part of it.

As a chief inspector of police at Derby, I worked alongside lots of people with roots in Jamaica and had regular meetings with associations representing them. One thing I noticed at those meetings was if you had twenty people attending the meeting you would have at least twenty different opinions about what do and gaining agreement was just about impossible. I realised over the period of my visits to Jamaica that having strong opinions about virtually everything is a feature of the Jamaican culture. I often mused about the source of this attitude and I read widely about the history of Jamaica trying as often as possible to read books written by Jamaicans.

I recall a novel called "The Polished Hoe," which was written by a Canadian citizen with a background in the Caribbean (Austin Clarke). It provided an account of the life of a slave, starting when she was being interviewed by the police as a suspect for a murder. Whilst it was fiction, I have little doubt that the problems the heroine faced were typical of those faced by female slaves at the time. If you can find the book, it is well worth the read.

Jamaicans in their writings and in conversations indicate that they have not forgiven the British for our role in the whole slavery business. They make comparisons with the way we remember the holocaust but do not give similar emphasis to slavery. It is not that they want to belittle the evil perpetrated against the Jews rather that they consider the evil against Africans was on the same level but is rarely mentioned. It remains an unpalatable fact that the wealth of cities like Bristol and Liverpool was built upon what we now know to have been an evil business and some public apology is long overdue.

Most Jamaicans have a very 'in your face' mentality and I suspect that this is because such an attitude was the only way to stay alive as a slave. Certainly, any notion that Africans willingly submitted to an allegedly superior race is not indicated from any of the literature available.

One of the features of having worked in Africa and in Jamaica is the extent to which the latter have held onto many aspects of their African origins. This speaks volumes for the strength of the human spirit to overcome adversity.

In addition to the work developing training for supervisory officers, I also undertook a project to assist the JCF in developing modern methods of human resource management. Whilst I have generally been satisfied that the overseas work, I have undertaken has made a difference I was not so happy with my human resources work in Jamaica.

Another consultant had been out to Jamaica and produced a draft human resource policy document at quite considerable expense, but the organisation was making little progress in agreeing and promulgating the policy. The original consultant no longer being available and me being a Chartered Member of the Chartered Institute of Personnel and Development I was asked to pick up and progress the work.

Reading the policy document, I quickly realised that whilst it incorporated state of the art ideas about human resource management, it did not reflect the needs of the Jamaica Constabulary Force. For example, there was a detailed section about how to deal with industrial disputes, but the police in Jamaica, as in the UK are forbidden from striking or joining a trade union. One serious omission, given the nature of risk of a sudden and violent death for police officers in Jamaica was the lack of any policy on what to do in the event of a police officer, being killed on duty.

A local working group had been formed to consider any proposals for changes to policies for the JCF and in theory it was their responsibility to consider the proposals and approve them or return them for amendment and re-presentation. Reading through the minutes of previous meetings of this group revealed that they would have the same circular discussion about the policies, but never make any progress. This was partly due to the unsuitability of some of the policies but also the basic culture of Jamaicans where reaching agreement can be extraordinarily challenging. The task certainly proved too challenging for me and I made little progress.

Holidaying in Jamaica

As my former colleagues' RM and BD learned from me about the beauty of the island of Jamaica we decided that I should arrange an island holiday for the three of us and our wives and what follows is my record of that holiday.

On Friday morning, we set off for a drive across the island towards the North coast in the vehicle that we had hired for the purpose. Our hire car turned out to be the only aspect of our holiday that caused us a degree of dissatisfaction. We were told that the only vehicle available that was large enough to carry seven adults and their luggage was a twelve seat Toyota minibus, but we discovered, fairly early in our journeys that the suspension was rather unforgiving, and the seats upholstered more for short town journeys than island wide touring.

We selected the Stoney Hill route out of Kingston, rather than the main route via Spanish Town. This road quickly takes you into the mountains that run down to the outskirts of Kingston but skirting around the taller hills that comprise the Blue Mountains. The road is steep, and winding and traffic moves slowly given the nature of the highway. However, just occasionally some driver will display suicidal tendencies and try to overtake where the road does not allow and this is just as likely to be a huge tanker or a fully loaded bus as it is a private car, so it's a good idea to expect the unexpected when at the wheel.

On the way through the mountains, we spotted many examples of damage caused by 'Hurricane Ivan' that swept across the island in the summer of the previous year. Many trees had been blown down and the road has been washed away in many places. Temporary repairs had been affected so from time to time the smooth tarmac surface changed to rough limestone. Of greater concern were the places where there is a sheer drop down the mountainside and the floods brought by the storms have removed some of the supporting walls and part of the roadway. Not being the best person with heights I kept my hands firmly on the steering wheel and tried to make sure that I kept away from the area of road that I suspect may now be in danger of giving way. In many places, repairs were already being undertaken but it will be some time before the road is restored to the state it was in before the hurricane.

As we leave Kingston behind so the scenery changes along with the roadside houses. There are more of the original wooden houses built into the side of the hill so that at the front the entrance is at ground level, but the rear of the same house may be elevated as much as 20 feet from the ground. Often these wooden houses are brightly painted. The modern houses are mostly single story and constructed from blocks that have been covered over with plaster and painted.

Trees, flowers, and plants grow in profusion in gardens and at the roadsides, the trees include some that tourists will easily recognise such as bamboo and coconut, but some would be more difficult for a new visitor to recognise. For example, the ackee tree which is bearing fruit during our visit. The bright red fruits have a black centre and when opened-up, reveal a sort of pulp that looks for all the world like scrambled egg. This food forms the basis of a typical Jamaican breakfast and is traditionally eaten with saltfish.

The latter is imported from Newfoundland and has been eaten here since the slave masters imported it to provide food for their slaves. Like most other Jamaican food, I enjoy saltfish and ackee very much but that means that I put on weight during every visit. Apparently the ackee was brought from West Africa but the fruit is only eaten in Jamaica, it is a funny world sometimes. Other less familiar trees include breadfruit.

We cross over the mountains and follow a river valley down the other side as we continue our drive towards the coast. Naturally as we get further down the valley the river widens and gives us some indication of the fact that we will reach the sea at some stage. Eventually the river valley begins to broaden out and the vegetation now includes banana and its cousin plantain. I love plantain fried for breakfast as an extra to the ackee and saltfish. We pass by some large banana plantations and a roadside sign indicates that they have been funded by a European Aid Programme.

Traditionally Britain has had a special arrangement whereby we purchase bananas from the Caribbean at a rate which is above the normal market price, but this no longer appertains, and the Jamaicans find it difficult to compete with the 'Chivita' bananas that are grown in the US under subsidies. They have similar problems with their sugar because of European subsidies.

I have travelled this route previously and know roughly where we will be at lunch time, so I have arranged for our gastronomic tour to include a lunchtime stop at Harmony Hall on the coast road near to Ocho Rhios. We eventually hit the coast road and turn left heading towards our destination, Montego Bay. We have occasional glances of the azure blue colour of the Caribbean and the holiday feeling starts to develop. Before reaching our lunch-time rendezvous place we pass through Oraccabessa where Ian Flemming settled, and which is also featured in one of the James Bond films.

It is better known now as James Bond Beach and his house Golden Eye has been converted into a luxurious and extremely expensive hotel in the same 'Island Outposts' chain as two of our intended destinations.

At Harmony Hall, we stop at our intended lunchtime destination, a beautiful old colonial building that used to be a Methodist Manse and is famous for being the house in which the writer of the Jamaican national anthem was brought up. Their national anthem unlike ours extols the nation and seeks God's blessing upon it rather than the monarch, which I think is how national anthems should be. Upstairs is a gallery with pictures and other objects de art and downstairs an Italian restaurant run by a lady who spent her formative years in England, half Italian, and half Portuguese she has lived on the island for a long time. The food is excellent, and we sat outside enjoying the tranquillity of the garden.

I chose some local fish cooked in white wine with tomatoes and olives it was wonderful. Fish is always a good option and on a previous visit to this restaurant I thoroughly enjoyed a salad with marinated smoked marlin. Whilst we were there a huge Jackfish was delivered which had just been caught and would be on the menu for dinner that evening—it would have been nice to stay.

After lunch, we continued along the coast road travelling first through Ocho Rhios where we saw a large cruise liner birthed in the harbour. The coast road to Montego Bay is a lovely stretch of road with many miles of it alongside the seashore. This makes for an attractive journey but one which is difficult to describe to people who have not experienced undeveloped coastline. For the greater part the seaside villages are occupied by the locals and their brightly painted wooden houses and boats are dotted about the higher points of the seashore.

Some of the buildings are painted in the colours of the flag of Ethiopia indicating the Rastafarian beliefs of their occupants. There is a tendency for places to be rather untidy but for me this adds to the attraction, rather than diminishing it.

The road is being converted into a modern dual carriageway, but in typical Jamaican fashion some sections have not yet been completed and there is a total absence of workmen around. The link between the new and old road is sometimes quite difficult to find and as we bump over the ramps and unmade sections we are reminded of the unforgiving nature of the suspension of the vehicle and the thin upholstery of the seats. There are roadside stalls, bars, and cafes at which the locals hang out listening to reggae music and smoking ganja.

From time to time, we pass large private holiday developments where the all-inclusive tourists spend their time. They have wonderful facilities, and their visitors enjoy the Caribbean beaches and weather to the full, but they do not see the Jamaica that we will see, the real Jamaica. During the final approach to Montego Bay these large holiday centres increase in both size and number.

Montego Bay was one of the first places in Jamaica to be developed as a tourist resort and the name seems to me to be synonymous with palm trees, beaches, and island paradise. It is Jamaica's second city, and some areas of the town are not suitable places to visit having a high crime rate and frequent shootings. However, the part alongside the famous beaches known locally as 'Hip strip' is well policed and safe, indeed a delightful place to visit day or night.

Our destination for the first three nights of the holiday is in the countryside about half an hours' drive from Montego Bay. It is a very local Jamaican development called 'Countryside Villa.' We travel through the town and head towards the coast again, stopping first at a supermarket where we obtain food for the evening.

Supermarkets in Jamaica are much the same as they would be in England but with the fresh food representing the greatest departure with exotic fruits in abundance. Although the locals sometimes describe Jamaica as 'third world,' it is not, the standard of living for the wealthier Jamaicans being comparable to people at home. Conversely the countryside dwellers do not live to the same standard and there are some extremely poor areas in the cities that are shanty towns and worse than anything we know in Britain, and it is these that are the breeding ground for the violence and gang activities that blight the island.

At Reading (there are many places on the island with English place names) we turn inland and drive up into some mountains. As we near Countryside Villa we pass through a large citrus fruit plantation. Orange groves as far as the eye can see in an extensive and picturesque mountain basin surrounded by tree covered hills.

The villa is approached down a long, winding, and rough lane where we pass by a collection of local premises including one wooden shack which is the local bar and another which is the local shop. There are small farms dotted around the place and the fields are fertile with melons, peppers, bananas, and oranges being grown. Countryside Villa occupies a plot of land which must be about five acres in size. There are three main residential buildings each two-storey and brightly painted. Margaret and I have stayed here before and know what to expect, people have the typical relaxed Jamaican attitude to life which does not always go down well with people from our part of the world.

Although I made a personal visit a couple of weekends before to make specific reservations of selected suites, I was not sure that what we got would be what we booked, or that it would turn out totally suitable.

Margaret and I were accommodated on the ground floor of one of the buildings and there was a separate bedroom for our daughter Barbara who was to join us there. We were happy with our suite, and it was the one I had booked for our previous stay but turned out not to be available because someone else had been allocated it despite my specific reservation. Roger and Daphne and Pam and Blair were in one of the other buildings. The suite allocated to Pam and Blair turned out to be unsatisfactory, but the management quickly agreed to provide another that was more appropriate.

In a similar self-catering establishment in Britain, you would find that all the necessary equipment would be in your room, but that is not the case here. Each of us passed through a phase of identifying things that we needed and then asking for them, things like enough crockery and cutlery, a kettle etc. Every time we asked for something there was no complaint just an unhurried but effective trip to bring the missing item. Some may find this frustrating, but it is better to settle down to the Jamaica pace of doing things. None of my friends seemed to mind too much and we were happy to go along with the relaxed Jamaican approach to life—that is why I chose the place anyway.

Once we had settled into our room and unpacked Margaret and I shot off to the airport in Montego Bay to meet Barbara off the flight from Gatwick and on our return with her we enjoyed the product of our shopping in the local supermarket before retiring to bed. Countryside Villa has a selection of facilities for the visitor all of which are adequate in a slightly rundown Jamaican sort of style. There is a tennis court, a four-hole golf course, a swimming pool, games room and Jacuzzi. The main amenity block has a bar come games room and a covered area around the pool where we sampled a nice breakfast on the first morning of our stay. The remainder of our meals were either taken on our own balconies or in Montego Bay.

The villa is set in beautiful rolling countryside and is quiet and peaceful. The large hammocks dotted around the place encourage relaxation and there was one big enough and strong enough for me to use, it is a very pleasant way to spend an hour or two with a book. We never felt energetic enough to play tennis or golf but did manage a session in the Jacuzzi, which we thoroughly enjoyed. Margaret and I managed a substantial walk further along the lane where there are more small farms and another bar, one that we visited on the previous occasion and played dominoes with the locals, whilst some of them smoked ganja.

During the daytime on both Saturday and Sunday we visited Doctor's Cave Beech in Montego Bay. This was considered the fashionable place to sunbathe and swim when Montego Bay was first developed as a tourist resort and is featured on one of Jamaica's bank notes. It is a private beach, so you pay for admission, but it is not expensive, and the beach patrols mean that your safety is secured, and you are not pestered by salesmen or beggars. The beach stretches for perhaps half a mile. The land side is occupied by various buildings that provide shops, bars, and restaurants, whilst shade is provided by an area of coconut palms at the Eastern end and parasols may be hired inexpensively along with loungers, deck chairs etc.

It is a lovely safe beach to swim from and swimming in the Caribbean is amazing, not least because of the colourful tropical fish that abound in the ocean, the sea temperature helps as well, in fact dipping in the sea from time to time is essential given the heat of the day. Jamaica is hot but there is often a pleasant breeze especially at the coast, in fact the climate is just about my ideal.

Our periods on the beach were interspersed with visits to the Groovy Grouper, my favourite bar/restaurant. They have a regular 'busker band' that play good, old fashioned reggae and calypso numbers with great enthusiasm and were joined from time to time by us. They also do a Planters Punch speciality drink that goes down well provided you do not have too many given that it contains liberal amounts of the local speciality Appleton Estate rum. Both food and drink are relatively inexpensive by comparison with UK prices but slightly more than you would get charged at a bar in the town.

Montego Bay gets the name from an extensive bay with a backdrop of hills in which it is located. I find the place attractive although some people refer to it as the Blackpool of Jamaica. It is a very lively place and even when you are sitting on the beach there are numerous reminders of this. Boats of all shapes and sizes pass by including those with glass bottoms to allow viewing of the coral and sea life and large oceangoing yachts. The international airport is close by and holiday flights from all over the world come in over the sea. Some might find this disturbing but for me it just adds to the excitement of being here and the planes are not immediately overhead, so noise disturbance is minimal. It is not unusual to be able to snap a photograph with a cruise liner at sea, a flotilla of smaller boats inshore and an aeroplane in the sky.

Although Doctor's Cave is a private beach there are many public ones around the bay and judging by the numbers of people who I have observed using them they are each pleasant enough for sunbathing and swimming. On the Western limits of the bay there are many new buildings including the docking facility for cruise liners and the shops and entertainment centres that service their needs.

Saturday night on the 'Hip Strip' is lively and that was where we headed for our evening entertainment. Occupying a prime position on the seashore is 'Margaritaville' a leisure and entertainment complex. In the daytime families enjoy various water sport activities and long chutes deposit the users into the Caribbean at an alarming speed. At night, the atmosphere changes and a wide range of tastes are catered for. The open-air night club features things like skimpy costume competitions and other hedonistic delights. That is not where we headed.

Our tastes were more than met by the fish restaurant that has been built over the sea. They have an extensive menu but most of us went for the lobster which was simply unbelievable. The setting is very romantic looking out across the bay with lights reflected from the ocean and whilst we were there a huge cruise liner jewelled with numerous coloured lights that twinkled in the sea set out for some other exotic Caribbean destination.

Across the road is a smaller entertainment complex called Coral Cliffs. It is a bit brash but the live band that plays there every evening is extremely good and they play music that will satisfy just about every taste between 9.00 p.m. and 1.00 a.m. in five slots of about half an hour. That was where we ended our evening, not that we stayed for the final session by the band, given that some of my guests were beginning to fall asleep.

On the Monday, we set off back in the direction that we had travelled out that is, back along the coast road in the direction of Ocho Rhios our intended destination for the next three nights. At about the halfway point we left the coast road at Falmouth to visit one of Jamaica's historic houses 'Good Hope Great House.' The road led us into the hills and the nearer we got to the estate the more interesting the roadside scenery became. During the final few miles, we passed extensive sugar, pawpaw, banana, and citrus fruit plantations.

Good Hope Great House is a jewel and well worth a visit; a beautiful old plantation owner's house that has been sympathetically restored. We arrived to find that the owners had just commenced a daily visitor's programme where for a fixed sum you could undertake horse trekking, tour the old buildings, and have a gourmet lunch. We settled for a reduced version, and you can guess that we included the gourmet lunch. The house is extensive, built from local stone and situated on the upper slopes of a hill with commanding views of the surrounding countryside. The rooms are furnished with original furnishings and some interesting facts are displayed in each room which allow the visitor to get a feel for the place.

Adjacent to the main building is the former prison where unwilling slaves were kept shackled. That is one of the disturbing reminders of the terrors that our forefathers visited upon our brothers and sisters from Africa. We thoroughly enjoyed our tour of the house and the excellent gourmet meal. Most of our party opted to have a little of everything on the menu and we could not fault any of it. All washed down with a drop of good wine. What a life!

After lunch and a visit to some of the old industrial buildings on the estate where the sugar cane was processed, we resumed our journey to our next destination where we arrived late afternoon.

Our first venue had been deliberately down market and cost each couple around twenty-five pounds per night, but there was nothing down market about our second stopping off point. Jamaica Inn at Ocho Rhios oozes old world charm and the class of the establishment can be judged by the fact that Marylyn Munroe was a visitor in the fifties and more recently Mr & Mrs John Major and Liz Hurley amongst others. I am lost for words to describe the place; 'heaven on earth' immediately comes to mind and that is not an exaggeration. The visitor is charmed from the moment he/she arrives by car at the vehicle dropping off point, which leads straight to a covered reception area which offers a view straight out over the beach and sea below. The paint everywhere is maintained in a pristine state and the uniformed staff friendly, efficient, and relaxed. Generally, as if by magic the wife of one of the joint owners appears whilst you are checking in and gives you a personal welcome. Having stayed here before and made the reservation I was greeted by name.

The three couples were all located in what are described in the brochure as Deluxe Sea View Rooms all on the ground floor and Barbara was located upstairs in a room that was identical except for the fact that we had a terrace, and she had a balcony. The buildings that comprise the Jamaica Inn are all built in colonial style on two floors. The main residential block runs parallel to the sea, about 600 metres from the waters' edge. At either end, additional residential buildings set at right angles to the sea complete three side of a rectangle, the open side being the sea. The wing on the western side comprises exclusive accommodation that tends to be used by the rich and famous who may wish to have a level of privacy beyond that available elsewhere—they have exclusive access to a small private beach that cannot even be seen from the hotel because it is hidden away in a cove of rocks.

The moment you step into a Jamaican Inn room you cannot avoid being impressed; beautiful arrangements of exotic flowers grace the bedroom, bathroom, and terrace; the terrace is equal in size to the large bedroom and comes complete with a three-piece suite, and you look out over wonderful gardens, a crocket lawn, the beach and of course the Caribbean Sea. The limits of the private beach of the Jamaican Inn are defined by rocky tree covered promontories to the East and West. The effect of this is that the beach may only be approached through the hotel reception area or from the sea and this preserves the feeling of privacy.

Most of the hotel amenities like the bar, restaurant and other dining areas are located to the western end of the premises. Dining is usually undertaken outdoors, but there are facilities to move inside when it rains. The area set out for breakfast is right over the sea and Margaret and I love to sit at the corner table and watch the brightly coloured fish as we eat our breakfast. In the mornings, large shoals of yellow and black striped fish make their way to that part of the bay knowing that the waiters throw scrap food into the sea. We follow their example and love to see how the enthusiasm of the fish for Jamaican ginger cake make it look as though the sea is boiling over around where the cake landed.

The comfortable lounge areas feature pictorial records of the life of this hotel including those of some of the famous visitors and aspects of the life stories of the American family that have owned and operated the hotel for around 50 years.

Jamaica Inn is not so much about modern world luxury as old world charm, and this means that you are expected to dress for dinner in the evenings; not in a suit and tie or evening dress but at least a shirt with collar and proper trousers. The information leaflets do point out that you can dress as you like on your own terrace and be served with your meal there if you so desire. For our part, we chose to dine together at the restaurant which is also in the open air. There is a different set menu for each day featuring a six-course meal with choices for each course and many Jamaican specialities.

The food is excellent as is the service and general atmosphere. There is often live music provided whilst you eat your meal. The wine list is also extensive, and we sampled a reasonable proportion of what was available.

One of my pre-breakfast delights whenever I have stayed at the Jamaica Inn has been to swim for a good half an hour. I recommend this as a method both of gaining an appetite for breakfast and working off some of the calories from the dinner the night before. In any case swimming from this beach is always a delight. Sunbathing on the same beach during the day is most relaxing and it is never crowded so you can have space to yourself and not be shoulder to shoulder with other holiday makers.

During our stay in Ocho Rhios we set off one morning immediately after breakfast to visit Dunns River Falls one of Jamaica's most popular tourist attractions. I know from personal experience that if you wish to see the falls at their best it is a good idea to arrive as soon as the place opens around 9am. By about 10.30am thousands of people arrive from the cruise liners birthed in the harbour and you cannot move then for grossly obese elderly and middle-aged Americans which is not my idea of fun.

Standard fare for a visit to the falls is to walk down to the beach via the steps that have been provided and then with the help of a guide to walk back up the falls. It's a little more complicated because you would probably not survive walking the falls in your bare feet or your own shoes, so you are invited to hire special rubber shoes that have non-slip soles a very essential feature that prevent you from falling back down the falls.

Language is always inadequate to describe the most meaningful experiences of life. How would you set out to describe in words your feelings when you see your child come into the world or the pleasures of taking out your grandchildren for the day? Difficult, isn't it? Where do I start so far as the falls are concerned?

At the bottom, I suppose which is where the falls end on the pleasant but not spectacular beach.

The falls do not feature a spectacular drop as in the case of the Victoria or Niagara Falls; indeed, if they did there would be little chance in attempting to climb them and you cannot see the entire falls from your first view on the beach. I would guess that climbing the falls involves a walk of about half a mile and the typical rate of ascent will be around forty-five degrees. The falls vary in width between narrows of around ten or twelve feet to parts where they must be about twenty feet wide. A huge volume of crystal-clear water falls over large smooth boulders. Typical tropical vegetation grows on either side of the falls and sometimes trees sprout from amongst the falls themselves. The vegetation includes spectacularly colourful flowers. From time to time the falls level out into a flat area where there are large rock pools into which the water flows.

If you intend to visit the falls and do the walk (which is essential) expect to get soaked to the skin because it is impossible not to and your guide will encourage it to the extent of showing you how to stand in a rock pool under an overhanging rock and turn your head into a part of the waterfall. It is a strange but exhilarating experience to look out through a large volume of water that is flowing out from your forehead.

Your guide will agree to carry your cameras and take photographs of you in these positions which all adds to the experience and provides a more accurate record of what you see than these simple words can express. I do say what you **see** because photographs have their own disadvantages; they do not convey feelings and words do have that capability at least in part if not in totality. So, the word here is 'exhilarating,' certainly the experience is not something you should miss if you visit Jamaica.

On this occasion, I declined the opportunity to climb the falls for a second time, offering to take photographs of the others from the walkway that runs alongside the falls. I don't like heights and got quite frightened when I previously did the falls, so I was happy to find an excuse. However, those of you who are like me scared of heights should take note of the fact that I did do it and would not have missed the experience for all the tea in China or all the Blue Mountain coffee in Jamaica, so do not be put off!

As I had anticipated by the time that our group had reached the top of the falls the place was packed solid with busloads of mainly American tourists from the cruise liners proving my point that it was best to arrive just as the gates opened.

Although some tourist places in Jamaica are extremely busy others are just the opposite and one of these may also be undertaken whilst staying at the Jamaica Inn. A visit to the former home of the late Sir Noel Coward is well worth the effort of a drive of about forty-five minutes and unlike Dunns River Falls it is extremely quiet. His house called Firefly is located on a hill overlooking the sea on the site of a house that was originally occupied by Captain Henry Morgan an English pirate who was one of the first European visitors, not a nice man I fear and not a good advert for the English.

Noel Coward built his house there in the 1950's and remained until his death, leaving the house to his lover who in turn gave it to the nation. It is now officially a museum but not stuffy like museums often are and it remains just the house that he lived in and has been left just like it was during his lifetime with some of his clothes in the wardrobes, his music at the piano and the dining table set out just as it was when he entertained Queen Elizabeth the Queen Mother.

You can sit in the window where he wrote the words and music for the song 'A room with a view.' It is essential that you do, and you will then observe what he was writing about, a fabulous view down to the sea and around the extensive bay. It allows history to come to life and I find myself imitating him singing the song as I write this piece as I did when I sat in the window.

What remains of Captain Morgan's house (more a lookout post) has now been turned into a bar and it's nice to end the tour with a very cold Red Stripe Beer. As a Derbyshire man, I found it interesting to see that one of the pictures on the wall shows a visit by the then Duchess of Devonshire (now deceased). As Deborah Mitford one of the Mitford sisters, I am sure that she would have known Noel Coward in her younger high society days before the war.

After our three lovely nights at the Jamaica Inn, Ocho Rhios we set off again for our next destination Jakes on the less visited South Coast of the island. Our drive to the South took us by way of yet another route through the mountains that form the hinterland of the island. Our route was chosen because it was new to me and gave us the opportunity to observe the mountain scenery in yet another part of the island.

It provided us with an interesting and ever-changing tableau of the Jamaican countryside although the fact that the route was tortuous and the road in places quite rough the lack of suitable upholstery to the seats and the unforgiving nature of the vehicle suspension made us ready for a stop along the journey and towards the end look forward to our arrival at the intended destination.

Our rest and recreation point on this journey was differed widely from the Italian Restaurant at Harmony Hall and the Good Hope Great House, but just as interesting an insight into the real Jamaica. It was a simple roadside bar, part of a small house where the lady proprietor clearly lived because that is where she came from when we alighted from the vehicle and walked into the bar and it was in her house where we were invited to use the bathroom (not being American here just explaining that it was the bathroom of this small local house that doubled as the toilet for the bar).

The area around the South Coast of the island is not as developed as the North Coast but it has an attraction all the same. It is a little on the barren side with far more rocky outcrops than sandy beaches. Jakes is a bit of a one off, quite unique, and distinctly bohemian in character and appearance. Margaret and I had visited before just to look round and have a meal, but we had never stayed there before. The place does not feel like a hotel. Residents are lodged in individual houses ranging in size from those with three and four bedrooms to ones that are little more than a double room with an open veranda looking straight out over the sea.

Jakes specialises in honeymoon holidays and a selection of the individual chalets are specifically designed for that purpose. They have bedrooms that are in the open air on the roof with just a canopy over and with shower facilities also out in the open and large enough for a couple to use together! I should stress that they are not open to public view.

By the time we arrived at Jakes we seemed to have developed a certain Jamaican attitude to life. Margaret and I had this notion in the plan for this part of the holiday that we would take advantage of some local tours from the hotel including boat trips up the Black River and out to a sandbar where a local has built a bar and restaurant on stilts, but the relaxing nature of the island and especially Jakes took over and we made just one trip ourselves and no tours.

We did spend a lot of time just chilling out, sitting on the rocks right over the sea and listening to the waves breaking against them and occasionally hitting us with their cooling sprays. In fact, wherever you are at Jakes, the restaurant, the bar, or your own rooms you are adjacent to the sea. The sound of the sea, the smell of the ocean and the feel on your body of the sea breeze along with the sunshine that seems permanent are all, star features of a visit to Jakes. The food is good but not expensive and the barman will stay open, as long as you wish, mixing you rum based cocktails until the cows come home.

There are no lovely beaches in the immediate vicinity of Jakes, but there is a small swimming pool, and the absences of beaches did not bother us—neither did much else—says a lot for the atmosphere that this hotel creates.

Our one trip out was to a small fishing village that has the unlikely name of Alligator Pond. I had been told that there was the best fish restaurant in the world located there, so we thought that it was an absolute must as part of a gourmet adventure. I had also been warned that the roads were steep and winding with uneven surface and an absence of signs. All that was said about the route proved to be correct, but we did eventually arrive there.

The restaurant was not remotely what we had expected but we were not disappointed with the food. After parking our vehicle with many others including many coaches we walked in the direction of the beach where all the activity seemed to be taking place. There was a large warehouse type of building at the head of the beach, and this housed a bar and the kitchens of the restaurant. The tables were spread across the beach on raised areas some in old boats that were on wooden stands to stop them from falling over and others inside circular wooden structures that looked like the framework for old fashioned fairground roundabouts but minus the roundabout.

Adjacent to the kitchens were two huge cabinet chillers that contained fish and seafood of all types and colours. This is where you selected what you wanted for your meal and placed your order. The price depended on the amount that you selected and your choice. We all went for lobster tails cooked with garlic and served with rice and peas—very Jamaican and some of us added a load of prawns as well—all washed down with cold Red Stripe Beer.

Perhaps now is the time to remind you that I had been told that this was the best fish restaurant in the world and I guess we were all expecting something very plush which is the last word you would use to describe 'Little Ochi,' however the food was most definitely equal to the best in the world and the atmosphere was great and very Jamaica with lots of reggae music and lively banter.

One of the special features of our stay at Jakes was the beautiful sunsets when the sea and the coastline seemed to be bathed in a red glow.

Barbara returned to Kingston by taxi during our three nights at Jakes and we ourselves left in good time on the Sunday because I wanted my friends to sample the delights of a Sunday Brunch at the Strawberry Hill Hotel, Kingston our final holiday destination. Our journey to Kingston took us through Mandeville, the administrative capital of the parish of Manchester. Unlike in Britain where parishes are the smallest administrative units in Jamaica they are amongst the largest in size.

Mandeville is a fine town with many beautiful new houses most of them occupied by 'returning residents'; people who have lived mainly in the UK for a lifetime of work and then sold up and moved back home where the money they obtained from their London houses and their public service pensions allow them to live out their days in comparative comfort. Good for them!

Strawberry Hill is gem of a hotel situated in the Blue Mountains overlooking Kingston and about half an hour's drive from the city centre. Sunday Brunch is a weekly special that is extremely popular and requires advanced booking. On one of my previous visits that coincided with the birthday party of the opposition leader (Jamaica Labour Party), some of the more important guests arrived and departed in a helicopter.

The hotel is part of the Island Outposts chain and is owned by Chris Blackwell who was the founder of Island Records. Record memorabilia may be found around the buildings. The main amenity block is made up of a collection of timber buildings each with balconies where tables are set out for the diners.

Set high in the mountains the air is crisp and the views over the mountains or the harbour and Kingston are quite remarkable. During the Test Match series against England when the game was being played at Sabina Park in Kingston, the BBC had a satellite camera located by the poolside showing the view whenever there was a break in play.

Sunday Brunch is a buffet of the highest standard imaginable. Self-service so you may go back as many times as you wish. Whilst the cuisine satisfies European tastes it certainly has a Caribbean flavour. I just love to have a plateful of seafood as a starter and always major on the green lipped mussels. The meat for the main course has always been 'jerked'; a Jamaican way of marinating the meat in a spicy dressing before it is cooked, but you would not describe it as very spicy.

The surroundings in which the food is eaten cannot be explained fully given the inadequacy of words, but my own personal experiences include sitting just a few feet away from humming birds extracting the nectar from the most exotic flowers imaginable so bright in colour, dramatic in shape and excessive in quantity that you just have to touch them to make sure that they are not artificial. So, it is not just the food that is wonderful it is the entire experience.

The residential accommodation at Strawberry Hill is all discretely built from mainly wooden constructions into the sides of the mountain offering a view either over Kingston or the surrounding mountains. Our houses looked out over the mountains and apart from the different vegetation and lack of snow we could have imagined that we were in the Alpine regions of Europe. The buildings blend into the hillside and have wonderful balconies that allow you to sit outside and just bask in the beauty of the place.

By the time we got to Strawberry Hill the cumulative effect of the previous part of our holiday was starting to turn us from relaxed into downright lazy and we spent the entire three days lazing around the hotel; if you have found perfection and are living in it there is not much point in moving on.

Strawberry Hill has a swimming pool that is known as an infinity pool because it appears to have no edge but to just drop over the edge of the mountain. It is quite an experience to swim up to a sheer drop down the mountain side, a bit like swimming up to a waterfall but without the certain knowledge that you will be washed over the edge.

The houses at Strawberry Hill are furnished with local antiques and everything makes the best of the surroundings in a very tasteful way. Beautiful arrangements of tropical flowers complete the picture.

Strawberry Hill is surrounded by gardens that have been expertly landscaped to make the best of the hillside location. Exotic trees and flowers abound, and birds and butterflies make use of them and add to the kaleidoscope of colour that surrounds the visitor. The place has an aura of peace and tranquillity, and it is indeed far from the madding crowd. The food is excellent, and the staff are friendly and efficient in fact just the place to continue to wind down and build up reserves for the busy lives that lay ahead on our return to the everyday life.

Nigeria Does Lightning Strike Twice in the Same Place?

Here I am lying in my hotel bedroom in Abuja, the capital of Nigeria. I have just arrived along with my colleagues Blair and Roger. Having completed our work together in Ethiopia we each followed our own independent working routes around the world, before coming together again for a long-term project here in Nigeria.

After the long journey out, I was tired and fell asleep quickly and started to have a nightmare which commenced as a dream but became reality. In my dream Addis Ababa and Abuja were being linked. I remembered that a colleague in Ethiopia who had been a resident in the Hilton Hotel in Addis Ababa when the communist government of Mengistu Haille Mariam collapsed, described to me his experiences.

The communist forces were located on a hill to one side of the hotel and the 'liberating' forces led by Meles Zenawi were on the other side. They were firing at each other and some of the shells were travelling through the Hilton Hotel. Unfortunately, the floor on which my friend was sleeping was the level at which the shells were passing through and he had to dive for the floor and stay there for quite a long time until the shelling stopped. He described how he flattened himself against the floor of the hotel and every time he heard the of crack gun fire and the whoosh of a shell thought that he would be hit.

Here I was in this hotel room in Abuja, and I could hear the crack of heavy and continual gun fire in the distance. Any moment I expected to hear the tell-tale whoosh of a shell passing through my room. Was this a dream or was I awake? Sometimes dreams can be so vivid that it is difficult to determine where dreams end, and reality begins. At some stage I realised that I was awake and that the gun, fire was real. Strange to say, my first thought was: "How will I

310

explain to my wife and family that on my first day back in Africa history has repeated itself?"

A confusion of thoughts entered my mind as I lay there. Nigeria has become democratic, but they have had a series of military cues in the past, and this might be another one. Surely this is not real, and it cannot be happening to me? What do I do to protect myself?

My mind was made up and I decided that this was real and any minute now shells may be erupting around my room, so I must get as close as possible to the floor and away from the window with some protection from the outer walls of the room. I am going to say that I slithered out of bed snake like, but at sixty plus years and one hundred and twenty kilograms, I am not much like a snake, hippo more than snake if you see what I mean, but it is surprising what a small target a big old man can make if he really tries hard.

I lay as flat as possible on the floor of my hotel room. My heart was beating like a two-stroke engine and I was scared that this time I was going to die all alone. The gun fire continued as I lay there but there were no signs of any shells or bullets connecting with buildings and I gradually realised that all the bangs were coming from one direction, which was strange if this was a battle between opposing forces.

I decided that I needed to do a little investigation, so I slithered along the floor maintaining the mental illusion of a snake, towards the window. At last, after the effort of dragging my body along the floor my breath failing for physical effort and fear, I slowly raised my head and pulled the curtain back slightly. At first it looked as though my suspicions were confirmed when I saw the flashes caused by the firing of large calibre weapons. But then I realised slowly that the noise and the flashes were from a huge firework display in the distance.

I flung back the curtains in relief and saw for the first time that my room looked straight out at the Nigerian National Sports Stadium, where the fireworks were signalling the end of the Pan African games. I pulled up a chair, opened the curtains fully and enjoyed the display. What a greeting to a new country.

Africa is a huge continent yet we in Britain often link the entire continent, when making comments about government, culture, or economics. Having lived for substantial periods in Ethiopia and Nigeria, I can say that there are far more differences between these two African countries than there are similarities. Ethiopians although justifiably proud of their history are often guilty of understating their ability and potential whereas Nigerians often have a very inflated opinion of themselves and overstate what they have achieved. Ethiopians are generally quiet and unassuming whereas Nigerians are often noisy and demanding.

Most of the populations of both countries have a strong belief in God, but how that faith displays itself is manifestly different. A poor Ethiopian Christian will be inclined to think that his or her poverty must be accepted as a part of God's plan and purpose and may in fact be a punishment for some sin. Conversely most Nigerian Christians are convinced that God's desire is to bless his children with wealth and success and the poor person stays poor only because they do not have sufficient faith in God.

Our purpose in Nigeria was to assist the Nigerian Police and the Government of Nigeria in the development of community policing. You may wonder what we mean by 'Community Policing' and you would not be alone. There is no universal definition for this style of policing and one recent extensive manual on the subject, indicates the level of confusion about community policing. In the work that we do, our starting point is frequently one of developing a style of policing more appropriate for a democracy. Consequently, the material that we have produced starts with the theme of democratic policing and compares this with alternative models.

I would say that what sets democratic policing apart from other systems is that the police should see their primary role as being to protect the public, whereas the police in a totalitarian regime would see their primary function as being to protect the state. Admittedly any police force exercises social control on behalf of the government, so the difference is a question of degree.

The democratisation process that swept across the former Soviet Union and Africa meant that the governments of these countries recognised that they needed to change the orientation of their police forces and often looked for help to countries like the UK. In turn our government has an aid programme that is focussed on the "Millennium Goals" which have at their core the eradication of poverty by the year 2015.

The goals include universal rights to education, access to clean drinking water and access to justice. Our work was concerned broadly with improving access to justice for the poor and we formed a part of a much bigger project.

A quick reminder of the history of Nigeria since independence about forty years earlier is probably a useful starting point for what we were doing, and we certainly discussed this history as an important part of our training programme.

Nigeria has had a succession of military governments and has rarely remotely resembled a democracy.

The Nigeria Police was originally created by the colonising powers, and I can assure you the last thing that our government were thinking about was the protection of the people. They simply created a paramilitary police force to protect their interests which not infrequently meant that this resulted in the police oppressing the people and infringing their human rights.

Following independence one set of rulers replaced another, the colour of their skin changed but they had learned well and carried on oppressing the people just like we had done before. What else could be expected when that was the model of government, we had dictated to them for over a century? Well would you believe it we were trying to teach them about democracy—a great pity that we left it so late!

The story of our project with the police began about two years earlier when Blair one of the team I worked with in Ethiopia was appointed as Police Adviser to the Nigeria Police. He had just established a working relationship with the previous Inspector General when the guy was removed from office. Community Policing had already been talked about and was therefore the idea of the previous IG and the present one did not want to know.

Nigeria has a population of over one hundred and twenty million people and a police organisation that is believed to be about three hundred thousand strong. It is a vast country with some thirty-six States each with a State Government. Policing is provided as a Federal (national) responsibility. So, the Inspector General at Police HQ in Abuja is accountable to central government for policing across the nation and a local Police Commissioner is accountable to the IG and to the State Government.

Nigeria is believed to be one of the most corrupt countries in the world and has the unenviable reputation for generating more worldwide scams or frauds than any other part of the world. People are on the take in every situation that you come across. It is a pervasive and destructive tendency, and it is hard to equate with the fact that a larger percentage of the population attend a Christian church than anywhere else in the world.

Blair worked at Federal level in Abuja and Roger, and I worked at State level, initially in Enugu. We had a Project Team of nineteen senior Nigeria police working with us. The Project Team plus the three of us, two influential civilians and an Assistant Inspector General acted as the Steering Group for the Implementation of Community Policing in Nigeria.

Roger and I worked at State level initially in Enugu, but later expanding into another five pilot states. Our approach was to create a pool of locally based Community Policing Developers with three or four being trained for each major police station. Using the skills, we had imparted they would then implement the project, supported by the Project Team.

Roger and I ran the first three courses for Community Policing Developers whilst at the same time we selected candidates to become the future local trainers who then took over from us.

Baseline studies were initiated in Enugu at the commencement of our work there and amongst other disturbing facts they revealed that 96% of the population had some personal experience of police corruption. Most frequently this meant being stopped by the police on the highway and being instructed to provide money to the police. Another frequently occurring example was being asked to provide money for relatives in custody to be granted bail. Generally, the arrests giving rise to the requests for money would not have been based upon reasonable suspicion that they had committed a crime. Thus, arrests were frequently made of groups of innocent people for the sole purpose of collecting money.

Air Travel Nigeria Style

My most regular air journeys were between Abuja the capital and Enugu. At the time just one airline operated from Enugu having the strange name: 'Sossolisso.' Whether the repeated combination of the letters SOS is intentional or not I will leave you to decide. When I first travelled with them, they were operating three aeroplanes each of them being former Yugoslav Airlines DC9's. Now I am no expert on aircraft, but I calculate that these machines must have been approaching thirty years in service and it showed. I remember one of their planes always seemed to come in to land on full engine power and it does not feel right somehow. It may be that I was also influenced by the fact that the regular pilot at the time was a former Yugoslav air force pilot who happened to live at the same hotel, and I used to see how much alcohol he consumed the night before he was due to fly.

Let me try and describe Enugu airport. It is spacious and the buildings are reasonably modern. It can be noisy when busy but when I was waiting to get back to Abuja on a Saturday on a flight that had been scheduled to depart at 8am but eventually left about 4pm it was as quiet as a mortuary. You just work it out for yourself—if the airline is servicing Enugu, Port Harcourt, and Lagos with just 2 or 3 planes it follows that for a greater part of every day the tarmac at Enugu is empty. This is not very encouraging when you are waiting for a flight!

The airline had a habit of making the return journey free seating which means that it is a free for all in selecting a seat. Now regulars like me know that some of the seats are broken and we all try to get on the plane early so we can make sure that the seat backrest does not col/lapse just as the plane leaves the ground. There is a lot of pushing and shoving and the women are the worst especially those who are large and generously endowed. They tend to use their excessively large bosoms to push you out of the way like I remember doing with the bumpers on a dodgem car at the fairground when I was a teenager.

It is difficult to know how to react; if I smile, I feel in danger of them thinking I am a pervert, if I complain I am likely to get more of the same, so I try to do the Buster Keeton bit by not showing any reaction at all.

There are some seats that one tries to avoid at all costs. The rearmost seats are next to the toilets and because the engines are at the rear end (not on wings) it's very noisy at the back, so on noise and smell they are to be avoided. The best seats are in rows 12 and 13 because they cover for the emergency exits so there is more leg room, and you get the opportunity to get out first in an emergency.

Once you have overcome the propensity of the large women to bump you out of the way in the queue you are just as likely to find yourself sitting next to an extremely large Nigerian male. Now I am not small, but I do have the capacity to sit on one normal aircraft seat, but some of the local men need one and a half so they overhang into your seat and cannot get the seat belt to fasten around their girth. You can imagine what it is like whilst they work their shoulders around trying to get more seat belt, the emergency exit looks increasingly attractive.

Another thing that I notice about Nigerians who travel by air is that they seem to have an absolute requirement to contact every person on their mobile phone address book and tell them that they are sitting on an aeroplane about to depart for wherever, when the crew have already announced that they are to be switched off because they may affect the instruments of the aircraft. Now that would be difficult enough if they had just one mobile phone in use at a time, but they often have as many as three and they all seem to think that it is crucially important to have the latest chimes. When they all start shutting down at the same time it feels like you are operating in the timpani section of a huge orchestra.

If Enugu local airport was quiet, the opposite was true of Lagos domestic airport which is noisy and busy to the point of being chaotic. There are at least half a dozen small domestic airlines operating out of the airport, so competition is stiff. The outstanding feature of Lagos airport is that everyone you meet tends to want to either; rob you, defraud you, befriend you, provide you with company for the night or an unbelievably good investment opportunity or sell you something.

It is simply a marketplace with planes and many destinations. Add to this that the journey between the domestic and international terminals traverses a dual carriageway where you may purchase any commodity or service from the comfort of your car, and you will begin to gain a picture of what it is like.

My advice if you ever find yourself travelling this road is to keep your eyes focused on an imaginary point in the middle distance and do not deviate your stare for one moment to either side, because in this part of Lagos even the most minimal eye contact is assumed to be a potential sale. Next piece of advice is, wind your window down for the minimal space to look at the item, in the unlikely event that you have been foolish enough to consider making a purchase.

You would be surprised what little space is required for a Nigerian would be Sir Richard Branson, to be through the window and your business partner for the next twenty years, when all you wanted to do was to look at a pair of fake D & G sunglasses.

Always have the exactly the right change available for the item, because they never have any or you end up with this young man running alongside your car sorting out the change whilst he is negotiating his palls selling similar rubbish and cars travelling along the next traffic lane. When this happens the temptation after a while is to say, "Keep the change." Another successful business transaction he thinks as you discover that the sunglasses were made for someone with a face half the size of yours!

Abuja domestic terminal clearly started life as the international airport but when a new terminal was developed got downgraded to cater just for internal flights. It is not as busy as Lagos or as chaotic, but it does have people who will pray on ignorance or unfamiliarity to relieve you of your money. For example, the guy who took my suitcases subsequently asked for N1500 excess baggage charge. I gave him the money and asked for a receipt, but he told me to collect it when I identified my case before boarding. You can guess that no receipt was forthcoming, and the money obviously went into his pocket and not into the coffers of the airline. They tried it on again subsequently but when I held up the money and said it would not be handed over until I saw the receipt being written out, I stopped having to pay for excess baggage.

I recall well arriving at the Abuja domestic terminal with a view to flying on the 4.00 p.m. direct flight to Enugu, scheduled to arrive well before 5.00 p.m. and therefore giving about an hour leeway to ensure arrival at the hotel before dark. There are no streetlights in Enugu, and we had an embargo on after dark road travel because of the high incidence of vehicle high jacking in the town.

The first surprise was that the checking in desks that I had used on my very recent flight were now a pile of rubble and no redirection signs. After a few minutes of wondering around apparently lost I managed to find a Nigerian who appeared to know what he was doing so I tucked in behind him.

We found ourselves in the open air under the hot sun between two rows of shipping containers that were being used as temporary buildings. This was where the various internal airlines had moved their operations to, but the normal chaotic set up had been multiplied a thousand times.

I was already getting concerned when I saw that my suitcase was dumped with a load of others on the rubble and mine was the only one with a Sossolisso Enugu tag. I pointed this out and it was quickly moved to another place on the rubble where there was at least one other piece of luggage labelled the same as mine. Having satisfied myself that there was half a chance that my suitcase and I would end up in the same location I returned to the terminal building and made my way through the security checks to the departure lounge.

I guess that by the time I had got through to the lounge it would be about 3.30 p.m. and my flight would be about half an hour away, so not too long to wait. I have often said to people here that Sossolisso is the most reliable airline operating in Nigeria; I have never known them to fly on time so you can rely on them to be late whereas the other airlines are sometime on time, so you cannot rely on them. I was therefore quite surprised to see a Sossolisso plane already on the apron, but my pleasure and anticipation was quickly dispelled when I saw that there was no sign of any flight activity. A closer scrutiny revealed that the tires on one side of the main wheels were very flat!

For two hours I sat in the departure lounge and watched flights depart for various internal destinations across the country; Lagos, Port Harcourt, Ibadon, Kano and Calabar, not forgetting that very soon after I sat down the EAS flight departed for Enugu and I realised that I could have been at my intended destination for just after 4.00 p.m. For the entire two hours there was not a single announcement about the flight to Enugu although a Sossolisso flight came in from Lagos and went out again to Port Harcourt. By the end of the two hours of waiting without news I had been able to locate some of my fellow intended passengers to Enugu and being thrown together, we inevitably shared our feelings about flying just a few hours after a recent crash. We were all a bit concerned and getting more so as darkness approached.

It just shows that you should take nothing for granted because when I eventually boarded the aircraft, I was told that we were flying to Enugu via Port Harcourt and the flight crew was not even prepared to give me an estimated time of arrival. I imagined that I might find myself sleeping in the departure lounge of the airport at Port Harcourt. I have never flown into Enugu after dark and was not sure of the extent to which it is equipped for night flights, whereas Port Harcourt and Abuja both share the facilities with an international terminal. Boarding the aircraft had been interesting because the tarmac was not illuminated so we used the aircraft headlights to find our way to the steps!

On the way into Port Harcourt, we had bounced about a bit and there had been some flashes of lightning in the sky indicating the presence of a storm and on taking off again for our destination, I quickly realised that the storm was directly over Enugu! We ran into some of the worst turbulence I have experienced, and this was combined with spectacular flashes of lightning that illuminated the complete sky in a vivid blue aura. You can guess that I was spending a fair bit of time praying and the fellow behind me was also calling on the Lord. I know this because every time the plane dropped into an air pocket or the lightning flashed, he exclaimed "Jesus Christ"!

You always know there is a problem when after the announcement that you are about to land and having descended significantly, you do not land but continue to fly around. That is what happened, and it was clear that the pilot was flying around the worst of the storm and trying to avoid being struck by lightning which can apparently bring an aircraft down. In fact, the newspapers had been suggesting that the reason for the Lagos crash was a lightning strike on the plane!

When we eventually landed it was still raining on the ground and the electric storm was still evident in the sky. There were only a few of us on this final leg of the journey and our relief was evident as we exchanged farewells and shook hands thanking the Lord for safe arrival in Enugu.

Lorries Die Too!

It has been recorded that there are certain towns in England where people go to die. They are the places that are noted for people living in retirement and therefore, inevitably the places where they die: Eastbourne and Bakewell to name but two such places.

I spent a part of my time in Nigeria along with my wife staying in the city of Ibadan, which despite there being a capital city Abuja, and a former capital Lagos, it remains the largest city in Nigeria. It is also famous in these parts for being the home of the first university in Nigeria. What we did not know before we went there is that it has at least three other claims to fame.

Ibadan, I have decided is the dirtiest city on earth. Everywhere you go the roadside and central reservations are covered with huge piles of litter and during the rainy season stagnant water. As you approach some parts of the city the pollution hangs in the air as poisonous, noxious clouds waiting to fill your lungs with asthma inducing fog.

Ibadan also has some of the longest traffic jams to be found anywhere in the world. On my return journey from work one day, it took us around an hour to travel about a mile and we only achieved that by driving a Toyota Prado through gaps and along surfaces not intended even for such a robust vehicle. The pollution was so bad during this part of the journey that I ended up with asthma for a couple of days afterwards.

The traffic jam leads me to the final reason for Ibadan having a unique characteristic; it is the place where lorries go to die!

However, despite the obvious difficulties which I have already given some clues about, I want to start with the positive aspects of our stay in Ibadan. We were accommodated at the International Institute for Tropical Agriculture (IITA) which turned out to be an oasis of beauty, comfort, and cleanliness in a desert of dirt and grime.

The Institute occupies a huge site close to the university campus and less than a mile from the largest lorry cemetery in the world! When you drive through the security gates and enter the compound it is really like you enter an entirely different world. In a way, it is an extremely sad reminder that all that is required to clean up Africa is investment and organisation.

Driving along the road to the main reception building on either side there are large palm trees set in large areas of lawns that are closely cropped and very green at the time of my visit which was towards the end of the tropical rainy season. Although I would not know which species of palm trees they are, it needs to be said that it was predominantly because of palm oil that the British colonised Nigeria in the first place and they still provide a source of income and cooking oil for the locals.

At the time Margaret and I had recently been reading the current edition of a magazine "New African," which had impressed us and reminded us of the gross inaccuracies that we were taught in school as facts about Africa. We clearly remember growing up with the notion that prior to the white man bringing Christianity and education to the Africans they were but savages. Recent discoveries in the former Kingdom of Benin (South West, Nigeria) have revealed that they had craftsmen and architects as skilled as those in the ancient Greek and Roman civilisations.

Even more disturbing news than the fact that we were taught lies as facts is contained in an article describing slavery and the role of the Church of England in propagating it! The Codrington Plantation covering seven hundred acres of rich red soil on the island of Barbados kept detailed accounts for its absentee landlord in England. In 1781 the headcount of slaves was two hundred and seventy-six men, women, and children, valued at between £70 and £15 per person. The disturbing fact is that the absentee landlord was the Church of England. True, and worthy of praise is the fact that Rowan Williams the previous Archbishop of Canterbury has publicly repented of the sins of the church, both their role in slavery and the robbing of Africa of its history.

When slavery ended in the British West Indies, total slave imports of well over two million left a surviving slave population of about six hundred and seventy thousand. It can at least be some source of thankfulness for English Christians that most of those from our country who led the fight against slavery were motivated by their commitment to Christ.

The IITA has been developed since the 1960's and the buildings reflect the architecture of that period, but because they were constructed using the best standards and fittings are still in relatively good condition. We stayed in a one-bedroom flat with large living room and bedroom along with adequate kitchen and bathroom. Although the fittings were original and therefore showing the signs of wear they still worked, a lasting tribute to the investment in quality in the first place. It was comfortable without being luxurious.

The grounds of the IITA proved to be an absolute delight; spacious and well planned in the style of park land and including a nine-hole golf course complete with lakes and other natural obstacles. We did not play golf, but we did walk around the estate including the golf course and nature lined up an amazing experience for us. As we walked between two sections of the golf course along a track surrounded by a mass of tropical trees and plants, we spotted a large and beautiful butterfly.

It had a wingspan of around five inches when fully open. The background of the open wings was medium brown in colour but on the leading edge trimmed with a pale fluorescent blue colour, the same colour appearing as a substantial flash on both halves of the wings. We had a camera with us and for a little while tried to get near enough to take a picture using the zoom facility when the butterfly decided to settle on the muddy ground about a couple of inches from my foot and I took a good photograph of it. We also saw another magnificent butterfly which came close enough for us to take a photograph.

This one was slightly smaller with fluorescent blue, yellow and oranges flashes on a black background. A little later Margaret said, "I am a bit worried there might be snakes here," and I looked to the ground close to her and saw one about four feet in length, which I pointed out to her. It was just the shed skin of a snake, but a bit of a shock initially.

There are some quite unbelievable trees in the park. One huge one had a trunk that looked for all-the-world like an elephant's skin. The trunk also had ribs or flaps sticking out creating seven or eight alcoves each large enough to accommodate Margaret. The tree was probably two hundred feet high. There are still huge rain forests in Nigeria with trees like mahogany in profusion. They are exploiting them to a limited extent but thankfully not using the slash and burn techniques found in South America and some other tropical areas.

On the Sunday morning of our stay in Ibadan we met up with a friend, Rev A, a young Methodist Minister who I met in Enugu, where he was undertaking his probationary training. He is now attending the Emmanuel Theological College (joint Anglican and Methodist) with a view to obtaining a degree in theology. He took us to the college chapel where they were celebrating their fortieth anniversary.

We arrived for 10am and stayed till after 1pm but left before the end because there was no sign of the service ending and we had already listened to the sermon and given our offering. The church was full, with about three hundred people and some "great and good" representing the fact that it was a special anniversary. The formal speeches and welcomes tended to distract from the spirituality of the occasion in my mind. To be honest I tire of the endless paying tribute to traditional rulers, judges and others considered to be worthy of praise, here in Nigeria. There is far too much of it and the church should in my opinion reflect the fact that all men and women are equal before God. I do not mean to be disrespectful of leaders, it's just that there is too much of it and it consumes large proportions of all public occasions and distracts from the overall objectives of the events.

An extensive brochure was produced to celebrate the anniversary and I will quote from one of the articles that describe the history of the Methodist Church in Nigeria.

"James Fergusun a freed slave travelled from Freetown in Sierra-Leone to Lagos in Nigeria and in 1841 appealed to Rev Thomas Dove a Methodist Minister in Freetown to send a missionary to Nigeria. Thomas Birch Freeman arrived in response in September 1842. The early Methodists in the West of Nigeria (Yuroba) were from the Wesleyan Branch of the church whereas those in the East (Igbo) were from the Primitive Methodist tradition."

Methodism remains strong in Nigeria and today combines traditional conservative styles of worship with more African charismatic praise and worship. However, like all traditional denominations it is losing out to the new charismatic Pentecostal churches which have experienced phenomenal growth in Nigeria over the last 30 years.

Well, I guess you are thinking that I have forgotten the so-called theme of this chapter, a place where lorries die! What do I mean by this? It is just that the description seems so appropriate. For a stretch of about two miles of roadway through a suburb of Ibadan the wide verges are littered with trucks in various states of decay. These are the ones that have died but are being kept in a state of suspended animation so that their body parts can be used to bring life back to their nearly dead brothers.

In total there must be five thousand or more of these wrecked vehicles. Why are they all there? The answer is that hundreds of mechanics ply their trade along the road; here they do not have fancy workshops, they just wait by the roadside like vultures waiting for animals to die in the desert. Unfortunately, some machines lose consciousness before making it to the verge, so they require major surgery whilst on the highway. I kid you not—we saw one such lorry virtually blocking the carriageway for about three days whilst they did a major engine repair! That is why the traffic jams are so frequent and long.

The slow death of a lorry can be observed as you pass along the road—starts with the removal of small parts like wheels and mirrors etc, but then gains momentum as the vehicle slips downhill leaving what is left as a lump of scrap metal. Some days, palls of black smoke rise into the sky indicating that tires that cannot be re-used are being burnt. Now to be burnt a tire must be in a sorry state judging by the state of those that are still being used entirely devoid of tread and often with cuts or bulges in the side walls.

Consequently, although Ibadan is a special place for lorries to die, others just die alongside an expressway where a tire bursts and they turn over shedding their load in the process. One time I saw a full load of tomatoes strewn across the highway, another time a load of oranges. Often lorry loads of goods are topped with numerous people hitching a cheap ride. No doubt they end up just as crushed and broken as the oranges and tomatoes that make a colourful squash on the road surface. Does not bear thinking about, does it?

A Nigerian Arrangement

There is a tendency throughout Africa for events to be planned at short notice or seemingly not planned at all and it is not unusual to find yourself invited to an event after it has occurred. About 11.30 a.m. one Tuesday morning I was working in the office processing questionnaires from a public attitude survey when Assistant Commissioner of Police A called me and said, "You are expected at Central Police Station." I quickly replied, "What for?" and he then said, "You remember on Saturday that the DPO (Divisional Police Officer) told us about a community engagement session that he had arranged, well it's happening now, and you are required."

I arrived at Central Police Station (CPS) a few minutes later and found it a hive of industry. A series of marquees with open sides had been erected and there were hundreds of people milling around the police station compound. The police band was playing, and it was obvious that the community engagement session was going to be big. That was a problem for me because I was not dressed for a formal occasion. Never mind I thought, I will disappear to the rear of the crowd and then get away once I have seen the people that matter.

It was not to be the case because just as soon as I had found out from A what was happening, I was accosted by an usher who ushered me to my place on the front row in the centre section of the honoured guests and right next to the Chief Judge for Enugu State and alongside a collection of very impressively dressed traditional rulers. Here was me in my M & S casual style khaki trousers and casual shirt in between the boss of the legal profession in his pinstripes and tails and a traditional ruler in a cloak that would put "Joseph's Amazing Technicolour Dream-coat" to shame!

Whilst waiting for events to commence formally I chatted informally to the people sitting alongside me and got hold of a copy of the programme and the speech that was to be made by the host Divisional Commander (DPO). I established that the event was being called to commission some recent improvement work including a new "ULTRA MODERN FLAG STAND." Many of the recent improvements that have all taken place since the DPO arrived at the station were self-evident, a coat of paint around the building and a new security wall and gate being the most obvious. The improvements have all come about through local sponsorship schemes. We have been advocating such steps in our training courses for divisional management teams and it is encouraging to see them happening.

Speeches here in Nigeria are far more flowery than you are likely to get in the UK and I include below just the opening paragraphs of the speech.

[Today is remarkable and would remain memorable in the minds of those who crave for excellence, hard work, vision, good name, sacrifice, commitment, discipline, development, innovation, goodwill, and symbiotic human relations etc. these feelings properly articulating and harnessed, gave birth to this occasion—COMMISSIONING OF ULTRA MODERN FLAG STAND by our indefatigable and quintessential Commissioner of Police.

Permit me to go into memory lane on how these projects came into being. On 15th August 2005, when I assumed duty at CPS, Enugu, I was brought face to face with a premises supposedly dressed in "GRAVE CLOTH," not conducive for discharge and delivery of quality services to the citizenry. Especially residents and entrepreneurs within CPS jurisdiction.

I was psychologically challenged to re-dress the entire CPS with a RESURRECTION CLOTH. The story of GRAVE AND RESURRECTION CLOTH, you may wish to know, is the handiwork of our Lord Jesus Christ as exemplified in St JOHN Gospel Chapter 11 verses 11-44. This is when Christ raised Lazarus from the dead and ordered that the GRAVE CLOTH should be removed and replaced with the RESURRECTION CLOTH. The same Christ-like vision and legacy, I have borrowed to apply in CPS. To God be the glory!

Having been faced with these challenges, I now mapped out an ACTION PLAN comprising the following working strategies:

1. *Reduction of incidence of armed robbery and other violent crimes in CPS.*
2. *Reduction of Traffic Congestion within CPS jurisdiction noted for commercial activities.*
3. *Reduction in the level of corruption and indiscipline within the Division.*

4. *To improve the depreciating public relations between the Police and the members of the public within the Division.*

It is interesting to note that all these strategies are on course.

To actualize these strategies, I started by invoking the principles of COMMUNITY POLICING, one of which encourages PARTNERSHIP with trustworthy and reliable stakeholders. With the unalloyed loyalty and cooperation of my COMMUNITY POLICING DEVELOPERS, I was able to ignite the machinery of mobilisation and sensitisation of stakeholders. Today, the result of that initiative is what has given CPS a facelift and celebration for which we are gathered here.

His speech goes on to list what has been contributed and by whom which is the sort of transparency that we have been encouraging.

Shortly before the arrival of the Police Commissioner a large troop of traditional dancers and musicians came dancing into the compound of the police station and did a lengthy performance. They were led by a banner which indicated that they were representatives of the Coal Camp Vigilante Group. I was delighted to see that they were involved because only a few months previously I had been told that this group had so little trust of the police that they would have nothing to do with them. These groups are set up by local people to provide a citizen led local police service usually serving a quite small area. This one had been set up some years ago to counter armed robbery and killings that the police were not addressing, so their contribution to the event was something of an achievement.

Behind the banner came the dancers and musicians the latter using a wide variety of local percussion instruments both wooden and metal and providing a very African rhythm. At the rear of the troop, they were dragging along a goat which was later presented to the DPO (his Christmas dinner). The goat not surprisingly was more reluctant to join the parade, knowing that his contribution (it was a male) would be much more significant than all the others put together.

The dancers performed again after the Commissioner had arrived amidst fanfare and salutations. A dance troop of police wives also performed. I am pretty sure that if as the local police boss in the UK, I had asked my police officers get their partners to create a dance troupe I might have met with something more than a polite refusal, but Africa is different, and dancing is a very important part of everyday life.

I have previously explained about my attempts at dancing in Ethiopia and some of the comments of locals on my level of achievement. Something similar happened in Nigeria, when the most senior woman police officer complemented me on my dancing.

Dancing in most regions of Ethiopia largely involves upper body movement, but dancing in Nigeria is mainly made up of lower body movement. Most Nigerians are designed for their form of dancing due to their generously sized bottoms which they shake vigorously from side to side, whilst at the same time shuffling their feet to the rhythm of the music.

The comments about my dancing were made when I was running a course for executive grade officers of the Nigerian Police Force including the most senior woman police officer who at the time was an Assistant Inspector General. At the first break on the first day of the course she approached me and told me that we had met before. I was at a loss to remember when we had met previously but was saved any embarrassment when she explained that she had seen me dancing Nigerian style in the Methodist Cathedral in Abuja, when the then President of Nigeria had attended. Perhaps I should explain that native dancing is not a significant part of the role of an overseas police adviser, but understanding local culture certainly is.

Wherever I have been in my travels I have tried as much as possible to get to a church on a Sunday. In Addis Ababa it was St Matthews Anglican Church, but in my travels around Nigeria I generally found a Methodist Church. In Abuja it was the Methodist Cathedral about a twenty-minute walk from the Sheraton Hotel where I stayed. On the day of my unintended dancing demonstration my wife Margaret was out visiting me, and we walked together in the bright sunshine with the likely temperature being around 35 degrees. We passed by a filling station on the way and saw lots of cars waiting for fuel. This is a country which is the sixth largest producer of crude oil but has frequent fuel shortages.

Nearer to church we found the police were stopping traffic coming onto the main road and thought that this was some further exercise to control the petrol queues. That was until some motorcycle outriders came along the main road followed by a procession of police and other official vehicles, one of which was flying the flag of the President.

We were quite surprised to see them turn up the side street that we were heading for and then even more surprised that they headed straight for the Methodist Cathedral. Yes, the President visited our church that morning. Initially that created a few problems because we were prevented from going to the church entrance where the presidential procession had blocked the entire road. There were armed police and soldiers everywhere as you can imagine.

Once Mr President was inside then we managed to get to the church but had to walk around the back to an entrance on the far side. No one directed us we just went that way following a very well-dressed Nigerian lady. We halted close to the entrance for the Nigerian National Anthem played by an Army band that might sound better leading a carnival parade.

By this time Margaret was being bothered by the sun as we had spent about 25 minutes under its glare and she was trying to get close enough to the building to get in the shade whilst I was trying to mouth to her "National Anthem," and at the same time standing to attention like a good friend of Nigeria or retired policeman should! It was the first time that Margaret had heard the anthem, but I have had quite a lot of it, given the official functions I have attended here.

Security in the church was extremely high! However, nobody searched us, nor asked who we were, and we ended up amongst the VIP Guests/Presidents entourage on the fourth row from the front and directly behind the President. The head of the Anti-Bomb Squad was just behind us and the Head of the Police Mobile Unit in front of us. Standing by Mr President was a guy in dark glasses and a body that reminded us of 'Odd job' from one of the early Bond movies. Why do bodyguards always look like bodyguards? It might be more effective if they looked ordinary.

You might guess that it was a special service, and you would be correct. However, it was not to acknowledge the President but to pay tribute to the Methodist Archbishop of Abuja the Most Rev (Dr) Ebere O. Nze on his 68th birthday and the launch of his book "Reflection of Faith and Contemporary Issues."

The President read one of the lessons—Luke 12: 13—21. You can look it up, but it includes "A man's life does not consist in the abundance of his possessions" and "You fool. This very night your life will be demanded of you."

The preacher was a Professor at the University of Calabar, and also a Minister, a personal friend of the Archbishop. It was a good and direct message in line with what you would expect from such a reading. He looked at what constitutes a fool in scripture using a collection of examples from Proverbs and Psalms. He used Bible examples of people who had everything but did not remain faithful to God and encouraged the listeners to remain faithful to God.

The President also made a speech and talked about the importance of God. He mentioned that the Presidential residence has a chapel where the Archbishop joins himself and other leaders monthly for prayer for the nation. He also did a bit of political speech making but not so that it detracted from the sense of worship to God. In fact, the service was pretty much like services are generally with an absence of bowing and scraping to the President which we appreciated.

I had a slight shock at one stage when Margaret dropped a hymn book on the floor, and it made a loud bang, and I thought the 'Odd job' look-a-like might shoot us!

With services generally lasting more than three hours it is perhaps difficult for people in the UK to understand how one can string out a service for so long. Really the answer is very straight forward because each activity is undertaken to the full. The praise session for example when we sing and dance to African music may last for up to half an hour or more. Despite the use of African music for praise sessions we start and finish with traditional English style hymns from the Methodist Hymn Book sung with the backing of a robed choir and accompanied by a church organ. It is quite a strange mixture of styles with the African not quite eliminating the colonial influence.

When the main offering is taken up instead of the collection box coming to the congregation, we all go out to the front and deposit our offering there. Presumably on the basis that the Lord loves a cheerful giver, the worship band led us with their African music, and we are encouraged to dance with enthusiasm. This is when those of us with rather large bottoms have a distinct advantage. I did my absolute best that morning as I danced past Mr President and his entourage which included the most senior female officer in the Nigerian Police Force and that is where she had seen me before.

Trip to Benin

The journey from Enugu to Benin to visit a Nigerian colleague who was in hospital following a road traffic accident took about three and a half hours and is roughly in a South West direction, journeying through the States of Enugu, Anambra, Delta and Edo. What are now the States of Enugu, Anambra and Ebonyi were originally Eastern Nigeria or Biafra as it was called during the civil war that you may remember.

Most of the road for the entire journey was a dual carriageway, but in some small sections in a poor state of repair, particularly in Anambra State. For the first half an hour from Enugu, we travelled roads that I was completely familiar with as it forms the route back to Abuja, and to Nsukka and Oji River (where we had been delivering training). The scenery for that section is hilly or undulating and interesting without being spectacular. Most of the large centres of population are bypassed.

One of the memorable features of the journey was the crossing of the Niger River at Assaba which is in Delta State. Well to be completely accurate the Eastern side of the river has the City of Onitsha (former capital of Anambra State) and the Western side of the river has Assaba. I once read a book entitled "Strong Brown God" which was about the Niger River. It is the largest river that I have seen in my life. At the crossing point it must be a good three quarters of a mile wide.

On the delta side of the bridge, it opens wider and has numerous quite large and inhabited islands. And I could see large numbers of boats plying back and forth with passengers and goods. It was an impressive sight, and the colour of the water informed the name of the book I have just referred to. The brown of the water comes from the red soil that abounds in West Africa.

Soon after entering the State of Anambra we came to the new capital city, Awka, and on entering we had to negotiate two burnt out coaches, some of the remains of rioting that had occurred in the last few weeks when substantial numbers of people were killed and lots of houses burnt down as well. The riots had been politically motivated over the removal from office of the State Governor. Our progress through Awka was slow because we were (like every other traveller) subjected to road checks about every 800 yards.

Awka has lots of new buildings and it is easy to see why the politicians would prefer to live there than in Onitsha, of which there will be more, later. There are many large houses on hillsides overlooking the new capital City and I would guess that most of them are occupied by government officials!

Onitsha on the other hand is one of the scruffiest cities I have ever visited. I find it extremely difficult to describe. On the Saturday morning from one side of the city to the other side took us nearly an hour. On a bad working day at rush-hour, I am told that it can take well in excess of two hours to negotiate. Although the main road through Onitsha was a dual carriageway it was in an extremely poor state of repair. I am conscious that you will have an entirely inappropriate picture in your mind by my use of the expression dual carriageway.

What I mean in the case of this stretch of road is that there is space for two lanes of traffic in each direction and there is a gap between the two carriageways but is far removed from anything you will ever have seen. I will try to the limit of my descriptive powers to put you in the picture by selecting just a few assorted word pictures.

Firstly, please try and envisage the central reservation as being nothing like the ideas you have in your minds. All along the stretch of road the gap between the carriageways is un-surfaced, so that means red soil which now in the dry season results in loads of red dust. Further the edge of the metalled road is not properly completed, so from time to time it has broken away and there may be a sheer drop up to three or four feet in depth. From time to time some poor unfortunate motorist (cars, lorries, you name it) has been forced of the metalled road surface at an inappropriate point causing the vehicle to roll over and that is where the vehicles stay, getting covered in dust. There are very few proper crossing points, so vehicles just leave the road and drive across the land in between; some get stuck for good and remain there. Hope you are getting the picture.

Now just take a look at the surrounding buildings, they are mostly sixties style concrete boxes of apartments that have never been painted externally since they were built. Typically, they are between four and eight stories high and there are hundreds of them. Somewhere between the flats and the road is where the occupants of the flats dump their rubbish and there must be millions of tons of the stuff. Now and then the rubbish has been dumped on the central reservation with one pile so big that it was spilling into the road and had blocked one traffic lane of the two available.

There are markets, stalls, and sales pitches of one sort or another for almost the entire length of the road through the city. One section was almost entirely taken up with commercial motor vehicles. Either side of the road and in the central reservation. Car cleaning here takes on a new dimension, the guy was brushing about six inches of dust off the top of the vans that were for sale when we passed by. In another area it was a huge scrap yard of second-hand motor parts again taking up both sides of the road and the bit in the middle. It looked like another huge cemetery for automobiles.

One area of the city is given over to clothing with stalls spread out on either side and in the centre of the road and in another it is food of every type grown in West Africa. There are numerous motorcycle taxis that weave in and out of the traffic which seems always to be blocked as we drive through the city this Saturday morning. It is hot with the temperature gauge reading 35 degrees, but thankfully the air conditioning on the vehicle is working. As we get nearer to the Niger Bridge, the traffic becomes even more slow-moving and chaotic. The taxi cars are continually pulling out in front of us and blocking the road with consequential blasting of hooters from all directions.

So, if you can get the picture, there are two lanes of so-called moving traffic and to the roadside are large market areas selling everything under the sun. The taxis stop and start all the time without any warning and the motorcycles cut across you without any regard for life or limb. A motorcycle taxi will be used to convey anything you can imagine but think would never fit on two wheels. For example, I have observed whole families (mum dad and two kids) babies in arms, dining tables, a full set of carpenter's tools, baskets of live chickens—do I need to add any more? The strangest example of this was a full-length fridge freezer on the back of a motorcycle.

The nearer we got to the bridge the longer we remained static between moves and the shorter the distance we moved before stopping again. I noticed that immediately in front of the bridge three roads converged—a total bottle neck. The police are supposed to be directing traffic, but they just looked as though they had given up. A motorcycle taxi with a huge basket full of ripe tomatoes, on either side of the seat gets stuck between two cars and I imagine we are going to see some tomato sauce being made.

Eventually we do get onto the bridge and slowly cross the Strong Brown God and enter Delta State and the town of Asaba. In truth, we are crossing the Northern most tip of Delta State. As the name implies it contains the Niger Delta and a few miles down-river a boat is a more acceptable method of transport than a car. It is also quite dangerous with not infrequent kidnappings. Delta State contains a good proportion of Nigeria's oil resources, along with River State and there is a lot of jealousy about how the money from oil is spent.

One of the main problems is that in spite of having huge oil resources Nigeria has little or no refining capacity, so it has to buy back refined petroleum products at inflated prices. It makes no sense to me that they seem to be doing nothing about this.

The tip of Delta State is not as dangerous as the area where the oil is located, so I did not feel particularly scared. The scenery became different from what we had been passing through previously. Flatter and generally much better farming land. We passed numerous signs indicating commercial farming. The combination of abundant water and hot weather obviously produces rapid growth. The areas that had been cultivated were relatively free from weeds but elsewhere it was dense bush or jungle with lots of trees like bamboo, but also large creeping vines everywhere, even up the tallest of trees. There were also many forests of palm trees from which the locals extract palm wine, palm oil and palm kernels. Palm wine when first gathered from the tree is a very pleasant milky looking drink with no alcohol content. When it starts to ferment it becomes like fire water, I have only drunk it the same day it was gathered thus far and had no after-effects whatsoever.

As we passed from Delta State into Edo State the countryside changed again and there are some quite steep hills with the road cut into red sandstone rocks. The hills are clearly too much for some of the local lorries and quite a few have overturned spilling their loads, one of which was full of tomatoes.

Benin is the capital of Edo State and has a population of more than a million people. It is an ancient city that goes back well beyond colonial times and used to be the capital of the Kingdom of Benin. Look on a map of West Africa and you will observe that the country next to Nigeria to the North is Benin; a rather long and narrow stretch of land from the coast almost to the Sahara Desert, you will also observe that the piece of sea there is called the Bight of Benin and is part of the Gulf of Guinea.

As we entered the city, I received a telephone call to say that the man I was visiting had been moved to Lagos that morning, so I was not going to be able to see him. Back to Enugu then!

The Pilgrimage

After a few weeks of almost continually work seven days a week following our arrival in Enugu, Roger and I decided that we had earned a trip out and a discussion with P our driver ensued after which we decided that we would visit the Awhum waterfall. Our Access to Justice Welcome Pack described this as "More than 30 metres high; the fall is located close to a monastery. The water is said to be curative and capable of dispelling evil or satanic forces if and wherever sprinkled." As it happened this turned out to be a very inadequate description!

P picked us up at the hotel at about 10.45 a.m. (should have been 10.30 a.m.—but this is Africa). We drove for an hour into the countryside. The area is rolling more than hilly or mountainous and the flora changes depending upon the situation: The higher the ground the less dense the vegetation and the lower the ground the denser the vegetation. Some of the rolling hills just outside Enugu reveal outcrops of coal shale indicating the presence of coal in the area. I recognise these because of the similarity with those in Derbyshire.

Further on from Enugu the vegetation becomes lusher, and the areas at the side of the road are cultivated. The main crops are corn (maize) and cassava. We also observe banana plantations and a multitude of palm trees. The types that predominate are the trees from which palm oil is obtained, although we did spot a few coconut palms as well. Our route takes us along the original main road between Enugu and the capital Abuja, but which has now been superseded by a new road. P identified the village that he originated from and explained that as a child he would carry water from the river in a pot on his head—a forty-five minute, return trip. He was quite surprised to find that I also had to carry water as a child and impressed when I explained that in the winter, I also had to carry water for the cattle.

Eventually we turned off the main road onto a track that took us through an area with lush tropical plants and trees on both side of the road. Some small dwellings could be spotted and some small areas of land under cultivation. After about two or three miles travelling along the track we came to a monastery. It was then that we began to realise the inadequacy of the description supplied by Access to Justice. Awhum is a place of pilgrimage. There is a large area inside the compound of the monastery where cars were parked, and people were wondering around.

Some single-story buildings clearly housed accommodation for better off pilgrims who were staying overnight. The poorer pilgrims had less salubrious but still adequate arrangements. On the inside of the high boundary walls of the monastery a waterproof canopy had been provided and a concrete base. Clearly, they spread out their clothes on the concrete and slept there, under the stars. Other buildings advertised a Ministry Centre and administration facilities. We set off on our walk to the waterfall as the road from the monastery is unsuitable for vehicles.

The route was all downhill on the way to the waterfalls, but that made us aware that the return journey would be all uphill. Please consider that the temperature would be at least thirty-five degrees and you will realise that we had a slight concern about the return journey. You may note that I was wearing sandals—I had some trainers in the car but had preferred the sandals not knowing quite how far it was going to be to get to the waterfall and thinking it would not take long. In the event it turned out to be more than an hour each way, so probably about a six-mile return trip, perhaps the trainers would have been better?

Eventually we arrived near the bottom of the valley that we were walking into and had to cross a small river. From this stage onwards we began to meet groups of pilgrims returning from the waterfalls. Many of the groups were singing and clapping and we were greeted warmly. There seemed to be a special appreciation of the fact that two white men were joining them in their pilgrimage.

Having crossed the river, the ground rose again for a short distance. Near the river crossing point clothes were spread over the bushes—washday is Saturday (by the river). Before long we were again at the riverside but on this occasion walking on the riverbank. By now there was a continual stream of returning pilgrims, some with Bibles, others clutching rosaries in their hands and chanting prayers, and others singing, dancing, and clapping. After a little while alongside the river we had to get into it and walk in the water towards the waterfall. My sandals came into their own as I left them on and they protected my feet, whereas Roger had to take his shoes off. He left his socks on to shield his feet a little and looked very English!

Along the river path from time to time we came across shrines and a cave where we saw people praising and praying. The further along the river we went the narrower the channel became and the higher the rocks on either side. Eventually we were in a deep ravine at least sixty feet up to the top of the banks on either side both of which were overhanging and only a small amount of light getting through to us. By now we were frequently required to stop and allow those coming in the opposite direction to pass because of the narrowness of the channel (about four feet wide).

After walking along the riverbed for about ten minutes we reached the waterfall. A vast torrent of water was pouring from above us at a point where the ravine ended. This area was perhaps ten feet wide and there would be around about a dozen people dancing and singing under the torrent, all fully clothed and, so far as I could ascertain in their right mind. Nothing ventured, nothing gained so I joined them. It was quite an experience. I found the torrent to be further through than I had imagined, and I was trying to get beyond the water, but that proved impossible because of the numbers of people—a bit like the Baseball Ground, Derby in the good old days of Derby County success—and standing crowds—same smell of sweaty bodies as well!

Turning around in the torrent proved a bit problematic because people were pushing in from behind me—that was where I lost one of my sandals. I bent down to try and find it in the three or four feet of water, whilst under the torrent and it nearly washed me under. Whilst I was concerned about a three mile walk with one bare foot, I was also concerned not to get drowned, so I got out. A nice young man discovered my plight and went in and recovered my sandal. I felt great after coming out of the water, but I am not offering an explanation, perhaps it was relief!

On the way back, steep uphill and very exhausting we came across groups who were breaking their return journey to have open air services. One group of ladies were sat under a tree listening to another lady preaching. I shouted, "God is good" and they replied "Amen, Praise the Lord." Another group were engaging in the African praise songs and dancing that I have described as taking place at the Methodist Cathedral in Enugu.

At the car, we were approached by a couple who were both medical students at the university in Enugu and we gave them a lift back to Enugu. They seemed suitably impressed at our interest in their culture and also that we were working with the police.

The Inspector General's Workshop

Life has a habit of providing interesting reminders of previous experiences and sometimes of fulfilling an intent that was formed a long time ago. I cannot explain the reason, but I have had a long-term feeling for Africa. This came to fruition in the first instance during my stay in Ethiopia. It is being continued during my work in Nigeria and although the two countries are so different, they have that African feeling about them. What this means is difficult to define; it includes the smell, the climate, the soil, the dust, the roads, the driving and most definitely the people and their habits.

Walking into the Nigeria Police Staff College at Jos was a fulfilment of a desire that first came to me at least 25 years earlier. Around that time, I spotted an advertisement for a police training adviser to the Nigerian Police based at Jos. I sent off for the forms but decided that I could not really leave Margaret and the children at that time and neither could I sacrifice the children's education in moving all of us to Nigeria. It is also a fact worthy of note that when I was undertaking my masters' degree course at Birmingham University back in 1986, I submitted an essay on the history and development of policing in Nigeria. This means that I am more aware than your typical retired UK police officer would be that the colonial power produced a police force to protect the colonial interest, not to protect the people. Part of what we are now trying to do is to correct that fault, not to re-write history but to indicate that the world has thankfully moved on.

My reason for going to Jos was to help run and contribute to the Inspector Generals' Workshop on Community Policing. Originally, I had put together at Blairs'ss request a proposal for two workshops each of two-days duration, splitting the participants to create manageable numbers for group discussions and the like. These workshops were intended for all the executive ranks of the Nigeria Police and there are a lot of them, approximately ninety. They comprise the

Inspector General, six Deputy Inspector Generals, a load of Assistant Inspect Generals and another load of Police Commissioners.

My original proposals got changed, so many times and for so many different reasons that I would bore you if I tried to explain. Suffice to say, we wanted to confront in a sensitive way some of the problems that were being reported to us by the rank and file of the organisation and my reading of the situation was that the IG was not quite ready for that, or at least not in the format we had proposed.

What we ended up with, or at least what we looked like having as we made our final preparations on the Tuesday before the event took place on the Thursday was one workshop for ninety participants starting at 9.00 a.m. and ending at 5.00 p.m. That was when the late, late changes started to be imposed upon us. First the Minister for Police Affairs and the Chairman of the Police Services Commission and other senior government officials decided that they must be there. That dictated that the event started at 10.00 a.m. with a formal opening by the Minister. Further to that the IG decided that he wished the event to end at 4.00 p.m. and there were further hurried changes.

The journey from Abuja to Jos takes at least three hours to complete. For the first hour or so we travelled the same route that we do for Enugu. Our general direction was towards the North of Nigeria and into Plateau State where Jos is the capital city. As the name implies it is situated on a mountain plateau and therefore incorporates scenery that I had not previously experienced in Nigeria. For most of the last hour of the journey we could have been in Ethiopia. Long before you get to the plateau the mountains become a dominant feature of the landscape ahead. They initially look dark and rugged, the rocky craggy outline etched against the skyline. Eventually we passed through them and into the plateau. This is where it really looks like Ethiopia.

A vast area of countryside was revealed with a jigsaw of colours, mainly at this time of the year (rainy season) varying shades of green. Bright green patches appear frequently looking like teff fields in Ethiopia. However, the crop here is rice, hundreds if not thousands of acres of it. Which reminds me of what the chairman of the ruling party here said at a Security Summit I attended; he explained that previously no rice was imported into the country, but now rice was being imported from America where it is produced under subsidy. This means that the person or company that brings a shipload of rice from America makes a fortune, but also means that about three thousand farmers have no market for their rice.

There are also huge tracts of maize and root crops including potatoes, carrots, and onions. Passing through some of the villages in this area the roadsides represented a harvest festival style display of local produce for sale, beautiful carrots colourful red onions, potatoes, bananas, and other such things. My Nigerian colleagues on the project team tell me that Plateau State is noted for the excellent crops that are produced.

As we approached Jos the fertile plain gave way to an area where huge rock formations protruded out of the ground and there was little soil. The crops here were restricted mainly to yam and cassava, but another feature that was reminiscent of Ethiopia was the abundance of eucalyptus trees, like parts of the road to Sandafa where the Ethiopian Police College is located. In fact, the surroundings for both police institutions are quite similar.

We arrived at the police college during the afternoon and introduced ourselves to the Commandant who complained that he had been told nothing about the event. There were other signs of the usual chaos that surrounds major activities in Nigeria. No one seems to wish to take responsibility, despite prior arrangements made for that to happen. The hall was being set out for the event so I was able to make an initial appraisal as to where we would set up our equipment and how we would address the assembled company. I should not have bothered because we changed everything around the next day anyway as the programme became the subject of further amendments.

We checked into the hotel at about 6.00p.m. and I set up my room for a rehearsal with the project team using a 'PowerPoint' display that I had been updating over the two previous days. I started our session by explaining the nature of the changes that had taken place in our programme and how this would affect what we could achieve. I explained the reasons for the changes and additions to the presentation. Then we found that we could not get the video projector to work. Blind panic set in at this stage with calls going out all over the place to find a replacement video projector.

Fortunately, P one of the team had her niece staying with her and she sorted the problem out for us. We finished our rehearsals about 9.30 p.m. After they had left my room, I began to realise that I was hungry, I had left the hotel in Abuja soon after 7.00 a.m. and had no breakfast and now it was 9.30 p.m. and I had not eaten anything all day. The menu in the dining room did not leave me with a lot of choice. I had braised beef and vegetables. The beef was not up to much, but the green beans, carrots and potatoes were outstanding and had clearly been gathered that day.

Back in my room I continued preparation through to about 11.30 p.m. and then resumed at 6.30 a.m. when Blair visited for his speech to be copied out on my printer. We were on the road by 7.00 a.m. once again without breakfast.

I cannot begin to describe the chaos that greeted us at the police college. Each of the participants had come with his/her entourage which included escort vehicles and armed guards, at least half a dozen personnel for each participant. So much fire power I wanted to hide out of the way or find a bullet proof vest. You can imagine what it was like with all that lot arriving at around the same time and scrambling for the seats that they thought best reflected their seniority.

A former police commissioner who is a fellow member of Nigeria Police Community Policing Project Steering Committee acted as the master of ceremonies and did a great job. The proceedings commenced with a prayer and the singing of the national anthem. The Inspector General then welcomed the assembled company and delivered an excellent speech during which he made his commitment to community policing clear and his appreciation for what DFID were doing in supporting the programme. His speech was followed by a speech from the Minister for Police Affairs, who also nailed his and the governments colours to the mast in support of community policing.

What I have not explained and find most difficult is the complicated protocol that is followed in these speeches. Nigerians are very formal on these occasions which means, speeches take twice as long as they might otherwise take because of all the compliments to important people and so on. You can guess I am already beginning to realise that my programme will change yet again. The Minister concluded his speech by formally opening the workshop.

Blair followed with the aims and objectives for the day and some suitable comments designed to get the assembled company thinking appropriately. By the time he had completed his session the time was approaching 10.45 a.m. and we were supposed to have taken a tea break. Blair politely and correctly differed to the IG as to whether the break should be taken. A quick discussion on stage (that was where the High Table was located with all the bigwigs) and it was decided to go straight into the presentation by the project team, so that the Minister could hear the presentation. The presentation was good with some parts being exceptional, including fortunately the conclusions. It is always best to end on a high note. Six of the seven members of the team took part in the presentation and each one was given a reasonable amount of applause at the end of his/her session.

At the end of the presentation the Minister left the proceedings which meant that the IG had to formally accompany him to his car. This was the tea break but when I tried to get people to start drinking the tea (cold by now) they indicated they could not do this until the IG led the way (protocol again). By this time, I am wondering whether I would get to do anything personally. I half hoped that I did not but knew that there were some messages that I needed to get across without fail.

When we re-assemble the team, I took questions. First from the High Table (big bigwigs), then from the AIGs (lesser, but still bigwigs) and then the Police Commissioners (still bigwigs but not quite as big). This was potentially a minefield where we wondered if serious levels of honesty from the floor might get punished later by the IG. It went very well and the IG himself joined us in answering the questions.

By the time the question session was completed, and we stopped for lunch it was already 2.15 p.m. and we had been scheduled to take lunch at 1.00 p.m. My plan had been to run two sessions, one identifying the benefits and barriers to community policing, including splitting into groups and the other considering the nature of the culture of the Nigeria police. My discussions with the master of ceremonies indicated that I would need to complete my session by 4.00 p.m. with a 3.15 p.m. start time. So once again and for the umpteenth time, I changed my plans.

In the event, I incorporated both sessions into the one period. I spent the first twenty minutes or so talking about the nature of culture in organisations and explaining how change plans must address culture as well as the structure of an organisation. I drew on research into police operating cultures to explain how the hierarchical nature of police forces can inhibit the flow of information and prevent the empowerment that is a core value of community policing. I gave them illustrations from my UK experience and asked them to compare what I said with what they observed in Nigeria deliberately not making negative comments about Nigeria Police but getting them to create their own judgements.

I then got them actively involved by inviting them to shout out benefits and then barriers to the effective introduction of community policing. These were listed for me on a flip chart. I then illustrated how some of the barriers might be overcome and asked them to go away and consider how they would work to overcome the barriers. I ended spot on my allocated time and received an encouraging round of applause. The MC then called for more applause and congratulated me on the presentation.

The event concluded with closing speeches from both the IG and Blair. Both were excellent the former revealing his clear pleasure with the outcome of the day's activities and the latter providing the inspiration for the participants to commit themselves to the change. The IG was particularly complimentary of his own project team which was a useful motivational tool for them.

Rock City

Abeokuta is a town situated about one hundred kilometres east of Lagos and the capital of Ogun State which just happened to be the home State of the then President of Nigeria. I was there because the Nigeria Police Community Policing Project had started to expand.

During our pilot programme in Enugu State we (retired UK police officers) delivered the training to Community Policing Developers (CPDs) who work as change agents in their local police stations, but if that continued it would take us another couple of lifetimes to cover the entire country which was not acceptable to the President who wants things to develop rapidly. So do we, and in fact it had always been our plan to hand all our roles over to Nigerian Police officers.

We had been training twenty or so of the best trainers in the organisation to replace us. We delivered a four-week course to them at the Police Staff College in Jos. Half of them had been deployed to Kano in the North where Roger and another colleague was working with them and the other half were with me. We supervised the CPD Trainers as they delivered the course to selected staff who will become CPD's after six weeks.

Abeokuta is a small town and life here is somewhat limited so far as social activities are concerned. I asked about restaurants and apparently such a thing does not exist other than at the hotels of which there are just three of any significance. The Gateway, the largest hotel is government owned and run down so there is no point in going there. The Continental has a restaurant but people staying there eat at Wenby's Suites (where I was staying) because they find the food unacceptable so that left me with little choice but to stay there.

Wenby's Suites has only been open for a year, it is small with probably around twenty rooms and a restaurant that has seating for just fifteen people, and it is often crowed. Sometimes, to create the illusion of choice I choose room service, which is usually quicker than restaurant service, but just the same choice of food but one night the service was very speedy indeed because just before ordering my meal I had given the hotel manager a good roasting about the fact that at least fifty per cent of the items on the menu were not available.

I am sure that you think I am being unnecessarily critical but given that all the items that I would normally select are among the items not available it works out that I had been having a rotation of the same three meals since I arrived last week.

I was sick of the sights of spaghetti bolognaise, chicken and chips and chicken casserole. Tonight, following my protestations, I got goulash and parsley potatoes. This business of having a posh and extensive menu that bears no relationship to reality is common in Nigeria. The key card supplied at our hotel in Jos indicated that we could swim in the pool for free, but it is not even a hole in the ground yet. There is this habit of putting out an impressive front which is just a façade and hides incredible ineptitude and ineffectiveness. I guess this is also a related problem to the level of corruption and criminal deception.

If truth be known my anger at the hotel manager was influenced by other things. One of the waitresses was a lovely little Christian girl who was having problems with him; he has told her that she will get the sack if she does not sleep with him! She was collecting some money together to pay for her to train in computers so that she could leave of her own accord and ultimately get another job. I contributed significantly to her fund and it gave me some pleasure to shout at the source of her difficulties and make him feel insignificant in her presence.

The abuse of power is endemic in Nigeria and I have heard of policewomen having similar problems with their bosses. We confronted those issues daily, in our classroom and the common people are as upset by it as we are. However, it is possible that the waitress was conning me, but I am sure that she is genuine and deserving of the help.

Abeokuta means 'rock city' and if you were here you would see why, there are numerous large rocky outcrops often topped with trees all around the area. I would suspect that the area was volcanic a long time ago and these rocks are all that remains. It is a busy town with an extensive market and a part of it specialises in local tie-dyed clothes.

We delivered our training at a police school. This is a school for the children (infants and juniors) of police families. It was quite an interesting experience sharing our venue with small children, most of whom have clearly never seen a white man close-up before. At their breaks quite a number came close by and gawped at me. When I moved towards them to say hello! they ran away and I was tempted to roar like a lion and chase them.

They were not the only visitors we got, most mornings a cockerel and his collection of wives came and had a look in the class and in the afternoons, they were replaced by inquisitive goats. They caused me some alarm when they started to sniff inside the box containing our handouts but fortunately the paper was not to their taste. The schoolteachers were also interested in what we were doing and commented on the participative style of training which contrasted with their traditional didactic teaching methods.

The trainers had generally been doing very well indeed and I admit to feeling quite proud that they are having the same effect upon the aspiring CPDs as we did when we delivered the course. It is one thing for us to deliver it successfully but quite another for them to replicate our achievements; quite necessary if we are to sustain the developments long term.

The school was very run down. We were using two adjoining and quite large classrooms. The school was built in 1993 and clearly had never seen a lick of paint since then. The rooms are filthy, have concrete floors and louvered windows all of which are broken. Electricity was fitted originally but there was not a single fitting left, just holes with wires sticking out. Do not worry, there was no power anyway! The climate was hot and clearly the only cooling was that coming naturally through the windows and doors. My first task when I got back to the hotel was a cold shower and the consumption of a large amount of bottled water.

The police children's school is on a large site which is occupied by the State Police Headquarters and all the associated services that run alongside such a building here in Nigeria. That means more than it would in England. For example, there are barracks for a substantial proportion of the police personnel working in this part of the state. That means that enterprising people have put up shacks where they serve food and sell phone cards for mobile phones and the like. The school is at the perimeter of the police estate and we drive down a very rough dirt track to get to it. The deep potholes sometime cause the bottom of our car to scrape the floor.

The school is a two-storey concrete building with a corrugated iron roof which is in an advanced state of decomposition (rust if you prefer). The classrooms form three sides of a square and the fourth side consists of the administrative buildings including the Headmasters office. The quadrangle has a concrete base and serves as the playground for the children who occupy most of the classrooms. We are using two downstairs classrooms and we overspill into some upstairs ones when doing practical lessons. The upstairs ones are notable for the lack of roofs so in the rainy season that we are currently enjoying we are sometimes required to move rather quickly.

There is an area around the school where the undergrowth is cut back and we park our cars (as do the teachers) but beyond that there is African bush. I regularly observe all sorts of exotic birds. Frequent visitors to the classrooms have included chickens, goats, and geckoes (like bright coloured lizards). One day a poisonous snake arrived whereupon the Assistant Police Commissioner from the Project Team who was observing near the door, jumped on it causing it to be a rather flat and very dead poisonous snake.

Class started at nine and we had two groups of Community Policing Developers being trained by local trainers. My role was monitoring the work of the trainers to ensure that the same behaviour change required was being achieved. The first activity of the day was prayers with both a Christian and a Muslim prayer being said, a very important principle a multi=ethnic country with a recent history of fatal violence between the two parties.

I often made comments about my faith in Nigeria and applied this to the process of change that we were trying to create. They made frequent references to being 'born again police.' My comments were always carefully worded.

I ran a session with both groups trying to remove some common myths about leadership. One of these myths is that leadership is exclusively male. I asked the groups who was the leader in their homes and naturally got the reply, 'the man' (we have just 3 female participants). I then referred them to their agreed definition of leadership which is always about influencing others to do what the leader requires them to do. I asked who has the greatest influence over the children and the other members of the family and they always say, 'the mother.' That is when say, 'I rest my case.'

In one of the classes a very bright young Muslim quoted to me the scriptural passages about wives being subject to their husbands. There followed an extensive but positive discussion about the role of women in Islam and Christianity and the extent to which how we interpret the Bible has changed to reflect newer ideas. I used the example of Christians leading the campaign for the abolition of slavery, whereas the Bible at least condones slavery by giving instruction to slaves and their masters.

The Muslim guy who had quoted his scriptures was allowed extra time for the weekend so that he could prepare for and lead the naming ceremony for his newly born son. When he came back, he told us that his son's name was Mustafa, but he would be known in the home as John Bown Junior. Some compliment I thought!

At lunchtimes, I often sit in the classroom and as the children are on their way home some of them try to work out what I am doing with this strange machine called a laptop computer. Some try to touch my skin—they will never have been this close to a white skinned person before.

Sudanese Interlude

During the summer of 2007 I undertook a three-week project in Southern Sudan. My task was to work with members of the Southern Sudan Training Development Unit and build their skills in the design and production of training programmes. A police project had been underway for about three years, following the Comprehensive Peace Agreement which marked the end of a long period of civil war in Southern Sudan. I had been contracted at short notice to replace a consultant who was unavailable due to an illness.

The work was to be undertaken in Juba the capital of Southern Sudan, but I travelled into Sudan via Khartoum the capital. I was undertaking the work with B a serving constable from Durham who was having a career break to work as an overseas consultant. He had commenced working with police forces overseas when volunteers were requested to serve on secondment in the Balkans and then went to Sierra Leone to undertake similar work at the conclusion of hostilities there.

"Khartoum," the word conjures up images of exotic Middle Eastern dancers, camels crossing desert sand dunes and General Gordon fighting the locals. When we arrived at Khartoum airport having travelled through the day there was not much daylight left, but enough to see many signs of a country that had been at war with military planes in evidence amongst the civil airliners and a whole section of the apron featuring air services provided by various international aid agencies.

It was excessively hot and dusty, and I guess that Khartoum is like that for a substantial part of the year. There are lots of modern buildings housing hotels and businesses and lots of flat roofed houses alongside the roads, some of which are metalled but some of which are approached by sandy tracks.

We were driven to a two-bedroom apartment, part of the office block where the police project is based in Khartoum. It was pleasant enough in an African way and we had a wireless internet connection which helped us to keep in touch with home. The residential suburb looks and feels like a half-finished building site. We arrived just in time to see a Sudanese sunset but not over the Nile.

Feeling the need for a walk and something to eat we explored the area in the immediate vicinity of our accommodation and found a recently opened Chinese restaurant. Very local in nature with plastic tablecloths and curtains (Mickey Mouse patterns on them); it was full of aid workers from around the world most of them drinking beer (illegal here)—we were drinking diet coke. A guy who had worked with B in Seirra Leone came in and sat at our table. He was typical of the worst aspect of some people that follow the aid gravy train; prematurely aged from excessive amounts of alcohol and debauchery. We left him drinking and went back to our accommodation for a reasonably early night.

The apartment was comfortable and quite well equipped; the rooms are all high at least twelve feet which along with the white marble floors gave a feeling of spaciousness. I had a double bedroom, but the bed was a little hard for me; just like a thin layer of foam rubber on solid wood' which is probably as near to a technical description as possible.

We needed a travel permit to go to Southern Sudan so a substantial part of our first day in Khartoum was occupied with officialdom but W our driver also fitted in a 'city tour.' The city is clean by comparison with Nigerian cities and most roads are very wide and straight, but often the roadsides are dusty and unfinished.

The most attractive part of the city is around the confluence of the Blue and White Nile. The thing that impressed me most was that you instantly realise why the rivers are so called. The water from the Blue Nile is blue and the water from the White Nile is white and you can see the difference very clearly. The areas around both sides of the rivers are fertile and lots of small patches of different crops were being grown.

The next day we awoke early with breakfast soon after 7.00 a.m. to be ready to go to the airport for our flight to Juba in Southern Sudan. We were at the airport for 9.00 a.m. for a scheduled UN flight at 11.00 a.m. Khartoum airport seems to be notable for the numbers of old aircraft that are parked around the perimeter. The UN operates an air service for its own employees and others working on aid programmes. The plane was a twin-engine turbo prop Bombardia Dash 800. For those who are interested it is a modern aircraft seating about fifty people and we had a good flight of three hours before arriving in Juba.

Juba had been at the heart of a civil war for about twenty years out of the last thirty years and the biggest industry here is aid. I have never seen so much evidence of aid organisations as here. Most aid workers live in camps, and we were in one of these. My room comprised half of a small portacabin, size 8' by 10' with a single bed, small wardrobe, small table, and chair and fortunately a small air conditioning unit.

Juba has lots of similarities with towns in Ethiopia, for example, virtually all the roads are dirt. This means that always there are potholes, but sometimes the potholes are more like bomb craters. Everywhere there is the hint of a sewage smell (other than our camp thankfully), and away from the commercial areas nearly all the locals live in circular houses with conical roofs called 'tukuls.'

I had never previously seen so many vehicles belonging to NGOs and aid organisations, in fact if you were to remove their vehicles and those belonging to the government of Southern Sudan then there would hardly be a vehicle left on the road. Aid seems to be by far the biggest industry here and it is influenced strongly by the market economy. We were paying $100 per night just for our rooms which resemble poorly equipped prisoner cells! However, others are similarly priced but not as good.

We spent the first morning setting up everything for our course to commence the following day and the afternoon getting some supplies that we needed. We visited another camp on the banks of the Nile and had a cold drink looking across the river. It is beautiful with lots of vegetation growing on the banks. However, just across the river which is half a mile wide was territory controlled by the LRA rebel group, so we stayed on our side.

What we found when we arrived for our course was not exactly what we had been led to believe. We expected that we would have a group of thirteen members of the Southern Sudan Police Training Development Unit, but they were already running a trainers' course under the supervision of another consultant D. That course had already started, and she had split the participants into four groups and each working day, one group was delivering and another group preparing, so we had the others, but because of the rotation we had to take them as separate small groups. I had a small group and B had another small group (three or four per group). This meant in effect that we only had half the days available, but we worked faster because we just had three people.

Juba was in the centre of the fighting during the civil war and so there had been no development for more than twenty years and it showed. It was a very rundown place. We constantly saw soldiers of the Southern Peoples Liberation Army (SPLA) around the place the legitimate authority in Juba. As one outcome of the Comprehensive Peace Agreement (CPA) Southern Sudan has now become independent nation. At the time of my visit this had not happened, and the fighting was continuing across the border in Uganda where the Lords Republican Army stand indicted with war crimes including forcible abduction of boy soldiers and rape of local women. This spills over the border into Southern Sudan and the Democratic Republic of Congo.

When talking to the country representative for Total Oil, who was living in the same camp (a French man from Paris), he made it clear that much of the fighting over who has control here is due to oil. Apparently, there are likely to be huge reserves of oil in Southern Sudan. The Russians and the Chinese are already here and in the latter case they are buying up prospecting rights as fast as they can. Total, have the difficult situation that they purchased some plots from the government in Khartoum many years ago, but the government of Southern Sudan (GOSS) have sold the same areas to companies controlled by the Russians. Apparently Southern Sudan is also rich in lots of other mineral resources including diamonds and gold.

The camp where we stayed (RA International) was run by a company based in Dhubai that specialises in setting up operations for aid organisations in post conflict or post disaster situations. It is made up of probably around fifty or sixty portacabins that are set out around concrete paths. Each cabin is divided into two rooms, and they are clean but basic, the only luxury being reliable electricity and air conditioning.

A large marquee contains a dining area and a bar with large screen TV. The food is good but expensive as is everything else here in Juba because demand from aid organisation employees just about exceeds supply. Certainly, this camp seems fully booked and it is one of at least six similar establishments.

The introductions by our course participants had revealed some interesting information. Many of the police were formally soldiers in the SPLA (freedom fighters) some of whom were serving in that organisation from fourteen years of age. Most members of the police in Southern Sudan are illiterate. That did not apply to the people on the course, but a few only spoke Arabic or the local language, so some translation by the more fluent members was required from time to time.

My regular daily routine was to get up at around 6.00 a.m. and have a shower. The ablutions block is about twenty yards from my room. For the men, there are just six showers and a similar number of toilets. From 7.00 a.m. onwards until 8.30 a.m., you queue for a shower or to undertake your morning constitutional. I do not enjoy queues at the best of times, so getting up early was my only option.

At breakfast one morning I was watching the news when I had a bit of a shock, a rat ran across the frame of the marquee just above the TV, it was coming from the direction of the kitchen! The only comfort was that it was quite thin, so hopefully it had not been eating my food before me.

The Sudanese people we were working with were an interesting bunch. They had been brought together recently to form the Southern Sudan Training Development Unit. Their role was to develop training programmes and train trainers to deliver them. They were, however, not a happy bunch. Many had been moved from their homes some distance away and had left their families behind. They had not been provided with accommodation by the police authorities, but the project was paying them an allowance. However, given the high cost of accommodation some of them were just sleeping in tents.

We also had a couple of people from the Northern Sudan Training Development Unit working with us, one worked directly with B and I and the other with the Training of Trainers Course, alongside the other consultant.

We were scheduled to work six days a week but one Saturday a little incident made us decide that we should remove ourselves back to camp in the early afternoon. Public sector employees including the police were being paid salaries for the first time since goodness knows when and this led to some drunkenness and high spirits, the outcome of which was some of them lobbing hand grenades about! Apparently, no one was injured but we did not stop to find out.

B and I often took a walk on both Saturday and Sunday but there were not that much to report; very dusty and dirty roads, snotty nosed poorly dressed kids, the smells of open sewers and rotting vegetation and the usual street side traders. We did not feel threatened in any way, even though there is evidence of ex-military weapons everywhere. In fact, in the showers of a morning I often see young men stuffing their 9mm pistols back in the waistband of their trousers as they leave the toilet or with an AK47 rifle slung over their shoulders as they have a shave. I am very polite to them and do not pick any fights.

I had read in a newspaper that there was Ethiopian dancing at one of the other residential camps. The two members of the Northern Training Development Unit

M and F stay in our camp and have access to the vehicle over the weekend so we decided we would go there one night. We got lost on the way so asked some fellows in a jeep and they said to follow them. When we got to the location there was no dancing programme, so we went next door to a restaurant that overlooks the Nile. The guys who directed us joined us for a drink and the meal and they turned out to be Ethiopian, along with the waitresses at the restaurant, so I had a lovely time conversing in Amharic, which made up a little for not being able to do some Ethiopian dancing.

We watched the sun go down over the Nile and it was beautiful and peaceful. Immediately in front of the restaurant and about midway between the banks of the river was some small islands and we saw flocks of cattle egrets come to roost there.

The area where we were eating was like a garden filled with lots of large trees under which we sat. The food was quite good too and Dh and I treated our Sudanese colleagues and Ethiopian guests. The Ethiopians were quite pleased to be listening to a forenji using some Amharic and I was quite surprised at how much I remembered. It was lovely to meet Ethiopians again and made me realise how much I miss them. I did demonstrate a bit of Ethiopian dancing for them, even without music and we all had a good laugh Ethiopian style.

The RA International Camp where we lodged, looked as though it had probably been built around a couple of years and the company that own and operate it specialize in establishing such camps, immediately after conflicts such as had been taking place here. It covers an area about one hundred and fifty yards long by one hundred yards wide and is tidy and well organised. There are plant pots with flowering plants outside the rooms and some of the sitting areas outside have been landscaped to a certain extent; well perhaps that is an exaggeration, they have planted some flowering trees like frangipani. There is also one extremely large mango tree and seats and tables have been set out under the shade of the tree. It is very pleasant to sit there of an evening and watch the sun go down over a cup of coffee, real filtered stuff not instant. A very tall razor wire topped wall keeps out unwelcome visitors.

The restaurant and bar area is inside a steel frame oblong marquee which is set out quite nicely with a bar and comfortable seats at one end and the restaurant at the other. Another marquee is located along the back of the first which houses the cooking facilities and in front of the point where the two join is an extensive serving area with heated food cabinets for the buffet meals. There is usually a choice of two or three meat dishes, lots of vegetables and a wide selection of salads at lunch and dinner.

Despite the very nice meals, you do tend to get tired of the same place, so some nights B and I left the camp about 6.30 p.m. and walked to a pizza parlour that we had visited by car on a previous occasion. It was light for the walk there and still hot, but dark and still hot on the way back. We always enjoyed the change and appreciated the walk even though it made us both sweat.

All the food at the camp is brought in by truck from nearby Uganda. It looks like the economy there is on the up and the business they are doing with Southern Sudan will surely help. A brand name "Out of Africa" is used on all sort of things including coffee and tea bags and I bought some fabulous cashew nuts under the same label recently.

Our course was hard work, and the participants were generally not as bright as those I worked with in Nigeria, nor for that matter in Ethiopia. Clearly the war here has meant that a lot of children could not be educated properly over a long period and many of the policemen and women are illiterate. There is, however, a willingness to learn, but getting them to work at a detailed level is difficult, a common problem throughout Africa.

We three UK consultants can list a wide range of African experience including Rwanda, Sierra Leone, Nigeria, Uganda, Kenya, South Africa, and Ethiopia between us. We have lots of deep discussions about both the needs and the blessings of the continent.

One night on our regular walk, B and I came across some fellows playing football in the street, so I decided to join them. I approached one of them who had the ball with a view to gaining possession with a degree of confidence due to my substantial experience playing in defence, but he had the body swerves of a George Best, or if you are old, a Stanley Mathews. I tried to match his swerve but somehow although my body moved my feet did not and I ended up hitting the deck sustaining grazing down my right thigh and elbow and a peach of a bruise on the right cheek (lower).

I did manager to recover some of my image by eventually winning the ball and making a beautiful cross field pass straight to the feet of B. His return pass left a little to be desired though and went straight into the open sewer at the roadside which is when we decided to resume our walk.

It was a bit uncomfortable lying on my right side that night and lying on my left side puts me facing the wall of my hut which is just a thin partition that creates two rooms out of one standard portacabin. The fellow in the one next door is lying in a similar bed (folding camp type) right behind the same partition and he snores all the time. Sometimes when he reaches a high point in his snoring it wakes me up with a start. It happened quite a lot, last night.

This closeness of the person who is in the adjoining room means that you get to know something of the other persons' foibles without ever seeing them. I am sure that my neighbour would tell you that though I do not snore, I do get up in the middle of the night a lot (elderly man syndrome). I confess that he may also know that I suffer a little from flatulence! I have let off one or two that caused the walls to rattle a little.

A man I spoke to was staying in one of the cabins with a room on either side and they were occupied by two Sudanese who regularly entertained the opposite sex at night. It was quite disturbing for him to have to put up with the groans of ecstasy coming from either side when he just wanted to get to sleep.

May be the management should take account of the effects of such close proximity and ask their clients to declare their particular anti-social habits on booking the rooms so that they can match people up appropriately. What anti-social sleeping habit would you declare? Makes you think, doesn't it?

One day we got back to the training room following lunch at about 2.00 p.m. and B and I were busy looking at some stuff on my computer when M the policeman from Khartoum that I have mentioned before walked in and told us that there had been a bit of an incident and we should go back to the hotel. I shut down my computer as quickly as possible and got into the back of our vehicle with F and B. Before we had chance to get everybody in the vehicle a fuselage of shots rang out from close by and the three of us hit the deck in double quick time. The deck in this case meaning the space on the floor of the vehicle between the lateral bench seats that run down the length of the vehicle on each side.

Now it may be the case that one does not believe in getting too close to people that you don't know particularly well, but I assure you that if you think your life may depend on it, getting close is not a problem. B is pretty big, and I have been described by my son-in-law as size FE which he says means 'flaming enormous,' but given the motivation that was present at this particular time it's amazing how little space a size FE can fit into. Fortunately, I was not suffering from the flatulence problem that I identified previously so my prone colleagues did not have to suffer gassing as well as the stress of thinking that any time there may be bullets flying through the vehicle. Had the bullets really arrived the problem may have produced substantially more than wind for all of us!

Our Sudanese friend F is small, and I got the impression that he had squeezed between the two of us which I think would be a very good idea. Wish I had thought about it first. We stayed in that position for a little while waiting for more shots. Whilst there was no evidence of the shots hitting anything and were most likely being fired in the air as a warning, I was not poking my head up to have a look that is for sure. One by one the vehicle emptied leaving me on the floor and being invited back into the classroom but not wanting to exchange the comfort of my, by now familiar position on the deck for a vertical one where I represent a much bigger target, along a route to a classroom which is just a larger version of my portacabin room the walls of which offers much less protection than the sides of a motor vehicle.

Eventually I did tumble out onto the floor and keeping as low as it is possible for a 63 year old with a big belly and a bad back, I shot back into the classroom (perhaps I should have used a better word) and tried to identify the place there that afforded the highest level of protection.

People in uniform with guns were by this time arriving from all points of the compass and the big question was should we leave or stay. One problem we noted was that our driver had disappeared; it looked as though he just pulled the keys from the vehicle and ran when the first shots were fired; perhaps a sensible and experienced response, but not one that helped us get back to the camp. Eventually one of our police colleagues packed us into a vehicle designed for far fewer people and we exited back to camp.

The problem at the police headquarters apparently arose from an accident in which a policeman belonging to the Nuer tribe died. Other members of his tribe think that the senior officer in charge has not dealt with the driver (a Dinka) as he should have done, and in a post conflict situation where the men have been conditioned to see a gun as an everyday weapon then these things happen. I don't really think that we were in danger of being shot, other than getting caught in friendly fire from people who join in the shooting, but do not know where it is coming from or who it is targeted towards.

It was interesting arriving back at the police headquarters after the previous afternoon's fracas when we all had to 'run for it' so to speak. We were met with hugs from everybody and lots of laughing. A sign perhaps of the tension and stress we had felt when the incident occurred. As the morning progressed a few stories emerged. Our driver, had been told that all drivers were going to be shot and that is what caused him the grab the car keys and run. He obviously has a good turn of speed in such circumstances because he caught up with K one of the policemen on our course who was also running away. K is very clearly a Dinka with both the traditional looks of his tribe and the facial scarification that they are given from childhood. He told P that he had heard that they (Nuers) had killed someone, so they both continued to run together. I told them that we should enter them for the London Olympics and there was a whole lot more of laughing.

Whilst we did see the funny side of what happened it was quite serious, so we did a risk analysis yesterday morning before deciding that it was safe to continue the training. There was much more evidence of armed police and members of the SPLA (Army) around to ensure that the inter-tribal hostility did not get the chance to kick off again.

Certainly, whilst I was lying on the floor of the vehicle and getting as close as possible to the others in the same situation, it was not at all funny and I was offering a prayer for protection, but God is good and looking back on the event inevitably brings a chuckle or two.

The Trainer Development Unit has been established with help from the British Government with a view to developing training courses that will help take the Southern Sudan Police from the immediate post conflict confusion of military and police roles to a properly constituted service orientated civil police. Everyone admits that there is a long way to go. B and I have been training thirteen members of the TDU, whilst they have in turn been delivering trainer training to another group of eleven who will become local trainers. The trainer of trainer courses has been supervised by another consultant D.

We have been attempting to equip the participants to design new training programmes, which is a bit of a tall order in the space of seven training days. It is clear they will need further support and it is also a fact that unless they apply soon what they have learned by designing a new course they will forget what they have learned. We have built the activities around the creation of a new course for NCO's (junior supervisors).

The members of the TDU are all lovely people, but their academic achievements are fairly low due to the influence of the long years of civil war. Most of them were educated in refugee camps in Uganda, Kenya, or Ethiopia. Some were former boy soldiers who joined the SPLA (Southern Peoples Liberation Army) to fight against the government forces. What they lack in learning they make up for in enthusiasm to see their country live at peace. There is a general weariness with war amongst the people here, which is not surprising.

The course concluded with a graduation ceremony which was scheduled to commence at 3.00 p.m. The woman who is responsible for resources had purchased a large supply of snacks and drinks for the event before leaving for a period of leave at her home in Jordon a week or so ago. The guest of honour was the Inspector General of Police. During the morning, the generator ran out of fuel and we were unable to purchase any because of a shortage.

This meant that the air conditioning in the classrooms was not working and that meant we were going to be extremely hot. The classrooms have been put up by the British Government and are portacabins, so with no electricity they become useless because they are totally unsuitable for the local climate. I compare this with what we did in Ethiopia when drawing up a model for regional police training centres. Ours were built using local materials and were designed with lots of doors and window holes with shutters (not windows with glass) so that they remained as cool as possible, and we made sure that the training was all low tech' capable of being delivered without electricity.

When the staff officer to the IG arrived to look over things, he blew a bit of a cylinder head gasket at the lack of air conditioning and intervened to send out staff to purchase diesel from roadside stalls in quarter of pint plastic bottles at an incredibly high price.

At about 3.00 p.m. on the dot the IG arrived but the staff was still fiddling with the generator. They did get it going and the air conditioning started to work, but naturally it had little impact on rooms that had heated up over a considerable period of the day. Sweat was running off my face down my shirt and down the middle of my back, my three clean handkerchiefs were quickly little better than wet mops. A series of speeches were made by members of the TDU team and some of the senior entourage accompanying the IG. D also said a word on behalf of the consultants/British Government. The TDU members took the opportunity to air some of their grievances' which I thought was quite brave. Some speeches were in Arabic and some in English and some speakers used both languages.

I wondered what the IG would say, having been kept waiting before we could start and then being provided with a catalogue of woes. In Nigeria, the IG would have gone berserk and fired all the staff on the spot. I was impressed by the Inspector General, he displayed an understanding of the problems presented to him and promised to look into them, he described the political situation in

Southern Sudan and identified the need for the trainers to apply what they had learned due to the desperately poor state of police performance that had come about as a result of the war.

He is a new appointment and came across as a lovely, committed, and able man and what he said suggested that there is hope that policing will improve, at the same time he was realistic about the lack of resources and poor infrastructure.

After the conclusion of the ceremony and the presentation of the certificates to the participants, we the consultants were presented with gifts; a stick and a carved giraffe for me. I am always humbled on such occasions by the generosity of people who have so little.

The partying then began, and I got some of my African music playing on my computer. There was a lot of laughing when I demonstrated West African (Nigerian) dancing styles and Ethiopian dancing and that encouraged others to join in. The celebrations continued for about an hour and a half, and the conversations indicated that the TDU members had also been impressed by the IG.

Afterwards one of the Sudanese we had been working with invited us back to his brother's home. We had an enchanting couple of hours with them and I will do my limited best to describe the events to you. We were driven to a suburb of the city of Juba called Kator where the houses are mainly traditional 'tukals' about which more will follow. On the way S, our host related to us how his family had been forced to leave the area and go to the north (Darfur), many of the residents of Kator had been killed and many houses had been burned to the ground. He had left as a boy and eventually returned many years later as a middle ranking police officer and his brother as an engineer.

In other words, their education and work training had all been undertaken in the North. In fact, S's wife and children still live in Khartoum where he has a house, a car and land and has done well for himself. Nonetheless he has volunteered to come back home to his roots but will within the next two years have to decide whether peace is permanent enough to sell up in Khartoum and move his family back to Juba. Such are the decisions that people face here in Southern Sudan and in any post conflict situation.

On arrival at the compound that housed S and his brother and family we saw that most of the buildings in the area are traditional, meaning that the walls are built from mud and the roofs are thatched, most are round, but some are square.

Each compound is delineated by fencing which is constructed from thin bamboo type material and stands about seven feet high.

We entered a large compound with at least four traditional houses and the shell of a larger house in the process of being built from local bricks made from a red clay material. We were greeted by various members of the family including quite a few children, one of whom could not come to terms with the presence of the white people and showed obvious signs of terror.

Grandmother was lounging outside her 'tuckul' on a mat before getting up to greet us, she had white hair and showed signs of considerable age but was not feeble. The whole family (other than the terrified infant) made us very welcome, and we then entered the tukul occupied by S a police officer and our host.

We all sat inside his house and the greetings and discussion continued, before we were brought chilled bottled water and then a large circular metal platter about a yard in diameter was placed on a table in front of us onto which was placed a dazzling array of local dishes.

There were pieces of fried chicken, a large bowl of dried fish that had been cooked in a stew, a potato and a beef dish cooked in a mildly spiced sauce, rice, a large lump of something that looked like pounded yam but was made from maize meal, a very tasty bean dish containing large white beans similar in flavour and texture to the ones in baked beans, two or three vegetable dishes and a large plate of salad. We all ate our fill and from time to time the children came to have a look at us and I think to see whether there would be food left for them.

When we had finished eating, we moved outside and sat and chatted and drank beer until the sun started to go down. We talked of many different things; the importance of cattle amongst the local population, the experience of local people during the war, the return to the area by those who had been forced to flee due to the fighting, the life expectancy of the roof of a 'tukul' and many other related topics. It was a quite remarkable day and one which we will all reflect upon for years to come.

It is sad to reflect that the animosity between the Nuers and the Dinkas has subsequently developed into a civil war in the newly dependent country of South Sudan.

Catching Up on Life Outside of Work

In 1987, we purchased a seven-bedroom semi-detached Victorian house in Matlock. We converted the top floor into a self-contained apartment for my father-in-law. He sold the country cottage where my wife had grown up and put the money into the purchase of the house. I was happy that my mother came to see the house, soon after we moved in but on 21st December, she passed away at the age of 85. I have written extensively about my mother in the opening parts of this record of my life, but I will add a little more about her.

My mother had not done very well with menfolk. As a teenager she fell pregnant to a man who then emigrated to Canada. At the age of 37 she married my father, with whom she had two children, my brother Sam and me, but when I was 4 and my brother 7, he died, leaving her to bring us up on an income of such a low level that she never paid income tax. Although we were relatively poor, we always had food on the table, a warm bed to sleep in and lots of love. I have never felt that we missed out on anything important.

My mother was a bit of a character, and she had many sayings that made me laugh and sometimes she slipped into the vernacular. A good example was when an official came to our home with a key for an old people's bungalow. She said to him, "Tha' knows what tha' can do with them keys?"

To which he replied, "Would you like to be specific, and it's really my boss that you should be making your statement to." Mother responded, "Tha' can tell him to shove them up his arse." He then asked if she would put that in writing and she indicated that she would write it on his paperwork, but she had to go into the house to find out how to spell the vernacular word for backside, or bottom.

Another example was when unknown to mother my brother purchased a bright yellow Morgan 3-wheeler. It was a strange looking machine with a motorcycle engine at the front, an open top with two seats and no doors, so you had to climb in. When the vehicle was delivered mother was convinced that the man had the wrong house, but when it became clear that her son had purchased this strange looking vehicle, she said to him, "Well to think that I gave belly room for nine months to someone who would buy a useless thing like that."

Mother's hard life was not made easier by the activities of the local authority who were going around the countryside condemning old farmhouses as being unfit to live in because they had no water supply, windows were too small or ceilings too low. They were using an act of parliament designed to achieve slum clearance which was hardly appropriate for isolated farm workers cottages. Interestingly when the properties were vacated because the owners could not afford to make the improvements, a wealthy businessman often purchased them at a throw away price and then made a fortune out of developing them.

I suspected that some monkey business was involved. For a time, my mother faced the prospect of court action and fines in relation to a farm she owned where there was a tenant farmer in residence. Fortunately, she found a loophole in the law and I now live in this beautifully restored grade two listed farmhouse that would have been demolished had the local authority had their way.

We moved into the farmhouse in 1994, two years after I had retired from the police. I have always wished that my mother could have seen us living here and I often thank her in my mind, for what she did to resist the local authority. I also thank my father for making the investment to buy the farm in 1939 for £650. I am not sure that I believe in ghosts, but a strange thing happened when we first moved in. On occasions, when I sat down in the lounge, I could smell the distinctive odour of old-fashioned pipe tobacco.

There was no logical explanation for this because everything had been stripped back to the bare stonework. It just felt that my father was communicating his pleasure that we were living at the farm. Quite recently I also had a very vivid dream where I met my father in heaven. He was accompanied by my mother and brother Sam. He was not an old man and looked pleased. I asked him if I could give him a hug and he seemed to agree. I walked up to him and discovered that he was taller than me and I said, "That's a surprise, you are taller than me," and then I woke up and cried. I am not saying this was a super spiritual moment, just that it felt good, and I thought it possible that my father had experienced a death-bed conversion and I would meet him in glory. Who knows?

At Matlock, our children were growing up and we had an active life with loads of Christian things happening. I started organising an annual "March for Jesus" event, which ran for a few years until some of the local vicars decided that it should be left to them to organise, and surprise, it stopped happening. By the time we moved to the farm Joanne had been to university and qualified as a nurse, Gareth was working as a gamekeeper, Barbara was starting at university studying physiotherapy. Our monthly YouthReach event was no longer attracting the crowds that had once attended and it was no longer viable. One of the problems with Christian events is knowing when to stop them. I called our management group together and although we knew that individuals and churches would have continued to supply financial support it was time to bring it to an end.

I had become a Circuit Steward for the Matlock Methodist Circuit of churches and eventually became Senior Circuit Steward. One of our main jobs was to lead the selection process for replacement ministers, which in theory occurred every five years. Going back to the time of John and Charles Wesley they had developed the idea of "itinerant ministry," where ministers we expected to move on every five years.

This practise reflected their experience in the Anglican church, where a family might hold the living in a parish for generations, they were ill equipped to lead a church. I concluded that the system was no longer fit for purpose, and I became increasingly frustrated by the state of terminal decline in the Methodist churches. Margaret and I had never been ones for flitting about from church to church but by 2010 we decided to join our daughter Joanne and her husband and family at St John's Church, Walton, Chesterfield where there had been quite remarkable growth over a period of ten years.

Once we started to get engaged with St John's Church, Walton, Chesterfield our ministry moved away from Matlock to Chesterfield, and I started to get involved in "Christian's Together for Chesterfield." Through this contact I discovered that they were trying to establish Street Pastors in Chesterfield. I offered to help them and produced a job description, person specification and recruitment process for a paid coordinator. I was keen on becoming a Street Pastor and excited at the prospect of patrolling late at night, looking after the needs of those who were sometimes incapable of looking after themselves.

As we advertised for a coordinator and interviewed prospective candidates, we could not find anyone remotely fitting the job description and I increasingly realised that my background, experience, and qualifications fitted me for the job, but I was reluctant to take on such a potentially demanding role when I was not far short of seventy and looking to wind down rather give myself more responsibility. After praying over the issue, I offered to become the coordinator without pay, but indicated that I only wanted to stay in the role for the first year, whilst we looked again for a suitable person to appoint.

Street Pastors originated in London as a Christian response to increasing knife crime and violence. They exist in more than three hundred cities and towns across the UK. Generally, they are deployed alongside the police and other agencies amongst the night-time economy between the hours of 10pm and 4am. They are not permitted to preach, but are there to help, care and listen. At the time we formed Street Pastors in Chesterfield, we had a very enthusiastic and talented Community Safety Officer who worked out of the Town Hall. He was our leading advocate and contributed funding from his budget.

During the developmental phase of Street Pastors, along with others from Christians Together for Chesterfield, we visited the local police commander, Chief Superintendent K, who I knew very well. The chairman of our group introduced me to K, and he replied, "You have no need to introduce John to me, he made a significant contribution to my development when I was a probationary constable in Derby." He was happy io make a significant contribution to the budget of Chesterfield Street Pastors and to offer police assistance in the training of our volunteers.

I have many wonderful memories of working in Chesterfield, along with my wife who also became a Street Pastor and others. It would be difficult to identify how many times our interventions have saved the lives of people who were under the influence of alcohol or drugs. Our presence on the street has a calming effect and is greatly appreciated by the other agencies.

Walking out on patrol one night when I was introducing a friend from our church to Street Pastors, and he was a bit nervous about what sort of reception we would receive. A group of lads greeted us across the street when one of them shouted, "You Street Pastors you know what you are don't you—you're a f'ing legend that's what you are."

Quite often we find ourselves looking after someone until we can safely get them home, so spotting people that are vulnerable is a critical skill to be deployed. One night we came across a very drunk young man in the church yard. He had been sick, and we cleaned him up, sat with him as he sobered up, and helped to contact his parents to arrange for him to be picked up and taken home. During the time we had been helping him a group of men had been watching us as they sat outside a nearby pub. Walking past them, as we arm in arm escorted the young man to an agreed pickup point one of the men said, "Can I book you for 2am for the same treatment?" We often had similar amusing incidents.

On another occasion we were outside a night club when two sisters who were a little the worse for drink were trying unsuccessfully to be admitted to the premises. We engaged them in conversation and gave them a lollipop sweat to suck. It turned out that they had come out to take their minds off things that were worrying them. They had been told that their father had been diagnosed with terminal cancer and did not have long to live, and the husband of one of the ladies was a serving soldier in Afghanistan. We ended up praying for them, just where we were on the street.

Over the years that Street Pastors have operated in Chesterfield, there have been many unsolicited expressions of appreciation for what we have achieved. At one church in Chesterfield, a guy knocked on the door of the rectory, When the vicar opened the door, he observed a heavily tattooed, muscular man, unlike any member of his congregation and when the man asked if he could arrange for the baptism of his baby son, the vicar was intrigued to establish what had prompted the request. The man explained that he was a bouncer at a night club in Chesterfield and had been so impressed by what he had seen of Street Pastors on duty he had decided he wanted his child to be brought up as a Christian.

On one occasion when I was doing a presentation about Street Pastors at a local Anglican church, a lady in the congregation asked if she could say a few words, although she was clearly nervous about speaking in public. She explained that part of her job was to view the Chesterfield Town Centre videos on a Monday morning. She said that viewing Street Pastors doing their work, she realised how many lives they had potentially saved and how she was hugely impressed.

The success of Street Pastors led to other initiatives including a comprehensive summer holiday club, we called Community Young Stars. The scheme was suggested by the Community Safety Officer, who said that he could find some money for funding, if we could provide volunteers to run the scheme. He offered the free use of Queen's Park Annexe. When it was first developed around 1960, it was a "state of the art" sports ground and pavilion but was now little used and in a state of terminal decline. The only problem was that the money had only become available in April and planning and delivering the event for the forthcoming schools summer holidays, was going to be a major challenge.

Using the auspices of Christians Together for Chesterfield we found considerable support for the project, although quite a few of the formal church leaders in the town were expressing their opinion that what we planned could not possibly be achieved within the available timescale. The areas immediately to the south of Queen's Park Annex, included areas of high social depravation and these were our targets. M, a children's evangelist who had developed a ministry to schools in the target area over many years, joined the planning team and we were able to use some of the funding to provide him with an honorarium for delivering the teaching sessions.

Volunteers from local churches were recruited, vetted, and trained for their roles. Our programme included morning sessions for 5-11 year olds, afternoon sessions for 11-15 year olds and evening sessions for teenagers. I scoured e-bay for sports equipment including, pool, table tennis, football, nets, footballs etc. Volunteers cleaned and painted the sports pavilion which had been almost abandoned. We engaged qualified sports coaches to deliver training sessions, and a mobile computer games provider to deliver computer game sessions.

After a while the local authorities discovered that we were going to be creating a safe learning and playing environment where they could bring children with behavioural problems and learning difficulties and leave them in our care, as did parents. I remember that one mother told us that her son had brought more things home from our craft sessions than he had done in the preceding three years of school life. After the school holidays, the teachers at his school reported that his behaviour in school had improved beyond recognition. We had a lovely team of volunteers who had time to spend with individuals who needed more attention. I certainly would not like to give the impression that entertaining and controlling the behaviour of the children was easy. Half-way through the morning and afternoon sessions we provided healthy snacks.

Our morning sessions were always the most popular, the afternoon sessions were not so well attended, and the evening sessions usually took the form of games outside and music and games inside. After six weeks of the play scheme, I was completely exhausted, but proud of what we had achieved, and we repeated the process a year later. After that the Queen's Park Annexe site was redeveloped so no longer available and we were unable to find any suitable replacement site.

Our next Community Safety Officer inspired initiative involved us setting up a drop-in centre for teenagers who were under the influence of drugs that at the time were not controlled by law. The main one, 'Spice' continues to be the drug of choice for homeless people, although it is now a controlled drug.

At the time. The youngsters involved gathered in the bus shelter in the town centre at what they called 'heaters,' because warm air from a supermarket provided a relatively warm and dry environment. This was also where most of Chesterfield's homeless people spent their nights. Often there would be a group of between ten and twenty youngsters, many of whom were completely spaced out and appearing to the elderly folk awaiting their busses to be challenging in the extreme. Our challenge was to get them off the street into a safe environment where they could be looked after and exposed to a positive influence.

The pastor, elders, and members of Grace Chapel kindly offered their premises for that purpose. It was ideal because in addition to a separate worship area there was an extensive coffee bar where we located table tennis, pool, and other games. It was housed in a former warehouse just outside the town centre. Whilst most of our volunteers remained at the premises, those who were also Street Pastors, patrolled in our uniforms, dealing with youngsters who had lost consciousness due the drugs and inviting them back to Grace Chapel where they could have free food and drink. We also patrolled Queen's Park and the Skate Park where young people congregated. During these patrols, we also provided a litter picking service which gave us a reason to be on the streets and parks and provided another useful service. We got to know the young people well and gained their trust. There were times when we prayed with them and saw God answer our prayers. Many of the young people who came knew us from the holiday club days and as they grew up, we would see the same young people, out in the town centre on Saturday evenings when we patrolled the streets as Street Pastors.

When Grace Chapel relocated to new premises right in the town centre in a former bank, we became even more popular and eventually our popularity led to our closure. We were regularly entertaining up to one hundred youngsters and our youth event was the main attraction for youngsters in the town centre. This caused concern for the police because of bad behaviour in the town centre and for us because we found it difficult to control them in the premises. Sadly, we eventually had to close.

I was becoming increasingly aware that by the time I reached seventy I was nowhere near as fit as I had been previously. I had been diagnosed with heart failure and could no longer cope with walking the town centre until the early hours of Sunday mornings and had to retire from being a Street Pastor. I had remained Chairman of the Management Committee but was finding that stressful and after a period in hospital, I decided that I would have to change my lifestyle and avoid putting myself in stressful situations. I resigned from most of my responsibilities with a view to extending my life for as long as possible.

One of the new developments for me was working with a good friend Will, in establishing a prayer stall on Chesterfield Market. Prior to the lockdown we could be found manning a stall on the main part of the open-air market near the burger van where there are seats for the customers. We wear high visibility tabards with "Ask 4 Prayer?" emblazoned on the front and rear and perhaps surprisingly, people do ask us to pray for them and we do regularly get feedback about answered prayers. One story is worthy of recording. The first week we set up our stall, we saw a small group of elderly blokes taking together as they drunk their tea or coffee. Seeing our tabards one of them shouted, "Don't bloody well expect me to ask for prayer, I'm an atheist." We thought that was a good start—not! We discovered that R spent most of the mornings six days week with his mates and his whole life revolved around that engagement, he had no other friends.

R made lots of far-fetched claims about what he had been in the past including that he was a former member of the SAS and could kill people with just the use of one finger! However, over time we got to know him very well and he shared with us the problems he was having over a proposed house move, and we offered to pray for him which he accepted. The situation with him experienced a complete turn around and sometimes when he arrived, and in front of his mates he would shout, "Hey that God of yours answered those prayers."

Sometime in late summer of 2019, when I was not able to join Will one Friday, R told him that he had been referred to the Northern General Hospital, Sheffield, for a scan due to suspected lung cancer, but he did not know how he could get there. He was not up to getting on and off busses and could not afford to get a taxi to Sheffield. The following week, when I was there, I took R to one side and told him that I would take him to Sheffield and he then shouted, "Bloody hell, John's going to take me for that scan in Sheffield!"

Over a period of two or three months, I made three journeys to the Northern General Hospital with Ray. The first time I took him for the scan, the second time I took him to see the consultant for the diagnosis and proposal for treatment (having a part of his lung removed) and the third time, I took him for the operation. During the long journeys I had many conversations with R and was able to share something of my faith with him. Before taking him to the ward where he was to have his operation, I asked him if I could pray for him, and he agreed that I could. Having prayed he said, "John, I know that I might die over this operation, but I am not scared, because I now know where I will be going to."

Following the operation, I picked up R and took him home. I had had not been inside his home before and what I saw did not surprise me but did sadden me. R had few possessions, his home was scruffy and untidy, with evidence of a chaotic lifestyle. When we got into the house, the electricity was not working, and we had to move around with torches. Later a neighbour came from across the road and helped him contact the energy company and re-activate the supply.

Over the next few weeks, just as the Covid 19 virus spreading, R was in and out of hospital at Chesterfield, being taken in by ambulance and then I would take him back home. Just before Christmas he called me and said he wanted to come to church with me so that he could thank God. My family were starting to worry that he would catch the virus and pass it on to me. I picked him up and took him to my church for our Christmas Carols by Candlelight service, which he clearly enjoyed. Early in the new year he came to church for our Sunday service and then joined us for Sunday lunch. R told us that he had not had a Sunday lunch for decades and he really appreciated being with us. On the way home he told me that in the whole of his life he had never had a friend like me, yet I felt I was doing so little for him.

He then asked if he could come to our Tuesday morning service and have lunch with us at church. In the event the lockdown was just beginning, and the church had decided that it was unsafe to put on lunch and that we would be closing the church and meeting thereafter online. After the service I took him a ride to Bakewell, where we had a take-away fish and chip meal. I was looking forward to building a longer-term relationship with R, but it was not to be.

I kept in touch with him by telephone for a while, but then he no longer answered. I worried about him and travelled over to see him, but found his bungalow locked up. Enquiring with the neighbours across the road I discovered that he had died from a massive stroke about a week before but had not yet been buried. The local authority was arranging the funeral, so I contacted them and was invited to take part in the service, paying a tribute to him and selecting two old hymns I thought he would be familiar with. There was just three of his neighbours, my wife and I and the undertaker present. I wished I could have known Ray longer but thanked God that he had gone to a better place.

Final Reflection

About halfway through the Corvid 19 lockdown, I decided that I should do something useful and decided to write my story with as much detail as I could remember. I was motivated by a comment on a Nicky Gumbell Bible study when he indicated that our stories have power. I have tried to be as honest as possible, but I would not wish to give the impression that I have found living the Christian life easy. I identify with St Paul when he said, "The good that I would, I do not and the evil that I would not I do." In the words of an old hymn, "I'm only a sinner, saved by grace."

I will remain eternally thankful to God for a fulfilled, exciting, and interesting life. I also appreciate all the love and kindness that so many people have showered upon me. I acknowledge the guidance provided by so many others who have influenced my life.